Reinventing Leviathan:
The Politics of Administrative Reform
in Developing Countries

EDITED BY
BEN ROSS SCHNEIDER AND BLANCA HEREDIA

North·South Center Press
UNIVERSITY OF MIAMI

The publisher of this book is the North-South Center Press at the University of Miami.

The mission of the North-South Center is to promote better relations and serve as a catalyst for change among the United States, Canada, and the nations of Latin America and the Caribbean by advancing knowledge and understanding of the major political, social, economic, and cultural issues affecting the nations and peoples of the Western Hemisphere.

© 2003 North-South Center Press at the University of Miami.

Published by the North-South Center Press at the University of Miami and distributed by Lynne Rienner Publishers, Inc., 1800 30th Street, Suite 314, Boulder, CO 80301-1026. All rights reserved under International and Pan-American Conventions. No portion of the contents may be reproduced or transmitted in any form, or by any means, including photocopying, recording, or any information storage retrieval system, without prior permission in writing from the North-South Center Press.

All copyright inquiries should be addressed to the publisher: North-South Center Press, 1500 Monza Avenue, Coral Gables, Florida 33146-3027, U.S.A., phone 305-284-8912, fax 305-284-5089, or e-mail mmapes@nsc.msmail.miami.edu.

To order or to return books, contact Lynne Rienner Publishers, Inc., 1800 30th Street, Suite 314, Boulder, CO 80301-1026, 303-444-6684, fax 303-444-0824.

Library of Congress Cataloging-in-Publication Data

Reinventing Leviathan: the politics of administrative reform in developing countries / edited by Ben Ross Schneider and Blanca Heredia

   p. cm.

Includes bibliographical references and index.

ISBN 1-57454-101-3 (hc: alk. paper) — ISBN 1-57454-102-1 (pbk: alk. paper)

1. Administrative agencies—Developing countries—Reorganization. 2. Civil service reform—Developing countries. 3. Developing countries—Politics and government. I. Schneider, Ben Ross. II. Heredia, Blanca

JF60.R42 2003
351.172'4—dc21   2002044499

Printed in the United States of America/TS

08 07 06 05 04 03   6 5 4 3 2 1

To
Alicia Colomer Heredia
and
Catherine Mackay McCord

CONTENTS

COMPARISONS AND CONCLUSIONS

PREFACE AND ACKNOWLEDGMENTS

During the academic year 1995-1996, Blanca Heredia, Ben Schneider, and Kwang Woong Kim were, by coincidence, all housed at Northwestern's Center for International and Comparative Studies (CICS). We started talking about our common interests in bureaucracy and administrative reform, and out of these initial conversations grew a comparative research project that proved to be unexpectedly lengthy and complex. Over the course of these discussions, we came to two recurring observations on the growing literature on various kinds of structural reforms that convinced us of the value of undertaking the research presented in this book. First, most work on administrative reform had surprisingly little to say about politics, due apparently to a convergence of disinterest. On one hand, most "neutral" experts or scholars of public administration were more interested in debates on best practice than in the messy politics of bringing about that practice. On the other hand, administrative reform and bureaucracy rarely sustain for long the interest of most political scientists, despite the manifest political importance of bureaucracy, especially in most developing countries.

The second observation was that a series of recently published studies on the politics of first wave reforms had generated a list of plausible hypotheses for building more general theories of reform politics. This list of hypotheses seemed to be a good starting point for a collaborative project on the politics of administrative reform, though even at the outset we suspected that many of the arguments about the politics of carrying through major structural reforms of the state and the economy would not be useful in understanding the process of administrative reform. These hypotheses, derived from the broader reform literature, informed the original working papers; however, many of them fell by the wayside as we developed better explanations for the peculiar politics of administrative reform in our final version of this book.

In the course of successive meetings, numerous drafts from country specialists, and interviews with policy reformers, we realized that available analytical schemes for the study of the politics of state reform needed to be substantially revised in order to account adequately for the distinctive challenges posed by second wave reforms. We realized, moreover, that before moving toward the formulation of more plausible causal hypotheses, we had to begin by developing a conceptual framework that allowed us to navigate through the intricacies of reforms aimed at rebuilding the administrative structure of the state. As we worked on this project, we consistently attempted to relate the singularities of individual countries' experiences to the broader regularities implicit in our evolving conceptual and analytical maps. This process, central to our whole endeavor, proved to be particularly challenging, however, given the paucity of empirical information on the actual implementation and results of reform processes.

This project benefited from numerous and diverse sources of support and guidance. Our peripatetic venture included meetings at the Center for International and Comparative Studies (CICS) at Northwestern University; Escola Nacional de Administração Pública (ENAP) in Brasília; the Centro de Investigación y Docencia Económicas (CIDE) in Mexico City; and The World Bank in Washington, D.C. We thank these institutions for their help in sponsoring and organizing these meetings. Major funding for the project came from the Tinker Foundation. The World Bank, The Korea Foundation, and an Alumni Initiatives Award from the Fulbright Program provided additional support. The intellectual framework of the project was jointly developed by both of us, but the project as a whole was organized for the most part through Northwestern University, hence, the reverse ordering of the names on the cover.

Our successive meetings were greatly enhanced by presentations and commentary by Fernando Abrucio, Sergio Berensztein, Renato Boschi, Javier Corrales, Fernando Filgueira, Peter Evans, José Maria Ghio, Edward Gibson, Stephan Haggard, Kwang Woong Kim, Evelyn Levy, Edson Nunes, Guillermo O'Donnell, Regina Pacheco, Susan Rose-Ackerman, Bernard Silberman, Barbara Stallings, Judith Tendler, and Meredith Woo-Cumings. We are also grateful to other colleagues who provided suggestions and feedback at various points in the project's development: Andres Fontana, Peter Siavelis, and Miguel Vatter. Kathleen Hamman, our editor at the North-South Center Press, was enthusiastic about this project from the start. Her hard work with our far-flung authors added much needed polish and coherence to the volume. We also wish to thank Mary Mapes for her cover design and formatting of the book and Susan Holler for the index.

Blanca Heredia, Mexico City
Ben Ross Schneider, Berlin

Chapter One

THE POLITICAL ECONOMY OF ADMINISTRATIVE REFORM IN DEVELOPING COUNTRIES

Blanca Heredia and Ben Ross Schneider

INTRODUCTION: BUILDING STATE CAPACITY[1]

Over the past decades, many developing nations recast their states, both in terms of what they do and how they do it. Initial changes tended to focus on the elimination of governmental functions, cuts in spending and investment, reductions in personnel, privatization, deregulation, and devolution of central state responsibilities to state or local levels of government. The often large costs of downsizing, in terms of bureaucratic coherence, effectiveness, and efficiency produced, according to one overview, a "disintegrated state," . . . "with demoralized and barely functioning state agencies" (Nelson 1994, 20, 27). These administrative costs of the first wave of economic restructuring, along with the novel pressures and demands placed upon governmental bureaucracies by increasingly competitive markets and politics, have led governments to focus on a second generation of administrative reform efforts. This later type of reform focuses on building or rebuilding institutional and administrative capacities.

In the 1990s, the needs for capacity-building reforms and "good government" rapidly became focal points in analyses of development.[2] Administrative reform also became part of the evolving "Washington consensus."[3] The World Bank devoted its flagship publication, the 1997 *World Development Report: The State in a Changing World*, to demonstrating how important bureaucratic capacity is. In a section entitled "Good Government Is Not a Luxury — It Is a Vital Necessity for Development," the report urges reform in alarmist terms: "People living with ineffective states have long suffered the consequences in terms of postponed growth and social development. But an even bigger cost may now threaten states that postpone reforms: political and social unrest and, in some cases, disintegration, exacting a tremendous toll on stability, productive capacity, and human life" (1997, 15).

However, there is no consensus and little research on how to go about getting more state capacity. Many studies note that politics has to be taken into account, but systematic comparative work on the politics of administrative reform is rare.[4] Our goal is to provide political explanations for why some governments are able to enact significant administrative reforms, while others cannot. Our point of departure is that significant administrative change redistributes power resources. Therefore, explanations for the success or failure of a particular country's reforms have to account for who wins and who loses and why the political settlement came about in the way it did. Our optic more generally is one of political economy, though in our view economic factors usually affect public bureaucracies indirectly by influencing the opportunities and constraints faced by political power holders. The question is, how do economic factors, fiscal crises in particular, alter preexisting political incentives and practices? Thus, we embed our analysis of administrative reform in its broader political economic context.[5]

Recent literature on first and second generation reforms offers four major sets of factors that might be expected to affect the process of administrative reform (see especially Kaufman 1999). First, some authors privilege a political perspective. For example, Stephan Haggard (1997) outlined a conceptual and analytical scheme that emphasizes the centrality of politico-institutional factors in shaping state reform. Haggard conceives of administrative reform as "a process of re-writing the contract between elected politicians and bureaucratic officials" (1995, 12), whose outcome is strongly shaped by two main variables: the balance of power between the executive and the legislative and the nature of the party system, particularly its degree of party fragmentation and level of party discipline.[6]

Others scholars concentrate more on a second set of economic pressures for or against reform. Fiscal crises and constraints pressure governments directly to reform government bureaucracies, though these pressures do not necessarily translate into reform efforts designed to increase state capacity. More generally, historically, and theoretically since Max Weber (Gerth and Mills 1958), capitalism and modern bureaucracy have flourished together. In the current context of increased international competition and volatile capital flows, capitalists have strong incentives to push for administrative reforms that reduce transaction costs (ports, customs, courts); level the competitive playing field (monopoly and trade regulations); and enhance investor confidence through greater transparency in budgets, international reserves, and monetary policy (see Maxfield 1997 and Mahon 1996).

Available empirical work on state reform suggests the importance of looking at a third set of strategic factors (see, for example, Prats 1999, especially 178-181). The strategic choices of state reformers, such as policy design and coalition building, shaped the political costs of different types of reforms, though less formally articulated in the literature. The preferences and strategies of state reformers or "change teams" should figure more prominently, at least initially, in explanations of reform because the distributional implications of "technical" reforms in the public sector are often not apparent immediately to other political actors.

The fourth set of influences is international. International financial institutions (IFIs) can have influence in domestic reform initiatives through conditionality in emergency lending and ongoing program lending. The rapid circulation of ideas on administrative reform constitutes another international factor. As earlier in the first wave of neoliberal economic restructuring, a predominant international thinking on administrative reform — called managerialism or "new public administration" — influenced the design of some reform programs. These four sets of influences include many of the factors thought to affect the politics of reforms of all sorts. As subsequent sections and chapters discuss, not all of these factors had the expected intensity or direction of influence.

Beyond these influences commonly cited in the literature on both first and second wave reforms, our project generated, more inductively, two further hypotheses. First, the prospects for administrative reform are dimmer in countries where the bureaucratic and political elites are fused, as they were for decades in Mexico and Thailand. Conversely, when political outsiders come to power, they are more likely to embark on administrative reform. Second, the programmatic commitments of political outsiders matter. Where these commitments (for example, expanding social programs or gaining access to the European Union - EU) require complementary administrative changes, then governments are more likely to sustain investments in administrative reform.

Our project was initially designed to assess these influences and arguments in several countries of Asia, Eastern Europe, and Latin America. However, in order to make these assessments, given the state of available work on the subject, we first had to develop a more precise conceptual map of the problem. This task proved crucial as we framed the central issues and questions that resulted in a set of key conceptual distinctions we have found to be particularly productive analytically. This introductory chapter starts off laying out these conceptual distinctions. The second section of this chapter examines the major differences between first and second wave reforms, emphasizing that second wave reforms, which concentrate especially on administrative reform, tend to be more costly, to take longer, and not to create support coalitions. This chapter's third section provides a typology of three major models of reform. *Civil service reforms*, including merit recruitment and promotion as well as tenure, are designed to reduce particularism and politicization in the bureaucracy. *Accountability reforms*, including measures to enhance legislative oversight and transparency, are designed to make the bureaucracy more accountable to politicians and other groups outside the executive branch. *Managerial reforms*, such as decentralizing authority and enhancing incentives in more flexible pay and employment schemes, seek to make the bureaucracy more efficient and customer oriented.

Sections two and three of this chapter delimit the dependent variable. A large number of discrete measures fall under the general rubric of administrative reform. Many re-engineering reforms, such as revamping information systems, training programs, publicity campaigns, and the like, fall outside our purview because they do not redistribute power and hence do not require extensive political analysis. More generally, we largely exclude *institutional reforms* of both the first wave (privatization, decentralizing central government functions to local governments, and eliminating government functions) and the second wave (creating new regulatory agencies, for example) to focus on changes within the remaining central government agencies.[7] Within central government agencies, our focus is on the middle and top officials rather than the operational workforce at lower levels of the administrative hierarchy.

Section four of this chapter provides some background on our six cases: Argentina, Brazil, Chile, Hungary, Mexico, and Thailand. Among developing countries, our cases rank high in terms of size and socioeconomic development. However, variation is wide in terms of pre-reform bureaucracies, political systems, and the progress of administrative reform. In a simplified overall ranking, administrative reform in the 1990s was most extensive in Chile and Hungary, significant but stalled (or medium) in Brazil and Argentina, and only incipient (or low) in Mexico and Thailand, though the potential was enormous in Thailand.

This chapter's fifth section turns to the assessment of the causal variables that were prominent in explaining reform outcomes in the empirical chapters. The weight of these factors generally varied over the course of reform. Among pre-reform conditions, the extent of fusion between political and bureaucratic elites and the programmatic orientation of the incoming government shaped the initial likelihood of reform. Fiscal crises often accelerated reforms. Institutional variables, such as the strength and cohesion of parties, were less important in the initial design of reform but affected the pace and alterations in the process of implementing it. Coalitions were important in the initial enactment but usually in the negative sense of overcoming opposition. International actors were generally not evident, yet ideas on best practice permeated many programs of reform. Strategic factors, especially packaging administrative reform with other top political priorities, helped overcome initial institutional and coalitional obstacles; however, packaging may turn into a liability over time. This chapter's sixth section takes a more speculative look at factors that are likely to affect longer-term sustainability of reform efforts.

THE POST-DEVELOPMENTAL STATE
AND THE SECOND WAVE OF REFORMS

First wave or first generation reforms, such as privatization and deregulation, reduced and redefined core state functions.[8] Such reforms also produced important transformations in administrative structures, though mostly as byproducts of larger institutional transformations that lacked a deliberate concern for administration as such. First wave reforms focused on shedding state functions and personnel and tended to proceed relatively swiftly. Three factors help explain the relative ease, compared with the second wave, of these reforms. In most cases, first wave reforms were introduced in the context of economic emergency that muted opposition and tended to generate broad support for nonroutine, drastic policy action.[9] Second, small groups of insulated reformers implemented these reforms. These groups were answerable only to the executive and, thus, insulated from both established bureaucratic procedures as well as from particularistic pressures entrenched in the political process. Third, by eliminating agencies and firing personnel, downsizing directly deprived losers of the institutional levers through which to resist or reverse reforms. Market-oriented reforms had the additional virtue of generating, almost automatically, strong support coalitions made up of clear and concentrated winners (Schamis 1999). Implementing first wave reforms was not easy and cost free; however, relative to second wave reforms, the costs and obstacles were lower and shorter term.

Once the shedding of public functions, firms, and agencies came to a close, two things became obvious. First, despite major reductions in functions, states retained central responsibility for providing a significant number of vital public goods and services. Second, the administrative machinery for carrying out such tasks exhibited a plethora of problems and deficiencies. In the post-adjustment period, core state functions, such as tax collection, maintaining monetary stability, and law enforcement, whose effective delivery had been historically weak in many developing countries, have risen to the top of government reform agendas. Tasks such as regulation, traditionally overridden by direct state participation in the economy, have also become increasingly central. In addition to devoting renewed energies to fulfilling long neglected core state functions, administrators have responsibility for new tasks, such as environmental protection, and in some cases must plan for major shifts in social priorities. Economic liberalization has reduced the space for direct state intervention in the promotion of economic growth, as it simultaneously generates strong pressures for new modes of state action capable of enhancing international competitiveness.

Among economists, there is a widespread consensus, especially for Latin America, that increasing growth and exports requires increasing savings and investment in human capital. The state or, more narrowly, public administration is crucial for both. For Sebastian Edwards, "the most direct and effective way to raise aggregate domestic savings is to increase public sector savings" (1997, 97). Public sector savings have averaged only 1 to 2 percent of gross domestic product (GDP) in Latin America, compared with 8 percent in East Asia. Administrative reform, beyond blunt downsizing, has a role to play. In fact, many post-developmental states are fairly lean by international standards; public sector employment and salaries are comparatively low (see Table 3 below). Therefore, future fiscal gains are more likely to come with better administration of existing resources rather than cutting the public payroll. Similarly, the state will continue to be a major investor in human capital in most developing countries, and the quality of that investment is as important as the quantity. Again, according to Edwards, "public sector spending on education is 3.7 percent of GDP in Latin America, versus 3.4 percent in Asia. Yet the quality of Latin American education is among the poorest in the world" (1997, 100). Thus, reforms of the administration of public spending on education are paramount. In sum, the administrative machinery inherited from the developmental era, often carelessly slashed during first wave reforms, was ill equipped for the challenges that confronted political leaders after initial market-oriented adjustment.

Though the costs of effective administrative reforms vary across policy areas, overall, they tend to be quite daunting. Reshaping administrative structures and personnel practices is, for one, much more time consuming than eliminating agencies and firing personnel. Putting together an administrative reform scheme and introducing it against the open and, typically, veiled resistance of most of those working within the state apparatus tend be lengthy, difficult processes. In addition to their long periods of gestation and maturation, second wave reforms usually require very intensive use of political and administrative resources. In contrast with first wave reforms that do not rely on altering bureaucratic behavior, successful administrative modernization fundamentally depends on changing bureaucrats' incentives so that they are convinced that it is rational and personally beneficial for them to behave in ways consistent with enhanced bureaucratic performance. However, reshaping the incentive structures governing state bureaucracies is a bit like attempting to fix a car's engine while the vehicle is moving. Basically, what reform initiatives tend to do in the short run is to multiply administrative tasks and to disrupt established procedures that, even if suboptimal, allow bureaucrats to deliver expected goods and services. One of the first major hurdles administrative reformers must overcome is finding ways to sustain reformist efforts in spite of bureaucrats' resistance, often masked by the legitimate need to perform the organization's routine functions.

Sustainability is obviously crucial to the success of any reform initiative. In the case of second wave reforms, however, it is particularly central, given the long periods of time necessary to change large bureaucracies and the fact that many of the obstacles to and opponents of reform do not automatically fade away.[10] The initiation and institutionalization phases of reform programs exhibit, regardless of the specific reform in question, distinct logics and dynamics. Based on the analysis of market-oriented economic reforms, a number of studies have argued that the key distinction between the two phases is that successful initiation hinges on strategies that insulate reformers from losers, while consolidation depends on reformers' ability to generate winners (Haggard 1997). Although useful perhaps as a broad point of departure, this view is insufficient in accounting for the specific problems associated with the institutionalization of capacity-building administrative reform.

In contrast with market-oriented economic reform, most of the strategies employed to alter the incentives facing bureaucrats tend not to be self-enforcing. This means that reformers must spend considerable time and energy directly monitoring the behavior of bureaucrats to ensure that reforms are carried out. The often huge monitoring and enforcement costs of bureaucratic reforms help explain why these processes tend to be so difficult to sustain over time. Moreover, as most capacity-enhancing reforms entail a reduction of superiors' discretion, their commitment is difficult to sustain, especially when superiors are faced with competing demands for their attention. Information asymmetries generate opportunities for simulation and noncompliance on the part of subordinates. These elements along with the absence of natural and concentrated support coalitions tend to make administrative reforms particularly difficult to sustain.[11]

In sum, second wave reforms are decidedly more costly and difficult to achieve than first wave reforms. Because institutionalization, particularly in the case of capacity-enhancing administrative change, critically hinges on maintaining the reform impulse over relatively long periods of time, one can understand why so many bureaucratic reform initiatives languish and die after brief, intense spasms of reformist fury. Most second wave reforms take decades or generations to become institutionalized, and many things can derail them.

MODELS OF ADMINISTRATIVE REFORM

Most complaints about bureaucracy fall under three common diagnoses: that it is corrupt or clientelist, that it is inefficient, or that it is arbitrary and unaccountable. The corresponding models of reform to remedy these pathologies are civil service, managerial, and accountability reforms. In practice, each model is composed of many discrete and sometimes overlapping administrative measures (see Table 1). Analytically, though, overall reform strategies can usually be characterized by the predominance of one diagnosis and one model of reform to remedy the situation.

Table 1. Three Models of Administrative Reform

Model	Civil Service	Accountability	Managerial
Diagnosis	personalism, clientelism, patrimonialism, corruption	abuse of power, arbitrariness, lack of accountability, unresponsiveness (to citizens)	inefficiency, red tape, inflexibility
Goals of Reform	universalism, professionalism, meritocracy, honesty	external control, responsiveness to civil society or legislatures	efficiency, responsiveness to clients, flexibility
Administrative Measures	entrance exams, tenure, promotion by merit, oversight, salary increases, rules	legislative oversight, nominee confirmation, accountability agencies, transparency	management contracts, competition among agencies, decentralization, end tenure
Potential Negative Byproducts	rigidity, loss of accountability, inefficiency	politicization, excessive delays, cumbersome procedures	clientelism, loss of accountability

Civil service or Weberian reforms were chronologically the first model adopted to enhance bureaucratic performance. Defined conceptually by Weber as legal-rational authority and embodied visibly in the progressive era's civil service laws in the United States, the primary goal of this model of reform was to eliminate patrimonial, amateur, and spoils-system administration. The common components of civil service reform include entrance by examination or other professionally sanctioned qualifications, promotion by merit, job tenure, reasonable and predictable salaries, and administration based on written rules.[12] By taking personnel decisions out of the hands of politicians, these reforms reduce patronage and clientelism. Stable employment and income diminished the temptations of corruption, while detailed rules and extensive paper trails provided means for rooting out malfeasance. However, at the same time these reforms reduced corruption and clientelism, they created new bureaucratic pathologies (such as over regulation, rigidity, and emphasis on complying with rules rather than achieving results) that became the bases for other models of reform.

A second model of reform, accountability or democratizing reform, views the problem as excessive power in the executive administration; the cures are greater democratic control, transparency, and accountability. Civil service reforms deprive clientelist politicians of influence over appointments and consequently limit their power over how agencies are run. However, politicians often return collectively, as legitimately elected representatives, and demand greater formal and institutional controls over the executive branch. One form of accountability reform is thus greater legislative control over the bureaucracy. This control can take several forms, including confirmation of top appointees to head agencies, regular hearings on agency activities, and extensive rules on the execution of laws the legislature passes.[13] In addition to direct assertion of legislative controls, other measures make agencies accountable to other oversight or ombudsman agencies or require greater transparency by making information on administrative procedures and decisions publicly available.

A third type of reform views inefficiency as the greatest problem in admin-istration and proposes several managerial remedies. The rules of Weberian admin-istration combined with the rules imposed by legislatures tend to absorb more of a bureaucrat's time than actually implementing policies or providing services (Garvey and DiIulio 1994). Moreover, job tenure and rigid rules for promotion, which often depend more on seniority than merit and performance, deprive managers of the ability to use promotions and firings to motivate subordinates. The cure for proponents of managerial reform consists of many instruments borrowed from the private sector, including decentralized personnel management and elimination of civil service tenure; management by results, including management contracts and performance based pay; and elimination of red tape and excessive regulation.

In recent decades, managerial diagnoses and reforms have gained interna-tional preeminence among the three models. David Osborne and Ted Gaebler's (1993) *Reinventing Government* is the touchstone of most managerialists, having been translated into dozens of languages and used as a handbook for many reformers around the world. It inspired former Vice President Al Gore's program for administrative reform and was prominent in several reform proposals in Latin America (Bresser-Pereira and Spink 1999).[14] Gerald Garvey and John DiIulio (1994, 26-28) provide a good indication of the predominance of managerialism in debates over reform in the United States. In their review, they note the disputes among four types of managerialist strategies without mentioning civil service or accountability reforms. However, transferring managerialist models directly to developing countries may pose the risk of misdiagnosing the problem. Where clientelism and corruption predominate, managerialism may not be the optimal remedy. As Gaebler noted, "You have to invent government before you can reinvent it" (interview 1997).

In practice, many reform programs combine elements of the three models or attempt to address all bureaucratic maladies at once (see Table 1 for a summary). The World Bank, for example, advocates three mechanisms for enhancing state capability: rules and restraints, competitive pressures, and voice and partnership — which correspond roughly to our civil service, managerial, and accountability models — and sees relatively few problems in pursuing all three at once (1997,

7-11). This multifront attack on the bureaucracy downplays trade-offs among the models of reform and minimizes the negative byproducts of each model. For proponents of civil service reform, inefficiency and unresponsiveness to citizens and clients are unfortunate costs of securing the essential depoliticization of bureaucracy. For managerialists, the efficiency benefits of deregulation and eliminating tenure justify the new exposure to clientelist and patronage temptations. For advocates of accountability, delay and inefficiency are an acceptable price to pay in the effort to promote participation and democratic control of the bureaucracy.

The emphasis in much of the technical literature of public administration of "best practice" and "optimal" administration neglects the fact that reformed state structures are not the products of "optimizing" strategies on the part of state reformers, but rather the result of protracted and intense political struggles. Each model of reform shifts power in significant ways. All of them shift power away from presidents and their inner circles. Civil service reforms take appointments out of the president's hands. Accountability reforms shift power away from the executive toward the legislature or other citizens' bodies. And managerial reforms increase the discretion of lower level managers, at the expense of their erstwhile bosses.

Table 2. Social and Economic Indicators

	Population (millions)	GNP per capita (1995 dollars)	Adult Illiteracy (%)
Thailand	58	7,540	6
Chile	14	9,520	5
Argentina	35	8,310	4
Mexico	92	6,400	10
Brazil	160	5,400	17
Hungary	10	6,410	na

Source: World Bank, 1997, 215. Gross national product (GNP) per capita is in purchasing power parity.

BACKGROUND AND VARIATIONS IN REFORM

Most of the six countries analyzed in this book are in the upper range of size and income for developing countries (see Table 2). For some periods during the second half of the twentieth century, most of these countries have turned in above average economic performance. Over the past several decades, these countries have advanced significantly in establishing market-oriented economic reforms. These are states with at least modest capacity to promote growth and adjust to international shocks and opportunities. Additionally, all these countries became democratic, or at least more democratic, in the last two decades of the twentieth century.[15] Along these broad dimensions, the case selection allows us to control for some extremes of poverty, size, social development, and political system. Our "sample" is probably

biased toward countries with a higher likelihood of reforming their public administrations, or at least attempting to, so our conclusions may not apply smoothly or
completely to smaller, poorer, and less democratic countries.[16]

Pre-reform bureaucracies in these countries also showed wide variation on
basic quantitative measures. The measures in Table 3 capture some of these
differences as well as the conclusion that, by the 1990s, there was still room for
significant reform. Government employment was not large in many of our cases,
especially by the 1990s, and was a very low 2.4 percent of the labor force in Chile.
Public sector employment was much higher in Argentina and Hungary, 12.6 and
15.4 percent respectively, and probably helped move downsizing up the agenda of
policy options in those countries. In most OECD countries, general government
employment is over 15 percent of total employment: for example, 15.3 percent in
the United States and 33 percent in Sweden, according to the Organization for
Economic Cooperation and Development (OECD) Analytic Databank. Total government spending was also low by international standards in Thailand, Argentina,
and Mexico; medium in Chile and Brazil, though data from Brazil from the early
1990s fluctuate dramatically; and highest in Hungary. Total spending was a primary
concern for Brazilian reformers and increased the attractiveness of downsizing
reforms, even if total employment was comparatively low.

Table 3. Some Background Administrative Variations

	Civilian Government Employment (percent)	Public Sector Spending (percent of GNP)	Corruption 1995	Corruption 1999	Ratio of Public to Private Salaries (percent)
Thailand	5.3	15	2.8	3.2	47
Chile	2.4	33	7.9	6.9	70
Argentina	12.6	16	5.2	3.0	24
Mexico	16.7	18	3.2	3.4	na
Brazil	4.7	36	2.7	4.1	na
Hungary	15.4	55	4.1	5.2	na

Sources: General civilian government employment as a percent of the labor force is from Shiavo-
    Campo et al. (1997) and includes non-central government administration, which is nearly
    half the total in Argentina. Data for Thailand refer to 1992, for Chile 1990, for Argentina
    1993, and for Hungary 1993. The figure for Brazil is from IBGE (1996). The figure for
    Mexico, from the OECD's Analytic Databank, is for general government employment as
    a percent of total employment for 1990.
      Data on government spending are for the central government only for 1990 (*World
    Development Report* 1992, 239). The corruption scale is inverted from 0 for corrupt to 10
    for uncorrupt from the Corruption Perceptions Index of Transparency International 1995
    (http://www.gwdg.de/~uwvw/rank-95.htm) and 1999 (http://www.transparency.de/docu-
    ments/cpi/index.html). Salary data are from Campos and Root (1996, 144).

Prevailing bureaucratic practices presumably feed into the perceptions of corruption quantified in the indices compiled by Transparency International, and administrative reform would be one of the measures to raise a country's score. In 1999, Chile ranked second highest among developing countries (after Singapore), and Hungary was one of the highest ranked among transition economies. The substantial changes in the scores from 1995 to 1999 for Brazil and Argentina presumably reflect the different personal styles of Presidents Fernando Henrique Cardoso and Carlos Saúl Menem and may hint at the limits of how much one president can shift the index up or down in the absence of more structural reforms. In any case, the perception of corruption was an issue for reformers in the lowest ranking countries of Brazil, Mexico, and Thailand. Relative salaries between comparable management-level positions in the public and private sectors are difficult to gauge, but even spotty comparisons reveal what bureaucrats in most countries would readily complain of, namely, that employment in the public sector was not financially attractive. In sum, even at this very aggregate macro level, the characteristics of and challenges for public administration in our six countries varied substantially, as did their strategies for reform.

Drawing on the country chapters, we turn to thumbnail sketches of the pre-reform bureaucracies and the progress of plans for reforming the central administrations in the 1990s (summarized below in Table 4). In Brazil, the bureaucracy throughout the postwar period has been characterized by a mix of different kinds of agencies, some predominantly clientelist, others more Weberian, and others, especially at top levels, informally managerialist (see Bresser-Pereira 1999; Evans 1995; Geddes 1994; Schneider 1991). Since the return of democracy in 1985, each successive government has attempted major reforms. The 1988 Constitution included a number of articles that extended fairly rigid Weberian reforms, such as entrance only by examination and tenure for all civil servants. Fernando Collor de Mello (1990-1992) attempted to undo some of the provisions of the Constitution in a radical, damaging, and ultimately unsuccessful program of downsizing. The reforms did not progress mostly because Collor could not get Congress to pass the necessary amendments to the Constitution. The Cardoso (1995-2003) government succeeded in amending the Constitution in 1997-1998 to allow for downsizing and enacting the managerial Bresser Plan. Beyond the significant political feat of passing the constitutional amendments, implementation of managerialist reforms has been uneven, and the ultimate outcome is still uncertain.

In Argentina, historically the bureaucracy also used a mix of administrative practices: clientelist, Weberian, and corporatist (in which groups, such as the military or labor unions, captured various parts of the state). Frequent political turnover and instability in the postwar period precluded any systematic and sustained reform of government administration. Raúl Alfonsín's government (1983-1989) tried to create an elite administrative corps, along the French model, but these efforts were sidelined by chronic economic crisis. Reforms in the Menem government (1989-1999) initially concentrated on downsizing as part of a drastic stabilization program. The reform package also included measures to enhance Weberian features, such as meritocratic entrance and promotion and salary increases, yet at the same time, in a more managerial vein, make tenure conditional on performance and provide incentive pay for outstanding performance (Fontdevila

1994). At the beginning of Menem's second term, reformers introduced a more managerial program of reform, but it did not get very far.

In Mexico, bureaucratic and political elites have historically been fused (see Camp 1984, Grindle 1977, and Centeno 1994). Given the hegemony of the Institutional Revolutionary Party (Partido Revolucionario Institucional — PRI) until the election of Vicente Fox in 2000, the bureaucracy became the central arena for the political system as a whole. Various programs to reform lower levels of the civil service were common from the 1970s on and created a fairly rigid and inefficient civil service. Administrative reform was absent on the crowded agenda of first wave reforms, but resurfaced in the first years of the Ernesto Zedillo government (1994-2000). Civil service and managerial reforms both had adherents, though neither side won a decisive victory. Civil service reforms were supported by an unlikely alliance of modernizers who wanted to reduce corruption and by bureaucratic incumbents who wanted to ensure their place in government. Advocates of managerial reform wanted to capitalize on the historical effectiveness of the non-Weberian, informal practices at the top of the bureaucracy. Overall, Chapter Six authors, David Arrellano and Juan Pablo Guerrero, argue that managerialism of a superficial sort was least disruptive to political leaders when the bureaucracy was the center of politics.

In Thailand, the bureaucracy has similarly been the center of politics, not because of party hegemony, but more due to the weakness of parties and groups outside the bureaucracy (see the classic text by Fred Riggs 1964). At the same time, Thailand has had a long-standing tradition of Weberian administration, though at the top levels clientelism and politicization were rife. By the 1980s, rapid economic growth highlighted the deficiencies of a formally Weberian bureaucracy whose effective operation came to be increasingly burdened by the coexistence of rigidity, a lack of coordination, and pervasive particularism (despite its formal Weberian features). The strongest push for administrative reform came in the late 1990s from a surprisingly strong middle-class movement. This movement was primarily interested in reducing patronage by enhancing transparency and citizen oversight over the bureaucracy rather than enhancing state capacity. Far-reaching accountability reforms were a key part of the 1997 Constitution. Again, though, implementation has been slow, and it is too early to say how far and well these constitutional provisions will work in practice.

Hungary also had a long tradition of Weberian bureaucracy. Communist rule though fused political and bureaucratic elites, and politics trumped Weberian procedure. After the fall of communism, administrative reform was a component of the overall political and economic transformation. The fiscal problems of the mid-1990s set in motion concentrated efforts to reform the bureaucracy. The Lajos Bokros program did not reduce overall employment by much but did reduce the wage bill significantly. Additionally, employment was shifted among agencies in so-called "rightsizing" measures. At the same time, governments of the late 1990s made important Weberian and managerial reforms, mostly designed to pave the way for eventual accession to the European Union (EU).

In Chile, the bureaucracy historically has been one of the most professional in Latin America, though it became increasingly politicized in the 1960s and 1970s

Table 4. Summary of the Types, Extent, and Timing of Administrative Reform in the 1990s (in descending order)

	Civil Service	Accountability	Managerial	Downsizing
Chile	Medium (salary increases and professionalization, 1990-1995)	Medium (National Commissions, 1990-1994)	High (1995-1999, 60+% of officials covered by performance pay)	High (employment reduced by half under military; 14% increase 1990-1997)
Hungary	Medium	Medium (lustration)	Low (reorganization, and some pre-existing managerial characteristics reinforced)	High (11% reduction in wage bill with major "rightsizing" shifts among agencies)
Argentina	Medium (Alfonsín's elite corps, Sinapa, and pay increases in 1990s)	Low	Low (reforms proposed but stalled in Menem's second term, 1995-1999)	High (1991-1992) but public employment increases after 1993
Brazil	Medium (tenure and exams in 1988 Constitution; professionalization in 1990s)	Medium (1988 Constitution; and oversight boards in Bresser Plan)	Medium (enacted but still in progress, 1997-)	Medium (1990-1996)
Thailand	Low (long history of Weberian practices with some further reforms in the 1990s)	Medium (major reforms in 1997 Constitution, but still in progress)	Low	Low?
Mexico	Low (reforms of some agencies)	Low (IFE)	Low (proposal from SECODAM but very little action)	Low

(see Cleaves 1974). After 1973, the military government drastically reduced public sector and government employment. After the return to democracy, center-left governments (Patricio Aylwin, 1990-1994, and Eduardo Frei, 1995-1999) undertook a series of reforms primarily in the context of fiscal balance and economic growth. The reforms undertaken by the Aylwin government were mostly Weberian, including professionalization, increased pay, and increased employment, with some accountability measures. Subsequent reforms under President Frei took a more managerial cast and have proceeded further by some measures than in any of the other cases. The process of reform was facilitated by the fact that civilian governments in the 1990s inherited a lean and comparatively effective bureaucracy from the outgoing military regime.

In sum, administrative reforms in these six countries have been frequent, varied, and complex. Although it simplifies the complexity of the reform efforts of the 1990s, Table 4 provides a rough ranking of the six countries, from highest to lowest. Reforms have been relatively high and sustained in Chile and Hungary. Reform efforts in Argentina and Brazil are best characterized as medium. Since the late 1980s, reformers in both countries have launched sweeping programs, but succeeding governments often let implementation lag or shifted the reform strategy. Reforms advanced the least in Thailand and Mexico, though the reforms in progress in Thailand may ultimately constitute the most significant accountability reforms of all the cases. These rough rankings are useful to initiate the discussion of causal variables, though much of the discussion that follows is more nuanced and disaggregates the types and processes of particular reform episodes.

WHY SOME REFORMS SUCCEED

The various sets of influences introduced at the outset filtered in at different stages in the process of the reforms of the 1990s in our six cases. To summarize the main findings of this section, reform programs usually originated in a small group in the executive. International influences, especially best-practice ideas on managerialism, came into initial designs. Initial support within the executive depended both on the absence of fusion between the bureaucratic and political elites and the packaging of administrative reform to other short- and long-term government goals. Fiscal crises accelerated reform initiatives, though most other economic factors had little broad influence. Institutional and coalitional factors illuminate the medium-term process of enacting and implementing reform proposals. Strategic factors and packaging were important at this stage in overcoming institutional obstacles and building coalitions.

Historically, proposals for administrative reform projects are commonplace. Incoming governments regularly generate plans for transforming the structure and operation of public administration.[17] In some countries, the generation of reform proposals is institutionalized in a cabinet-level agency responsible for public administration, such as the Ministry of Administrative Modernization and Control (Secretaria de Contraloría y Desarrollo Administrativo — SECODAM) in Mexico or the Ministry of Federal Administration and Reform of the State (Ministério da Administração Federal da Reforma do Estado — MARE) in Brazil. Few of the many proposals are later credited with having changed the way administration works. By this standard, the countries in our study are already remarkable; even in cases of medium or stalled reform, the reforms in all six countries, save Mexico, are likely to be remembered. Making ambitious proposals for administrative reform has become routine. Less common are cases in which bureaucratic reform receives high policy priority and reformers manage to implement it effectively.

Tracing reform proposals back to their origins usually leads to a small group of upper-level officials within the executive; Thailand is the exception of our cases. Proposals rarely emerge from electoral campaigns, party platforms, or legislative initiatives. These proposals are politically weak because to succeed they have to find allies among top bureaucratic elites, political parties, and other groups. Reformers and their "change teams" first need support from top officials in the executive: presidents and their inner circles, ministers, and other second-level officials. In contexts marked by close fusion between bureaucrats and politicians, policy elites will tend to have few incentives to award administrative reform a high priority. By fusion we mean the extent to which major political actors and their allies hold bureaucratic positions in the top several levels of the executive. Conversely, the extent of fusion can be gauged by the weakness of nonbureaucratic political actors. Mexico and Thailand are prime examples of fusion. As Unger describes traditional Thai politics, the principals are the agents and vice versa. In Mexico, the weakness of the PRI and the legislature, at least through 1997, was the flip side of the strength of the bureaucratic elite. From 1970 to 2000, Mexican presidents came from within the bureaucracy and had no prior elected office. As Arellano and Guerrero note, administrative reform in the context of fused elites is unlikely to generate support among bureaucratic insiders.

In contrast, elected officials with weak organic links to bureaucrats or political "outsiders" are more likely to be open to reform proposals. This outsider status is clearest in the case of the center-left coalition that came to power in Chile in 1990 after nearly two decades of dictatorship. It is also evident in Hungary after the fall of communism. The Cardoso and Menem governments are hybrids. In Brazil, the Party of Brazilian Social Democracy (Partido da Social Democracia Brasileira — PSDB) was a new party with fewer close links to the bureaucracy. However, its coalition partner, the Liberal Front Party (Partido da Frente Liberal — PFL), has long been ensconced in the bureaucracy. In Argentina, the Peronists had also been out of power for nearly two decades, and previous military governments had made an effort to purge Peronists from the bureaucracy. However, Menem's style was ultimately more clientelist and relied on bringing allies into appointed positions in the bureaucracy.

The extent of fusion influences the likelihood that bureaucratic elites will be receptive to reform proposals. Deeper commitment to reform depends, in turn, on the programmatic or ideological orientation of the government and the extent to which administrative reform serves the longer-term goals of the political elite. In general, policy elites with strong anti-state views (the government of Augusto Pinochet in Chile or the Collor administration in Brazil, for example) are less likely to push capacity-enhancing reforms than those with more positive, proactive expectations of the state. The latter (reformers in Cardoso and post-1990 govern-ments in Chile, for example) tend to give administrative reform a higher overall policy priority than anti-statists and, particularly, to see it as involving much more than sheer downsizing. In Hungary, as Nunberg notes in Chapter Three, ideologies were more fluid, yet governments formed by different parties shared the program-matic goals of breaking with the communist past and building a modern, European state.

Severe economic crises usually prompt state actors to rethink how states go about their business, especially how they go about developing their economies.[18] Economic crisis was prominent in the latest round of neoliberal reforms, as it was in previous changes in development strategies. Economic crisis was also crucial in triggering major administrative reforms in Brazil, Argentina, and Hungary, yet it operated primarily through the fiscal account.[19] Cutting costs, especially payroll costs, becomes the primary focus of reforms undertaken under fiscal duress. Cutting costs does not translate directly into any of the three models of administrative reform, especially in the short run. Reducing corruption through civil service reforms or increasing administrative efficiency through managerial reform both reduce costs but not in time to resolve the fiscal and balance of payments crises. Worse, in the short run, managerial, civil service, and accountability reforms all increase costs while simultaneously disrupting day-to-day operations. Therefore, initial responses to crises focus largely on firing people and reducing salaries. They are only the trigger for longer-term administrative reforms to the extent that state officials can link long-term reform strategies to short-term fiscal adjustment.

Fiscal crises accelerate reform by focusing the attention of policymakers and by overwhelming other factors (see Haggard 1997, 47). Top leaders focus on the immediate crisis to the exclusion of other political variables, like coalition building, that might otherwise feed into decisionmaking. Fragmented legislatures, or legislatures that normally block the executive, often pass major fiscal reforms under the gun of an unraveling economic crisis. Similarly, divisions within the executive are put on hold during crisis moments. Ministers who oppose one another are unlikely to let their animosities stall an emergency fiscal package. Economic crises in the 1980s and 1990s tended to centralize decisionmaking to presidents and their inner circles.[20]

Balance of payments crises and associated fiscal adjustments draw governments into closer contact with multilateral lending agencies responsible for emergency lending. In the 1990s, these IFIs invested considerable funds and human resources to think through issues of administrative reform (Mahon 1997; Nunberg 1997). So, a priori there are good reasons to expect the influence of IFIs to be great. However, IFI influence is variable and smaller than their influence in first wave reforms (see Nelson 1995). The IFIs were central actors in designing downsizing reforms in Argentina, however, importantly, as part of the overall first wave of reform in the early 1990s. There is little evidence of IFI influence in the other cases until the Asian currency crises in 1997. The lack of influence in Mexico is noteworthy because of the heavy involvement of IFIs in first wave reforms of the 1980s (Heredia 1996) and in the 1995 bailout. Outside of balance of payments crises, IFIs had a more limited impact through ongoing program lending to finance particular projects of reform.

Turning to political and institutional variables, the first set of obvious hypotheses is that governments backed by disciplined parties with majorities in the legislature in which party fragmentation is low will be better able to enact significant reforms (Haggard 1997). On a scale of party fragmentation, none of our six cases ranked low, meaning that in none of our cases did two major parties account for 80 or more percent of the total vote in the 1990s. Chile, Argentina, and Mexico (after

1997) had medium fragmentation, while Brazil, Hungary, and Thailand ranked high.[21] On the surface, a comparison of Chile and Argentina, where presidents enjoyed coherent legislative support, with Brazil and Thailand, with some of the world's most fragmented party systems, bears out these hypotheses. In Argentina, Menem's Peronist majority essentially gave the executive a free hand in decreeing rapid administrative change. In Brazil, it took the Cardoso government several years of protracted negotiation to get its fragmented support in Congress to enact a significantly altered program of administrative reform. However, that the Cardoso government was able to have any significant program approved seems to contradict the fragmentation hypothesis. The reasons that the government was able to overcome very unfavorable party and legislative constraints were due in part to the continuing fiscal crisis and to the packaging of administrative reform with the popular Real Plan. The Mexican case is even more problematic for these institutional hypotheses. The PRI was a highly disciplined majority (at least through 1997) party that for decades approved almost anything the executive sent its way. The lack of significant reforms in Mexico had more to do with the central role of discretion in the bureaucracy on the part of technocratic reformers who did not want to be constrained by bureaucratic reforms and the clientelist wing of the PRI that depended so heavily on patronage resources.

In this sense, Mexico provides a stronger confirmation of Barbara Geddes' (1994) hypotheses. Her argument is that when clientelist resources are pivotal in electoral politics, politicians will not approve civil service reforms, except under conditions when such reforms hurt patronage-dependent parties equally. This condition occurs when two major parties have almost equal power and hence equal access to patronage. Majority parties like the PRI have few incentives to give away one of their greatest advantages in electoral competition. However, the party-parity argument runs into problems in Argentina and Brazil. In Argentina, the majority Peronists relinquished patronage resources, despite the lack of parity, as did the fragmented Brazilian parties in the civil service reforms of 1988 as well as in some aspects of the managerial reforms of the 1990s. Politicians' interest in maintaining clientelist resources continues to be a significant factor in the success of civil service reforms — and may become more significant as governments enter the protracted process of institutionalizing reforms. However, the specific hypothesis that reform is likely only when two evenly matched parties face each other in Congress does not find strong confirmation in our cases. None of the six countries met the conditions of party parity, yet the extent of reform varied substantially.

Another institutional variable with more consistent explanatory power is coherence within the executive. Infighting within the executive stalled reforms in Mexico, Thailand, Hungary, and, to a lesser extent, in Brazil. In these countries, fragmentation of political support found expression within the executive, often manifested in the appointment of representatives from different factions or parties to key ministries and to some degree shifted contention among political factions from the legislature to the executive. In contrast, hyper-centralization in Argentina smoothed the path to reforms of all sorts.

Governments with support, usually captive, from labor and from peripheral or rural constituencies faced fewer obstacles to reform of central government administration. These conditions were clearest in the Argentine case, where one public sector union collaborated with government reformers and Menem maintained strong support from provincial Peronists.[22] In Brazil, unions opposed administrative reform, but politicians from the peripheral northeast helped pass the legislation. However, strong rural and union support is only a facilitating factor as demonstrated by Mexico, where the PRI enjoyed strong support but chose to avoid significant administrative reform.

A more positive, pro-reform group has traditionally been the amorphous and diffuse middle class. Governments competing for middle-class support often have more incentives to enact administrative reform, frequently in the direction of civil service reforms designed to reduce corruption and particularism in the delivery of basic services. In the United States, the middle class was the major force behind civil service reforms in the progressive era (see Shefter 1994). There is evidence of middle-class support for administrative reform of all types in Brazil, Thailand, Chile, and Mexico. However, this support does not seem to drive reform in our cases, largely due to the lack of direct intermediation between middle classes and parties. That is, many multiclass parties court middle-class voters as one of several constituencies, and in most countries it is impossible to identify any single party as the party of the middle class.[23] Moreover, few parties take up the cause of civil service reform as an electoral platform that might channel intense middle-class preferences. The Thai experience is especially revealing in that the middle class effectively bypassed intermediaries such as political parties to participate directly in decisionmaking on administrative reform.

Given the high costs of second wave reforms and daunting political obstacles, the strategies and leadership of reformers sometimes loom large in explaining reform outcomes. Skillful packaging increases chances reforms will be enacted. Linking contentious administrative reform to more consensual policies, such as electorally popular stabilization programs in Latin America or accession to the European Union in Hungary, reduces potential opposition to administrative reform. Good packaging can mobilize favorable public opinion, delegitimize opposition by losing groups, win over opponents within the bureaucracy, and enhance the leverage of external resources or pressures.

Opportunities for packaging naturally depend on what issues are at the top of the political agenda in each country. Reformers in Brazil and Argentina cast their administrative proposals in terms of essential measures to ensure the viability of popular stabilization programs. In Eastern Europe, supporters of administrative reform defended reform programs as essential components of their simultaneous political and economic liberalizations, as well as necessary conditions for entry into the European Union. Overall, of course, successful packaging is not costless. Packaging may help overcome short-term resistance yet leave reform without sustaining support over the longer run. When administrative reform succeeds initially because it is part of a larger agenda, then longer-term consolidation depends on the fortunes of that larger agenda. Tied to short-term stabilization, programs may barrage the bureaucracy with reform measures in the short run but flag once stabilization is achieved. Linked to longer-term programmatic goals, administrative reforms may take time to get off the ground yet benefit from sustained support over difficult periods of implementation.[24]

Internationally popular ideas, or "consensuses," also play a role in packaging. That administrative reform became part of the Washington consensus in the 1990s helped legitimate it in the eyes of some constituencies. The international imprimatur of managerialism, or the "new public administration," makes it appear more modern and high tech. Minister Bresser-Pereira worked to sell his reforms not only as the most modern but also as a strategy for Brazil to leap frog the stage of basic civil service reforms and land directly in the twenty-first century with the same reform strategies as those most popular in industrialized countries. This marketing strategy was less pronounced in other countries, though references to managerialism and "reinventing" government were common. As Robert Kaufman notes in this volume's concluding Chapter Ten, the Washington consensus on managerialism had a stronger influence in the Americas than in other regions.

Additionally, reformers can draw on international funding, through program loans rather than conditionality in emergency bailouts, to overcome resistance and implement reforms.[25] Funding from IFIs for specific programs of administrative reform does not have anything like the impact of IMF conditionality or the structural adjustment loans of the first wave. Nonetheless, even marginal international funding can help reformers leverage change. As noted above, administrative reform is costly in the short run, and most governments operate under tight fiscal restraints. International funds in this context can help reformers leverage more support from the government. In other cases, international funding allows reformers to undertake narrower pilot projects that, if successful, help reformers get domestic funds in subsequent efforts.

In sum, economic factors, especially fiscal crises, are triggers that help explain the timing of reforms. Reform proposals may be enacted under the duress of fiscal crises; however, their medium-term implementation depends more heavily on political factors, both institutional in the sense of the structure of the party system, as well as coalitional, in terms of which groups support reform and how strongly. The major determinants we started with are the degree of fusion — and hence the initial costs of reform — and the degree of programmatic commitment — or the willingness to bear costs over the longer term. In countries where the interests and careers of politicians and bureaucrats are closely linked, the likelihood of decisive action on administrative reform tends to be lower than in those in which a greater separation between the two groups exists. Where top political and policy elites hold anti-statist and strong pro-market views, the salience of administrative reform will tend to be lower and more focused around downsizing than in cases where elites hold more positive and pro-active views about the role of the state.

Our research also offers a number of specific conclusions on what to look at in order to understand the politics of administrative reform and what to look for in potential policy recommendations for furthering reform efforts. Since reform proposals rarely come out of party platforms, electoral campaigns, or civic mobilization, attention should focus, especially during the initial stages of reform, on politics within the executive. Core issues within the executive are the degree of fusion among political and bureaucratic elites, the programmatic commitments of the political elite in the executive, and the extent of cohesion (or lack of fragmentation or division) among the major groups represented in the executive. Contrary to some policy recommendations (Burki and Perry 1998, 136-137), our cases do not suggest any benefits from sequencing reforms or completing first wave reforms before embarking on second wave reforms. Given the benefits of packaging and the accelerating effects of economic crises, administrative reforms may progress further if conducted simultaneously with other major reforms. Reform advocates may well not be able to mobilize significant public and political support, and their time may be better spent seeking out captive coalitions and passive allies. In a related vein, reformers may be well advised to look for other reform programs to hitch onto rather than looking for ways to overcome the daunting problems of collective action that confront administrative reform (see Schneider 2000).

CONCLUSIONS: SUSTAINING REFORM EFFORTS

As noted at the outset, administrative reforms take a long time to become consolidated or institutionalized. Conversely, given political fluidity and turnover as well as the frequency of major reform initiatives, most rational bureaucrats, even in the countries where reforms have progressed the furthest, have good reason to doubt that current reforms will be institutionalized soon and in the same forms as they were initially enacted. What factors are likely to affect the institutionalization of reform, at least over the medium term? Variations in the level of elite motivation in favor of reform, strongly shaped by partisan views about the legitimate role of the state, are particularly important in the case of capacity-enhancing administrative change, given these reforms' long maturation periods and their high propensity toward reversibility. Two additional factors appear to be particularly important in conditioning the sustainability of reform efforts: the durability of the conditions under which reforms are initiated and the particular model of administrative reform enacted.

Conditions of initiation are important for consolidating reform efforts because variations in the specific causal factors driving administrative change tend to influence strongly the willingness and ability of reformers to sustain reform over time. For consolidation, the durability of the shifts triggering the introduction of administrative reform along with the number and relative political weight of initial winners seem especially important. Fiscal crises tend, for instance, to generate powerful incentives to embark upon bureaucratic modernization. The problems with financial stringency are that it tends to be short lived and it tends to produce, in the short run, many more losers than winners. As fiscal constraints relax, incentives to continue paying the costs of enforcing new rules diminish, and governments tend to return to pre-crisis administrative practices. The hike in public sector hiring in Argentina after the worst part of the fiscal crisis had passed is a good example of this pattern. Several factors, however, can, by prolonging the effects of fiscal constraints as levers of reform and/or by expanding the number of winners, make the automatic return to traditional practices less likely. For one, fiscal constraints have been fairly severe in developing countries for periods stretching up to a decade. Heavy indebtedness can force governments to devote a large proportion of government revenues merely to debt service. If governments maintain high interest rates to attract foreign investment and shore up the currency, then governments create their own ongoing fiscal constraint. Moreover, once macrostabilization becomes a trampoline to power (as it was for Menem and Cardoso), then politicians can emphasize fiscal austerity as a virtue and make it a political more than an economic variable.

The model of reform also shapes the nature, length, and complexity of the institutionalization process. In principle, managerial reform has a number of advantages. The reliance on market or quasi-market competition reduces monitoring and enforcement costs. What managerial reform does, in fact, is to delegate enforcement to competitive pressures, thereby reducing the time and effort reformers must spend in directly insuring compliance. If, for example, schools and health clinics, compete for "clients" and receive resources on the basis of the numbers of children they enroll or patients they treat, then central administrators do not have to assess the quality of the services. Budgeting should directly reward managerial behavior by redistributing resources to those agencies with more clients. An additional advantage of managerial reforms, especially when contrasted with civil service reforms, is that they can generate more concentrated groups of winners in a relatively short period of time. Winners of managerial reform strategies may include, among others, a small group of middle managers who gain autonomy as well as more concentrated groups of clients who experience dramatic changes in the services they receive.

Similarly, accountability reforms that grant the legislature more control over personnel and procedures in the executive branch may be easier to institutionalize, as legislators in principle constitute a powerful constituency with an enduring interest in maintaining its prerogatives.[26] Legislative oversight of the executive generates information for legislators and media attention, especially within specialized committees within the legislature that may otherwise have little importance or few political benefits for their members. Transparency reforms, in contrast, do not have semi-automatic, self-reinforcing tendencies to become institutionalized. The mere existence of transparency can alter bureaucratic behavior in the immediate run because bureaucrats will behave differently if they know that outsiders can monitor their decisions and performance. However, if bureaucrats perceive over time that no one is paying attention, then transparency has little impact. To be effective, transparency requires that someone be watching — that "someone" is usually composed of organized groups in civil society. The question for institutionalization is whether monitoring by civic organizations benefits the organizations, again by granting privileged information, by attracting media attention, and ultimately by helping to recruit new members. Although they did not receive very much attention in our project, organized groups such as neighborhood organizations, business associations, unions, ecology groups, and other NGOs, may take an interest in particular pieces of administrative reform or their application to agencies they watch. In such instances, institutional transparency can greatly reduce the cost of monitoring by these groups.

Of the three models of administrative reform, civil service reform appears to be the one most difficult to implement and institutionalize, especially initiatives designed to professionalize the civil service as a whole. The basic difficulty facing those seeking to professionalize the civil service is that moving from discretionary to merit-based recruitment and promotion deprives superiors of one of their most crucial levers of power and influence. This loss of power, in conjunction with the technical and administrative complexities implicit in setting up and operating a merit-based personnel system, make the enforcement costs of civil reform particularly high. As a result, gaining credibility for the new rules also tends to be especially difficult. The institutionalization of civil service reform hinges, in the first instance, on political powerholders' relinquishing discretionary control over the bureaucracy. Given the exceptional economic and political circumstances under which this type of reform is usually performed, surrendering the power to hire, promote, and fire personnel is politically quite costly and, in turn, generates strong incentives for inconsistent enforcement.

NOTES

1. We are grateful to Carlos Gil, Javier Parra, and Christa Van Wijnbergen for research assistance and to Guillermo O'Donnell, Herman Schwartz, Peter Siavelis, and the project participants for comments on earlier versions.

2. See Bradford (1994); Bresser-Pereira et al. (1993); Grindle (1997); Nelson (1994); Haggard (1997); Tendler (1997); and Turner and Hulme (1997).

3. See Mahon's chapter and Chaudry et al. (1994); Edwards (1997); and Burki and Perry (1998).

4. The Inter-American Development Bank's annual report on Latin America (BID 2000) highlighted the centrality of political variables in accounting for variations in the quality of public institutions. The report includes systematic comparisons of the effects on institutional quality of factors such as party fragmentation and electoral rules. The report does not, however, focus specifically on administrative reform.

5. However, we try to keep our focus narrow by excluding some elements of context such as culture or social networks, which admittedly are crucial elements of consolidating reform over the longer run. See the analyses in Grindle (1997) for more attention to culture and networks in specific reform initiatives. Tendler's (1997) analysis of "good government" in Northeastern Brazil is an excellent example of a fully embedded analysis of administrative reform.

6. At a higher level of abstraction, Haggard concludes that "the 'reform of the state' can thus be seen as a political process of striking a balance between the efficiency gains to be achieved by delegation, the interests of executives and legislators in controlling bureaucratic agents for political ends, and the need for politicians and bureaucrats to remain responsive to organized interest groups" (1997, 47). See also Geddes (1994) and Haggard and Kaufman (1995).

7. To illustrate, many countries have reformed tax collection. Our central focus in this area is not changes in tax rates or forms of collection (value added versus income taxes, for example) but on reforms within the tax collection agencies, especially those changes that affect career incentives for tax collectors.

8. In 1997, the *World Development Report* (World Bank 1997, 152), drawing on a paper by Moisés Naim, listed the "instruments" of the "first generation" of reform as "drastic budget cuts, tax reform, price liberalization, trade and foreign investment liberalization, deregulation, social funds, autonomous contracting agencies, some privatization." The second generation included "civil service reform, labor reform, restructuring of social ministries, judicial reform, modernizing of the legislature, upgrading regulatory capacity, improved tax collection, large-scale privatization, restructuring central-local government relationships."

9. Weyland (1998), for example, provides a persuasive argument linking hyperinflationary crisis to the willingness and ability of political elites to enact drastic reforms.

10. Some first wave reforms do generate political realignment. Hathaway (1998) documents how import liberalization in the United States turned previously protectionist sectors like shoe and textile manufacturers into advocates of free trade.

11. Geddes found that legislatures enacted civil service reforms only when the two or three largest parties achieved political parity. She also found that reforms were stalled or forgotten when, even in the space of a few years, parity collapsed (1994, 125-127). Institutionalized civil service reform required a generation of party parity in the case of the late nineteenth-century United States. In her view, institutionalization required the long-term maintenance of the initial conditions that triggered reform.

12. See Gerth and Mills (1946). Evans (1995) uses the shorthand "Weberian" to characterize these reforms and the resulting bureaucracies.

13. This has been a fairly steady process in the United States, especially in the last half of the twentieth century. See Lupia and McCubbins (1994) on the choice of various types of legislative oversight.

14. See Al Gore (1994) and other publications on Latin America by the National Performance Review. See also Bresser-Pereira and Spink (1999).

15. Argentina made the transition to democracy in 1983, Brazil in 1985, Thailand beginning in 1988 (and more solidly after 1993), Hungary in 1989, Chile in 1990, and Mexico in 2000.

16. Grindle (1997) covers more cases of reform in poorer and smaller countries.

17. Unger lists a string of reform proposals in Thailand. See Spink (1999) for a broad historical survey of reform attempts in Latin America. Reform proposals in the United States have been frequent since the late nineteenth century (Uveges and Keller 1998).

18. Economic crises have been common in our cases. From 1980 to 1997, growth was negative in Thailand, 1997; Chile, 1982-1983; Argentina, 1981-1982, 1985, 1988-1990, 1995; Mexico, 1982-1983, 1986, 1995; Brazil, 1981, 1983, 1988, 1990-1992 (IMF 1997, 144-147).

19. Currency or balance-of-payments crises by themselves do not necessarily shift attention to the bureaucracy. However, solutions in the short run to balance of payments problems usually do run through fiscal adjustment (in combination with higher interest rates and domestic recession). It is then that state officials begin looking more closely at what can be done with the bureaucracy.

20. Other economic factors have more indirect and segmented effects on administrative reform. Concern over balance of payments as well as more open economies strengthen liquid asset holders and exporters who then develop specific demands for reforming those parts of the government that oversee or affect domestic and international markets. Demands to make regulatory bodies more efficient and transparent or to streamline customs, taxation, and port administration are common. Reforms in these parts of the bureaucracy resemble first wave reforms in that they involve small numbers of bureaucrats and can often be resolved through the simpler institutional task of creating new agencies. Moreover, these reforms rarely generate widespread opposition from parties, unions, and other political actors who may oppose universal reforms. Pressures for these partial reforms are fairly constant and have built-in supporters once enacted.

21. The rankings for party fragmentation, by one rough measure, were the number of parties that accounted in the 1990s for 80 percent of the vote: two parties means low fragmentation, three parties indicates medium fragmentation, and four or more parties, high

fragmentation. Sources include Beyme (1993, 430) for Eastern Europe; Catiglioni and Medina (1998, 61-64) for Argentina; Aguirre (1998, 157-158) for Mexico; Mainwaring (1999) on Brazil and generally; and Chapter Seven on Thailand by Unger in this volume. Haggard and Kaufman (1995, 351-352) use a different indicator, the "effective number of parties," measured by the number of seats controlled by parties in the lower chamber of the legislature, to derive similar rankings: Chile, 2.0; Argentina, 2.9; Brazil, 5.5; and Thailand, 6.6. In the case of Chile, Haggard and Kaufman used a special measure of party coalitions rather than parties.

22. To revisit the Geddes hypothesis, what is striking in the Argentine case is that Menem was able to split support within an overall clientelist party between the over represented rural (or peripheral, non-Buenos Aires) faction, which continued to receive significant patronage resources, and the metropolitan faction, including labor unions, which did not (Gibson 1997). This strategy of course was closely related to Menem's strategy for resolving the fiscal crisis, and, counterfactually, the impetus for reforms that hurt the metropolitan clientelists would probably have been much weaker in the absence of fiscal crisis.

23. The PAN in northern Mexico may be an exception. Urban middle classes, acting as the center-right PAN's core constituency in Mexico's northern states, appear to have played a role in making it politically profitable for aspiring elites to push through anti-clientelistic administrative reforms in a number of municipal and provincial governments in Mexico (Mizrahi 1996).

24. Advocates of reform can also anticipate the obstacles created by fragmented party support or potential intra-executive infighting. Bresser-Pereira convinced President Cardoso to establish an interministerial council for state reform that included all major ministries. Bresser-Pereira then submitted his proposal first to this council. Once the council had approved it, it was harder for individual ministers to oppose the proposal openly. In Mexico, in contrast, President Zedillo charged the Ministry of Finance and Public Credit, also called the Treasury (Secretaría de Hacienda y Crédito Público — SHCP), with the task of elaborating a proposal for reform but granted the Ministry of Administrative Modernization and Control (Secretaría de Contraloría y Desarrollo Administrativo — SECODAM) veto power and never created a mechanism for resolving conflicts between the two.

25. The World Bank notes four ways that international agencies "can encourage and help sustain reform:" technical advice, cross-country experience, financial assistance, and "mechanisms for countries to make external commitments" (1997, 14-15). In our cases, technical assistance, expert foreign advice, and external commitments were not important, with the partial exception of Argentina. The Harvard Institute for International Development sponsored research on the success of their technical assistance programs and published the results in Grindle (1997).

26. Institutionalizing administrative changes aimed at increasing citizen participation in public management tends, in general, to be more lengthy and difficult. Reforms designed to incorporate direct citizen participation tend to increase administrative costs greatly by enlarging the number of participants and by lengthening the process of policy formulation. These reforms also tend to be, at least in the short run, strongly resisted and resented by most bureaucrats because citizen participation provides superiors with alternative sources of information concerning their behavior. As an enforcement and monitoring device, however, citizen participation is not quite as effective as market competition. First, citizen participation tends to be too irregular and variable to act as a reliable self-enforcing mechanism. Second, in the absence of conditions limiting the political benefits of the discretionary and particularistic exercise of political and bureaucratic power, expanded citizen participation can easily degenerate into booming clientelism.

References

Aguirre, Pedro. 1998. "El sistema de partidos mexicanos en el umbral de una nueva era." In *Partidos políticos y representación en América Latina*, eds. Thomas Manz and Moira Zuazo. Caracas: Nueva Sociedad.

Beyme, Klaus von. 1993. "Regime Transition and Recruitment of Elites in Eastern Europe." *Governance* 6: 3 (July): 409-425.

BID (Banco Interamericano de Desarrollo). 2000. *Desarrollo más allá de la economía. Progreso económico y social en América Latina.* Washington, D.C.: BID.

Bresser-Pereira, Luiz Carlos. 1996. *Economic Crisis and State Reform in Brazil.* Boulder, Colo.: Lynne Rienner Publishers.

Bresser-Pereira, Luiz Carlos. 1999. "From Bureaucratic to Managerial Public Administration in Brazil." In *Reforming the State: Managerial Public Administration in Latin America*, eds. Luiz Carlos Bresser-Pereira and Peter Spink. Boulder, Colo.: Lynne Rienner Publishers.

Bresser-Pereira, Luiz Carlos, José María Maravall, and Adam Przeworski. 1993. *Economic Reforms in New Democracies.* New York: Cambridge University Press.

Bresser-Pereira, Luiz Carlos, and Peter Spink, eds. 1999. *Reforming the State: Managerial Public Administration in Latin America.* Boulder, Colo.: Lynne Rienner Publishers.

Burki, Shahid, and Guillermo Perry. 1998. *Beyond the Washington Consensus: Institutions Matter.* Washington, D.C.: World Bank.

Cabrero, Enrique, and Teresita Escotto. 1992. *Evolución Reciente de los Procesos de Reforma de la Administración Pública y su Efecto en los Modelos Organizacionales.* Documento de Trabajo 8. Mexico City: CIDE.

Camp, Roderic. 1984. *The Making of a Government: Political Leaders in Modern Mexico.* Tucson, Ariz.: Arizona University Press.

Campos, José, and Hilton Root. 1996. *The Key to the Asian Miracle.* Washington, D.C.: The Brookings Institution.

Castiglioni, Franco, and Juan Abal Medina. 1998. "Transformaciones recientes del sistema de partidos argentinos." In *Partidos políticos y representación en América Latina*, eds. Thomas Manz and Moira Zuazo. Caracas: Nueva Sociedad.

Centeno, Miguel. 1994. *Democracy within Reason: Technocratic Revolution in Mexico.* University Park, Pa.: Pennsylvania State University Press.

Chaudry, Shahid, Gary Reid, and Waleed Malik. 1994. *Civil Service Reform in Latin America and the Caribbean.* Washington, D.C.: World Bank.

Cleaves, Peter. 1974. *Bureaucratic Politics and Administration in Chile.* Berkeley, Calif.: University of California Press.

DiIulio, John, ed. 1994. *Deregulating the Public Service.* Washington, D.C.: The Brookings Institution.

Edwards, Sebastian. 1997. "Latin America's Underperformance." *Foreign Affairs* 76: 2 (March/April): 93-103.

Evans, Peter. 1995. *Embedded Autonomy*. Princeton, N.J.: Princeton University Press.

Fontdevila, Pablo. 1994. "Downsizing the State: The Argentina Experience." In *Civil Service Reform in Latin America and the Caribbean*, eds. Shahid Chaudry, Gary Reid, and Waleed Malik. Washington, D.C.: World Bank.

Garman, Christopher, Stephan Haggard, and Eliza Willis. 1996. "Decentralization in Latin America." Paper presented at the annual meeting of the American Political Science Association.

Garvey, Gerald, and John DiIulio. 1994. "Sources of Public Service Overregulation." In *Deregulating the Public Service*, ed. John DiIulio. Washington, D.C.: The Brookings Institution.

Geddes, Barbara. 1994. *Politician's Dilemma*. Berkeley, Calif.: University of California Press.

Gerth, H.H., and C. Wright Mills, eds. [1946] 1958. *From Max Weber: Essays in Sociology*. New York: Oxford University Press.

Gibson, Edward. 1997. "The Populist Road to Market Reform." *World Politics* 49: 3 (April): 339-370.

Gore, Al. 1994. *Creating a Government That Works Better & Costs Less*. Washington, D.C.: National Performance Review.

Graham, Lawrence. 1998. "The State in Retreat in the Administrative Field." In *The Changing Role of the State in Latin America*, ed. Menno Vellinga. Boulder, Colo.: Westview Press.

Grindle, Merilee. 1977. *Bureaucrats, Politicians, and Peasants in Mexico*. Berkeley, Calif.: University of California Press.

Grindle, Merilee, ed. 1997. *Getting Good Government*. Cambridge, Mass.: Harvard University Press.

Grindle, Merilee. 2000. *Audacious Reforms: Institutional Invention and Democracy in Latin America*. Baltimore: The Johns Hopkins University Press.

Haggard, Stephan. 1995. "Reform of the State in Latin America." Paper.

Haggard, Stephan. 1997. "Reform of the State in Latin America." In *Development in Latin America and the Caribbean*, eds. Shahid Javed Burki and Guillermo Perry. Washington, D.C.: World Bank.

Haggard, Stephan, and Robert Kaufman. 1995. *The Political Economy of Democratic Transitions*. Princeton, N.J.: Princeton University Press.

Haggard, Stephan, and Sylvia Maxfield. 1996. "The Political Economy of Financial Internationalization in the Developing World." *International Organization* 50 (1): 35-68.

Hathaway, Oona. 1998. "Positive Feedback: The Impact of Trade Liberalization on Industry Demands for Protection." *International Organization* 52 (3): 575-613.

Instituto Brasileiro de Geografia e Estatística (IBGE). 1996. *Pesquisa Nacional por Amostra de Domicilios*. Rio de Janeiro: IBGE.

International Monetary Fund (IMF). 1997. *International Statistics Yearbook*. Washington, D.C.: IMF.

Johnson, Chalmers A. 1982. *MITI and the Japanese Miracle: The Growth of Industrial Policy*. Stanford, Calif.: Stanford University Press.

Kaufman, Robert. 1999. "Approaches to the Study of State Reform in Latin America and Postsocialist Countries." *Comparative Politics* 31: 3 (April): 357-376.

Krasner, Stephen D. 1984. "Approaches to the State: Alternative Conceptions and Historical Dynamics." *Comparative Politics* 16: 2 (January): 223-246.

Lupia, Arthur, and Mathew McCubbins. 1994. "Learning from Oversight: Fire Alarms and Police Patrols Reconstructed." *Journal of Law, Economics, and Organization* 10 (1): 96-125.

Mahon, James. 1996. *Mobile Capital and Latin American Development*. University Park, Pa.: Pennsylvania State University Press.

Mainwaring, Scott. 1999. *Rethinking Party Systems in the Third Wave of Democratization: The Case of Brazil*. Stanford, Calif.: Stanford University Press.

Maxfield, Sylvia. 1997. *Gatekeepers of Growth*. Princeton, N.J.: Princeton University Press.

Ministério da Administração Federal e da Reforma do Estado (MARE). 1995. *Plano Diretor da Reforma do Aparelho do Estado*. Brasília: MARE.

Mizrahi, Yemile. 1996. "Administrar o gobernar: El reto del gobierno panista en Chihuahua." Mimeo.

Moe, Terry. 1984. "The New Economics of Organization." *American Journal of Political Science* 28 (November): 739-777.

Nelson, Joan. 1994. "How Market Reforms and Democratic Consolidation Affect Each Other." In *Intricate Links*, ed. Joan Nelson. Washington, D.C.: Overseas Development Council (ODC).

Nelson, Joan. 1995. *Is the Era of Conditionality Past?* Working Paper 1995/72. Madrid: Instituto Juan March de Estudios e Investigaciones.

O'Donnell, Guillermo. 1993. "On the State, Democratization and Some Conceptual Problems." *World Development* 21 (8): 1355-1369.

Osborne, David, and Ted Gaebler. 1993. *Reinventing Government*. New York: Plume.

Prats i Català, Joan. 1999. "Democratic Governability in Latin America at the End of the Twentieth Century." In *Reforming the State: Managerial Public Administration in Latin America*, eds. Luiz Carlos Bresser-Pereira and Peter Spink. Boulder, Colo.: Lynne Rienner Publishers.

Riggs, Fred. 1964. *Administration in Developing Countries: The Theory of Prismatic Society*. Boston: Houghton Mifflin.

Schamis, Hector. 1999. "Distributional Coalitions and the Politics of Economic Reform in Latin America." *World Politics* 51 (2): 236-268.

Schneider, Ben Ross. 1991. *Politics within the State*. Pittsburgh: University of Pittsburgh Press.

Schneider, Ben Ross. 2000. "The Politics of Administrative Reform: Intractable Dilemmas and Improbable Solutions." Paper presented at the 1999 conference on *Sustainable Public Sector Finance*. Atlanta: Federal Reserve Bank of Atlanta. Available at <http://www.frbatlanta.org/invokecfm?objectid =CBC39D21-B434-11D5>.

Shefter, Martin. 1994. *Political Parties and the State: The American Political Experience*. Princeton, N.J.: Princeton University Press.

Schiavo-Campo, Salvatore, Giulio de Tommaso, and Amitabha Mukerjee. 1997. "An International Statistical Survey of Government Employment and Wages." Background paper for *World Development Report*. Washington, D.C.: World Bank.

Silberman, Bernard. 1993. *Cages of Reason: The Rise of the Rational State in France, Japan, the United States, and Great Britain*. Chicago: University of Chicago Press.

Spink, Peter. 1999. "Possibilities and Political Imperatives: Seventy Years of Administrative Reform in Latin America." In *Reforming the State: Managerial Public Administra-*

tion in Latin America, eds. Luiz Carlos Bresser-Pereira and Peter Spink. Boulder, Colo.: Lynne Rienner Publishers.

Tendler, Judith. 1997. *Good Government in the Tropics*. Baltimore: The Johns Hopkins University Press.

Turner, Mark, and David Hulme. 1997. *Governance, Administration, and Development: Making the State Work*. West Hartford, Conn.: Kumarian Press.

Uveges, Joseph, and Lawrence Keller. 1998. "One Hundred Years of American Public Administration and Counting." In *Handbook of Public Administration*, eds. Jack Robin, W. Bartely Hildrath, and Gerald Miller. New York: Marcel Dekker.

Weyland, Kurt. 1998. "The Political Fate of Market Reform in Latin America, Africa and Eastern Europe." *International Studies Quarterly* 42: 645-674.

Woo, Jung-en. 1991. *Race to the Swift: State and Finance in Korean Industrialization*. New York: Columbia University Press.

Woo-Cumings, Meredith. 1993. *Developmental Bureaucracy in Comparative Perspective: The Evolution of the Korean Civil Service*. EDI Working Paper 93-40. Washington, D.C.: World Bank.

World Bank. 1997. *World Development Report: The State in a Changing World*. New York: Oxford University Press.

EMPIRICAL STUDIES IN THE POLITICAL ECONOMY OF REFORM

Governo do Estado de Pernambuco. 2000. *Plano Diretor da Reforma do Estado*. January. Recife: Comissão Diretora de Reforma do Estado.

Habermas, Jürgen. 1984. *The Theory of Communicative Action,* volumes I and II. Boston: Beacon Press. Originally published in German, 1981.

Instituto de Estudos Políticos. 1997. *Os formadores de opinião no país e a Reforma do Estado*. February. Brasilia: Instituto Brasileiro de Estudos Políticos.

Melo, Marcus André. 1998. "When Institutions Matter: The Politics of Administrative, Social Security, and Tax Reform in Brazil." Paper included in this volume, Chapter Eight, originally presented at the Latin American Studies Association (LASA) Conference, Chicago, September 24-26, 1998.

MARE (Ministry of Federal Administration and State Reform). 1995. *Plano Diretor da Reforma do Aparelho do Estado*. November. Brasilia: Imprensa Nacional.

Osborne, David, and Ted Gaebler. 1992. *Reinventing Government*. Reading, Mass.: Addison-Wesley.

Petrucci, Vera, and Letícia Schwarz, eds. 1999. *Administração Pública Gerencial: A Reforma de 1995*. Brasilia: Editora da Universidade de Brasilia.

Chapter Five

FROM THE DISARTICULATION OF THE STATE TO THE MODERNIZATION OF PUBLIC MANAGEMENT IN CHILE: ADMINISTRATIVE REFORM WITHOUT A STATE PROJECT

Manuel Antonio Garretón and Gonzalo Cáceres

GENERAL ISSUES IN STATE REFORM

In recent years, the theme of the state in Latin America has been one of the most important in debates among domestic political actors, international organizations, researchers in the social sciences, and the scholarly community in general. The two main streams in these debates and studies on state reform have been 1) a focus on the changing nature of the state, including its new role and functions in a transformed society and 2) concrete policies and political processes oriented toward what is called the "modernization of the state."[1] Unfortunately, the proponents of these two streams or schools of thought have hardly communicated and have not worked together. The majority of policymakers and international organizations clearly prefer the second stream, the practical concept called "modernization." The drawbacks of modernization are that its narrow vision reduces reform to the explicit agendas of governments and international organizations, and its effects on states' apparatus are isolated from the social context. Under this second stream, everything happens as if the reforms or modernization were a neutral set of recommendations and practices that the state, also something neutral, should comply with to adapt itself to a new model of development.

This narrow, prescriptive view of the administrative reform of the state, with its specific policies for restructuring administration, does not question the nature of the state and its new relations with society. The modernization stream reduces reforms to formal descriptions of policies, evaluations of policies' effects, and analytic classifications of what are considered today as standard schemes or models of reform, such as bureaucratic (civil service) reforms, accountability reforms, and managerial reforms. Associated with the idea of models or types of reform is a sequential view of reforms in terms of "waves," for example, downsizing, rebuilding, or modernizing (see Heredia and Schneider and Kaufman, both chapters in this volume).

There are several problems with modernization's narrow vision. First, it reduces the reform of the state to a deterministic set of policies and isolates them from transformations occurring in society. Second, and more important, is that thinking of state reform in terms of waves assumes that there is an optimal sequential model with obligatory phases that every state should follow. This way of thinking and operating makes several normative and ideological assumptions. The sequence starts with the structural reform of the economy (the "transition to a market economy," according to the recipes followed by international institutions), which includes in its package of reforms the downsizing of the state. In practice, downsizing has not caused an across-the-board reduction of the size and resources of the state (some functions of the state, such as the military, may receive more resources than before); instead, a particular type of state is dismantled in order to rebuild another. That is, we are not dealing here simply with some neutral, technical measures. Modernization as a mode of state reform is actually the installation of a new mode of development that corresponds in part to a new mode of domination (O'Donnell 1978 and 1980).

Under modernization's sequenced view, the problems raised by the "first wave" of reforms lead to a second wave that attempts to redress the disastrous effects of the downsizing, organized around the ideas of the subsidiary role of the state while rebuilding its capacity to intervene in society. But all of this must be done according to the principles of the new economic model that emphasizes efficiency and views individuals more as consumers than as citizens. This means that the state must accomplish its own process of modernization, which corresponds to the "last wave" of state reform, that is, managerial modernization (see World Bank 1997; Bresser and Spink 1999; and Heredia and Schneider in this volume).

In the same way that downsizing obscured the policy goal of dismantling the state, the "second wave" confuses rebuilding state capacity with the process of strengthening citizens' rights. Similarly, an exclusive focus on the "third wave," which is managerial modernization of the state, though undoubtedly important and indeed indispensable, tends to neglect the real transformations in the broader society and polity that affect the state. When governments undertake reforms using the model of modernization, it is as if they are saying, "Let's do everything better without thinking about what we are going to do and why we are doing it." When this favored approach to reform is selected, both policies and analyses often look like little more than ideological and practical adaptations to the dominant neoliberal model (Bradford 1994).

SOME BASIC CONCEPTUAL ELEMENTS

In this chapter, we start from a somewhat different perspective, that is, we do not accept the idea that administrative reform is a positive subproduct of the hallowed neoliberal reforms. First, the state is defined herein as

1. The set of public institutions and organizations with the legitimate monopoly of coercion in a given territory;
2. The locus of crystallization of power relations in the society; and
3. The main agent and actor able to bring about national unity, social integration, economic development, and social change.

Any transformation in these functions and tasks creates effects in the administrative apparatus, and, vice versa, changes in the administrative apparatus tend to alter the role of the state and its relations with society. Therefore, when we refer to a transformation of the state, we should always consider four levels:

1. The state's general role and functions in development, national unity, domination, and integration;

2. State institutions and organizations;

3. Personnel, including the executive branch and techno-bureaucracy, the legislative and judicial branches, and all of the other people who make up the federal bureaucracy; and

4. Specific relations with citizens (as the customers of the state's services).

Administrative reform is always based on some changes in the first level and consists of modifications of structure, norms, procedures, and practices in any of the other three levels.

Second, we define *state administrative reform* as any partial or global formal change in the state apparatus, institutions, organizations, or procedures, based on an official decision by a state authority that may or may not be part of an explicit general agenda or intended policy. In this sense, administrative reform should not be confused with the more general concepts of state reform (the deliberate and explicit dimension) or state transformation (the factual or implicit dimension) that concerns the changing relations between the state and society and that embrace the different functions and tasks that the state plays in these relations and in the general mode of development. In this sense, *administrative reform of the state is only a partial and particular part of state reform or transformation.* However, in turn, administrative reforms always express some deeper transformation of the state — this dimension should be highlighted before a state faces administrative changes and when we study this process (Garretón and Espinosa 1992; Garretón 2000; Melo 1999). Therefore, we will consider what have been called "waves" not as a sequence but rather as particular and specific types of policies directed toward the state, which are part of a transformation of the relations of the state with society and are guided by specific ideological visions about the role of the state.

Third, we must place the administrative reform of the state in Latin America in the context of the more general changes occurring in what we have called the "socio-political matrix," that is, the relations among the state, its system of representation, civil society and social actors, and a particular political regime (Garretón 1996; Garretón and Espinosa 1992).

The following questions then arise: How have changes in the last decades in the economic model, political regimes, and relations among social actors affected and transformed the state? How has this transformation in turn affected the other elements?

THE CRISIS OF THE NATIONAL-POPULAR STATE AND CHILE'S ADMINISTRATIVE REFORM

Our main hypothesis is that we are witnessing a radical change of the national-popular state, which prevailed in Latin America for several decades after the 1930s. The national-popular state played a key role in nation building, industrialization, the organization of the internal order, and social integration and redistribution. This type of state expanded progressively in size and resources and became the main referent of collective action, thus politicizing society (Touraine 1989).

Various causes and phenomena lie behind the crisis or rupture of the national-popular state, including economic reforms that led to a new economic model, the integration of states' economies into the global economy and into an increasingly integrated region, authoritarian regimes giving way to democratization processes, social disintegration, and contradictory cultural tendencies that combined globalization with new identities and forms of collective action. However, a new coherent state model has not emerged to replace the national-popular one, given the total failure of the early neoliberal attempts and also of later corrections. In this regard, what we see are different attempts at partially replacing the old, classical "state of compromise." Administrative reform is one aspect of these attempts but is not in and of itself a new, successful pattern.[2]

The rest of this chapter presents the main policies of administrative reform of the state in Chile.[3] First, the situation of the state is described under the previous democratic regime until its break with the military coup of 1973; then the legacy of authoritarian rule is covered, continuing with the programs of the first democratic government (1990-1994), followed by an analysis of the explicit policies of state modernization under the government of Eduardo Frei Ruiz-Tagle (1994-1999). The chapter concludes with a preliminary analysis of state reform promised by the third government of the Alliance of Parties for Democracy (Concertación de Partidos por la Democracia — CPD), led by President Ricardo Lagos (2000-2001).

TRAJECTORY AND CRISIS OF THE NATIONAL-POPULAR DEMOCRATIC STATE[4]

From the 1930s until the violent change of government in 1973, the Chilean state played a decisive role in nearly every aspect of Chilean society.[5] Starting in the 1930s, three types of ideological influences filtered into debates among Chilean elites. First, various versions of the New Deal, among other plans, were designed to revive economies after the 1929 crisis and later on, those of the welfare state, also linked to the post-war reconstruction of national states. Second, statist visions arising from ideologies as different and contradictory as corporativism, Soviet socialism, and social democracy gained currency. A third and final ideological influence, more exclusively Latin American, was the expansion of the state, giving it a populist and reformist character, with the decisive presence of the middle class as well as of popular sectors. This has been called the "state of compromise" (Touraine 1989).

The confluence of these three ideological views validated the strategic role of the state in Chile's economic, social, and cultural development. It also served both as a theoretical and a practical justification for general and sectoral development plans (at the moment when they were being set in motion), making them capable of reactivating the economy and driving industrialization after the 1929 crisis. These development plans substantially broadened educational opportunities after 1938, provided a small but dynamic housing supply from mid-century onward, and activated processes of agrarian, educational, and urban structural reform through the 1960s.[6]

Developmentalism combined with labor populism reaffirmed the proactive role of a centralized and dirigiste state in the creation of big public companies, dedicated to the exploitation of natural monopolies (the entrepreneurial state) and to the adoption of a national system of social policies. Although explicitly and formally universal, these social policies were, in practice, concentrated on the middle sectors (the social state). This broad range of policies and activities generated an extensive bureaucratic apparatus, which was embedded in partisan politics yet simultaneously endowed with a relative autonomy and a vocation of public service.

From 1964 to 1973, the mesocratic (middle-class) bias of public policies broadened to include agrarian and urban popular sectors, which, either through their own mobilization or stimulated by the state, had induced the state to meet some of their demands. This expansion of coverage in social policies translated into the institutionalization of a series of state entities of support for the agrarian and urban popular worlds. At the same time, economic policies sought to expand the internal market, create a great commercial block of Andean countries, and strengthen the state's role in the planning of development. The economic side of state intervention required the creation of a technocratic — rather than welfare — structure within the state apparatus. The expansion of the state's size via the multiplication of new responsibilities and the aggregation of tasks and dependencies — without an internal reformulation and restructuring of the state apparatus — not only created more jobs in the bureaucratic corps but also deepened rigidities that were a drag on individual and collective performance in many divisions. Most of these divisions lacked mechanisms for performance evaluations of public employees.

The culminating point in this history of the progressive expansion of the state came in 1970, when the left-wing coalition forming the Popular Unity (Unidad Popular) came to power. Public services and companies expanded, and a massive operation of nationalizations, buyouts, and interventions in private companies of diverse sizes and quality in all sectors created what was called the "Social Property Area." The crisis and end of the government of the Unidad Popular in 1973 was also the terminal crisis of the national-popular state.[7]

The expansion of the state's developmental and social responsibilities and the administrative apparatus to execute them also had profound effects on the organization of politics and civil society. The process of state expansion was part of a broader process that could be called the "statization" of society, whereby the state increasingly became the main practical and symbolic referent for collective action.

THE DISMANTLING OF THE NATIONAL-POPULAR STATE (1973-1990) AND THE LEGACIES OF AUTHORITARIAN RULE

The structural reforms undertaken by the military regime of General Augusto Pinochet Ugarte, under the auspices of authoritarianism and neoliberalism, set the basis for a dramatic reduction in fiscal spending. From 45 percent of gross domestic product (GDP) in 1973, fiscal spending fell by more than half to 20 percent in 1987 and to 17 percent in 1989.[8] The Chilean tax system in place at the end of the 1980s was the product of tax reforms in 1974 and 1984. The 1974 Tax Reform fully indexed the tax system and eliminated a broad spectrum of exemptions and special tax treatments. The 1974 reform also created an additional rate of 40 percent on corporate revenues and established a value added tax (VAT or *impuesto al valor agregado* — IVA) to replace the older, inefficient sales tax. The 1984 Tax Reform, for its part, mainly affected the direct taxpaying system, introducing the principle of taxing expenses instead of incomes.[9]

In the period prior to the 1988 plebiscite, following an electoral strategy designed to appeal to most citizens, the Pinochet government made important cuts in major tax rates. Among these cuts were reductions in the special VAT for luxury items and fuels, an overall reduction of the VAT from 20 percent to 16 percent, reduction of foreign trade tariffs from 20 to 15 percent, reduction of the tax on seals and stamps, and suppression of the 2 percent tax on remuneration schedules. Together these cuts made up a fiscal cost of nearly $US600 million (Marcel 1997). The tax cuts during the last two years of military rule, combined with the ongoing costs of the state's intervention in solving the financial crisis of 1982, created a heavy burden for the consolidation of fiscal discipline for democratic governments after 1990.

Together with the introduction of radical changes in the economy — liberalization, external opening, and privatization — the military government transformed social policies. These changes moved in six main directions:[10]

1. Drastic reduction of resources, affecting with particular intensity housing, health, and education (and within these, major reductions in investment and remuneration for personnel in these sectors);

2. Transference of executive functions and relocation of services to the private sector and geographic deconcentration of ministries and services;

3. Introduction of market mechanisms in the allocation of public resources (to subsidize demands);

4. Implementation of concrete measures directed at reducing nominally universal programs and targeting fiscal resources to be spent on the poorer segments of the population;

5. Development of compensatory social programs for situations of extreme poverty; and

6. Weakening the power of workers and unions together with strict controls on the collective expression of social demands.

Despite the lack of a coherent "package of administrative reforms," as such, the military government, from the moment of the first adjustment policy in 1975, executed a group of measures that deeply transformed the apparatus of the state. Among these are the massive privatizations of public ventures — leaving some privatizations "pending" and exempting large-scale copper mining — as well as privatizations of public services, especially social security; the relocation of public services' functions; the relocation of the fiscal deficit to municipalities in the areas of education and health; the drastic reduction of public servants and the elimination of agencies; the restructuring and weakening of the "social" ministries and the modernization of the "economic" ones; the new regionalization of the country with a military seal; administrative legislation that generated increasing instability; and the establishment of an organic constitutional law, which made the modification of this legal corpus enormously difficult.[11]

Consequently, in spite of some initial measures of financial and administrative rationalization, in practice, a pronounced deterioration of public management resulted, given that the economic authorities of the military regime considered the state, by definition, inefficient. The pervasive arbitrariness, authoritarianism, and devaluation of public functions devastated bureaucrats' morale. Their salaries were reduced disproportionately by fiscal adjustments. The Pinochet government, obsessed with privatizations, abandoned public services employees to their fate (Marcel 1994, 14).

Thus, an extremely negative notion of the role of state was disseminated, claiming that modernization and efficient management were synonymous with the private sector. The dominant political thinking associated the public sector with antiquated, bureaucratic, and anachronistic ideas and images. As a consequence, all public servants were unfairly considered to be inefficient. This prejudiced vision, which rejected the functions and effectiveness of public policies, continued under ensuing democratic governments, among right-wing political groups and business sectors. Behind these arguments were, on the one hand, an interest in impeding the generation of regulating devices and, on the other, an interest in privatizing all the available public capital and services (Díaz 1988, 2). But here, in addition, there is also a larger ideological-political aspect: punishing a sector that is seen as responsible for the crisis of 1973 and eliminating state intervention, understood as the main cause of the politicization of the society. Neoliberals and neo-conservatives, by underlining the inefficacy of state action and its supposedly harmful effects on economic growth, in fact became a powerful brake on the endogenous modernization of the public administration, opposing various reform initiatives attempted by the democratic governments (Oyarce 1997).

In synthesis, the democratic governments did not inherit an economic crisis as such, but they did inherit a model of economic growth with enormous social imbalances and a profoundly transformed state apparatus.[12] This transformation had two main implications. The first was structural: the state was adapting to a new model of development through drastic reductions in its size, resources, and functions.[13] The second was political-cultural: a dominant ideology of negative criticism of state functions and a marked deterioration of public management, and, in turn, drastic reductions in services provided.

DEMOCRATIC CORRECTIONS AND
ADAPTATION TO NEW SOCIAL POLICIES

In March 1990, Patricio Aylwin became president with the support of the center-left coalition of parties called the Coalition of Parties for Democracy (Concertación de Partidos por la Democracia), composed mainly by the Christian Democrats, the Radical Party (UCR), Socialists, and the Party for Democracy (Partido por la Democracia). The central axes of the first democratic government's actions were two: 1) to maintain the macroeconomic stability of the last phase of the neoliberal economic plan that was undertaken by the military regime, while accelerating growth and correcting social inequalities; and 2) to consolidate the democratic government elected in 1989 after the 1988 Plebiscite, avoiding the possibility of an authoritarian regression by the *pinochetist* forces and establishing some truth and justice concerning torture, murders, and other human rights abuses of citizens. The socioeconomic model was labeled as "growth with equity," and the political dimension as "transition (to democracy) government," both encompassed by the strategy of so-called "democracy of agreements or consensus."[14]

Given these primary priorities, the modernization of the state remained a secondary matter on the new government's agenda. In fact, it was rarely mentioned in the Coalition for Democracy's program. Moreover, the matter of state reform was later dropped, and government officials even made declarations against the possibility of reform. Behind this anti-reform position were, in part, the two core programmatic priorities, with stability and economic growth as the predominant factor. Proponents of the anti-reform position also harbored political concerns: the desire to avoid confrontation with the bureaucrats and the institutions inherited from the dictatorship, as they feared destabilizing opposition from business and military leaders. Simultaneously, many leaders in the new government had an ideological-cultural tendency to view past experiences of global or radical social change as traumatic (for example, some measures undertaken by the Allende government) and, therefore, advocated gradual, incremental alternatives (Flisfisch 1993; Garretón and Espinosa 1992; Boeninger 1997).

In spite of this hesitation, one may distinguish some lines of action that signaled a clear break with the vision of the state dominant under the military regime and in neoliberal ideology, although they were not part of a systematic package of measures, nor do they quite add up to a coherent alternative vision.

Reinforcement of the State's Capacity

The weakened state inherited from the military regime generated the need for reinforcing the state in three areas: reorganization at the central executive decision-making level, new state agencies for social policies, and national commissions and councils to develop new relationships with sectors of civil society.

1. *Reorganization at the central executive decision-making level.* During a good part of the twentieth century, the Chilean presidential system was based on the premise that the highly personalized power of the president was sufficient to coordinate a decision-making system that comprehended both a very limited

number of actors and matters of great simplicity. By eliminating the democratic partisan character of the government and by tailoring the decision-making system to a hierarchic model of a military nature, the military regime used the personalized and relatively absolute power of General Pinochet to operate as an effective coordinating factor that gave coherence to governmental action. One of the institutional mechanisms that made this control effective was derived from military institutions: the Presidential General Staff (Estado Mayor), later called the Secretary-General of the Presidency (Secretaría General de la Presidencia — SEGPRES).

The Aylwin government elevated SEGPRES to the category of a Ministry in 1990. Subsequently, SEGPRES successfully assumed a leading role in the programs and actions of the Ministries of the Political Area and in general government coordination.[15] Additionally, an issue that would later be very important for the process of modernizing the state was that SEGPRES had as one of its basic objectives to "evaluate the need to introduce innovations into the organization and procedures of the administration of the state, in order to propose them to the Ministry of Interior" (Aylwin 1991, 390). However, because the creation and elevation of SEGPRES was a short-term measure not accompanied by a more general restructuring of the high-level state apparatus, some other new agencies, such as those designed to work on environmental problems, for example, CONAMA (Comisión Nacional del Medio Ambiente), were placed under SEGPRES' jurisdiction, while other functions such as information remained in other ministries. This disorganization weakened SEGPRES' leadership on the general affairs of the government.

Alongside this ministerial restructuring, which included the reorganization of the Ministries of the Secretary-General of the Government (Secretaría General de Gobierno) and of Planning and International Cooperation (MIDEPLAN), two further mechanisms of coordination were implemented: the setting of ministerial goals (or groups of tasks or priority plans) for a determined period with periodic follow-up and evaluation (Metas ministeriales 1990; and Chateau 1997) and the formation of Inter-Ministerial Committees to ensure the coherence of governmental action (MIDEPLAN 1994 and 1996).

The issue of state reform was first limited to the activities of an ad-hoc Inter-Ministerial Committee called the Working Group on the Improvement of Public Management, established in November 1991. This group, composed primarily of second-level ministerial undersecretaries, lacked sufficient dynamism; by 1993, it became clear that its activities were of little relevance (MIDEPLAN 1993). Nevertheless, the Undersecretary of Regional Development and Administration (Subsecretaría de Desarrollo Regional y Administrativo), part of the Ministry of Interior, took some pioneering initiatives to streamline the bureaucracy and modernize public management. This Undersecretary's main initiatives included a) carrying out pilot programs under the Offices of Public Information at the central and local levels (107 of these offices were constituted by 1993), whose purpose was to assist citizens requiring services from the public sector; b) educating state employees in matters of public management; and c) consolidating a group concerned with information technology issues, aiming to produce norms for equipment acquisition and consulting, as well as the establishment of public sector networks for communications and database access (Aylwin 1991, 16; Aylwin 1992, 17; and Aylwin 1993, 15).

2. *New state agencies for social policies.* Patricio Aylwin's administration concentrated, as has been noted, a substantial part of its actions on the correction of the economic model's social effects of poverty and inequality, focusing on those social groups most punished by structural adjustment policies (Raczynski 1994). To this end, the Aylwin government reinforced the existing agencies and created additional state agencies to assist vulnerable groups, drawing on significant support from international cooperation. Among others, the Fund for Solidarity and Social Investment (Fondo de Solidaridad e Inversión Social — FOSIS), the National Institute for Youth (Instituto Nacional para la Juventud — INJ), the National Women's Service (Servicio Nacional de Mujeres — SERNAM), the National Corporation for the Development of Indigenous Peoples (Corporación Nacional de Desarrollo Indígena — CONADI) and the National Fund for Citizens with Disabilities (Fondo Nacional para los Discapacitados — FONADIS) were created and integrated into the Ministry of Planning and Cooperation.

After a few years, the combined effect of economic growth, new targeted programs, and previous assistance plans steadily reduced the adverse indexes of poverty and extreme poverty in Chile (MIDEPLAN 1996). Between 1987 and 1994, the percentage of the national population living in poverty fell from 45 to 28 percent. Between 1990 and 1994, the population under the poverty line fell almost 12 percentage points, and the number of poor people dropped from 5.2 to 3.9 million, a significant reduction in a total population of close to 14 million. No less significant was the reduction in the index for "extreme poverty," which fell from 17 to 8 percent between the mid-1980s to the mid-1990s. These achievements are remarkable, considering the short period of time when they were achieved, and even more impressive if compared with the poverty levels of other Latin American countries (Consejo Nacional para la Superación de la Pobreza 1996, 52). More recent figures show a consolidation of the diminishing tendency of the indicators for poverty and extreme poverty. While in 1994 the percentage of poor people reached 27.5 percent, in 1996 this figure fell to 23.3 percent. The percentage of those in extreme poverty fell from 7.6 percent in 1994 to 5.8 percent in 1996 ("Las paradojas de la encuesta CASEN 96," 1997). Complying with its principles of growth with equity, the government raised these targeted programs to the level of stable policies (Garretón 1996, 7).

3. *National commissions and councils to develop new relationships with sectors of civil society.* In areas where debate or consensus-building was needed, either because the government did not have a clear policy or because officials perceived a need to legitimate its policy ideas between the executive and legislative branches, the Aylwin government introduced the innovative idea of National Commissions. These commissions are composed of representatives from the executive, the legislative, the political class, and civil society and are charged with debating or proposing policies in sensitive areas such as human rights or higher education. Frei's administration deepened this practice, spreading it to a wider variety of problems, such as public ethics, poverty, education, productive development, savings, and information technologies. These were key efforts in democra-

tizing or accountability reforms, according to Heredia and Schneider's classification (see Chapter One of this volume).

It is evident that this system of National Commissions allows for an integration of representative sectors of civil society into the state and makes a necessary distinction between state policies and governmental policies, which form part of an ongoing redefinition of the role of the state. However, unlike countries with parliamentary regimes where such national commissions respond to their Congresses and their decisions are much more than mere suggestions, in Chile these commissions have a debating, consultative, and symbolic function, often serving only to legitimize or delegitimize particular policies of the executive. When institutions actually have to make policy decisions, such as the National Television Council, they tend to reproduce the political-partisan correlation of forces, so that their autonomy is minimal and their debate is often just a prolongation of the options already presented by different political parties.

Additionally, between 1994 and 1998, the government created a great number of Inter-Ministerial Committees and Counseling Commissions for dealing with specific problems, such as development of certain regions, modernization of education, dealing with child abuse, and modernizing the regulatory role of the state. Usually, these committees would reach beyond the executive to include representatives from Congress, but, in contrast with the National Commissions, these groups rarely included representatives from civil society (*El Mercurio* 1998, D4).

Improvement of Working Conditions for the Public Sector

Public Salaries

In 1990, the public sector's low salaries and poor working conditions, along with distortions in personnel administration and the overall salary system, constituted a potential source of conflict and an obstacle to appropriate usage of the state apparatus. The responses of the incoming democratic governments had several components (Flisfisch 1993):

1. *General readjustments of remunerations and leveling of incomes of the most delayed sectors and rationalization of the remuneration system in the public sector.* Between 1990 and 1997, the fiscal expenditures on personnel rose by 118 percent or approximately $661 million dollars. In the same period, the average annual spending on personnel grew more than the ordinary expenditure: 11.7 percent versus 10.3 percent, meaning that, in relative terms, the state's yearly budgets have privileged remunerations over social or investment programs. Aylwin's government gave four salary adjustments to the public sector: in 1990, 25 percent; in 1991, 18 percent; in 1992, 14 percent; and in 1993, 15 percent. After an initial reduction in salaries caused by the great inflation of 1990, a gradual and sustained increase of real remunerations was achieved in the public sector as a whole. In fact, between 1990 and 1993, total remunerations of public employees — including the armed forces and police personnel — grew nearly 30 percent in real terms, doubling the real growth of the general index of wages for the same period. Within this across-the-board increase, the improvement in the remunerations of the central adminis-

tration was remarkable, reaching 36 percent in real terms. With this growth, salaries in the central administration recovered the highest levels of remuneration registered since 1978.

2. *Improvement of the working conditions of public administration personnel and their performance*, via career tracks, elimination of distortion in remunerations, improvement of evaluation systems, and so on.

3. *Strict control of the expansion of public employment, limiting increases in personnel to the most deficient sectors of the public administration.* Between 1990 and 1997, the total number of public servants, excluding the armed forces, grew by 14 percent. While in 1990 the number of civil servants in the central government reached 114,023, by 1997, the number had risen to 132,485. This number translates into a yearly increase of 2.4 percent. Nevertheless, if it is a question of measuring the state's size, it has remained relatively stable, with public spending around 20 percent of GDP, with the sole exception of 1993, when it reached 21.4 percent.

4. *A regular system of consultation and information with the main workers' organizations in the public sector*, through the establishment of specific technical commissions and the promotion of annual agreements on labor issues within the public sector.

Employment Conditions

With regard to the organization of the public administration, between 1973 and 1989 a decree law on public administration established that all administrative positions were subject to the rule of flexibility and hence temporary. Before turning over power to the incoming democratic government, the military regime modified this situation with the application of a group of norms on tenure, which acquired the rank of Organic Constitutional Law (Ley de Bases de la Administración Pública), thus making its modification very difficult. These norms, which generated a situation of almost absolute employment tenure, in principle reduced the number of positions of exclusive reliance on the president to fewer than 500 for the new administration. However, through negotiations between the exiting regime and the opposition, those positions were increased to approximately 2,000. In order to attenuate the consequences for rigidity of these measures, the Frei Administration, after 1994, attempted to ameliorate the evaluation system, linking individual performance bonuses with collective performance in order to create an incentive for those services that fulfilled the established goals.

Before 1990, public employees naturally developed and internalized strategic defensive attitudes and behaviors to counter their experiences of precariousness, insecurity, and arbitrariness they suffered under the military regime. On the one hand, public employees endorsed corporative actions designed to modify the current legal framework to accentuate its rigidity even more, and, on the other hand, they evinced a generalized hostility toward innovative ideas and initiatives that implied greater demands for employee productivity and autonomous responsible performance, often perceived as threats to employment stability and automatic promotion based on seniority.

Improvements in the Health, Education, Municipal, and Regional Administrations

Health and Education

In the health and education sectors, neoliberal policies initially executed by the military regime with a high level of centralization resulted in these same policies being transferred to municipal governments. The state acted much like a regulating entity toward the municipal governments and financed them through a system of transferences (subventions). One of the effects of this decentralization was to pull personnel from both sectors out of previously statutory normative frameworks; in both cases, this constituted a variant of the administrative statute of the Central Administration. Labor relations for these employees thus became essentially the same as the contractual model of common labor law. As a consequence, during the 1980s, employees in the health and education sectors experienced a process that could be described as a proletarization, informalization, and marginalization.

The Aylwin government confronted these problems by increasing spending on infrastructure and some technological innovations; it also created special statutes covering teaching and health personnel. The first of these statutes (Estatuto Docente) was more significant, as it implied a political rupture in the coherence with which Aylwin's economic team wanted to treat the labor issues, that is, without special treatment for any sector, and it involved a long negotiation with the teachers' union.

Municipalization[16]

The military regime strengthened municipal governments by transferring three types of activity to them: public education, both basic and mid-level; primary health care; and the administration and management of diverse subsidies, including those for housing. In addition, during the economic crisis starting toward the end of 1981, municipal governments were also responsible for administering two important employment programs, designed to mitigate rapidly rising unemployment levels, which ran over 30 percent in some periods. The challenge of developing these activities gave dynamism to many municipalities, not only in traditional administrative functions, but also in areas such as cultural activities. All of this was done within the framework of a strict municipal authoritarianism and verticalism; the military regime eliminated local elected bodies, introduced deliberative councils of unelected "notables," and mayors were directly appointed by Pinochet in all municipalities.

After 1990, the Aylwin government sought to strengthen municipal competence and autonomy in matters of health and education through two legal projects, one on revenues and the other on health care. At the same time, the only constitutional reform aimed at overcoming the authoritarian enclaves (in this case, the central government's appointment of mayors; see Garretón 1995) was precisely the one terminating the appointment of mayors and generating a new democratic structure of communal government, relatively similar to the pre-1973 system.

Regionalization

The regionalization process carried out by the military regime had different ideological origins from municipalization. Municipalization, based on a developmentalist discourse, attempted to balance a weakening of the central state with a strengthening of the municipalities, with the intension of expanding collective decisionmaking so that individuals would have greater control (this complemented the goal of market expansion). In contrast, though regionalization was also inspired by right-wing, developmentalist ideology, it advocated some geopolitical concerns along with elements taken from the national security doctrine. This exercise culminated in a division of the country into 13 regions that exist to this day. With some exceptions, these artificial regions have been weak political-territorial units that lack true regional cultural identities to hold them together.

The Aylwin government pushed regional reforms further and provided regional governments with a sui generis political structure, which no doubt constitutes one of the most innovative contemporary modifications of the state. However, these new political structures were unable to resolve the problem of regional government in terms of effective decentralization and regional autonomy. In synthesis, this reform gives juridical personality and independent resources to the regions and endows them with a mixed system of government. The mixed system is composed of an executive, including the governor and his or her cabinet of regional ministerial secretaries — all of whom are centrally designated by the President — and a regional council elected by a provincial election board whose members are the councilors from the municipalities in each province.

THE MODERNIZATION OF PUBLIC MANAGEMENT UNDER THE FREI GOVERNMENT (1994-2000)

B eginning with the second government of the Concertación, the emphasis in matters of state reform changed substantively. One of the 13 inter-party commissions charged with elaborating the new government's program was explicitly dedicated to the issue of the state and its reform, using the term "reform" in the official language of the program for the first time. As we have seen, during the military regime, the issue of the state and its reform was an instrument of a new mode of domination and development. Under the Aylwin government, the issue of state reform was seen as a means toward the achievement of other democratization aims. In contrast, the Frei government made state reform an integral part of a general modernization project.

Thus, among the major, long-term projects of the Frei government, the subjects of the state and its modernization appear fundamental.[17] For example, the *Presidential Instructions* given at the creation of the Inter-ministerial Committee on Modernization of Public Management from December 1994, to which we will refer later, state:

> The development of the country requires the gradual perfecting of our administration, making it more efficient both in its organization and its management. Such perfecting must be made within the framework of the existing legality and

constitute itself in an effective means for the execution of public policies. . . . It is indispensable for the achievement of this objective . . . to move gradually toward a management style oriented by results and centered on the service to the citizenry, and . . . that the mission, goals, and results of the public organisms be known by the citizens, so that they may evaluate their management in terms of relevance, effectiveness, and efficiency" (Frei 1994).

Four years later, in his *Message before the Congress* in May 1998, the President consecrated an explicit chapter for the "the necessary modernization of the state." Frei advocated "reinforcing the state" through modernization. To implement this policy, his message announced the introduction of management indicators for public services and independent technical evaluations of governmental programs. Frei set a goal for the end of his term that the 100 most important programs would be subjected to this type of evaluation. This argument was reinforced by announcing the installation of a control system for the performance of public functions. Finally, he mentioned different laws or regulatory projects concerning public probity, public management of the state, and management and financing policies for public enterprises (Frei 1998).

The central idea of state efficiency has been permeated by some ambivalence concerning the role and size of the state. In the beginning of its administration, the Frei government had great difficulty defining its primary goals and place in history; thus, for a long period, the definition revolved around the shift from "political democracy" to "modernization" as the axis of governmental action. This shift, however, did not help the administration set priorities, form a strategy for action, nor fix a clear image of what the central problematique was for the government (Garretón 1995). Consequently, the government discourse about the state oscillated between, at the beginning, an emphasis on the idea of reducing the state's size, considering any reduction of public spending as a success, and, after some years, some emphasis on the defense of a strong state, which included reversing its earlier stance advocating its reduction in size.

In any case, the central task of state reform was "modernization," understood as the flexibility, rationalization, and efficiency of public management, and consisting of ". . . (a) a management committed to results, (b) transparency in the application of resources, (c) a quality public service for the people. This is how the government understood it, setting in motion modernization programs which involve the identification of strategic objectives, construction of management control systems, establishment of management performance indicators, commitment to specific goals, greater resources and equipment, up to the necessary and unavoidable education programs for public servants" (Aninat 1996).

While this vision of the modernization of the state concentrates on perfecting its administrative management, through efficiency and efficacy, the debate over the size of the state has not been neglected by the government. In spite of some initial oscillations already mentioned, government discourse increasingly emphasized (and in so doing confronted business and right-wing pressures) the need for a state of greater relative weight and supported the argument with reference to comparative studies that demonstrated that the Chilean state was smaller than many European ones (World Bank 1997; International Competitiveness of National Report 1997).

In his "Mensajes Presidenciales" ("State of the Nation" speech) to Congress, Frei went beyond the government's defensive vision on the issue of the state size, mentioning again its comparatively small size, and insisted that it was not a question of reducing but rather strengthening the state, even increasing its size in order to avoid both "its dismantlement or the total deregulation of activities."[18]

Similar opinions were systematically repeated by the ministers of the Secretary-General of the Presidency. On questions of how to resolve some of the pressing issues in the country's future agenda, such as social inequality, poverty, and lack of investment in human capital, Minister Juan Villarzú called on the citizenry to "defend the role of the state with greater force, even without fear of speaking of its growth. It is precisely this aspect that marks the greatest difference from the neoliberal vision of society that promotes a diminution in size and attributions of the public sector."[19]

Throughout the Frei government, then, the central issue was the modernization of public management. The lines of action implemented from the government point toward a modernization that can bring public service and state action in general as close as possible to the management criteria in the private sector. Thus, in his "State of the Nation" speech to Congress in May 1998, cited above, President Frei emphasized that public enterprises "must be efficient and competitive, will not receive any financial support from the state, and should comply with the same obligations that the laws impose on the private sector" (Frei 1998).

The Question of Corruption and the Debate on Privatization

At the end of the Aylwin government, the problem of corruption acquired prominence because an executive at the national copper company verified an embezzlement that amounted to millions of dollars. However, corruption was not a new issue. The denunciation of corruption and lack of transparency predate the return to democracy and were major issues at the end of the military government. According to a study conducted by the main public auditing office (Contraloría General de la República) during 1988, a total of 4,089 million pesos related to actions by public officials and departments were questioned. Although that figure decreased ostensibly under democracy (in 1996, the same auditing office objected to only 291 million pesos related to state actions), the menace of a lengthening of the tentacles of a practice usually assumed to be marginal within the public corps remained latent. Particular scandals in Chilean state and military offices, while comparatively less significant than those occurring in the rest of Latin America, are publicized by the media and contribute to a growing concern among the public, even though corruption was never a central issue for most people. A very important scandal about high pensions (*idemnizaciones*), established by the Frei government for state companies' high executives, who by the time of the discovery had left their jobs, burst out in 2000, the first year of President Lagos' term, and generated an intense new debate on the subject of corruption.

At the decentralized level of the state, the Frei government created two special bodies. The first was the National Commission on Public Ethics and included jurists and politicians from all sectors. The Frei government created this commission even as it acknowledged the low level of corruption in Chile (see the comparative rankings by Transparency International in Chapter One, this volume). The Ethics

Commission's final report gave rise to some legal projects that have yet to prosper. The second body was the Interministerial Committee of Modernization of Public Management. This Committee worked along two converging lines. First, it sought to de-politicize and simultaneously "technify" (use technical criteria and procedures for gathering information and making decisions) the activity of the executives of public or semi-public companies, as well as of the main administrators of state institutions. Second, by understanding that the more transparent the processes of hiring, acquisition, and public bidding are, the better the possibilities for efficacy in and scrutiny of the use of public resources, the government contemplated a legal framework for perfecting the regulations and procedures for state acquisitions, with clear rules and principles regarding external contracting (including studies, consulting, bids, and other services).

Another issue pertinent to the topic of state reform was the culmination of the privatization process begun under the military. The Frei government reaffirmed the decision not to privatize large-scale copper mining, even though it accepted the system of concessions for related industries and services, and has accepted, with conditions, the privatization of sanitary enterprises and concessions for road works. The debate, especially in Congress, shifted in the late 1990s from privatizations as such to the normative and regulatory frameworks that should govern privatized services, designed to impede monopolist practices, while preventing them from harming the most vulnerable social sectors. These problems became dramatic at the end of 1998 and during 1999, when the privatized electric enterprises were unable to cope with the energy crisis. The result was an emergency law increasing the regulatory and intervening capacity of the state in this energy sector.

The Management Reform Process under the Frei Administration

We have pointed out how, from the beginning of the second Concertación government, modernization of the public apparatus was oriented toward a substantive transformation of management.[20] Some months later, in December 1994, such intentions crystallized with the creation of the Inter-Ministerial Committee of Modernization of Public Management with the mission of promoting and coordinating modernizing efforts in public institutions (MIDEPLAN 1995). Another institutional manifestation of this modernization drive was the creation of the Commission on New Information Technologies (mentioned earlier). Since its creation, the Committee of Modernization of Public Management included the ministers of Interior and Finance and the secretary-general of the presidency, who chairs it. The under secretary-general of the presidency acts as the executive secretary of the Committee. The Committee's task was to propose the general policies of modernization of public administration to the president of the Republic; to foster and generate mechanisms of coordination and exchange among public institutions in the realms of perfecting, developing, rationalizing and modernizing public functions; and to identify and promote the tasks demanded by the development of a state "truly committed to the citizenry."

The guiding principles of the modernization of public administration were further defined from 1993 through 1995. Beginning in 1993, the assistant director of Rationalization and Public Function of the Dirección de Presupuestos (the

Chilean equivalent of the Internal Revenue Service) of the Ministry of Finance under Aylwin's administration synthesized views from various parts of the state elite and, by 1995, clearly defined them as 1) gradually increasing the efficacy of public services within the current constitutional context; 2) promoting, within the ministries and services, leaders capable of carrying out the process of modernization of the public sector's organizational culture; 3) adapting and applying new organizational and management technologies; 4) moving gradually and steadily toward a management style oriented by results; 5) focusing management style to meet the demands and needs of the users; 6) opening management to greater transparency; 7) optimizing the use of public resources; 8) qualitatively improving the human resources of the public sector and dignifying individuals' functions (Marcel 1993; Flisfisch 1995).

While the Frei government continued to clarify the objectives of its modernization, the practical reorganization of work plans for better user service suffered delays in some areas and progress in others. Among the delays, the most evident was the one that associated salary incentives with improvements in performance. After a long wait, it was assumed that during 1998, the system of employee evaluation, based upon results and performance, would come into effect. One of the government's advocates of the modernizing process has announced the implementation of new Law 19.553, which will give monetary awards to the best performing employees. However, the unpopular half of the evaluation system, which provides for the flexibility of norms to allow firing those with the worst evaluations, is still pending.

Despite uneven progress in the modernizing process, the extension and consolidation of the so-called Pilot Plan of Modernization of Management in Public Services is noteworthy. This plan, begun in 1993 and widened in 1994, was designed by the Internal Revenue Service of Chile to improve the management of public resources and establish performance measurements for the quality and delivery of services provided. The orienting methodology of the pilot plan was based on establishing the mission of each agency or office, upon which its objectives were elaborated, products and users of the service identified, and goals of management improvement set for the short and mid-terms. Then the agency committed itself to achieve the performance of those goals.

Complementing this performance commitment, government offices and ministries, in addition to presenting their goals and objectives for the year, had to commit to management indicators classified in four broad categories: coverage, service opportunity, efficiency, and self-financing indicators. These indicators had been established by a process that began in 1995, in the context of elaborating the government budget. In 1995, 80 performance indicators were experimentally introduced into 26 public services. This experiment generated a methodological discussion in those divisions regarding their management and specific areas of quality improvement. In 1996, the participating services expanded to 50 with 104 indicators. In 1997, the Internal Revenue Service, under the Finance Ministry, sent to Congress information on 75 services with 291 indices of performance and associated goals, which covered around 80 percent of the state apparatus.

As for the measurement of management goals, during the first semester of 1996, evaluated units achieved positive results along 76 of the 104 performance indicators (or 73 percent of goals reached). Furthermore, many of the management indicators, the tangible results of an effort of strategic planning, turn into savings through better or more opportunely expended resources, expansions in coverage or service, and reduction in the time needed to serve the user — all implying an improvement in the quality of the service.[21] Concerning the savings due to better or more opportunely expended resources, it is remarkable in the 1997 evaluation that the Production Promotion Corporation (Corporación de Fomento a la Producción — CORFO) reduced its expenditures on central administration and salaries from 111 percent of the allocation for programs in 1995 to 56 percent by the end of 1996. Likewise, administrative expenditures in the Technical Cooperation Service of the Ministry of Economy decreased from 76 percent of program costs in 1995 to 30 percent in 1996.

With regard to the extension of services, the number of bonuses for banking access given by the Solidarity and Social Investment Fund more than tripled, from 6,058 in 1995 to 19,043 in 1996. Similarly, the coverage scope of the National Board of Child Care Centers increased by 14 percent between 1994 and 1997. Its service capacity, measured by the number of children cared for per year, also rose by 67 percent between 1990 and 1997.

As for reduction in the time spent to serve users, among other relevant cases, the Office of Labor (Dirección del Trabajo) reduced the time between the receipt of a complaint and the inspection of the problem from 34 days in 1994 to 23 in 1996. The presence of qualified personnel, aided by new information equipment (acquired thanks to the modernizing process of the state), reduced the processing time for a customs declaration from 13 hours to 15 minutes. For its part, at the National Institute of Social Security (Instituto de Normalización Previsional) the rendering of benefits for the participants in the former Private Employees Social Security Department (Ex- Caja Empart) was shortened from 66 to 41 days and at the former Public Employees Social Security Department (Ex-Caja de Empleados Públicos), from 109 to 70 days. At the Civil Registry Service, 92 offices for the immediate delivery of birth certificates were established. Finally, among the most remarkable results, was the 60-percent reduction of processing time for special circulation permits by the Engineering Department (Dirección de Vialidad), part of the Ministry of Public Works. For 1997, goals as ambitious as having at least 55 percent of taxpayers served by the Internal Revenue Service report an improvement in the quality of the service were set. At present, an average of 4 to 5 indicators per institution has been reached, basically measuring the effectiveness, efficiency, and quality of services provided.[22]

In sum, what under the first democratic administration was but one line among other existing ones, started to become a transversal axis entirely synchronized with the modernizing rhetoric of the second coalition government. Of course, it is still premature to argue that the endogenous modernization of the public bureaucracy has been consolidated. Nevertheless, it can be stated that many segments of the bureaucratic sector at least have added to their daily work a corpus of instruments and practices that have improved the state's management without reforming its basic matrix and disposition. This shows the ability of the ad-hoc committee to sidestep the discussion on the reform of the structures of ministries and other institutions of the state and to focus instead on the issue of the adaptation of the state to the role of an efficient interlocutor of an increasingly demanding and distrustful "citizen-customer." However, by the same token, the debate neglects the deeper problems of state transformation in its functions and structures.

Indeed, very few overall structural changes in the state were introduced, such as lowering the institutional profile of CORFO. The suppression of the Ministry of Planning and Cooperation, announced in a confused manner, was never achieved. The real structural changes inside the state apparatus have occurred without reference to an explicit project of state modernization; instead, they have been linked to some fundamental and substantive reforms, as in the education sector, where the initial advising staff was incorporated into the administrative line, and in the judicial sector, where reforms were designed to transform the practices, selection, and careers of members of the judiciary.[23]

Certainly, the predominant strategic vision throughout the public administration was to reorient all services and sectors toward emphases on the user; obtaining results and measuring performance; the quality of service; increasing levels of transparency; and flexibility in the handling of resources. However, herein lies the main weakness of state reform policy during this period — its lack of relation with state-society transformations and thus the reduction of these policies to a set of computerized programs on the state side and to the notion of state users or customers on the society side.

REFORM AND MODERNIZATION OF THE STATE IN THE THIRD CONCERTACIÓN ADMINISTRATION: A PROVISIONAL ASSESSMENT

Ricardo Lagos' electoral victory in the hard-fought second round of the presidential election in early 2000 was the third consecutive presidential win by the Coalition of Parties for Democracy (Concertación de Partidos por la Democracia).[24] President Lagos is the first president of Chile in this coalition not from the Christian Democrat wing. Lagos belongs to the center-left axis of the coalition of three parties (the Socialist Party, the Party for Democracy, and the Radical Party) and has a social democratic ideological orientation. In his first two Presidential Messages (Mensajes Presidenciales) to the Congress, President Lagos announced that the main goal of his administration was to make Chile a developed country by 2010, the bicentennial of Chile's independence. He told the nation that he was the "reform president" and mentioned state reform as one of his administration's main reforms.[25]

The Lagos administration has laid out its work in the area of reform and modernization of the state in three complementary orientations. First, it has sought to regain for the state — not always with the intensity that his administration showed at the beginning and always with the opposition of the business sector and the political right wing — the regulatory and socially compensatory function that was hinted at in the cycle of democratizing reforms that characterized the Aylwin administration. Second, it has launched different programs to reinforce the relations between the state and civil society. Third, it has deepened the managerial reform promoted by the Frei administration; however, this reform is now oriented much more emphatically toward the idea of "electronic government."

A New Phase of Democratizing Reforms

Given the existing political and institutional obstacles to broad political reforms, including the enactment of substantive reforms to the political-electoral system[26] and the discussion of a new constitution, the Lagos administration has sought and apparently will continue to strengthen its regulatory attributes, as the first post-authoritarian administration did. As social equality (something different from equity) was the main priority of Lagos' campaign, the government was interested in correcting the inequalities and injustices created by a neoliberal economic model. So the new administration has sought to increase the resources of the state and increase social spending without privatizing the strategic companies that it still owns. In this way, instead of opening CODELCO (Chilean Copper Commission) to the participation of the private sector, the government had already managed to get Congress to pass a law, in spite of fierce resistance, that tightened control over tax evasion. The law, sharply criticized by the business community, gives new powers to public agencies that investigate large-scale tax evaders. With a similar compensatory orientation in the area of relations between capital and labor, unemployment insurance was created. Additionally, a new law for labor reforms was approved, after some concessions to business associations, that will improve unions' ability to negotiate in an environment of growing flexibility for employers in hiring, contracting, and other areas.

In the longer term, yet still linked to the idea of growth with social equity, the administration has sped up a series of structural reforms, which seek to expand cultural capital, to improve the quality of education, to improve the state's medical assistance coverage, and to promote and protect the rights of individuals in conflict with the justice system. Specifically, these apply to deepening reform of the courts (criminal trial reform); education (lengthening the school day); and a complete reform of the health system, including the creation of a public solidarity fund to pay for health care for the poor, which is currently being studied by a special presidential commission.

In spite of advances in the above areas, some other areas are lagging, one of which is the redistributive role of the state. In mid-2001, after a difficult debate, Congress approved a tax reform that reduced taxes, especially on high incomes; granted some minor benefits for some levels of low income; and increased very slightly the tax rates for private companies, which had been very low (about half of what companies pay in the United States). The 2001 tax reform was proposed by a former minister of finance and a current senator in the government's coalition. While the government did not want to reduce the state's income and resources, it also did not try to increase revenues through taxes. These measures were a concession to the private sector, whose leaders fought any tax reform that could possibly decrease their incomes or increase the state's resources, even though they demanded that the state resolve the problem of unemployment.

The other weak areas are the ethnic minorities' geographical decentralization, de-concentration, development, and autonomy. Although the Chilean government's land conflict with an organized, belligerent segment of the Mapuche people has not reached the characteristics and dimensions of the Mexican case, and the government has made a special effort to create a commission to discuss the historical debt with the ethnic minorities, the state is clearly behind in the restitution of lands and the expansion of benefits and compensation after decades of neglect. Even more important is the prospect of creating a bi- or pluri-national-state.

Reinforcement of Relations between the State and Civil Society

One of the main concerns of the government is the extent to which civil society or the citizenry has the capacity to access and share control of the state without damaging the autonomy of public policies. In this sense, there are at least three main initiatives. One is the creation of the Council of the Defense of the Citizen, which is charged with safeguarding the rights of citizens before state agencies. The second is the Presidential Instruction for Citizen Participation, which promotes the social participation and consultation of citizens on different policies that are close to their concerns. The third is a special loan from the Inter-American Development Bank (IDB) to "Strengthen Alliances between the Civil Society and the State," which operates through a special competitive fund for projects that originate in civil society institutions.[27]

Reinforcing Decisionmaking and Performance in the State

Reinforcing State Policymaking

As far as modifications of the management of the state apparatus are concerned, the main initiatives seek to consolidate the actions of an increasingly strong state without expanding its size, even though the recruitment of professionals and technicians for justice, health, and education reforms are likely to increase the size of the labor force in public administration. The Lagos administration, aware of citizens' demands for greater streamlining of bureaucracy, has distinguished itself by simplifying ministerial management. The most outstanding instance of this is the decrease in separate ministerial portfolios by assigning one minister responsibility for two or three thematically similar departments. This designation of bi- and tri-ministers is not a totally original strategy in Chilean history. At this time, there is no way to predict how far into the future it will last and whether this measure is part of a process of institutional transition toward a future fusion of portfolios in related fields. Anyway, the designations of the tri-minister of Finance, the Economy, and Energy; the bi-minister of Housing, Urban Development, and National Property; and the bi-minister of Public Works and Transport and Telecommunications at the beginning of the government were welcomed by a citizenry desirous of governmental actions that result in greater accessibility, simplicity, and austerity in public administration.

Management Control and Electronic Government

During the Aylwin and particularly the Frei administrations, three main tools for management control were used: the establishment of performance indicators of volume and quality of services, which was especially successful in "window agencies," the areas of the state with direct contact with the public, such as the Tax Service, Civil Registry, and the National Institute of Social Security (Instituto de Normalización Previsional — INP); the evaluation of governmental programs through independent committees of experts (102 programs evaluated since 1997); and the Program of Management Improvement, issued after the government made an agreement with the Public Employees Association that established some economic incentives for productivity and efficiency. Along with maintaining and reinforcing these tools, the Lagos administration introduced in the budget a competitive fund for projects presented by states agencies or services that are not part of the official budget. All these measures have been positively evaluated by the public and the political class, even if the opposition says that Congress does not always perform the necessary follow-up and permanent evaluations. High officials claim that these measures have been successful since public spending on these activities has increased by 6 percent and public employment has increased by only 2 percent.[28]

The Lagos administration, acknowledging public interest in making state action more efficient and effective, has focused on three specific areas: 1) improving the exchange of information between state and society through intensive use of new information technology, 2) professionalizing all those decisions related to the recruitment and qualifications of the management of state and semi-state agencies and state companies, and 3) consolidating and deepening the procedures and philosophy of strategic planning in all public agencies.

Of these three areas, this administration has taken a special interest in everything related to the electronic accessibility and visibility of the state. The intensive use of the Internet, exemplified in the opening of a state portal and of "single windows" meant to reduce processing time (public purchases, retirement, applications for subsidies, calls for bids, and so on), has brought more and better coordination among different public agencies (ministries, services, units, and semi-state institutions) and expansion of informational transparency. Although the idea of electronic government still seems distant, the advances in various areas are important and have elicited general recognition. The role of the Internal Tax Service (Servicio de Impuestos Internos) and its modern remote tax filing system is particularly outstanding.[29]

Professionalization of State Functions

While the maxim "The state is to serve and not to be used" is a foundation of President Lagos' communications strategy, the scandal caused by the compensations (*indemnizaciones*) received by a group of high executives of state companies forced an acceleration of the process of professionalization and depoliticization of public administration. The *Manual de trámites en la administración pública* (*Manual of Procedures in Public Administration*) and the interest in drafting rigorous rules of probity in state management were joined by a set of measures that seek to "improve the service that the public administration delivers to the citizenry."[30] Publicly formulated in May 2001, the initiative seeks to construct a set of procedures that minimize the risk of corruption in a country where influence peddling and the lack of legality are minor in comparison with other Latin American nations. The set of measures announced on May 11, 2001, includes, in addition to the Instructions on Electronic Government and the creation of the Council for the Defense of the Citizen, the Public Management Statute, which defines a formal system of selection and hiring public managers; the Public Purchasing Act, which requires that calls for bids and their results must be published on a web page for citizen access to these processes; the Administrative Procedures Act, which regulates administrative processes and so-called "administrative silence" under certain circumstances; and the assimilation of public enterprises to the norms and responsibilities that rule private enterprises.[31]

Summing up, the direction and controlling elements of the Lagos administration's agenda, usually dominated by the figure of the dynamic and always-present president, suggest that this administration will seek to balance social policies with its interest in improving state administration. In this area, difficulties associated with a slow recovery from the economic crisis of 1997, which for some people have been more psychological than economic, have created an excellent opportunity to expand state intervention in favor of job-creation programs.

In spite of the deployment of resources and projects that at times have been more media-oriented than effective, it is worth noting that one of the principal vacuums of the Lagos administration is the absence of a sufficiently explicit map of the kind of state the administration eventually wants to create. Lacking this, neither the substantive orientation of the current undefined or hybrid model of the state nor the basic neoliberal elements of the model of economic growth (indeed it is not possible to talk of a model of development), eagerly defended by business sectors and the right-wing opposition, can be considered susceptible to profound change. This situation makes us presume more continuity than change for the remaining years of the Concertación government.

BALANCE AND CONCLUSIONS

The main conclusion of this study is that the ongoing administrative reforms, some of them very important and in general very successful, have not acknowledged the profound transformations in the concept and function of the state and its relations with society in the last decade. If we view the long historical period since the 1930s, Chile has moved between the expansion and the reduction of the state apparatus, on the one hand, and the restructuring and modernization of the state's capacity, on the other.

If we consider Heredia and Schneider's scheme that distinguishes among downsizing, Weberian (civil service), accountability, and managerial reforms in the course of the four periods studied, some types of administrative reform have been mixed during each period. During the military dictatorship, the "first wave of reforms" and "downsizing" were prominent results of the regime's economic model; these reforms also coincided with its ideological-political perspective (Heredia and Schneider, Chapter One in this volume). Additionally, some important de-concentration and fake decentralization linked to geopolitical and military criteria took place under the military dictatorship. This is the only period in which a drastic reform or transformation of the state occurred, in the sense that we defined the concept in the first paragraph of this chapter, led by a project that removed an inward development model from the national-popular state.

Under the modernizing and democratizing process inaugurated in 1990, at least three distinct reforms of the state apparatus took place: 1) institutional reforms, associated with the creation and restructuring of ministries and other state organizations and the correction of municipalization and regionalization made by the military; 2) reform of state policies on health, education, judiciary, environment, and poverty reduction that generated important administrative changes; and 3) modernization of management, partially linked to the introduction of management patterns from the private world into the public sphere. In the first democratic government, the idea of strengthening the state's capacity to fulfill tasks in other fields, with an emphasis on what Heredia and Schneider have called civil service and accountability reforms, was dominant. In the second government of the Concertación, what was foremost was managerial reform, considered as a primary objective in and of itself. During the current third Concertación government, the private sector and the right-wing opposition have been fighting to retake the democratizing role of the state. At the same time, this administration has deepened managerial reforms, in particular, their electronic and technological dimensions.

Usually, the concrete plans for administrative reforms such as regionalization and municipalization, public management modernization, anticorruption measures, goal-oriented public programs, personnel training, customer service improvements, restructuring of some services due to new social policies, electronic management, and so forth, have all run separately and not as integrated programs. Thus, the transformations that have occurred in the state have been more a question of effective results of separate, different processes than of planned design. On the other side, all of these processes have been only partially realized, giving the ex-post, so-called reform of the state or administrative reform the seal of isolated, erratic, slow and ad hoc solutions.

It is likely that the partial, segmented, and uneven character of state reform is the norm because, while some isolated political, economic, or social goals may be clear, the state model sought and the type of internal restructuring necessary for implementing that model have never been formulated in a coherent way. Perhaps this lack of coherence has its origin in the transformation of the role of the state from an agent of national economic development and social integration to the vehicle for the installation of a market-economy model, linked to the process of globalization. Thus, modernization of the state has become part of this general modality of modernization.

In the phase of inward-oriented development, there existed a state project that we called national-popular. Under the neoliberal mode of development, the project changed to one of dismantling the state combined with the expansion of coercive functions at the beginning and the subsidiary state model afterward. Today, the main challenges for the government are to figure out how to control the economy socially and how to reconstruct the political capacity of society so that it can contend successfully with globalized market forces. In order to accomplish these things, there is no comparable state model, good or bad, as there was in the past. This means that there is no clarity about the role and structure of the state and that administrative reform is left to a formal, abstract set of measures without substantive content.

Thus, the main question is: Why have democratic governments, based on a majoritarian coalition, not been able to go beyond partial reforms and undertake real state transformations? First, the state lacks a new development model. Second, in this vacuum, the electoral agenda (elections take place almost every two years) pressures the government to spend inordinate amounts of time and energy on immediate, urgent problems and demands and to delay deep reforms, which seem very abstract and can create new counter-demands and criticisms. Third, the current economic model and the private sector both challenge and pressure the state to prove that it is performing well.

This critique of the dominant perspective of administrative reform policies in Chile, lacking a compass determined by a state project, can be extended to some restricted perspectives on the study of the reform of the state. We have attempted to show how, in all the periods analyzed, what is called administrative reform never comes from the requirements of an economic growth model alone, and that, in this sense, it is incorrect to speak of "first wave" reforms, which would be a script written from some economic reforms based on a partial and ideological vision. The problematique confronted by the transformation of the state cannot be seen from one dimension, because it is simultaneously economic, political, and cultural. The state is not only an administrative machine to be reformed to satisfy economic requirements but is also a sphere of domination, an agent of national unity and social integration, an actor in society, and a space for action and representation by society's actors.[32]

The problematique today is that the models of political representation, social participation, economic growth, modernization, and modernity are all in search of definition.[33] The same lack of a coherent vision is likely to happen with the type or model of the state in future decades, thus leaving administrative reforms to the immediate requirements of one or another sphere of social life, particularly of the dominant economic requirements for globalization. And this will continue to be so as long as the state is considered only a dependent variable and no autonomous state project is developed. The lack of a project that defines the desired state, combined with the predominance of a vision that defines the state simply as an apparatus to be "adapted" to the economy, is the consequence of the decline of the meaning and importance of politics among the ruling sectors in society and within the mainstream of social science.

NOTES

1. For examples of the first stream, see Bradford 1988; O'Donnell 1993; Instituto de Estudios para la Transición Democrática 1997; Evans 1995; Calderón and Dos Santos 1991; Cunill 1997; Garretón 2000; Garretón and Espinosa 1994; Bradford 1994; For examples of the second stream, see World Bank 1997; Klicksberg 1995; Klicksberg 1994; and Heredia and Schneider, Chapter One of this volume. An attempt to link these different perspectives, although conceptualized differently, may be found in Kaufman, Chapter Ten of this volume.

2. Summarized here are ideas and arguments that have been developed in Garretón 1995; and Garretón 2000. A broad bibliography about the subjects mentioned in this paragraph exists, especially on the transformations of the Latin American state and society over the last two decades. See Touraine 1989; Smith 1995; Smith, Acuña, and Gamarra 1994; Díaz 1994; and Sosa, 1996.

3. The reform of the state as a specific subject has been the theme of debate only recently. There exist many official reports, which will be cited in this work, but there has been little academic research and literature produced on state reform. Among recent works on the subject from an analytical perspective, there are some articles published in collective volumes more concerned with the general transformations of Chilean society and economy that also discuss the subject of state reform or change. From a perspective relatively close to governmental positions, see Muñoz 1998; Bitrán and Sáez 1998; Marfán 1998; Marcel and Tohá 1998; Ahumada 1998; and Meneses and Fuentes 1998. For a vision coming from more neoliberal economists who are linked politically to the right-wing opposition to government, see Larraín and Vergara 2000. For other views, see Arrau 1997/1998; and Garretón and Espinosa 1992.

4. For the general characteristics of Chilean society in the twentieth century from a historical perspective, see Drake 1993; Angell 1993; Aylwin et al. 1990; and Correa et al. 2001.

5. On the relations among the economy, politics, and society and the role of the state, see Ahumada 1958; Pinto 1971; Góngora 1986; Moulián 1982; and Garretón and Espinosa 1995.

6. On economic development and policies and state participation, see Ffrench-Davis 1973; Meller 1996; Ffrench-Davis 1990; and Tironi 1984.

7. For information on the specific period of 1970-1973, see Martner 1986; and Bitar 1979.

8. For 1973, the figure is taken from Costa 1994, 445. For 1987 and 1989, figures are taken from Aninat 1994, 40.

9. The 1984 reform eliminated the additional tax on corporate revenues and unified the first category tax into the Impuesto Global Complementario (Complementary Global Tax), thereby eliminating double taxation on business. Distributed profits were established as the basis of the first category tax, although without eliminating social security payments. Figures and observations taken from Marcel 1997, 36.

10. We follow here the analysis of Raczynski 1994, 14. For more information on aspects of state policy of the military regime, see Garretón and Espinosa 1992.

11. On the privatization process, see Marcel 1989. An account of how this process was politically made appears in Monckeberg 2001. A partial defense of this process is discussed in Hachette 2000. On the more general characteristics and effects of the dismantling of the state, euphemistically called "downsizing," see Ffrench-Davis and Raczynski 1990; and Suárez 1990.

12. A general balance of the neoliberal experiment and its impact on the state and economic policies can be found in Foxley 1982; Vergara 1985; and Ffrench-Davis 1999. A positive view appears in Larraín and Vergara 2000.

13. An apologetic document published by the National Planning Office (Oficina de Planificación Nacional — ODEPLAN) before the plebiscite of 1988 affirms the success of the military regime in ending the "socialist state," illustrating it with some figures about the downsizing of the public administration. For example, in 1974 almost 300,000 people, excluding teachers and military, were part of the state apparatus; by 1987, this number was reduced to 146,800 (ODEPLAN, *Chile modernización 1973-1987*, Santiago, 160).

14. On the idea of "transition government" and "democracy of consensus," see Boeninger 1997. About the "growth with equity" program, see Aylwin 1994. For a more analytical point of view that includes the first and a great part of the second democratic government, see Garretón 1995; Garretón 1999; Drake and Jaksic 1999; Toloza and Lahera 1998; and Menendez and Joignant 1999. For a critical vision from the left outside the governmental coalition, see Moulián 1997.

15. In 1990, there were six so-called Ministries of Political Areas: Interior, Foreign Relations, Defense, Justice, General Secretary of Government, and General Secretary of the Presidency. The other areas were Economy and Social (Finance, Labor and Social Security, Education, Health, Housing and Urbanism, Planning, and International Cooperation); Infrastructure (Public Works, National Goods, Transport and Communications, and Energy); and Productive Development (Economy, Agriculture, Mining, and CORFO).

16. For this section and the following, see Ahumada 1998.

17. It is perhaps too early for an adequate analysis of the Frei period. At the end of the Frei administration, a series of studies that were made during the ongoing process appeared, covering four or five years of that government. See the following volumes previously cited: Menendez and Joignant1999; Drake and Jaksic1999; Cortazar and Vial 1998; Muñoz 1998; Bitrán and Sáez 1998; Marfán 1998; Marcel and Tohá 1998; Ahumada 1998; and Meneses and Fuentes 1998. Every year, FLACSO publishes an annual report, entitled *Annuarium*, which mentions the most important events that occurred and contains some analyses of specific aspects of that year. Also, FLACSO is completing a collected volume on the Frei government that includes an article by Garretón, "La (in)conducción política del segundo gobierno democrático" (forthcoming 2002 or 2003).

18. "Declaración del Primer Mandatario durante su visita a la Región del Bío-Bío," *El Mercurio* 1997a, C5; *El Mercurio* 1997c, C7. See also, the Messages of the President to the Congress, 21st May 1997 and 21st May 1998.

19. *El Mercurio* 1997b.

20. Unless other sources of information are mentioned explicitly, all the data we present in this section are taken from the Ministro de Hacienda, 1995-1997, and from the web page designated by the government to describe the state modernization process,

<www.modernización.cl>. Some information on the process of state modernization based on the improvement of management can be found in Novoa 2001.

21. Most of the changes relate to everyday encounters between members of the public administration and the citizenry. For example, the users of the public health care service (FONASA) in 1997 were given a high level of information about the service, compared with a very low level of information in 1989. Likewise, during the 1998 tax collection operation, businesses could send their documents via the Internet, opening the way for receipts showing electronic sales and services rendered.

22. It is accepted that the more successful experiences in the improvement of management and beneficiaries' satisfaction with these improvements are the Servicio de Impuestos Internos (Tax Service), the Registro Civil (Civil Registry), FONASA (National Fund for Health), and the INP (National Institute of Social Security). A complete study of the INP can be found in Villanueva 2000.

23. Perhaps a more important state reform in the 1990s of the judiciary was the reform of laws for criminal trials (reforma a la Ley Penal), which created the Ministerio Público (attorney system) and the adversarial system. Both started in 2000, but this is beyond the scope of this chapter.

24. For President Lagos' general vision of his government, see Lagos 2000; and Lagos 2001. For the context of this presidency, see Garretón 2000. For an analysis of the first year of Lagos' presidency, see Garretón 2001; *Asuntos Públicos* 2001a; *Asuntos Públicos* 2001b; and *Asuntos Públicos* 2001c. The information for this section is taken from Lagos 2000 and Lagos 2001; Ministerio Secretaría General de la Presidencia 2001; and Novoa 2001.

25. One year after the beginning of Lagos' presidency, the administration defined the modernization of the state as among its priorities. See <www.presidencia.cl>.

26. The most notable but not the only reforms are those relative to expansion of presidential power over the armed forces; modification of the National Security Council; reform of the Constitutional Court; an end to the practice of naming designated senators and to naming senators for life; replacement of the current binominal system of elections; a law limiting election campaign spending; a law limiting the powers of the military justice system; and a law regarding citizenship for Chileans residing abroad.

27. The Council was one of the announcements of May 2001, mentioned below. For the Participation Program, see *Instructivo Presidencial para la Participación Ciudadana*, Ministerio Secretaría General de Gobierno. For the BID loan, see *Programa para fortalecer Alianzas entre la sociedad civil y el Estado. Préstamo BID*, Ministerio Secretaría General de Gobierno, División de Organizaciones Sociales.

28. Interview with Mario Marcel in Novoa 2001.

29. The electronic addresses are state portal, <www.estado.cl>; unique window, <www.tramitefacil.gov.cl>; and Servicio de Impuestos Internos, <www.sii.cl>.

30. Lagos 2001.

31. See *La Segunda* 2001, 19.

32. For the need of a state reform vision that encompasses the different dimensions of society, see Garretón 2000; and for a type of analysis that encompasses these dimensions, see Kaufman, Chapter Ten in this volume.

33. About the redefinition of development, see PNUD 1994; and Garretón 2000.

REFERENCES

Ahumada, Jorge. 1958. *En vez de la miseria*. Santiago: Editorial del Pacífico.

Ahumada, Jaime. 1998. "El proceso de descentralización." In *Chile en los noventa*, eds. Cristian Toloza and Eugenio Lahera. Santiago: Dolmen Ediciones.

Angell, Alan. 1993. "Chile Since 1958." In *Chile Since Independence*, ed. Leslie Bethell. Cambridge, UK: Cambridge University Press.

Aninat, Eduardo. 1994. *Exposición sobre el estado de la Hacienda Pública*. Santiago: Ministerio de Hacienda, Dirección de Presupuestos.

Aninat, Eduardo. 1996. *Intervención en el II encuentro sobre modernización del Estado*. Santiago: Ministerio de Hacienda, Dirección de Presupuestos.

Arrau, Alfonso. 1997/1998. "Sociología de la modernización del Estado y relaciones laborales en Chile." *Revista de Sociología*, Universidad de Chile, 11/12.

Asuntos Públicos. 2001a. "Balance y desafíos económicos a un año del gobierno de Lagos." Informe No. 67 (May).

Asuntos Públicos. 2001b. "El liderazgo de Lagos frente a la Derecha y las dos almas de la Concertación." Informe No. 68 (May).

Asuntos Públicos. 2001c. "El gobierno de Lagos frente al dilema moral y cultural de Chile." Informe No. 69 (May).

Aylwin, Mariana, et al. 1990. *Chile en el siglo XX*. Santiago: Editorial Planeta.

Aylwin, Patricio. 1991. *Mensaje Presidencial 21 de mayo de 1990 y del 21 de mayo de 1991*. Santiago: Secretaría de Comunicación y Cultura.

Aylwin, Patricio. 1992. *Mensaje Presidencial 21 de mayo de 199 y del 21 de mayo de 1992*. Santiago: Secretaría de Comunicación y Cultura.

Aylwin, Patricio. 1993. *Mensaje Presidencial 21 de mayo de 1992 y del 21 de mayo de 1993*. Santiago: Secretaría de Comunicación y Cultura.

Aylwin, Patricio. 1994a. "Conferencia de S.E. el Presidente de la República, don Patricio Aylwin, sobre el proceso de modernización del Estado." In *Proyecto Chile. Modernización del Estado*. Seminario taller. Santiago: MIDEPLAN.

Aylwin, Patricio. 1994b. *Crecimiento con equidad. Discursos escogidos. 1992-1994*. Santiago: Editorial Andrés Bello.

Azevedo, Sergio De. 1999. "Reforma do estado e mudança institucional, variaveis exógenas e endógenas." In *Reforma do Estado e mudanca institucional en Brasil*, ed. Marcus Melo. Recife, Brazil: Fundação Joaquim Nabuco.

Banco Central de Chile. 1995. *Modernización de la gestión pública en Chile. Antecedentes, orientaciones actuales y avances.* Paper presented at Seminario Experiencias Internacionales de la Gestión Pública y su Relevancia para Chile, Santiago, March.

Bitar, Sergio. 1979. *Transición, socialismo y democracia. La experiencia chilena.* Mexico City: Fondo de Cultura Económica (FCE).

Bitrán, Eduardo, and Raul Eduardo Sáez. 1998. "Mercado, estado y regulación." In *Construyendo Opciones. Propuestas Económicas y Sociales para el Cambio de Siglo*, eds. René Cortazar and Joaquín Vial. Santiago: CIEPLAN-DOMEN.

Boeninger, Edgardo. 1997. *Democracia en Chile. Lecciones para la gobernabilidad.* Santiago: Editorial Andrés Bello.

Bradford, Colin. 1987. "Forms of State and Socio-economic Change." In *The Political Economy of Law: A Third-World Reader*, eds. Yash P. Ghai, Robin Luckham, and Francis G. Snyder. Delhi and New York: Oxford University Press.

Bradford, Colin, ed. 1994. *Redefining the State in Latin America.* Paris: OECD.

Bresser-Pereira, Luiz Carlos, and Peter Spink, eds. 1999. *Reforming the State: Managerial Public Administration in Latin America.* Boulder, Colo.: Lynne Rienner Publishers.

Calderón, Fernando, and Mario Dos Santos. 1991. *Hacia un nuevo orden estatal en América Latina. Veinte tesis socio-políticas y un corolario.* Santiago: Fondo de Cultura Económica (FCE).

Chateau, Jorge. 1997. "Sobre la modernización de la gestión pública en Chile hoy." In *Chile 96: análisis y opiniones.* Santiago: FLACSO.

Correa S., Sofía et al. 2001. *Historia del siglo XX chileno: balance paradojal.* Santiago: Editorial Sudamericana.

Cortazar, René, and Joaquín Vial, eds. 1998. *Construyendo Opciones. Propuestas Económicas y Sociales para el Cambio de Siglo.* Santiago: CIEPLAN-DOMEN.

Costa, Rosanna. 1994. "Hacia un Estado que favorezca la competitividad." In *Las tareas de hoy. Políticas sociales y económicas para una sociedad libre*, eds. Cristián Larroulet and Carlos F. Cáceres. Santiago: Editorial Zig-Zag; Instituto Libertad y Desarrollo.

Cunill, Nuria. 1997. *Repensando lo público a través de la sociedad. Nuevas formar de gestión pública y representación social.* Caracas: Nueva Sociedad.

Díaz, Álvaro. 1988. "El Estado neoliberal intervencionista. Cinco razones para no creer en el mito del Estado subsidiario." *Análisis* 2 (August 22-28).

Díaz, Álvaro. 1994. "Tendencias de la reestructuración económica y social en Latinoamérica." *Revista Mexicana de Sociología* No. 14 (October-December).

Drake, Paul. 1993. "Chile 1930-1958." In *Chile Since Independence*, ed. Leslie Bethell. Cambridge, UK: Cambridge University Press.

Drake, Paul, and Iván Jaksic, eds. 1999. *El modelo chileno: democracia y desarrollo en los noventa.* Santiago: LOM Ediciones.

Evans, Peter. 1995. *Embedded Autonomy: States and Industrial Transformation.* Princeton, N.J.: Princeton University Press.

Ffrench-Davis, Ricardo. 1973. *Políticas Económicas en Chile 1957-1970.* Santiago: CIEPLAN-Universidad Católica de Chile.

Ffrench-Davis, Ricardo. 1990. *Desarrollo económico, inestabilidad y desequilibrios políticos en Chile. 1950-1989.* Colección Estudios No. 28. Santiago: CIEPLAN.

Ffrench-Davis, Ricardo. 1999. *Entre el neoliberalismo y el crecimiento con equidad. Tres décadas de política económica en Chile.* Caracas and Santiago: Dolmen Ediciones.

Ffrench-Davis, Ricardo, and Dagmar Raczynski. 1990. *The Impact of Global Recession and National Policies on Living Standards: Chile 1973-1989.* Notas Técnicas No. 97 (November). Santiago: CIEPLAN.

Flisfisch, Angel. 1993. "Los desafíos del Estado chileno en la década de los noventa." In *La reforma del Estado: más allá de la privatización*, ed. Klaus Bodemer. Montevideo: FESUR.

Flisfisch, Angel. 1995. "La modernización de la gestión pública." In *Revista Chilena de Administración Pública* No. 5.

Foxley, Alejandro. 1982. *Experimentos neoliberales en América Latina.* Colección Estudios No. 7. Santiago: CIEPLAN.

Frei Ruiz-Tagle, Eduardo. 1994. *Instructivo presidencial del 6 de Diciembre de 1994 que crea el Comité Interministerial de Modernización de la Gestión Pública.* Pamphlet.

Frei, Eduardo. 1998. *Mensaje ante el Congreso Nacional, 21 Mayo 1998.* Santiago: Ministerio Secretaría General de Gobierno.

Fundación Nacional para la Superación de la Pobreza (FNSP). 1996. *La pobreza en Chile. Un desafío de equidad e integración social* 1: 52. Santiago: FNSP.

Ghai,Yash P., Robin Luckham, and Francis G. Snyder, eds. 1988. *The Political Economy of Law: A Third-World Reader.* Delhi and New York: Oxford University Press.

Garretón, Manuel Antonio. 1994. "New Relations between State and Society in Latin America." In *Redefining the State in Latin America,* ed. Colin Bradford. Paris: OECD.

Garretón, Manuel Antonio. 1995. *Hacia una nueva era política. Estudio sobre las democratizaciones.* Santiago: Fondo de Cultura Económica.

Garretón, Manuel Antonio. 1996. "Transformación del Estado en América Latina." *Espacios Revista Centroamericana de Cultura Política.* No. 6 (October-December).

Garretón, Manuel Antonio. 1999. "Balance y perspectivas de la democratización política chilena." In *La caja de Pandora el retorno de la transición chilena,* Amparo Menéndez-Carrión and Alfredo Joignant Rondón. Santiago: Planeta/ Ariel.

Garretón, Manuel Antonio. 2000a. *La sociedad en que vivi(re)mos. Introducción sociológica al fin de siglo.* Santiago: LOM Editores.

Garretón, Manuel Antonio. 2000b. *Política y sociedad entre dos épocas: América Latina en el cambio de siglo.* Rosario, Argentina: Ediciones Homo Sapiens.

Garretón, Manuel Antonio. Forthcoming 2002 or 2003. "La (in)conducción política del segundo gobierno democrático." Collected volume on the Frei government in process. Santiago: FLACSO.

Garretón, Manuel Antonio, and Malva Espinosa. 1992. "Reforma del Estado o cambio en la matriz socio-política." *Perfiles Latinoamericanos.* Mexico.

Garretón, Manuel Antonio, and Malva Espinosa. 1994. *From the Adjustment Policies to the New Relations between the State and Society.* Paris: Independent Commission for Population and Quality of Life.

Garretón, Manuel Antonio, and Malva Espinosa. 1995. *Tendencias de cambio en la matriz socio-política chilena. Una aproximación empírica.* Informe final Proyecto Fondecyt. Santiago (Marzo).

Góngora, Mario. 1986. *Ensayo histórico sobre la noción de Estado en Chile en los siglos XIX y XX.* Santiago: Editorial Universitaria.

Hachette, Dominique. 2000. "Privatizaciones: Reforma estructural pero inconclusa." In *La transformación económica,* eds. Felipe Larraín and Rodrigo Vergara. Santiago: CEP.

Heredia, Blanca, and Ben Ross Schneider. 2003. "The Political Economy of Administrative Reform in Developing Countries." Chapter One, this volume.

Instituto de Estudios para la Transición Democrática. 1997. *Un Estado para la democracia.* Mexico City: Grupo Editorial Miguel Angel Porrúa.

International Competitiveness of Nations Report. 1997. *La Época.* June 27: E1- E2.

Kaufman, Robert. 2003. "The Comparative Politics of Administrative Reform: Some Implications for Theory and Policy." Chapter Ten, this volume.

Klicksberg, Bernardo. 1994. *El rediseño del Estado.* Mexico City: Fondo de Cultura Económica.

Klicksberg, Bernardo. 1995. "Problemas estratégicos en la reforma del Estado en la década de los noventa." In *América Latina a fines de siglo,* ed. José Luis Reyna, Mexico City: Consejo Nacional para la Cultura y las Artes, Fondo de Cultura Económica.

Lagos, Ricardo. 2000. *Mensaje presidencial 21 de Mayo del año 2000.* Santiago: Ministerio Secretaría General de Gobierno.

Lagos, Ricardo. 2001. *Mensaje presidencial del 21 de Mayo del 2001.* Santiago: Ministerio Secretaría General de Gobierno.

Larraín, Felipe, and Rodrigo Vergara, eds. 2000. *La transformación económica de Chile.* Santiago: CEP.

Marcel, Mario. 1989. "Privatización y finanzas públicas." *Colección Estudios* No. 26. Santiago: CIEPLAN.

Marcel, Mario. 1993. "Mitos y recetas en la reforma de la gestión pública." In *Cómo mejorar la gestión pública,* ed. Eugenio Lahera. Santiago: CIEPLAN-FLACSO-Foro 90.

Marcel, Mario. 1994. "La modernización del Estado y la gestión pública: un desafío también para la autoridad económica." *Vida y Derecho* 6 (15).

Marcel, Mario. 1997. *Políticas en democracia: el caso de la reforma tributaria de 1990 en Chile.* Colección Estudios No. 45. Santiago: CIEPLAN.

Marcel, Mario. 2001. Interview by Sandra Novoa, "La tramitada modernización del Estado," *El Mercurio,* September 1: D4-D5.

Marcel, Mario, and Carolina Tohá. 1998. "Reforma del Estado y la gestión pública." In *Construyendo Opciones. Propuestas Económicas y Sociales para el Cambio de Siglo,* eds. René Cortazar and Joaquín Vial. Santiago: CIEPLAN-DOMEN.

Marfán, Manuel. 1998. "El financiamiento fiscal en los años 90." In *Construyendo opciones. Propuestas económicas y sociales para el Cambio de siglo,* eds. René Cortazar and Joaquín Vial. Santiago: CIEPLAN-DOMEN.

Martner, Gonzalo. 1988. *El gobierno del presidente Salvador Allende, 1970-1973: una evaluación.* Concepción, Chile: Programa de Estudios del Desarrollo Nacional: Ediciones Literatura Americana Reunida.

Meller, Patricio. 1996. *Un siglo de economía política chilena. 1880-1990.* Santiago: Editorial Andrés Bello.

Melo, Marcus. 1999. "Reforma do Estado e mudança institucional: a agenda de pesquisas para nos años 80 e 90." In *Reforma do Estado e mudanca institucional en Brasil*, ed. Marcus Melo. Recife, Brazil: Fundação Joaquim Nabuco.

Menendez-Carrión, Amparo, and Alfredo Joignant Rondón. 1999. *La caja de Pandora el retorno de la transición chilena*. Santiago: Editorial Planeta/Ariel.

Meneses, Francisco Javier, and José María Fuentes. 1998. "Estado y proceso económico," In *Chile en los noventa*, eds. Cristián Toloza and Eugenio Lahera. Santiago: Dolmen Ediciones.

El Mercurio. 1997a. March 12, C5.

El Mercurio. 1997b. July 19, C7.

El Mercurio. 1998. July 12, D4.

MIDEPLAN. 1993. *Modernización de la gestión pública bajo el gobierno del presidente Patricio Aylwin*.

MIDEPLAN. 1995. *Balance económico social 1994-1995*.

MIDEPLAN. 1996. *Balance de seis años de Políticas Sociales. 1990-1996*.

Ministerio de Hacienda. 1997. *Exposición del ministro de hacienda en el seminario internacional de modernización del Estado*. Dirección de Presupuestos, Ministerio de Hacienda y Comisión para la Modernización del Estado, years 1995, 1996, 1997.

Ministerio Secretaría General de Gobierno. *Instructivo presidencial sobre participación ciudadana*. Santiago: Gobierno de Chile. See <http://www.segegob.cl>.

Ministerio Secretaría General de Gobierno. *Programa para fortalecer Alianzas entre la sociedad civil y el Estado*. Santiago: Préstamo BID. See also <http://www.icnl.org/library/lamerica/reports/Chigovreport%5Bspa%5D.htm>.

Ministerio Secretaría General de la Presidencia. 1990. *Metas ministeriales. Segundo semestre de 1990*. Santiago: Gobierno de Chile.

Ministerio Secretaria General de la Presidencia. 2001. *Balance gestión 2000*. Santiago: Proyecto de Reforma y Modernización del Estado. April 26.

Monckeberg, María Olivia. 2001. *El saqueo de los grupos económicos al Estado chileno*. Santiago: Ediciones B, Grupo Z.

Moulián, Tomás. 1982. *Desarrollo político en Chile*. Colección de Estudios No. 18. Santiago: CIEPLAN.

Moulián, Tomás. 1997. *Chile actual. Anatomía de un mito*. Santiago: Ediciones LOM.

Muñoz, Oscar. 1998. "Estado, mercado y política. Chile en los años noventa." In *Construyendo Opciones. Propuestas Económicas y Sociales para el Cambio de Siglo*, eds. René Cortazar and Joaquín Vial. Santiago: CIEPLAN-DOMEN.

Novoa, Sandra. 2001. "La tramitada modernización del Estado." *El Mercurio*, September 1, D4-D5.

O'Donnell, Guillermo. 1978. "Apuntes para una teoría del Estado." *Revista Mexicana de Sociología* 40 (4).

O'Donnell, Guillermo. 1980. "El aparato estatal en los países del Tercer Mundo y su relación con el cambio socioeconómico." *Revista Internacional de Ciencias Sociales* 32 (4).

O'Donnell, Guillermo. 1993. "On the State, Democratization and Some Conceptual Problems." *World Development* 21 (8).

Oyarce, Héctor. 1997. "Los procesos de modernización, el Estado y la política." Santiago. Manuscript.

Pinto, Anibal. 1971. *Tres ensayos sobre América Latina y Chile*. Buenos Aires: Solar-Hachette.

Presidencia de la República. 1988. *Chile modernización 1973-1987*. Santiago: Oficina de Planificación Nacional (ODEPLAN).

Programa de las Naciones Unidas para el Desarrollo (PNUD). 1994. *Informe sobre Desarrollo Humano*. New York: United Nations Development Programme (UNDP).

Raczynski, Dagmar. 1994. "Políticas sociales y programas de combate a la pobreza en Chile: balance y desafíos." *Colección de Estudios* No. 39. Santiago: CIEPLAN.

Reyna, José Luis, ed. 1995. *América Latina a fines de siglo*. Mexico City: Consejo Nacional para la Cultura y las Artes, Fondo de Cultura Económica.

La Segunda. 2001. May 11: 19.

Smith, Peter H., ed. 1995. *Latin America in Comparative Perspective: New Approaches to Method and Analysis*. Boulder, Colo.: Westview Press.

Smith, William C., Carlos H. Acuña, and Eduardo A. Gamarra, eds. 1994. *Latin American Political Economy in the Age of Neoliberal Reform: Theoretical and Comparative Perspectives for the 1990s*. Coral Gables, Fla.: North-South Center Press at the University of Miami.

Sosa, Raquel, ed. 1996. *América Latina y el Caribe. Perspectivas de su reconstrucción*. Mexico City: ALAS UNAM.

Suárez, Christian. 1990. "Reseza del Gobierno de Chile." *Selección de Documentos Clave* 7 (12). Caracas: CLAD.

Tironi, Ernesto. 1984. *Evolución Socioeconómica de Chile antes del Neoliberalismo. Una Reinterpretación.* Documento de Trabajo No. 19 (October). Santiago: CED.

Toloza, Cristián, and Eugenio Lahera. 1998. *Chile en los noventa.* Santiago: Dolmen Ediciones.

Touraine, Alain. 1989. *Política y Sociedad en América Latina.* Madrid: Espasa.

Vergara, Pilar. 1985. *Auge y caída del neoliberalismo en Chile.* Santiago: FLACSO.

Villanueva, Tamara. 2000. *Cambio organizacional planificado en servicios públicos Memoria de Título.* Santiago: Departamento de Sociología, Universidad de Chile.

World Bank. 1997. *World Development Report: The State in a Changing World.* New York: Oxford University Press.

<www.modernización.cl>.

<www.presidencia.cl>.

<www.estado.cl>.

<www.tramitefacil.gov.cl>.

<www.sii.cl>.

Zona Pública. 1997. "Las paradojas de la encuesta CASEN 96." No. 21.

Chapter Six

STALLED ADMINISTRATIVE REFORMS OF THE MEXICAN STATE

David Arellano Gault and

Juan Pablo Guerrero Amparán

INTRODUCTION

In the 1990s, Mexico's administrative reform was at best superficial because it did not change or alter the institutional and political factors that have made the country's public administration an instrument of the ruling political group. In contrast to other cases in this volume, the Mexican experience highlights the fact that, in the context of limited democratic development (as in Mexico prior to the elections of 2000), administrative reform is inevitably linked to fundamental political changes. This argument will be developed in the following sections of this chapter.

The first section provides some basic background on the Mexican political system and the important transition currently underway. While the old political system is almost dead, some of its institutions are still important and influential, even as the new political system is taking shape. Studying this period of transition is crucial in understanding the characteristics of past and current administrative reform attempts, and the interregnum itself provides a rich and complex environment for reform efforts.

Within the context of transition, the second section of this chapter argues that administrative reform has been propelled by both economic and political reforms. Reforms in each of these areas have their separate histories, strategies, and timings, making it difficult to argue that there exists a coherent and explicit general project of reform for the administrative system in Mexico. In any case, the reforms classified in this volume's introductory chapter, by Blanca Heredia and Ben Ross Schneider, either failed (civil service and managerial reforms) or were completely absent (accountability reforms) in Mexico. The third section explores further the concept of *managerialist* administrative reform. According to this concept, the improvement of administrative procedures and the implementation of some advanced administrative techniques substitute, at least temporarily, for a deeper transformation of the administrative structure. Thus, a managerialist administrative reform may simply be a strategy for changing some administrative institutions and mechanisms without disturbing the traditional relationship between the political system and the public administration in Mexico.

The fourth section analyzes a recent attempt to implement a civil service system for Mexican public servants. This case study corroborates the general arguments of the preceding sections regarding the difficulties in overcoming the resistance of the political system to changes in the role of the public administration in a framework of strong, nondemocratic, presidential power. The concluding section proposes several hypotheses concerning the necessary conditions for successful administrative reforms in countries similar to Mexico.

THE POLITICAL TRANSITION IN MEXICO

In the 1980s and 1990s, the Mexican state underwent a major transformation in its economic role, and reforms advanced significantly in the electoral and political arena — through a defensive governmental position[1] allowing the opposition to take an increasingly active role — but progress was slow on social issues and even slower in the administrative system. There is some basis for thinking that the main explanation for this lack of administrative reform is that the economic and political reforms have generated new dynamics, allowing the formation and strengthening of new groups and transforming old networks of power. In one view, then, to the extent that the old administrative system was tied to previous patterns of authoritarian politics and state-led industrialization, once these patterns were changed, the public administration would also change automatically, with little need for specific reform efforts. In other words, the different dynamics generated through the other reforms would force the administrative system to adapt to these new conditions. According to this view, administrative reform (how government works) is an inevitable consequence and inseparable part of economic and political reforms. If we accept this explanation, then a separate administrative reform might not be necessary as a goal in and of itself.

However, at least for Mexico, and perhaps for other countries in Latin America as well, the transformation of the administrative system will probably be as difficult to achieve as other types of reforms. The most important reason why the difficulty of administrative reform has been so underestimated is that analysts often think of the governmental apparatus as an instrument: as a set of organizations, rules, institutions, and people that automatically obey orders (Denhardt 1993; Gortner, Mahler, and Nicholson 1987). Nothing could be further from the truth, as can be seen from the following brief description of the old Mexican political system.

The Old Political System

Traditionally, Mexico has been known as a presidential regime because the three-branch system did not work in practice. The executive branch has had so many formal and informal powers that the legislative and the judicial branches have had to accept presidential dominance. Before 1997, the system of political parties consisted of one hegemonic party, the Institutional Revolutionary Party (Partido Revolucionario Institucional — PRI), which controlled the presidency, Congress, most of the states, and a number of fragmented and weak opposition parties. Prior to 1997, electoral processes existed but were not crucial to defining political representation or distributing power among political groups, because of the particular government and party relationship that existed with all other sectors of society. For example, groups representing peasants, workers, members of the middle class, teachers, and bureaucrats were included in the central party structure. These groups, and, in particular, their leaders, were all looking for something — a job, connections, political support, or a recommendation. As government and party were the same, the PRI was able to fulfill most of these expectations in return for political support.

The relationship between high administrative officials and politicians was not clear under this system, because a political career was synonymous with an administrative one. The political system made this possible because presidential authority prevailed over legislative power and was supported by strategies of competition for power other than democratic electoral mechanisms. Consequently, the unchallenged power of the Mexican presidency as an institution affected the administrative structure primarily because executive power determined political institutions and their procedures. Real opposition did not exist at the national level until recently. Without an opposition, presidential control over the federal administration was practically absolute. Such overwhelming political power allowed the president the freedom to appoint (or at least influence the appointment of) the highest administrative officials, ministers, governors, deputies, senators, and judges, and to use all national resources freely to run a reward and punishment system. As a consequence, the administrative structure became the arena in which contenders competed for the presidency and became the main channel through which conflict among social sectors was managed.

In this sense, the Mexican bureaucracy seems more in tune with political than administrative procedures and activities. However, the Mexican bureaucracy can be considered more or less effective and stable, because an informal system of different levels of bureaucrats that rotate among the different government agencies and ministries with some regularity exists. In any event, mobility and political influence over the administrative apparatus is very high, despite the informal system described above.

To analyze this system, we can designate three semiformal levels of bureaucracy: high, medium, and base. High-level officials are politically involved with their bosses (the president and ministers). If a minister is moved to another agency or ministry, all high-level staff members accompany him or her to the new position. Semi-independent professionals in charge of the technical, legal, and administrative functions of the agency form the medium level of Mexican bureaucracy. Usually, these officials do not have political attachments to their bosses. They are hired because of their technical capacity or experience. For the most part, they leave the agency or ministry when their bosses are moved (formally, they "resign for personal reasons") but without necessarily having a promise from the former boss of a new position. In time, these medium-level bureaucrats often find a similar position in another agency. Generally speaking, they are hard workers who earn fairly decent salaries and work long hours, typically from 10 a.m. to 10 p.m. and often on weekends. The low-level bureaucrats who belong to a "corporatist" union form the base level. Usually, these officials receive very low salaries and hardly work at all. Movements among bureaucrats at the middle and upper levels do not affect them. Therefore, we cannot speak of a single bureaucracy; rather, we must analyze the several bureaucracies supporting different groups and particular interests.[2]

Thus, in general terms, the bureaucracy is highly attached to the political system, is subordinate to presidential political will, and changes every six years, creating uncertainty throughout the public sector. Additionally, public administration is overregulated; this complex legal framework allows bureaucrats' control over citizens who do not know about administrative processes and rules. Altogether, these factors — political interest, labor uncertainty, and overregulation — generate corruption, inefficiency, and obstacles to control and performance supervision.

Important changes in the political system began to consolidate during President Miguel de la Madrid's term (1982-1988). During his presidency and in the years thereafter, several political changes occurred: two opposition political parties consolidated their position against the PRI; economic constraints reduced the president's ability to manage a reward-punishment system over the whole political structure; policies of downsizing and decentralization reduced the size of the state's administrative structure; and, after the 1997 federal elections, Congress was no longer the president's unconditional servant. In addition, Mexico City was ruled by a member of an opposition party. In the 2000 presidential elections, the PRI lost the presidency for the first time in seven decades, the culmination of a long process of democratization, with the election of President Vicente Fox of the National Action Party (Partido Acción Nacional — PAN).[3]

Yet, until the year 2000, all these changes did not result in a new political system. At that time, the Mexican state, the political system, and the public administration as a whole entered a complex transition process. Several features of the old system remained and continue to coexist with new trends in the political, economical, and social spheres. For example, the president's image is still very important and, in many governmental areas, he remains the key decisionmaker. However, at this time, he faces new constraints in other areas, as Congress is no longer dominated by his own party. In addition, during the 1990s and parallel to the process of economic and trade liberalization, new independent agencies were created to regulate specific markets, and their performance was evaluated on technical rather than political criteria.[4] However, in 2000, the reward-punishment system continued to maintain clientelistic networks between government and organized groups, such as teachers, peasants, and workers. At the same time, the government's economic constraints have reduced its ability to reward supporters, and the rate at which new independent groups are appearing has increased, thus raising the demand for "rewards." In short, the transition process in Mexico seems to be leading to more open and transparent schemes of public decisionmaking and to more democratic, competitive, and fair electoral procedures. Nevertheless, all these remain emergent processes rather than consolidated realities, with both old and new systems coexisting.

Within this context, at least two further characteristics of the Mexican political system are important for an understanding of the complexity of administrative reform: 1) the government apparatus is still a basic part of the power structure, and 2) the government is not a harmonious set of organizations within a congruent network. In this chapter, we emphasize the first of these two characteristics. During the discussion that follows, it should be kept in mind that the Mexican political and administrative systems are changing rapidly, and several of the characteristics discussed here are being transformed. The following account is historical; it does not cover the current administration or events after the 2000 election unless specified.

Prior to 2000, the Mexican public administration was permeated and defined by corporativism and presidentialism. Since elected public officials were actually appointed by the PRI and particularly by the president, the structure of accountability and oversight was almost nonexistent. Congress's capacity for vigilance and control was still fragile and underdeveloped. Public officials remained accountable mainly to their bosses within a political or administrative and a formal or informal network. The president and his cabinet could appoint, remove, or redefine their teams almost at will.[5] Public resources could be manipulated with almost no constraints and could be used freely to support hidden political agendas.[6] Moreover, an open, complete system of government information accessible to the public was weak and untested; it was not clear to what extent government officials could be forced or persuaded to yield information to the public. In this sense, society and other political subjects did not have easy access to systematic and complete information regarding public programs, expenses, and the evaluation of the impact of public policies. Therefore, public resources were instruments for agendas of political teams (*camarillas*). Public organizations in Mexico were only rarely evaluated for their outcomes and impacts; more commonly, they were evaluated for the capacity of the administrator to perform particular political duties within the political network. All these gave hegemonic political groups a huge discretionary capacity for control. They could manipulate and use public resources and agendas without having a system that held them accountable to society.

In other words, public bureaucracy was a strategic tool for political control. This could also be said for other countries. However, in the Mexican political context it held particular significance, given the lack of checks and balances and the weakness of the legislative branch, the lack of transparency and absence of a system of accountability, and the weakness of the judicial branch, all of which explained the infrequent observance of the rule of law. Given this context and the assumption of administrative subordination, it is not surprising that administrative reform has been largely postponed. Put simply, generating a transparent, accountable, honest, and externally controlled public apparatus would have jeopardized the political control that the dominant political group enjoyed during past decades.

Until the PRI lost its hold on the presidency,[7] the following four main features characterized Mexico's federal public administration:

1. At least until 1994, the public administration was the arena for political struggles, especially presidential succession, where state secretaries (ministers) were the main contenders. This was the arena in which political groups mobilized resources and prepared strategies to fight for the presidency, compromising to a large extent the agencies under their command.

2. Public administration was the locus for corporatist and clientelist representation and, thus, displaced the representative role of Congress. In addition, apart from being the link between political power and social groups, such as labor unions and peasants groups, public administration was a means of channeling resources to those social sectors and the arena of distributional negotiation over the allocation of those resources. Social groups were not represented in Congress, and negotiations over public resources did not take place in the offices of congressional legislators. The allocation of resources was not negotiated by district representatives or on a territorial level either. All this negotiation and allocation went on in the departments of the secretaries of state and in their administrative apparatus. From the viewpoint of the secretaries of state, the loyalty of bureaucrats was essential to dealing with their clienteles and political support groups and to favoring their individual political ambitions, especially the fight for the presidency.

3. The structure of incentives for civil servants, individuals, and social groups (the high opportunity costs of fully obeying formal rules and the recurring failure to enforce sanctions) widely encouraged mutual arrangement through a hodgepodge of private, economic, and illegal channels. Public administration was the ideal means for the illicit enrichment of high-level appointees and their support groups. By the same token, thanks to its collusive transactions, the bureaucracy gained internal cohesion. Mutual complicity bred a powerful factor of internal cohesion within the bureaucracy and helped it show a united front to the outside world, while bureaucrats enjoyed little independence within the system and especially from their superiors.

4. The public administration apparatus was the president's unconditional right arm. This was a two-edged sword: on the good side, the secretaries and the president maintained strict, vertical control over administrators of programs and policies of most interest to the hierarchical chief. In such cases, because high-level administrators were closely supervised by ministers and the president himself, the risk that actions taken by these administrators would not reflect the wishes of those at the highest levels was fairly low. (Of course, the president's, ministers,' and top administrators' aims underlying various policies were not necessarily the most desirable for the people affected by the policies.) On the negative side, when the president, ministers, and ministerial team members did not personally supervise these same high-level administrators, they, in turn, found it extremely difficult to control lower-level administrators' execution of policies. Vast policy, law enforcement, and judicial areas left unsupervised by the president and his ministers were easy prey for minor bureaucrats and interest groups motivated only by self-interest. Corruption became the rule rather than the exception among police, the administration of justice, supervisory bodies, agencies responsible for granting permits, and others.

MEXICAN STATE REFORM: AN INCREMENTAL HISTORY

We agree with the perspective of Manuel Antonio Garretón and Gonzalo Cáceres (see Chapter Five, this volume), who describe state and governmental reforms in Chile as a set of different projects of political change that evolve through time and are shaped by different political and economical agendas. Due to the changeable nature of state reforms, it is not surprising that some programs and proposals for reforms achieve better results than others. The Mexican case is not an exception.

After the economic crisis that began in 1981, Mexico's government made enormous efforts to transform the rules, institutions, and actors that had characterized the economic and political system since the early post-revolutionary years. In 1981, the economic model could be characterized as typical for Latin America: highly protected industries dependent on a modest domestic market and an export sector mostly dedicated to primary products. Government intervention in the Mexican economy was very high, especially through more than 2,000 state enterprises, and was designed to promote endogenous development protected from international competition.[8]

In the political field, the Mexican system appeared democratic, with regular elections, a formal separation of powers, and a federal system of government. In reality, though, the system was centered on a dominant party, controlled by a set of elite groups linked by clientelistic advantages, making government domination a "right" and the legitimate "property" of some political groups. In this context, the administration of the state was flexible, with high-level bureaucrats firmly attached to political power structures and subordinate to political frameworks and their struggles. A government position was used to reward some players or was the result of a good relationship with key players. In other words, it was a spoils system, in which career accountability hardly existed and civil service careers were rare.

From 1982 to 1988, members of a new, reformist political group occupied key government positions in the administration of President de la Madrid. During this time, important state reforms were launched in various areas, most of them applied or designed in an incremental way and clearly affected by circumstantial political events. However, economic reform was clearly the priority for this group. Important transformations occurred, beginning with the idea that government could no longer be the unique "motor" for development. To implement this new strategy, De la Madrid's administration advocated privatization of public enterprises, downsizing (dismantling a "fat government"), balancing public finances, and economic transformation by opening the economy to international competition. At the same time, a severe economic and political crisis pressured the government to define new rules for elections, which led to opposition victories at the local level. As the composition of legislative power changed, discontent was reduced, and political legitimacy was recovered.

In terms of public administration, the de la Madrid government defined the decentralization of different institutions and resources (the health and education system were among the most important sectors to be reformed) as important objectives, even though efforts were limited in practice by political and administrative obstacles and resistance. In this context, reformers undertook a strengthening of the role of the municipalities, mainly vis-à-vis state-level government. Another proclaimed goal of the de la Madrid administration was the "moral restoration" of society, with corrupt public officials as the main targets. Basically, new controls were imposed on budget management and public servants' activities to constrain the possibilities for diverting public resources. To reach these goals, a new ministry was created, the Ministry of the Comptroller General of the Federation (Secretaría de la Contraloría General de la Federación — SECOGEF), and charged with investigating corruption scandals during the administration of José López Portillo (1976-1982).

The government of President Carlos Salinas de Gortari (1988-1994) consolidated the economic reforms and deepened the economic transformation undertaken by the de la Madrid administration. The economic recovery of the late 1980s allowed the Salinas administration to strengthen the new model of a "small" but agile government more capable of responding to social demands and supported by high levels of national and international private investment. In political terms, the Salinas administration negotiated three different political reforms in the organization, administration, and control of elections. These reforms sought to regain the political system's credibility after the broadly questioned 1988 presidential elections. Administratively, a decentralization effort was maintained, but it still faced strong opposition from actors such as unions, traditional leaders (*caciques*),[9] the administration itself, or pressure groups. Other factors also stalled or totally impeded reforms in areas such as education, health, and devolution of power. In addition, more precise ways to control the use of public resources were developed and defined through new norms and laws, mainly to reduce the public deficit by means of centralizing budget control in the Ministry of Finance and Public Credit, also called the Treasury (Secretaría de Hacienda y Crédito Público — SHCP).

The different initiatives designed during the Salinas administration can be characterized within what has been called Mexican state reform. However, this reform can hardly be explained as a single, rational, uniform process. Actually, the reform consists of a set of processes imposed by the higher levels of government, using the broad informal and formal discretional capacities of the President (Elizondo 1995, 95). Also very important is the fact that these processes have helped to generate a new system of alliances to redefine certain rules of the political and economic systems, often using the same clientelist, presidentialist, and authoritarian channels (Heredia 1994, 45).

As the Organisation for Economic Cooperation and Development (OECD) has stated, there is no unique model for a unique solution to the problems of governance and administration (OECD 1995, 19). For the Mexican case, the state reforms that began in 1982 have evolved in incremental and differentiated ways — firmly conducted in the economic field, defensive in political and electoral reforms, and limited and piecemeal in the administrative realm.[10] As Robert Kaufman (1997) explains, it seemed easier to change governmental objectives than legal and administrative frameworks.

Given the political changes experienced in Mexico since 1982, this situation of apparent unbalance among the different reforms launched in Mexico is understandable. First, the technocratic group that gained power in 1982 was part of the economic-financial network within the executive branch, concentrated in the Central Bank, the Ministry of Treasury, and the Ministry of Programming and Budgeting. This network was important because it promoted among them a common background and an economic ideology. Second, this group also developed a network of alliances with members of the international financial community. The struggle between so-called technocrats and traditional politicians and bureaucrats has been discussed at length since 1982 (see Pardo 1991; and Langston 1994). For the most part, all of these developments must be understood in a context of severe fiscal crisis, when government deficits clearly began to be a huge obstacle to growth. In other words, there were few alternatives but to fix the economic disarray.

A review of state economic reform clarifies that the goals of economic transformation have been transparent from the beginning: stabilization of the economy, balancing public finances, privatization, fiscal reform, economic deregulation, financial reform, trade liberalization, and renegotiation of the foreign debt (Aspe 1993, 11; Rebolledo 1993, 115-144). In contrast, political reform (basically electoral reform) was demanded by different pressure groups. The government and the dominant party (PRI) reacted defensively to these demands by making concessions designed to maintain control over resources, rules, and institutions. During the administration of President de la Madrid, a new code for the regulation of electoral activities was implemented after the electoral crisis of 1986, when an opposition candidate from the PAN lost the election for governor of the state of Chihuahua. Many opposition politicians and academic analysts thought that those elections were fraudulently manipulated by the federal government and the PRI. Under the administration of President Salinas, three electoral reforms took place (Prud'homme1996, 93), all driven by different political pressures and all facing strong resistance from some parts of the government and the PRI, who were unwilling to yield control over resources, rules, and electoral institutions.

Several political reforms have been enacted since 1978.[11] However, when social conflict and pressure increased after the conflictive and controversial elections in 1988 (when President Salinas came to power amid severe doubts regarding the legitimacy of his electoral victory), the most important advancements were made in electoral independence and transparency (Méndez 1994, 195-196). Political reforms in Mexico apparently had not been an integral part of the intentions of government reformers, at least not at the same level of intensity as economic reforms. Political reforms appeared to be part of a defensive strategy the government and PRI used to maintain control over the political system and government resources as long as possible, while maintaining legitimacy by deepening the democratization process.

Administrative reforms undertaken during the two administrations prior to 2000 are actually more difficult to understand than the economic and political reforms. Responsive and accountable government are concepts that have appeared only secondarily within all these processes of reform. Following the assumption that government institutions are designed and reformed to serve political ends (Haggard 1996, 4), the apparent relative insignificance of administrative reform efforts could be understood in light of the importance of economic and political reforms. Two contending interpretations might explain this situation. First, the costs, pressures, and demands generated by economic and political reforms normally lead political officials over time to realize that the government administrative apparatus also needs reforming (Heredia and Schneider in Chapter One, this volume). In other words, economic and political reforms had matured, and the time for an administrative reform had come. President Ernesto Zedillo's administration (1994-2000) included the official 1996 Program for the Modernization of Public Administration 1995-2000 (Programa de Modernización del Sector Público — PROMAP), which indicated the government's intentions (civil service, accountability systems, improvement of service culture within public offices, and indicators for performance evaluation, for example). This modernization program led to an increasing awareness that the time had come for a "second step" — an administrative reform that truly transforms the government apparatus into a responsive, professional, and accountable organization. However, the institutional, cultural, and political realities of public administration offer a different interpretation. Such a "second step" would by definition jeopardize political control over resources, institutions, and people that groups in power were accustomed to.

Among the administrative reforms proposed, one strategy under consideration could be implemented without excessively affecting the political structure embedded in Mexican public administration: managerialist strategy. This strategy emphasizes the implementation of better techniques to transform the bureaucracy into the canons of the post-bureaucratic paradigm (Barzelay 1992; Osborne and Gaebler 1992). Managerial reform attempts to free bureaucrats from micromanagement (in other words, reducing the overinvolvement of Congress or controller agencies in specific details of managing the agency), pushing them toward evaluation of performance and competition and making the administrative apparatus more efficient and responsive to society. This strategy, based on re-engineering, total quality management (TQM), and a service-oriented bureaucracy, might allow an administrative reform that would yield some improvements in efficiency and efficacy without jeopardizing the traditional political system of control.

In other words, a possible option might be to implement an intermediate, nonthreatening step, a "neutral" reform that technically improves government efficiency through administrative techniques. The managerialist agenda includes aspects such as corporate planning that clearly specifies what each department should do, budgetary planning that assures the efficient distribution of scarce resources, a service-driven bureaucracy that assumes that the citizen deserves value for money, and teamwork among bureaucrats to improve efficiency and motivation (Hughes 1994). It is likely that the "second step" administrative reforms launched by the Zedillo administration were unable to implement fully a civil service system and comprehensive procedures for effective accountability. If this is the case, the managerialist strategy seems an important option, not only because it is easier to implement and is apparently politically "neutral" (because its basic arguments are related to technical procedures), but also because, at least at the beginning, it does not jeopardize the traditional way the government controls the public administration nor does it affect the public administration's traditional ways of functioning.

MEXICAN ADMINISTRATIVE REFORM:
A MANAGERIALIST REFORM

The Zedillo administration launched important projects of administrative re-form, perhaps the most (at least formally) ambitious and comprehensive ever. They were known as PROMAP, the *Program for the Modernization of Public Administration 1995-2000*, published in 1996, and mentioned earlier in this chapter; the Integral System of Federal Financial Administration (Sistema Integral de Administración Financiera Federal — SIAFF); the New Programmatic Structure (Nueva Estructura Programática — NEP); and the Performance Evaluation System (Sistema de Evaluación del Desempeño — SED). PROMAP introduced words long forgotten in the Mexican public sector: "accountability," "citizens' rights," "infor-mation rights," and "evaluation." After a limited diagnostic analysis of existing problems, PROMAP proposed two objectives: 1) to transform the Federal Public Administration into an organization that acts efficiently and effectively through a new culture of service and 2) to fight against corruption and impunity, through control mechanisms and the promotion of human resources skills. The program proposed four different subprograms: Citizen Participation and Service, Adminis-trative Decentralization, Evaluation and Measurement of Public Management, and Professionalization and Ethics of Public Officials.

PROMAP's discourse emphasized accountability, both in its presentation and in the opening diagnostic analysis. However, the subprograms barely refer to the impact of proposed actions on accountability. Action in the citizen participation subprogram refers basically to better information regarding public services, the reduction of required procedures, and the need for public agencies to follow up with their "clients." There was no attempt to require a large transformation of the way government controls information regarding impacts, costs, and budgets assigned to programs or services. Also, there was no action planned so that clients could have real control over the process and results of the public agency's evaluation.

The actions of the decentralization subprogram emphasized the need to improve conditions for the supply of public services and the flexibility public institutions should have to attend to new needs efficiently. The apparent assumption was that more accountability would naturally be produced by better technical distribution of resources and responsibilities. In this plan, accountability was an internal affair, and efficiency was more important than openly providing informa-tion to the public. The plans for action of the Evaluation and Measurement of the public management subprogram described the need to develop an integral system of information and new performance indicators. However, the subprogram pro-posed the following systems for internal control: better information to improve internal management, clear objectives and measurable outcomes for internal evaluation, and performance indicators to guide management of the decision-making process. There was no proposal regarding better ways for citizens or Congress to control public actions, for example. No reference was made to an external evaluation of the impacts on society of public programs. The basic emphasis was exclusively on the internal management and decision-making process.

The subprogram for the Professionalization and Ethics of Public Service described a long-awaited mechanism for the implementation of a public service career in Mexico. Nevertheless, the program was very general, encouraging all public agencies to define their procedures for hiring and training their human resources. In addition, the Treasury Ministry developed a project for civil service reform in 1997. However, by the end of the Zedillo administration, no civil service career program had been implemented.

The SIAFF, NEP, and SED also were ambitious efforts to transform the traditional budgetary process into a performance-driven system. The basic idea was to provide public organizations with sufficient independence to avoid micromanagement by controlling agencies, such as the Ministry of Finance and Public Credit and the Ministry of Administrative Modernization and Control (Secretaría de Contraloría y Desarrollo Administrativo — SECODAM). The main instruments of modernization in this instance were the design and initial attempt to implement performance indicators, performance agreements, and budgets defined in terms of achievement of results, not solely based on expenditures. Implementation of the budgetary reform began in 1997 (three years before the end of the Zedillo administration). Gaining the necessary consensus and gathering sufficient technical capacity so that the entire public apparatus would wholeheartedly back the project was slow and met many obstacles. This budgetary part of the reform required a huge political and technical effort to induce hundreds of public agencies to implement the proposed system homogeneously. Performance-driven budgets face the complex challenge of giving public agencies large degrees of independence without losing macroeconomic and administrative consistency (Arellano et al. 2000). The implementation process was not completed by 2000, the last year of the Zedillo administration, so the future of this reform is uncertain.

The real possibilities and capacities of a proposal like this one, which started with high expectations and ended without major results, must be analyzed carefully. Our preliminary and speculative explanation for this reform's apparent inability to transform the public administration into an accountable and externally controlled apparatus is simple: such a transformation would jeopardize political control. An obligation to give the public information — not only on public services procedures but also on budgets, evaluations, outcomes, and the flow of resources within agencies and departments — would reduce the use of discretion by some top officials to support particular political agendas through their agencies. Moreover, it would give information to other political groups regarding official program outcomes and impacts on specific social groups. Providing this information would reduce flexibility in the reallocation of resources and manipulation (punishing or rewarding) of social and political groups. The development of specific regulations and institutional channels that would provide the public and Congress with the basic mechanisms for policy evaluation would impose severe restrictions and limits on top officials regarding the design and implementation of public policies. The public policy decision-making process, usually developed within the offices of the ministries, would be affected by the "intrusion" of new groups and actors, if a truly open system of information were implemented.

The implementation of an integral and legitimate civil service system would reduce the almost total discretion over the agencies' human and material resources that top officials now enjoy. This system would imply a different culture and values, in which appointed officials would have to negotiate with service bureaucracies, limiting their ability to manipulate resources for particular political agendas, legitimate or otherwise. Moreover, given the Mexican political culture at that time, a civil service reform could become the "hostage" of the existing clientelistic and corporatist political network, yielding inflexible and closed bureaucratic cadres (closely knit groups). Within the traditional civil service, bureaucratic groups were accountable only to their bosses and had few incentives to yield information to other parts of society; these groups formed a powerful, immovable, closed framework. The implementation of a performance-driven budget would increase the visibility of the results of public programs and make it more difficult to hide political agendas played out in the manipulation of public organizations.

However, the Zedillo government's administrative reform was clearly looking for an intermediate alternative. Following the U.S. model of managerial reforms would be common for Latin American countries (as Kaufman suggests in Chapter Ten, this volume). But it seems that the best solution in the eyes of government reformers would be to find a way of increasing efficiency and transforming the public apparatus by improving public agencies' behavior. In Mexico, the most important condition seemed to be to improve behavior without jeopardizing mechanisms of political control that traditionally depend on the manipulation of government agencies and power over information. The language used in the program and some of the experiences of the Zedillo administration seem to show that government reformers, as in many other countries, had found an alternative in "managerialism" (Lynn 1996). To be succinct, managerialism is a worldwide tide of faith in the capacity of private management techniques to resolve the problems of bureaucratization of governments that began in the 1990s and is still popular. Well-known documents such as those by David Osborne and Ted Gaebler (1992) and Michael Barzelay (1992) proclaim the end of the bureaucratic era and the beginning of the post-bureaucratic paradigm era.

This is not the time to go deeper into the critique and analysis of managerialism (see Arellano 1995). However, it is possible to say that for Mexican reformers, managerialism not only helps to improve efficiency and effectiveness but also allows "painless" administrative reforms to be defined and designed. Reform is relatively painless because managerialism, returning to the old politics-administration dichotomy, promises less politics and more administration through intensive doses of "neutral" techniques of management applied to public sector situations. Managerialist techniques are relatively easy to implement and, at least in their initial phases, do not require massive transformations of such issues as accountability and civil service reforms. Managerialism, by making some procedures simpler, supporting team thinking within public agencies, developing efficiency indicators, and asking bureaucrats to be concerned about the needs of their clients, assumes that it is possible to arrive at an efficient entrepreneurial government without changing the fundamental nature of the state, its policies, and its role in the political system.

Throughout this chapter, we have argued that the transformation of adminis-tration is also the transformation of politics. However, severe political limitations to the implementation of an in-depth transformation or reform of the Mexican public administration exist. As long as they remain basic elements of political control, public agencies and their political administrators will firmly resist yielding control over information and resources to society and to Congress. Administrative transfor-mation will surely be a long social struggle and will require several steps, as in economic and political reforms. The Mexican government, through the official modernization program of the Zedillo administration, took the first major compre-hensive step, using managerialist ideas yet avoiding the key problem of making government accountable.

In order to analyze the successes and failures of these managerial strategies, it is important to maintain the premise that an administrative transformation is also a political transformation. Thus, establishment of a professional civil service appears to be a strategic part of the reform and a prerequisite for the modernization of public administration. Both an efficient public sector and a performance-driven system of budgeting depend on public servants being held to a well-defined behavioral structure. The following section of this chapter is an in-depth analysis of the problems involved in creating a federal career civil service during the Zedillo administration. This case study is offered to aid in understanding the structural difficulties the Mexican administrative system faces when it launches substantive modernization programs. The importance of establishing a civil service in Mexico illustrates a fundamental difference between Mexico's managerialist reform and the managerial reform in Brazil, where political transformation of the administrative apparatus was a low priority for reformers (as explained by Luiz Carlos Bresser-Pereira in Chapter Four, this volume).

A CASE STUDY: THE OBSTACLES CONFRONTING IMPLEMENTATION OF A CAREER CIVIL SERVICE IN MEXICO

This case study examines efforts to create a federal civil service in Mexico, identifying and describing the main actors involved in the project, including their preferences (insofar as administrative reform is concerned), their interests, their strategies, and their specific proposals for administrative reform.[12] The analysis also considers some broader structural characteristics of the actors' social and political contexts, as well as the economic problems that affected their scope of action. A career civil service does not exist in Mexico at any level of government. The few areas where a civil service exists are isolated: the Foreign Service and teachers in the public school system. During the Zedillo administration, several public offices implemented or were in the process of implementing specific civil service systems: the Office of the Attorney for Agricultural Affairs, which resolves legal disputes involving land ownership; the National Statistics, Geography, and Informatics Institute (Instituto Nacional de Estadística, Geografía, e Informática — INEGI); the Judiciary; the Tax Administrative Service (newly created, following the model of Internal Revenue Service in the United States); and the Federal Electoral Institute (Instituto Federal de Electoral — IFE).[13]

The Mexican bureaucracy is organized formally into two categories of public officials. First, there are low-level employees (*empleados de base*), who are unionized and cannot be fired, including drivers, maintenance staff, secretaries, archivists, and lower-level technical staff who generally lack a university education. Second, there are the medium- and high-level public officials, called *funcionarios de confianza* (literally, "confidence officials," similar to political appointees in the United States) who are responsible for all the substantive areas of public administration. These appointees traditionally have been accountable for their performance only to the official who hired them and who can also fire them without difficulty when they cease to be useful or when they no longer have the trust of their boss.[14] The low-level employees have little chance of being promoted or making a career in public administration, while political appointees are in charge of making decisions and controlling budget and resource allocation. For the first group, the benefits are job security and stability. For members of the second group, benefits are better salaries and resources, as well as political protection and access as long as they are useful to their superiors in the hierarchy.

The federal government employed almost 2.9 million public employees in 1999, 30 percent of whom worked in the federal government; 24 percent in public entities, parastate agencies like the national oil company, Mexican Petroleum (Petróleos Mexicanos — PEMEX), and the federal electricity agency; and 46 percent, the largest group, in the health and education services, which were decentralized in the 1990s but remained on the federal payroll. In fact, a different breakdown of the same group shows that out of the total, 51 percent were in education either at the federal or local level, 23 percent in health and social security activities, and 10 percent in civil and military services for national and public security. Mainly unionized staff and political appointees occupied the remaining 16 percent, that is, 450,000 posts. Approximately 20,000 political appointees are employed in the federal government.[15]

The Federal Public Servants Act (1963), considered the main source of power for the public servants' union, regulates labor conditions. This law allows only one public workers' union, the Federation of Workers' Unions at the Service of the State (Federación de Sindicatos de los Trabajadores al Servicio del Estado — FSTSE).[16] In other words, this union holds a monopoly on representation of public servants. The right to strike is ruled out for public servants. A separate union for bureaucrats belongs to a countrywide union (Confederación de Trabajadores de México — CTM), which is one of the main sectors constituting the PRI.[17] Therefore, the power relationship traditionally has been between the presidency and the executive branch bureaucracy, considered part of Mexico's traditional corporatism, in which one group represents a complete sector, holds monopolistic representation, and assures social control in exchange for political and economic privileges for the leaders of the group.

The first attempt to establish a career civil service in Mexico took place during the early 1980s. The impetus behind the attempt was mainly an effort to reduce government spending on salaries, following the economic crisis that began in 1982. The huge public deficit made necessary a sharp reduction in government expenditures. In 1983, the General Bureau of the Civil Service was created in the Treasury

Ministry with the mandate to propose policies for more efficient management of bureaucratic personnel. Five months after the creation of this Bureau, an Inter-Ministerial Commission on the Civil Service was created, and put in charge of budgeting, legal reform, and follow-through, at least on the fiscal level, of the programs decided on by the General Directorate of the Civil Service.[18] The Commission was in charge of encouraging implementation of specific parts of a program to advance a career civil service and to standardize and systemize administrative methods, with the goal of eventually installing an integrated federal civil service. But neither a more specific mandate nor deadlines were ever decided upon.

Mainly for budgetary reasons, the Commission formulated a civil service program in 1984 that called for a centrally controlled civil service.[19] But since it proposed a single format for working conditions, eliminating de facto the special status of unionized workers, it was rejected by the FSTSE. Although the proposal recognized the need for a civil service for government workers, the union insisted that any such initiative comply with the rights of government workers, as enshrined in the Federal Responsibilities of Public Servants Act, which basically protects union workers from being fired.[20] As a result of this rejection, the Secretary of Budget and Programming (Secretaría de Programación y Presupuesto — SPP) project was put on hold, and no law was proposed.

When President Zedillo came to office in 1994, his term was soon marked by an economic crisis, which caused further delays in the civil service reform. However, a new modernization program for the administrative system was presented in 1995. The program called for a gradual implementation of a civil service system, based on a legal framework that was supposed to be in place by 1997. As already mentioned, the general outline of this public administration reform can be found in the Federal Public Administration Modernization Program (PROMAP 1995-2000).[21] Many actions were undertaken by different government agencies to launch and support the administrative reform. But the main actors for design and implementation were the offices of the Finance Secretary and the Comptroller and Administrative Development Secretary.

The primary role for establishing the civil service was given to a newly created Civil Service Unit (Unidad de Servicio Civil — USC) within the Finance Ministry. This unit had to design the draft bill, which would need the endorsement of the Comptroller General, before it could be presented to and discussed with the president.[22] A study that preceded the bill showed that public officials' salaries were too low and that the monetary compensation system, in which total payments are divided into a very low base salary and much higher bonus payments (the size of bonuses are determined by an employee's superiors) did not provide a clear incentive structure to improve bureaucrats' performances. The study also criticized the fact that hiring schemes varied among public organizations, so that training, staff development, and firing procedures were neither uniform nor regulated.

The main reforms proposed by the USC included an open and clear recruitment system, in which new aspirants to any branch of federal government must take a general examination, a psychometric test, and an examination specific to the job applied for. The first two tests would be the same for all public organizations, and the USC would be responsible for administering them. The last one would be developed by each public organization according to its specific technical needs. Other USC proposals included the generation of a new classification for nonunionized bureaucrats, a mechanism that would allow only half of the highest-level positions to be appointed by the ministry's head, while the other half would be career public servants. The monetary compensation system would have three parts, salary, incentives, and benefits, and would be regulated by the USC. Promotions would be of three types: by group, by increases in salary, and by increases in grade or responsibility (including group and salary). A new evaluation system, based on performance and better customer service and expertise, was to be implemented. Firing processes could be based on several possible causes: voluntary, misconduct, bad performance, lack of promotion in seven years, and economic constraints or downsizing. Training would be systematic for existing and new public servants at all hierarchical levels.

The Civil Service Unit's (USC) project provided three different options for unionized workers: 1) changing the status of union membership so that base employees could be integrated into the new civil service system; 2) keeping the separation between base employees and higher-level officials but allowing union members to resign their union membership in order to pursue a career in higher levels of administration; and 3) designing two civil service careers, one for political appointees and the other for base employees. This model left a great deal of responsibility in the hands of the USC, with centralized controls over three main areas: hiring, pay, and the criteria for job termination.

After the project was developed, it still needed the acceptance of the SECODAM. At this stage, the bill was stalled because both ministries, Finance (also called Treasury or SHCP) and SECODAM, could not reach an agreement. At first, the points of disagreement seemed to be mere legal points of little practical importance. But gradually, as negotiations progressed, it became clear that the difference of opinion was substantial.[23] For SECODAM, the Finance Ministry's civil service plan seemed too centralized. Throughout the process of personnel administration; opening new positions; setting criteria for hiring, approval of hiring, promotions, and pay scales; and formulating a system of incentives, training, control, and evaluation, the Finance Ministry reserved a central role for itself. It was not clear whether the USC had the administrative capacity and human resources to take on this responsibility or even whether it would be able to acquire these resources in the near future. In any case, the centralizing tendencies of the proposed program would cause the various secretaries to depend on the authorization of the USC, which did not seem to be the best way to increase efficiency from the SECODAM's viewpoint. The Treasury was emphasizing professionalization, which led to a centralized design, while SECODAM was emphasizing flexibility and efficiency, which called for a flexible scheme that would rescue some of the informal characteristics of the former organization and adjust to the specific condition of different public organizations. In terms of bureaucratic politics, the USC would gain a fair amount of control over the administration because its proposal would simultaneously highly complicate SECODAM's plans for public administration modernization.

As the diagnosis and objectives for the civil service plan differed, agreement on the rest of the agenda, particularly the implementation strategy, became unlikely. One of the sharpest points of disagreement concerned budgetary questions. SECODAM argued that the cost was too high, considering the evaluation, promotion and incentives, training, separation, and retirement systems linked to the Treasury's proposal. Concerning the payment system, the budgetary cost of generalizing previously informal bonus pay and other incentives, which are currently limited to a small group of officials, seemed also to be quite high.

This federal civil service project was stalled by severe problems.[24] The reasons fall into two areas: the first relates to policymaking, and the second concerns structural elements or the institutional framework. Regarding policymaking, the civil service project failed because of timing considerations. Zedillo promised that the bill would be passed in 1997, but that year was full of electoral events: congressional mid-term elections and elections for state and federal district governors and deputies. Other important matters contributed to the lack of progress in the civil service project: economic adjustments, the conflict in Chiapas, national security reform, and efforts to combat corruption.

As discussed earlier, two ministries were involved in the project's development: the Ministry of Finance and Public Credit (the Treasury) and SECODAM. Each ministry advocated for its own approach and different bureaucratic agendas. Finally, the process for building the civil service project may have ignored the most interested actors with the largest stake in its outcome: unionized mid-level and operative bureaucrats. Facing a common enemy, union leaders may have been able to gain new and revitalized support from their members. However, the two ministries found it impossible to build consensus on the real problems, their feasible solutions, and ways to implement them. The strategy to establish the civil service system was inadequate, lacking in political support, and badly timed.

After the 1997 elections, a number of changes directly affected the chances for implementation of a civil service reform. A change in the balance of power between the legislative and executive branches, favoring the Congress, made building consensus over presidential initiatives more difficult. Passing laws was no longer a simple process that went from executive proposals to congressional acceptance. Therefore, the institutional framework further decreased the civil service reform's chances of being passed by Congress. However, a new political group's ascendance to power after the 2000 elections substantially changes the former state of affairs. In particular, the main obstacle described in the first section of this chapter, the degree to which the ruling elite and civil servants were linked, has been overcome. In a general sense, it may be said that this break opens the way for new momentum for administrative reform in Mexico, including the professionalization of public office, efficiency-led managerial reforms, transparency, and accountability.

Despite these propitious changes and though conditions might be ripe, important problems and obstacles to reform remain. These include the following:

1. Although President Vicente Fox's National Action Party did not get a majority in Congress, there is a long way to go before the separation of powers is an everyday fact. Indeed, it is far from working properly. Those

in Congress will have to strengthen their parliamentary careers — finding incentives to make a career of legislation (through immediate reelection, for example) — and Congress must authorize for itself the support it needs, in terms of advisory bodies, agencies, and personnel, to professionalize legislative work.[25] Work remains to be done in professionalizing parliamentary advisory bodies and agencies.

2. The inefficiency (and discredit) of the judiciary must be redressed. An independent judiciary is vital if Mexico is to ensure that the Congress and executive are held fully legally responsible under the national Constitution. An independent judiciary must be able to interpret and enforce the provisions of the Constitution. Mexico lacks an independent, professional judiciary capable of creating a minimal rule of law to guarantee personal security, assets, and private property and to ensure compliance with laws and contracts. Because of past judiciary failures, no one believes that new legal reforms will be complied with. It is easy to write laws; however, after they have been written, they must be enforced, so that the citizens and the nation can enjoy the benefits that come with the rule of law.[26]

3. Systems of accountability have simply not existed, and they must be put in place. The lack of checks and balances has not allowed formal accountability to develop. The system that has prevailed has encouraged accountability only to one's immediate boss, often an accomplice, or at least a complacent spectator, in his subordinate's collusive transactions.

4. An overregulated public administration, with strict and traditional rules, works with unwritten logic and rules of the game. There is an excess of regulation — sometimes with contradictory laws — that serves only to cover up the prevalence of informal systems of operation, leaving room for civil servants to manipulate this system to their advantage instead of serving their fellow citizens efficiently. Arbitrariness is compounded by a terribly poor distribution of responsibility: working to rule, in some cases where decisions could simply follow common sense, requires the intervention of numerous bureaucratic agencies and hierarchical levels. However, when something does go wrong, no one is responsible.

This informality has become an institutional arrangement: corruption, fraud, bureaucratic patrimonialism, clientelism, opportunism, and inefficiency are institutionalized. At the same time, excessive rules and their complicated nature have substantially raised the costs of transactions through bureaucratic channels. In other areas where legal loopholes exist, informal arrangements help to conclude transactions. The system of groups and teams, regulated by these informal rules — binding friendships; complicity in mutual enrichment and inefficiency; and vertical group hiring, firing, and promotion for public positions — institutionalized a system that discouraged trust, objectivity, and the possibility of peer review. It also stood in the way of the professionalization of the system because it blocked those civil servants who otherwise would have climbed through the ranks on their merits. It also characterized the decision-making process, which was concentrated in a small number of individuals and agencies, where the delegation of responsibilities was infrequent. Once again, this shows the lack of cooperation and trust.

Overall, informality posed a dilemma for administrative reform in general and the installation of a meritocratic civil service. A reform of this type requires change in the formal and informal systems that govern institutions, the rules of the game, and the structures of incentives and penalties.

CONCLUSION

A repeated theme in this chapter is that implementing a successful administrative reform is a very complex political process. Reform represents significant changes in the power structure established by key decisionmakers at the top levels of government. In addition, a structured administrative reform implies modification of bureaucratic behavior. Thus, given the evidence presented in this paper, there are important remarks to be made regarding hypotheses common in the literature, some of which Heredia and Schneider review in Chapter One:

1. *The degree of convergence between the executive and the legislature. The common hypothesis is that where cooperation prevails, coherent state reform programs are more likely. When there is divided government, state reform efforts will be fragmented.* In other words, the relationship between the executive and the legislative branches affects the configuration and outcome of the reform. It is necessary to emphasize that this assumption works in a democratic context, implying free elections and conditions of fair competition, allowing different governments to alternate and a Congress relatively independent of the executive (a true separation of powers that allows equilibrium and specialization of state functions, especially in policymaking) to function. In Mexico, until the 1997 elections, the relationship between the executive and the legislative branches was not exactly cooperative; it could be better characterized as one of subordination, in which the bicameral Congress had to adjust to an incentive system imposed by the presidency.

2. *Level of party fragmentation. Fragmented party systems are thought to hinder state reform. Moves toward cohesive party systems may facilitate reform by providing legislative backing to presidential programs, but, in the case of long-standing cohesive systems, patronage may increase.* That is, a structured system of political parties with a long history of cooperation makes reform easier by allowing the legislature to support presidential programs. Once again, this hypothesis supposes a context in which political parties compete with each other and alternate in power.

3. *Degree of centralization of party control. The greater the centralization, the greater the chances for state reforms that strike an appropriate balance between efficiency and continued responsiveness to societal demands.* According to this hypothesis, the greater the centralization of the governing party, the greater the possibility of carrying out an administrative reform. The idea is that a decentralized party would face, among its congressional representatives at least, divergent interests that would reflect the diversity of their constituencies. Paradoxically, in the Mexican case, the centralization of the ruling party has obstructed the development

of an effective administrative reform, resulting in the bureaucracy's strategic role in the political system.

4. *A cooperative relationship between the executive branch and trade unions, especially the public workers' union, undermines administrative reform.* In principle, a cooperative relationship between the president and trade unions should benefit the implementation of reform. However, in the case of Mexico, even though the bureaucrats' union is an integral part of the PRI, far more than a cooperative relationship developed; instead, it was a relationship of patronage and subordination, which eventually marginalized the union in the negotiating process.

Considering these hypotheses and taking into consideration some of the experiences we studied here for the Mexican case, three more detailed arguments might be proposed in order to deal more effectively with the political peculiarities common in developing countries before or during the transition to democracy:

1. *The specific role of the high-level bureaucracy in the political system affects the chances for administrative reform. The more integrated this bureaucracy is in political power dynamics, the greater the probability that an administrative reform would affect the capacities and resources of the political system as a whole.* It seems that when competition for political power takes place in the electoral arena and when the political parties are the legitimate contenders, the bureaucracy is more likely to be concerned mainly with administrative affairs. In this case, as it is less affected by political matters, the bureaucracy is more likely to become independent and more professional. When political careers are conducted within the bureaucracy and public resources are also openly political resources, then administrative independence is very difficult to obtain.

2. *As the executive branch in Mexico is the designer, executor, and supervisor of all reforms and the legislative branch does not participate in policymaking, any administrative reform that might take aggressive steps toward reducing the discretionary powers exercised by diverse political groups over the public apparatus is not likely to be implemented.* An aggressive and comprehensive administrative reform program would be more likely to succeed if it were also promoted and controlled by institutions such as Congress and/or non-governmental organizations.

3. *The extent to which written rules and laws are followed is a prerequisite for an understanding of the outcome of an administrative reform.* When the rules of the game are basically informal (despite the fact that the actors involved might understand them perfectly), the bases for a formal administrative reform are weak because its new rules and procedures do not necessarily affect the unwritten rules.

In any case, it is clear that successful administrative reforms require complex transformations in the political arena. A successful administrative reform program involves more than just incentives, new institutions, and procedures. It must also change behaviors within organizational and institutional settings. This obviously makes success more difficult. Nevertheless, it must be said that the main obstacle to administrative reforms in Mexico was removed in one fell swoop with the electoral results of July 2000, when the PRI lost the presidency. This historical political event broke the traditional link between the political elite and public servants. It can be foreseen that in the years to come, the change of political regime will trigger a slow process of democratic reform of the administrative apparatus, which will certainly move in three directions: professionalization, managerialism, and transparency together with accountability.

As early as May 2001, the administration of President Fox was showing increasing interest in following strategies of both managerial and accountability reforms. Words such as "quality," "innovation," and "responsive and transparent government" were appearing in the rhetoric of the new administration. However, it is too soon to evaluate the potential changes this administration might achieve. First, the economic and political situation in Mexico requires that this administration "manage" its highest priorities: economic stability, tax reform, and political order are clearly more important than a new project of administrative reform. Second, the Fox administration must go through its own learning process. Potential reform projects appear to be very weak. Some of those in charge of these projects do not seem to have a clear perspective of how complex and difficult reforming the administrative apparatus will be. Others have offered a somewhat naïve analysis of the political implications of launching any managerial administrative reform.

NOTES

1. The government's position was defensive in the sense that politicians in power agreed to implement legal and political changes due to social pressure rather than to a specific plan for creating the conditions for an ordered democratic transition.

2. We will provide related information for these groups in the last section of this chapter.

3. The PRI's loss of the presidency encourages the emergence of a set of new rules for federal political/administrative operations in Mexico. However, the winning party in the July 2000 presidential elections, the National Action Party (Partido Acción Nacional — PAN), did not win an absolute majority in Congress nor did it take Mexico City, clearly limiting the presidency. In our view, these elections not only marked alternation in power, but a total change of political regime that will bring with it new rules and new actors. Where relations among the president, his party, and the public administration are concerned, this change is fundamental because it breaks the historical link between the political elite and the bureaucratic elite.

4. Since the early 1990s, several autonomous agencies with regulatory purposes have been created: the Federal Competition Commission (Comisión Federal de Competencia), the Energy Regulatory Commission (Comisión Reguladora de Energía — CRE), and the Federal Commission for Telecommunications (Comisión Federal de Telecomunicaciones). Some other existing agencies had their legal framework reformed in order to increase their administrative autonomy, such as the Central Bank, the Bank of Mexico (Banco de México), and the National Bank and Assets Commission (Comisión Nacional Bancaria y de Valores — CNBV).

5. Since the early 1990s, one exception is the attorney general, whose nomination requires Senate confirmation.

6. There has been a significant but still insufficient effort toward transparency in the budget, particularly in some controversial social programs. For more on this issue, see Casar et al. 2000.

7. A more detailed analysis of these points may be found in Guerrero 1997.

8. To illustrate, while total net spending, that is, the overall federal public spending including service of the debt, represented more than 43 percent of the gross domestic product (GDP) in 1987, with a public deficit greater than 15 percent of GDP, for fiscal year 2000, it is estimated that total net spending will represent only 22.8 percent of GDP, with a 1.25 percent deficit.

9. These local traditional leaders, who use clientelist strategies, enforcing them with patronizing and repressive actions, usually dominate local agendas at the state and municipal levels. See Alan Knight, 1996, "México bronco, México manso: Una reflexión sobre la cultura cívica mexicana," *Política y Gobierno* 3:1 (México City: Centro de Investigación y Docencia Económicas — CIDE).

10. Different administrative modernization efforts were undertaken in Mexico before 1982. For a detailed explanation, see Pardo 1991.

11. In 1978, a bill changing the electoral law was passed, allowing "minority" parties proportional representation in Congress.

12. However, this was not the first time the Mexican government proposed to implement a civil service. An important civil service program initiative appeared as a consequence of the 1982 economic crisis. However the proposal faced two main obstacles: trade union power and high-level officials' opposition to being closely controlled. In 1985, the government created a new commission to include union proposals in the civil service project; the central government pursued union cooperation because an administrative reform would change the legal framework decreasing public servants' union power. However, unionists did not agree with the reform proposal because they considered that government authorities controlled it too tightly. Later, the project was included in the agenda of the government of President Salinas, mainly due to the explicit goal of making Mexico a member of the OECD, thus complying with the Organization's standards. The union proposed that the president instead review public servants' responsibilities and salary structure. Salinas agreed in principle, but actually no review or changes were implemented during his administration.

13. The results of these attempts at professionalization have been variable. The most systematic, open, and meritocratic system is undoubtedly the independent agency that organizes elections, the IFE, due to this institution's independence of the federal government and the role played by the opposition parties in the Institute's decision-making body, the General Council, where they insistently pressed in favor of professionalization. It would be hard to evaluate the other career services at this time, but in general they suffer from design faults, especially endogamy and closedness. In all cases, including the IFE, accountability is undermined by design.

14. In 1997, there were 27 secretaries (ministers); 62 under-secretaries; 16 major officials (head officials for the administration of each ministry); 37 unit heads; 152 general coordinators; 343 directors general; 563 (area) directors; 5,463 under-directors; and 10,152 department heads at the federal government level, not counting the decentralized bodies of the administration. The total number is 19,986 public officials ("confidence" officials) from the first decision-making level (head of department) to minister. These positions, considered in the federal budget (1997), account for approximately one-tenth of the total costs of the centralized public sector, without counting base employees. Roughly, it is calculated that there are between 200,000 and 300,000 non-unionized bureaucrats in the central sector (excluding parastate companies like PEMEX or the Federal Commission for Electricity).

15. *Presupuesto de Egresos de la Federación*, 1999, Secretaría de Hacienda y Crédito Público, Gobierno Federal.

16. The FSTSE includes all the unions of low-level federal government workers. This monopoly on representation has its basis in a law passed during the corporativism years of the 1940s, which also imposes only one union in each area of the government. The FSTSE represents only lower-level government employees.

17. Until some reforms were undertaken by the ruling party (the PRI) in the 1990s, the party's system of representation was organized by three main social groups gathered in corporations or confederations: the bureaucrats in the CTM, the peasants in the National Confederation of Peasants, and urban and middle-class organizations in the National Confederation of Peoples' Organizations.

18. Members of the Commission included the Comptroller General of the Federation, the Secretary of Finance and Public Credit (SHCP), the Secretary of Labor, the Secretary of Budget and Programming (SPP), the Secretary of Public Education, and the General Secretary of the FSTSE. The objective of the Commission was to advise the president on the civil service. The SPP presided over the Commission, and a technical secretary from the General Directorate of Civil Service was coordinator.

19. See Haggard (1997, 15) generally on budgetary pressures. With very general objectives aimed at "modernizing public administration, promoting efficiency, and encouraging a vocation for service," this program had strong centralizing tendencies, which included centralized classification of posts, hiring of personnel, a single pay and promotions policy, information systems, and personnel development. The goal of this program was to guarantee a "meritocratic system and to encourage professionalization," by guaranteeing the job stability and security of public employees. See Jesús Amado Tiburcio, 1992, *Relaciones laborales en el sector público*, Documentos de Trabajo 37, Mexico City: Friedrich Ebert Stiftung, 32.

20. For efficiency reasons, the government proposal included the possibility of worker separation.

21. Some of the problems in public administration identified by the program itself are labor inequality between high and lower posts, overall low salaries, uncertainty regarding job permanence, lack of accountability, and a culture that encourages inefficiency, bureaucratic misbehavior, and corruption.

22. The reason why the office of the Finance Secretary was in charge of the civil service reform was because it was formally responsible for the general management of government personnel. Many other key tasks fell into the Finance Secretary's control, such as the budget allocation and implementation reform. In fact, this office is involved in all finance and budget issues, while the office of the Comptroller Secretary deals with administrative matters. Since both activities are constantly linked, there are frequent problems of coordination between the two offices.

23. From interviews with high-level officials in SECODAM, Mexico City, February, March, and April 1997.

24. In April 1988, a PRI senator presented an initiative on civil service to Congress, which rescued to a large extent the Treasury's USC proposal. Various factors meant that there was little time for the initiative to be discussed. There was an overloaded congressional agenda, and two weeks after introducing his initiative, the senator was appointed minister of Social Development, leaving the bill without a sponsor in the Senate.

25. It must be noted here, however, that support personnel can rely on a civil service system for job security to guard against the constant removal of members of their cadres, which, when it occurs, makes professionalization difficult. Nevertheless, as this is not an agency that executes policies, to some extent the main advantages of the system are lost.

26. See *World Development Report 1997: The State in a Changing World* (Washington, D.C.: World Bank), 265.

REFERENCES

Aguilar Villanueva, Luis. 1996. "La silenciosa, heterodoxa reforma de la administración pública mexicana." *Revista de Administración Pública* No. 91. Mexico City: Instituto Nacional de Administración Pública (INAP), 19-26.

Arellano, David. 1995. "Gestión pública en Estados Unidos: crisis y estado del arte." *Gestión y Política Pública* IV: 1. Mexico City: Centro de Investigación y Docencia Económicas (CIDE).

Arellano, David, Ramón Gil, Jesús Ramírez, and Angeles Rojano. 2000. "Nueva Gerencia Pública en Acción: procesos de modernización presupuestal. Un Análisis Inicial en Términos Organizativos: Nueva Zelanda, Reino Unido, Australia y México." *Revista Reforma y Democracia* June. Caracas: Centro Latinoamericano de Administración para el Desarrollo (CLAD).

Aspe, Pedro. 1993. *El camino mexicano de la transformación económica*. México: Fondo de Cultura Económica (FCE).

Barzelay, Michael. 1992. *Breaking through Bureaucracy*. Berkeley, Calif: University of California Press.

Casar, María Amparo, Juan Pablo Guerrero, and Eduardo Revilla. 2000. *Algunos aspectos relevantes del presupuesto 2000. Negociación política, análisis de ingresos, transparencia en gasto* (Information brochure of the Program on Budget and Public Spending). Mexico City: CIDE.

Denhardt, Robert B. 1993. *Theories of Public Organization*. Fort Worth, Texas: Harcourt Brace College Publishers.

Elizondo, Carlos. 1995. "El Estado mexicano después de su reforma." *Política y Gobierno* II: 1. Mexico City: CIDE.

Flores, Romeo. 1981. *Administración y política en la historia de México*. Mexico City: INAP.

Gortner, Harold F., Julianne Mahler, and Jeanne Bell Nicholson. 1987. *Organization Theory: A Public Perspective*. Chicago: Dorsey Press.

Guerrero, Juan Pablo, 1997. *Un estudio de caso de la reforma administrativa en México: los dilemas de la instauración de un servicio civil al nivel federal*. Documento de Trabajo 61. División de Administración Pública. Mexico City: CIDE.

Guerrero, Juan Pablo, 1998. "Oportunidades para la instauración del servicio civil en el México democratizado." In *Análisis multidimensional del servicio civil en México*, eds. Marcela Bravo Ahuja and Ricardo Uvalle. Mexico City: Universidad Nacional Autónoma de México (UNAM) and Plaza y Valdés.

Haggard, Stephan. 1997. "Reform of the State in Latin America." In *Development in Latin America and the Caribbean*, eds. Shahid Javed Burki and Guillermo Perry. Washington, D.C.: World Bank.

Haro Belchez, Guillermo. 1988. *Aportaciones para la Reforma de la Función Pública en México*. Madrid: Instituto de Administración Pública.

Heredia, Blanca. 1994. "Estructura política y reforma económica: el caso de México." *Política y Gobierno* 1: 1. Mexico City: CIDE.

Heredia, Blanca, Kwang Woong Kim, and Ben Ross Schneider. 1996. "Democratization, Economic Liberalization, and Reforming the State: Korea in Comparative Perspective." Project Proposal.

Hughes, Owen. 1994. *Public Management and Administration: An Introduction*. New York: St. Martin's Press.

Instituto Federal Electoral (IFE). 1996. *Código Federal de Instituciones y Procedimientos Electorales*. Mexico City: IFE.

Instituto Federal Electoral. 1999. *Estatuto del servicio profesional electoral*. Mexico City: IFE.

Kaufman, Robert. 1999. "Approaches to the Study of State Reform in Latin America and Postsocialist Countries." *Comparative Politics* 31: 3 (April): 357-376.

Kliksberg, Bernardo. 1994. *El rediseño del Estado. Una perspectiva internacional*. Mexico City: FCE.

Knight, Alan. 1996. "México bronco, México manso: Una reflexión sobre la cultura cívica mexicana." *Política y Gobierno* 3: 1. Mexico City: CIDE.

Langston, Joy. 1994. *An Empirical View of the Political Groups in México: The Camarillas*. Documento de Trabajo 15. Mexico City: CIDE.

Lynn, Laurance. 1996. "Reforma administrativa desde una perspectiva internacional: ley pública y la nueva administración pública." *Gestión y Política Pública* V: 2. Mexico City: CIDE.

Méndez, José Luis. 1994. "La reforma del Estado en México: alcances y límites." *Gestión y Política Pública*. Mexico City: CIDE.

Méndez, José Luis. 1996. "Reforma del Estado, democracia participativa y modelos de decisión." *Política y Cultura* 7. Mexico City: Universidad Autónoma Metropolitana-Unidad Xochimilco (UAM-X).

Merino, Mauricio. 1996. "De la lealtad individual a la responsabilidad pública." *Revista de Administración Pública* 91. Mexico City: Instituto Nacional de Administración Pública (INAP): 5-18.

Organisation for Economic Cooperation and Development (OECD). 1995. *Governance in Transition: Public Management Reform in OECD Countries.* Paris: OECD.

Osborne, David, and Ted Gaebler. 1992. *Reinventing Government.* New York: Addison Wesley.

Pardo, María del Carmen. 1991. *La modernización administrativa en México.* Mexico City: El Colegio de México (COLMEX).

Pichardo Pagaza, Ignacio. 1972. *Diez años de planificación y administración pública en México* (essays). Mexico City: Instituto de Administración Pública (IAP).

Presupuesto de Egresos de la Federación. 1999. Gobierno Federal: Secretaría de Hacienda y Crédito Público (SHCP).

Programa de Modernización de la Administración Pública 1995-2000 (PROMAP). 1996. Mexico City: Poder Ejecutivo Nacional.

Prud'Homme, Jean-Francois. 1996. "La negociación de las reglas del juego: tres reformas electorales (1988-1994)." *Política y Gobierno* III: 1.

Rebolledo, Juan. 1994. *La reforma del Estado en México.* Mexico City: FCE.

Secretaría de Contraloría y Desarrollo Administrativo (SECODAM). 1997. High-level officials interviewed by the authors in Mexico City. February, March, and April 1997.

Tiburcio, Jesús Amado. 1992. *Relaciones laborales en el sector público.* Documentos de Trabajo 37. Mexico City: Friedrich Ebert Stiftung.

World Bank. *World Development Report 1997: The State in a Changing World.* Washington, D.C.: World Bank.

Documents

Las Razones y las Obras. Crónica del sexenio 1982-1988. 1988. Mexico City: Presidencia de la República. Unidad de la Crónica Presidencial. FCE.

Crónica del Gobiemo de Carlos Salinas de Gortari 1988-1994. 1994. Síntesis e índice temático. Mexico City: Presidencia de la República. Unidad de la Crónica Presidencial. FCE.

Primer Informe de Gobierno de Carlos Salinas de Gortari. 1989. Mexico City: Poder Ejecutivo Federal. Presidencia República. FCE.

Segundo Informe de Gobierno de Carlos Salinas de Gortari. 1990. Mexico City: Poder Ejecutivo Federal. Presidencia República. FCE.

Tercer Informe de Gobierno de Carlos Salinas de Gortari. 1991. Mexico City: Poder Ejecutivo Federal. Presidencia República. FCE.

Cuarto Informe de Gobierno de Carlos Salinas de Gortari. 1992. Mexico City: Poder Ejecutivo Federal. Presidencia República. FCE.

Quinto Informe de Gobierno de Carlos Salinas de Gortari. 1993. Mexico City: Poder Ejecutivo Federal. Presidencia República. FCE.

Sexto Informe de Gobierno de Carlos Salinas de Gortari. 1994. Mexico City: Poder Ejecutivo Federal. Presidencia República. FCE.

Primer Informe de Gobierno de Ernesto Zedillo Ponce de León. Septiembre 1995. Mexico City: Poder Ejecutivo Federal. Presidencia República. FCE.

Segundo Informe de Gobierno de Ernesto Zedillo Ponce de León. Septiembre 1996. Mexico City: Poder Ejecutivo Federal. Presidencia República. FCE.

Tercer Informe de Gobierno de Ernesto Zedillo Ponce de León. Septiembre 1997. Mexico City: Poder Ejecutivo Federal. Presidencia República. FCE.

Chapter Seven

PRINCIPALS OF THE THAI STATE

Danny Unger

OVERVIEW OF THAI PUBLIC ADMINISTRATION

Thailand's public administration has pronounced Weberian features.[1] Merit largely determines recruitment and promotion, and bureaucrats enjoy job tenure secure from political influence. The public service displays the trade-offs inherent in what Blanca Heredia and Ben Ross Schneider call a civil service model of administration aimed at curbing corruption: rigidity and unresponsiveness. Thai state administration, however, also is rife with corruption, qualifying sharply the appropriateness of the "Weberian" or "civil service" label. Corruption in Thailand probably exceeds that in the other countries examined in this volume (see Table 1, Chapter One).[2]

In formal terms, the Thai state has been almost entirely free of accountability mechanisms. Most significantly, the Parliament has exercised little effective oversight of the bureaucracy. Mechanisms of vertical accountability also have been weak, although a relatively free press at times has been able to bring pressure to bear on state officials. Informal mechanisms, however, rooted in a loose but enduring balance among political forces, including bureaucrats, military officers, business leaders, and politicians, generally provided a measure of horizontal accountability. With the exception of brief periods during which the military leadership was relatively cohesive, for example, the early 1990s, no state institution, political party, or social group has been able to sustain dominance in Thai politics since the late 1960s. This political balance has held open the possibility that administrative malfeasance or poor performance might be exposed.

While the state bureaucracy had pronounced civil service features and only minimal and informal accountability traits, it was largely bereft of managerial characteristics.[3] For some time, Thai academics have called for imbuing bureaucrats with a service ethic. Officials have experimented with performance pay and other personnel policy innovations. By and large, however, with the very significant exception of administrative decentralization now being introduced in Thailand, would-be reformers of the state have not tended to emphasize reforms of the managerial type.

The key features of Thailand's state administration, its relatively limited size and responsiveness, are rooted in Thailand's traditional political economy. After the late 1950s, the state made no major moves to expand its presence in or control over production. Neither did the state significantly expand its provision of services.

The state's low level of penetration of society resulted, in part, from a largely atomistic social organization that afforded few organizational sites in which state and societal actors could negotiate the kind of "resources for institutions" bargains discussed by James E. Mahon (see Unger 1998 and Chapter Nine in this volume). Thailand poses a challenge to comparative analysis of administrative reform because its starting point diverges so sharply from most other countries, including those included in this volume. I elaborate on these differences below.

As Heredia and Schneider and Robert Kaufman note in this volume, Thailand's traditionally fused polity was, like Mexico's, unfavorable to administrative reform initiatives. Other institutional features also tended to militate against administrative reform in Thailand. The impetus for administrative reform, for example, in Argentina (see Chapter Two) or Brazil (see Chapters Four and Nine) came from small, insulated groups based in the executive branch. No comparable institutional space was available within Thailand's parliamentary system. Weak, multi-party coalitions enjoyed neither the secure terms of office available to Latin American presidents nor the strong political party and union backing available to President Carlos Saúl Menem (1989-1999) in Argentina. In Thailand, administrative reform could not be "packaged" together with the goal of entry into the European Union (EU) (see Chapter Three on Hungary) or that of economic stabilization, as in the case of Brazil (see Chapters Eight and Two). Thailand's geography and macroeconomic health precluded these strategies. By the 1980s, however, Thailand's increasing economic integration into the global economy generated pressures for limited administrative reforms of the kind described by Heredia and Schneider and by Kaufman.

The most fundamental reorientation in Thai politics, economics, and administration came in 1997 as a result of an economic crisis and the new Constitution made possible by the crisis. The Constitution introduced radical departures in administration and politics, as discussed below in some detail. The Constitution, however, did not aim to enhance state capacities, the goal Heredia and Schneider associate with "second wave" reforms. These authors note that where political elites are largely pro-market and anti-statist, administrative reform is likely to emphasize cutting back the state over enhancing its capacities (see Chapter Three on Hungary). In Thailand, the political forces that propelled the new Constitution were promarket forces, and, while not anti-statist, they were clearly anti-politician. As a result, their efforts focused on strengthening accountability mechanisms that depended not on the legislature but on organization at the grassroots level. As Kaufman and Heredia and Schneider note, the result of this emphasis on strengthening accountability mechanisms in order to curb corruption and clientelism could be additional administrative delays and inefficiency. In Thailand, however, the hope is that stronger accountability mechanisms might check bureaucrats' goal displacement and, therefore, enhance state capacities. Signs of the emergence of stronger political parties and greater policy competition among parties in the wake of new election laws hold out the promise of "spurring along this lumbering [administrative] juggernaut" (*Bangkok Post* 2001b).

The Thai state is neither large nor ambitious and controls few resources relative to other states. Reflecting specific historical conditions and contemporary isomorphisms in the second half of the nineteenth century (see Chapters Nine and One), the state early assumed formal Weberian features. Meritocracy within the state apparatus by and large reproduced existing social status gradations (the elite sought employment in the state and rose to its top positions) until about the 1970s. Recurrent plans for administrative reform produced little change. Administrative services, nonetheless, improved fairly dramatically between 1950 and 1980, as a result of higher education levels and the expansion of the polity. The 1997 Constitution set in motion profound changes in Thai politics and, potentially, public administration.

Thailand in Comparative Perspective

For many developing countries, the 1980s were a lost decade in terms of economic progress. For Thailand, however, the latter years of the decade were a time of boisterous growth. The drying up of resource transfers from rich to poor countries that hit many developing countries in the 1980s did not affect Thailand. Instead, 1987 marked the beginning of a boom in private capital inflows complementing high levels of Japanese economic assistance. The good times continued, as the further deregulation of capital flows in 1994 accelerated those flows and boosted domestic investment.

Stagnant economic growth and the severe contraction of states' access to foreign financing led many developing countries in the 1980s to retrench the roles of the state sharply. In Thailand, political elites effected loosely comparable reforms much earlier — in the late 1950s. These reforms helped to underpin relatively healthy fiscal conditions. As Table 3 in Chapter One illustrates, Thailand's state is relatively modest in size. Partly as a result of its size, unlike most other developing countries, Thailand did not experience deep, prolonged, or recurrent macroeconomic crises during the 1970s and 1980s. Thai officials, however, pushed through modest but important macroeconomic reforms in the 1980s. They imposed ceilings on foreign borrowing and devalued the baht in the early 1980s before running off a long string of fiscal surpluses beginning in the late 1980s.

With developing countries in the 1980s beset by chronic fiscal deficits, near-consensus policy prescriptions called for reducing the size of the state and implementing a variety of administrative reforms. Among these prescribed changes were entrance into the bureaucracy by competitive examination and autonomy from political interference in personnel matters. The Thai civil service, however, had long operated along such principles.

Heredia and Schneider (see Chapter One, Table 4) and Kaufman (see Chapter Ten) concur in describing Thailand, together with Mexico, as cases of low levels of administrative reform. These assessments may refer primarily to the relative changes in administrative practices that have occurred over recent decades. If we evaluate Thailand's public administration in static terms, rather than looking at rates of change, however, we might assess Thailand's administration more positively. Despite the state's modest level of service provision and extensive corruption, Thailand fares comparatively well in terms of education and health achievements, relative to countries with similar per capita incomes and levels of state expenditures for these services. Thailand also is unusual for the early date and sustained implementation of the civil service model of reform. However, it makes limited sense to refer to the civil service model's insulation from political pressures when bureaucrats themselves constituted the polity. Thailand's nominal agents were, in fact, *principals*; this factor explains why Thailand's experience — and that of many other East and Southeast Asian states — seems sufficiently different from other developing countries, including those covered in this volume, to justify a brief discussion here.

Popular Mobilization and State Response

Consider a caricature of the context within which at least some developing countries suffered severe administrative and economic pathologies that induced, by the 1980s, a "crisis of the state" (Bresser-Pereira 1999). In these societies, political competition was sufficiently intense and popular mobilization general enough to generate multiple demands that swamped limited state resources. Whether we view them as intent on serving the public good or their more private utilities, political leaders were trying to gain and hold political power. They struggled for access to state resources to generate and sustain political coalitions. Their efforts resulted in the mobilization of demands, outstripping the resources available to meet them. In brief outline, this picture, described by U.S. political scientist Samuel Huntington, constituted a pathology of developing societies. It did not, however, fit Thailand.

The political context of administrative reform in Thailand differed because the polity, until very recently, was severely restricted. The polity was small not only because the state suppressed popular groups, but also because of the nature of underlying socioeconomic conditions and limited associational activity (Unger 1998). Commerce, finance, and most manufacturing were in the hands of Chinese immigrants subject to state discrimination. Most farmers were surprisingly affected very little by their integration into the world market. They continued to own their own land, at least until the 1970s, and to grow rice inefficiently, exploiting conditions of land abundance. Neither Thai farmers, the bulk of the population, nor Chinese immigrants in the business sector were well placed to hold state officials accountable.

Thai state leaders also encountered only modest challenges after their successful administrative centralization beginning in the late nineteenth century. Officials derived much state revenue by taxing the Chinese at rest (opium, gambling, and liquor). The economy earned foreign exchange largely through the Chinese at work (exporting commodities). The requirements of raising revenue, therefore, produced incentives neither for an expanding state nor a particularly effective one. The state did not balloon in size, and the polity was contained within the ranks of state officials, hence scholar Fred Riggs' reference to Thailand as a "bureaucratic polity" (1966). With the end of the absolute monarchy in 1932, the civil service entirely escaped any political control. Thailand's political context differed strikingly from the scenario that disturbed Huntington's dreams.

In addition to the political, economic, and ecological factors cited above, how can we account for traditional state administration in Thailand? The development of a complex and effective bureaucracy surely depends in large part on the need for public administration. Only if powerful actors perceive such a need will they strike bargains with influential groups to raise revenue and devote the resources necessary to induce state officials to develop state capacities (see Mahon's discussion of "resources for institutions," Chapter Nine). In Thailand, the aristocrats of the nineteenth century and their bureaucratic successors after the overthrow of the absolute monarchy in 1932 were primarily concerned with maintaining a stable currency and consolidating control over the territory of Thailand. The polity's traditional leaders saw both of these missions as necessary to fend off encroachments by British and French colonialism.

To accomplish these limited goals, spirited Thai leaders in the late nineteenth century reformed Thailand's traditional administration. Working in the shadow of the British Empire, Thai administrative, fiscal, and monetary policies mimicked those of British colonial governments elsewhere (Anderson 1978). The Chakkri Reformation, initiated by King Chulalongkorn (1868-1910), beginning in 1892, reorganized the bureaucracy into functional departments along lines familiar today and established centralized control over Thai territory. An administrative system grafted from British colonial best practice and French civil law granted state agencies extensive autonomy (Wit 1961; Christensen, Dollar, Siamwalla, and Vichyanond 1993). Political mobilization, however, was no more evident in Thailand than it was in areas under British colonial rule. And while colonies developed anticolonial sentiments that eventually encouraged the creation of political movements linking elites and masses, Thailand's population remained politically unmoved. As a result, Thai officials could achieve their principals' goals of territorial control with only modest achievements in the administrative arts. Chinese immigrants worked within a partially self-sufficient rural economy to funnel surplus rice to Bangkok and overseas. Foreign exchange earnings did not generate a powerful rural-based political class until the 1970s.

Despite the modest scale of Thai state ambitions, at different times and in different agencies, officials exhibited elements of a spirit of service. Ultimately, however, with demands for administrative performance coming neither from political leaders above, after the overthrow of the absolute monarchy in 1932, nor citizens below, the dominant ethos of the Thai bureaucracy emerged as a formal expression of status hierarchy within Thai society. Over time, officials of Thai state agencies became principals in their own right. More pronounced elements of broader patronage — jobs for the boys — emerged only in the 1960s with the expansion of higher education and of state developmental goals. Until recent decades, jobs in Thailand were not scarce. Thailand had a frontier, and in a context of land abundance, most Thais stayed on the farm.

Formal bureaucratic features served, in the absence of any principals outside officialdom, to demand accountability and to reinforce the official status hierarchy. The state apparatus enjoyed autonomy from society's few demands and defined the boundaries of the polity. Thailand's bureaucracy assumed Weberian features, but the country's nominal agents were, in fact, its principals.

An Expanding Polity

In the 1960s, growing internal (Muslim and communist) insurgencies and external assistance helped to foster developmental goals among Thai military leaders. The insurgencies grew up under the thin veneer of central state administrative presence in the countryside. To combat the insurgencies, U.S.-financed road building helped to bolster the Thai state presence in the provinces. The roads also enhanced farmers' access to Bangkok's ports. Chinese middlemen supplied price information and helped to stimulate farmers' diversification of Thai agriculture.

As pressures to spur development and increase control over the countryside grew, the economy and society gradually changed. Chinese entrepreneurs drove economic growth, generating new economic and political pressures on the bureaucratic polity. By the late 1960s and early 1970s, business and elements of middle class organization emerged as new political forces, but power remained concentrated in the hands of state officials, the military in particular, into the 1980s. During that decade of relative political stability, business influence continued to expand both in Bangkok and in the provinces. Provincial businessmen (often in construction, contracting for the state, gambling, prostitution, and smuggling) increasingly used Parliament's rising powers as vehicles to accumulate wealth and exercise power through political parties. These new provincial figures financed their parties at rapidly expanding cost, buying candidates for office and voters to support them, in hopes of securing ministerial portfolios that controlled lucrative licenses, monopolies, and various contracts (Krongkaew 1997). Thailand's political and administrative elites were differentiating themselves, creating a less fused polity.

Business associations based in Bangkok and concentrated in finance, international trade, and manufacturing increasingly engaged state officials in agencies such as the central bank, the ministries of finance and commerce, and the state planning board. As late as the 1980s, Thai exports were concentrated in commodities such as rice, rubber, sugar, cassava, maize, and seafood. As business firms developed increasingly complex links with the international economy, they generated more forceful demands for effective and supportive state administration of trade, tariffs, customs procedures, market negotiations, and so on. These firms' concerns about lowering transaction costs (see Chapter One) constituted the strongest pressures for administrative reform. These pressures encouraged a reorientation in state administration away from its traditional territorial services (control and stability) to a trading mission (helping firms earn foreign exchange).

Very rapid economic growth in the late 1980s and 1990s also created demands for dramatic increases in spending on physical infrastructure. The scale of needs outstripped state fiscal capacities and eventually required collaborating effectively with private interests. The World Bank estimated, before the economic collapse in 1997, that the Association of South East Asian Nations Four (Indonesia, Malaysia, the Philippines, and Thailand — ASEAN Four) would spend around US$435 billion on infrastructure between 1995 and 2004 for power, telecommunications, transport, and water and sanitation services (World Bank 1995, 2-3, 23). Concerns about increasing government capacities to provide various services, including education and poverty alleviation, also boosted interest in administrative reform. In addition, the economic crisis in 1997 served to highlight the poor quality of regulatory oversight in the financial industry, adding new pressures for reform.

The remainder of this chapter is organized into four sections. In the first section, I expand on the above description of Thailand's bureaucracy, previous reform initiatives, and the general place of the public administrative system within

Thai politics. The second section examines Thai government performance in the areas of fiscal, industrial, market regulation, and social welfare policies. The third part covers the current state of the administrative reform agenda in Thailand, emphasizing the potential for the new Constitution to shift sharply existing administrative structures and practices. In the conclusion, I return to the issues identified in this book's introductory and concluding chapters and reflect on the issues that emerge from the consideration of the Thai case.

BUREAUCRACY AND POLITY IN THAILAND: A BRIEF HISTORY

Thai state officials under the monarchy kept Thailand independent while their neighbors fell under colonial rule. They used conservative fiscal and monetary policies to keep the baht stable. Despite the bureaucracy's formal Weberian features, behavior patterns changed little. Most of the bureaucracy functioned essentially as an elaborate court. Officials' identification as members of the bureaucracy was "too meaningful to be subjected to formal rules and regulations" (Mosel 1979, 349).

When officials seized the state in 1932, they entertained new ambitions and worked to expand education and stimulate economic growth. Among other concerns, they wanted to create jobs at a time when an economic depression threatened access to public salaries for the growing educated elite. The new leaders established various state enterprises and put them under the management of ethnic Thais rather than Chinese. Officials also closed off some occupations to foreigners, aiming to roll back Chinese control of the economy. While officials failed to dilute Chinese dominance of the economy, state enterprises became major sources of revenue for competing political factions within the bureaucracy. State enterprises proved to be a drag on the economy, deterring private investment. Not until the late 1950s, when a new political regime refrained from launching new ventures that would compete with private capital, did the Thai economy take off.

Field Marshal Sarit Thanarat (1959-1963) launched administrative reform and private, investment-led, import substituting industrialization in the late 1950s and early 1960s. By shifting resources away from the state enterprise sector, Sarit undercut political foes relying on state firms for funds to foster political followings. This was an early example of what Heredia and Schneider term "strategic choices," in which political and economic logics coincided. Sarit himself relied on select state monopolies and alliances with favored private firms to provide his own gargantuan financial needs. His government promoted both private Thai and foreign investment. State promotion and limits on competition from state firms created conditions conducive for the local Chinese to expand into new economic activities. With World Bank and U.S. assistance, Sarit created new centralized state agencies through which technocrats dominated macroeconomic policymaking. As a result, when party politicians' power grew in the 1970s and 1980s, they were compelled to seek rents from various line ministries under their control. Budgetary, financial, exchange rate, and monetary policies were largely beyond their reach.

Over time, political participation grew, new social groups mobilized, and extra-bureaucratic actors developed a degree of political influence. These developments threatened to undermine conservative macroeconomic policies. Combined with externally transmitted inflation, the result of these changes was higher fiscal and current account deficits in the 1970s. By the early 1980s, however, officials began to have some success grappling with macroeconomic imbalances. Under Prime Minister Prem Tinsulanonda (1980-1988), technocrats reestablished their sway over macroeconomic policymaking, even as political parties trawled at various line ministries.

In the 1980s, officials privatized a few state enterprises and streamlined export procedures, establishing duty drawback arrangements. They established one-stop regulatory centers and managed export quotas better. These latter adjustments hurt few powerful interests, while benefiting influential groups as well as the national economy. These administrative simplifications helped to increase foreign investment in Thai manufacturing and eventually increased exports. Manufacturing expansion spurred higher rates of growth later in the decade. Other administrative reform goals proved more elusive. Officials failed to meet the target of holding the overall growth in public personnel to 2 percent per year. Moreover, state enterprise unions blocked reform of port management. The unions' and port concessionaires' actions in the late 1980s produced lengthy shipping delays and nearly invoked sanctions against Thailand by a major international shipping conference.

Political parties and Parliament grew more robust over the 1980s, and at least symbolic redistributive politics assumed greater importance. The main political parties had rural electoral bases. Rural-based members of Parliament worked in Bangkok to obtain benefits for their voters and supporters, often in the construction sector, brokering the flow of resources from Bangkok to the provinces. Politicians' opportunities to serve as brokers benefited from the state's limited ability to provide services to rural clients. In some respects, Thailand was administratively centralized in the nineteenth century before it became politically unified in the twentieth century. The weight of administration, however, generally remained light and left ample room for the emergence of a new class of rural political brokers.

Most Thai constitutions limited parliamentary powers and included an appointed Senate. Members of the lower House faced limits on their abilities to introduce legislation. In general, Parliament had authority only to cut appropriations, not to raise them, and important legislation tended to bypass standing committees (Krongkaew 1997, 14). Parliament was not productive, a function of the time needed to pass legislation and the brief tenures of elected governments (Bowornwathana 1966c, 85-86). Episodic military seizures of power probably impeded the development of cohesive political parties that might have given parliamentary institutions more influence over policy.

Since the late nineteenth century, Thai administration had been highly centralized. Policies flowed down from Bangkok to field offices, where officials collided with the local agents of other ministries. Policy coordination either at the center or at local levels was weak. Despite the Ministry of Interior's dominance of local administration, efforts to impose rationality on the process from the center were ineffective. Even at the center, the National Economic and Social Development Board, for example, which was in charge of planning, had little ability to shape the implementation of policies carried out on the orders of department heads within different ministries. The administrative system remained highly centralized but with little coordination across agencies. Within ministries, departments retained autonomy and often failed to work with other departments.

The slow pace of change in the Thai public administrative system, following the overthrow of the absolute monarchy, reflected the entrenched power of largely unaccountable officials in a system according considerable autonomy to subministerial departments.[4] Officials operated in a context in which social groups were weakly organized and poorly placed to make demands of officials. Political parties were generally unable to control officials, though symbiotic links often developed between politicians and officials, particularly at the local level. On occasion, politicians also were able to bring misconduct to light, generally as part of efforts to bring down sitting governments. Labor unions and even business interest associations for the most part were too feeble to exercise effective control over bureaucrats. Here again, however, ad hoc patterns of accommodation for mutual advantage were not uncommon. Hence, it is not surprising to find very little impetus for administrative reform.

Administrative performance, of course, varied considerably across agencies. The importance of professional norms, for example, was suggested by the apparent relative cohesion and effectiveness of agencies such as the Ministry of Public Health, where higher level officials were all doctors, and the Ministry of Science, Technology, and Environment (Bowornwathana 1995, 408, 412-414). Other factors also account for these ministries' atypical service orientations. They differed from most other ministries in terms of their smaller size, the nature of their respective clients, and the limited opportunities available to officials in these ministries or to their clients for garnering rents.

Thai politicians, academics, business groups, and others argued for bureaucratic reforms. Especially after the fall of the "bureaucratic polity" in 1973 spurred demands for political participation and social equity, critics called for administrative decentralization and other reforms. While these calls produced occasional gestures, they never accomplished much. An Administrative Reform Committee survived for decades by achieving little (Samudhavanija 1990, 9-13). In 1978, Prime Minister Kriangsak Chomanand (1977-1980) issued an order on public facilitation. When officials complained, however, about the burdens the order imposed on them in the form of lengthy reports explaining their activities, the prime minister rescinded the order that same year (Samudhavanija 1986). Later initiatives in the 1980s aimed at advocating budgetary and accounting reforms, making changes in the major staff of agencies, increasing ministerial control over departments, coordinating national plans and implementation by line and local level agencies, and fostering better coordination among ministries (Samudhavanija 1990, 14). No groups were able to sustain pressures for reform, however, and reform movements typically came under the control of the bureaucrats themselves. Indeed, administrative reform generally came at the behest of bureaucrats themselves as they aimed, for example, to ease competition for promotion by boosting the number of high level positions available (Bowornwathana 2000, 398-399). Politicians, eager to win official favor, were receptive to such proposals, though central state agencies such as the Civil Service Commission were less so.

In general, then, in the decades following the overthrow of the absolute monarchy, sporadic but persistent administrative reform initiatives achieved little in Thailand. High level bureaucrats were not subject to much political control. The Thai state was less fused than it had been in the 1960s. Politicians, however, were unable to exercise effective control over bureaucrats.

Consistent with Heredia and Schneider's argument about the trade-offs inherent in selecting from among different models of administrative reform, many of the problems that beset the Thai bureaucracy reflect its Weberian features: red tape, excessive rigidity, and a lack of accountability. To a substantial degree, Thai public administration kept politicians from "interfering" in administrative policies on personnel issues. Politicians could not transfer or appoint top level bureaucrats. Neither could they interfere in departments without parliamentary approval. The Civil Service Commission's management of all departments' staffing plans induced rigidities (Bowornwathana 1996b, 43-46). Civil servants enjoyed secure tenures, and politicians often needed to curry their favor. Unable to wield much authority over officials, prime ministers often depended on informal advisers and kitchen cabinets. One student of the bureaucracy suggested that officials' power was so great as to make it all but inconceivable that politicians could implement reforms based on the "democratic governance paradigm" (Bowornwathana 1996a, 61-62). This, however, was what the authors of the 1997 Constitution set out to do. Instead of relying primarily on Parliament to provide for horizontal accountability, the new Constitution emphasizes vertical controls exercised by an active civil society and a new set of institutions to police politicians and bureaucrats.

Formal and rigid rules were hardly the sole pathologies afflicting the Thai bureaucracy. Those features were in part reflections of efforts to control pervasive clientelism and corruption.The costs in rigidity came without notable success in curbing the clientelism and corruption against which the civil service reform model aims. The model assumes that politicians act as principals and tries to limit their capacity to politicize administration. In Thailand's bureaucracy, at least until the 1970s, state officials were both principals and agents. Civil service reform kept the wolves at bay but left the hens to the foxes.

RECENT CHANGES IN STATE ADMINISTRATION

Fiscal Policies

S tudents of the Thai state long argued that while its macroeconomic policymaking was coherent and produced overall economic stability, institutions regulating other economic policies were riddled with corruption and incompetence. Even in fiscal policy, however, many Thais noted the need for better integrated budgetary procedures. This was true after the creation of the Bureau of the Budget in 1959 and the Fiscal Policy Office in 1960 afforded means of placing ceilings on ministries' budgetary demands. While these moves helped to secure a healthier macroeconomic future (by law, public borrowing could not exceed 20 percent of total expenditures, plus 80 percent of the amount of loan repayment), the budget process was inflexible and slow to respond to shifting policy priorities. The Bureau of the

Budget established overall budgetary ceilings not only for ministries but for their various agencies as well. These arrangements avoided problems of runaway public spending at the cost of significant budgetary rigidities. The Budget Bureau and the National Audit Office could rarely assess departmental needs (Campos and Pradhan 1996, 25-26). Centralized control over budget allocations — the civil service model — meant that implementing agencies had limited control over their own budgets, which may have undermined their accountability. Officials enacted no major budgetary reforms after the early 1960s other than an aggregate ceiling on public foreign borrowing in the early 1980s. The highly centralized system was largely immune to parliamentary or even cabinet oversight.

On the revenue side, observers long noted the distortional effects of various trade tariffs and the business (turnover) tax. In addition, authorities fared poorly in tax collection. The Chatichai Choonhavan government (1988-1991), however, managed significant improvements in the early 1990s, abandoning the business tax in favor of a value-added tax. Previously, as noted above, officials streamlined duty drawback schemes in the early and mid-1980s to help export-oriented firms. In the 1980s, revenue agencies began to consult more regularly with businesses on issues such as trade tariffs and quotas. These changes resulted in part from state-sponsored, quasi-corporatist arrangements during the 1980s, but the enhanced consultation survived the eclipse of these formal mechanisms.

Industrial Policy

In general, top Thai officials paid relatively little attention to industrial policymaking. The principal state institutions specific to this policy area were the Board of Investment and the Ministry of Industry (the Ministry of Commerce and, in particular, the Finance Ministry controlled trade policy instruments). The Board of Investment generally was profligate in granting promotional certificates to firms. Its criteria, however, often diverged from nominal policy goals. For example, in the 1970s and 1980s, while the Board began to call for more promotion of labor absorbing manufacturing industries, it overwhelmingly granted certificates to firms in capital-intensive sectors. Essentially, Board of Investment promotion served to offset disincentives embedded within tax and other policies. Reforms in more managerial directions in the 1980s established "one-stop" facilities and maximum time limits during which the Board of Investment pledged to make decisions on applications.

Traditionally, the Ministry of Industry had fallen under the control of party politicians. Significant changes in its orientation emerged in the 1990s, however. In part, this shift may have reflected the influence of Japanese technical assistance. More immediately, the change in focus reflected the urgent need to boost exports when they stagnated in 1996. For the first time, the Ministry of Industry developed broad industrial policy plans (the Industrial Restructuring Plan and the Industrial Master Plan of 1996) in cooperation with university economists (Krongkaew 1997, 35). The ministry also grew more active and innovative in pushing industrial decentralization. It worked closely with private firms and non-governmental organizations (NGOs) to push innovative, labor-intensive manufacturing schemes (Ministry of Industry Official 1997). The cabinet called for a reorganization of the agriculture, commerce, industry, and finance ministries and for the creation of a new Ministry of International Trade and Industry by 2001. The Chuan Leekpai cabinet (1992-1995; 1997-2001) fell from power before enacting these changes, but the government of Thaksin Shinawatra, elected in 2001, promised to revisit the issue (*Bangkok Post* 1999c; Chetchotiros and Santimetaneedol 2001).

Reflecting more quasi-corporatist developments that increased client partici-pation in policymaking, some business sectors were more successful in the 1990s in gaining state support. For example, the Thai Tapioca Trade Association success-fully pressured the Ministry of Commerce to set up a new institution, in cooperation with the association, to promote exports facing falling prices in European markets (Bowornwathana 1995, 393-394). In the textile industry, business associations worked with both commerce and finance officials on tariff and export policies and pushed for the creation of a Thai textile institute (Unger 1998, 133-134). In addition, the Thai Garment Manufacturers Association called for improved administration of export quotas (Bowornwathana 1995, 393).

Other than the Central Bank, Thailand did not have large public banks until 1997. Banks to stimulate housing development and small-scale firms were very much bit players. The Industrial Finance Corporation of Thailand was also small, and with the liberalization of Thai financial and capital markets in the 1980s and 1990s, its functions became increasingly obscure. Various public agencies devoted to the development of science and technology had limited funding or significance and had few effective links with industry or the Board of Investment (World Bank 1990, 9).

In general, administrative reforms in the industrial policy area moved toward greater coordination across state agencies and enhanced participation for affected firms. This trend resulted from broader political and attitudinal changes as much as successful adjustments in the incentive structures facing bureaucrats, that is, institutional tinkering. Business groups enhanced their abilities to pressure officials through the influence of politicians, business associations, and sympathetic press support. A diminishing status and ethnic gap between regulators and regulated also facilitated lobbying. Evidence of this change could be seen in the private sector committee working with the government on the Industry Ministry's reorganization.

Market Regulation

Pleas by exporting firms for greater coordination among agencies with overlapping areas of regulation induced changes in market regulation in Thailand. Thai firms, increasingly export dependent and, by 1996, facing a stagnant market for Thai exports, pushed for more effective state promotion and coordinated tariff policies. Officials' direct participation in international trade negotiations enhanced their understanding of firms' needs and also helped to shift their regulatory stances (Siamwalla 1998). Competition policy in Thailand is in its infancy. The Trade Competition Committee has a weak legal framework and is unable to impose credible penalties (*Bangkok Post* 2000b).

The 1997 economic crisis made clear the need for fundamental changes in the regulation of financial institutions in Thailand. The crisis revealed the effects of policy errors as well as the loss of fit between the domestic regulatory regime and a sharply altered global context of huge and volatile capital flows. Clearly, however, policy errors also showed that financial policy-making officials' autonomy was under challenge. By the late 1980s, prime ministers were less apt to delegate extensive financial policy-making authority to technocrats, and business interests were better able to bridge inadequate institutional barriers against capture of financial policy-making agencies by clients.

The Bangkok Bank of Commerce fiasco took place in 1996, when Central Bank officials covered up the Bangkok Bank of Commerce's parlous financial health, and a host of intense squabbles among finance sector officials prior to the baht crisis served notice that clientelism in this area was on the rise. Politicians in the Chavalit Yongchaiyudh government were able to fend off reforms even after the crisis hit, until their coalition collapsed late in 1997. Not only politicians were implicated in this debacle, however. Misconduct on the part of high level bureaucrats was also important. In 2000, the Bank of Thailand was still considering bringing charges against some of its former top officials (Yuthamanop 2000.) The Bank of Thailand's traditional autonomy clearly was compromised. In addition, the bank no longer attracted the depth of talent it had in the past (*The Nation* 1998c). In 1997, the Central Bank's external appraisals pointed to weaknesses in staff appraisal and promotion systems (Theparat 1998). Under Bank of Thailand Governor Chatumongkol Sonakul, the bank underwent considerable restructuring. The Financial Institutions Act of 1999 promised to enhance the Central Bank's prudential oversight of financial institutions and to bolster its independence from the finance ministry (*Bangkok Post* 1999b and 1999d).

The financial and economic crises of the late 1990s intensified political struggles over financial regulation. Government officials disposed of huge private assets, and their decisions had enormous effects on the fortunes of powerful figures. Even the International Finance Corporation was drawn into threats of legal action against debtors (*Bangkok Post* 1999b and 1999d).

In 1997-1998, the Democrat Party-led coalition, backed by the International Monetary Fund (IMF), pushed for macroeconomic and financial stabilization in Thailand. The scale of economic collapse sharpened Thai dependence on foreign capital. To draw in capital, officials were under pressure to adopt new, more transparent accounting procedures and to push through new bankruptcy and foreclosure laws. The first priority was cleaning up the financial mess. A financial restructuring authority was appointed to liquidate and sell off the assets of failed financial institutions. This financial institution's development fund incurred large losses, recapitalizing financial institutions and attempting to dispose of their nonperforming assets.

Addressing problems of nonfinancial corporate debts required the adoption of new bankruptcy and foreclosure laws as well as changes in the regulation of foreign investment. The overhang of nonperforming loans rose to half the total portfolios of surviving financial institutions in the late 1990s, which helped foreign banks gain entry into the market and led to revisions in the Alien Business Law (Ingrisawang 2000.) These changes aimed to increase transparency and facilitate more regulation by market institutions and independent commissions.

The second Chuan Leekpai government was able to push through the necessary legislation in 1998 only very slowly. Senate opposition, in particular, impeded the adoption of economic reforms. Existing regulatory instruments were inadequate to impose penalties and allow for a rapid cleanup of the mess. The government was unable, legally or politically, to force powerful interests to accept the dilution of their ownership or the loss of their management control over indebted firms. Nonperforming loans continued to climb through 1998 and into 1999. Divisions within the governing coalition and the Democrat Party itself aggravated the problem. Newly established bankruptcy courts saw little activity before 2000. The technical limitations of courts and their fragile insulation combined to set a very slow pace of implementation of these reforms. In 2000, however, the banks began to press foreclosure and bankruptcy proceedings against even some of their largest debtors (Ingrisawang 2000; Haggard and MacIntyre 2000, 57-79; MacIntyre 1999).

Social Welfare

Before the 1990s, social welfare programs in Thailand did not cover many Thais beyond those employed in the civil service. Thai politicians, officials, and academics have focused concerns about distribution on rural development schemes since at least the 1960s, when spreading communist and Muslim guerrilla movements helped fuel concerns to consolidate central control over Thailand's regions. Rural poverty, particularly in the Northeast, declined relatively slowly. Thai income inequality grew in the 1980s, and according to some measures, by the 1990s, it was the worst in East Asia and higher than that in Mexico (World Bank 1996, 14). Over the 1988-1996 period of rapid growth, however, the percentage of the population and even the absolute numbers of Thais living in poverty fell sharply.

We have little evidence that antipoverty programs achieved much success in Thailand. In 1998, a World Bank official in Bangkok argued that the Thai government was weak in "poverty-conscious decisionmaking and eval-uation"(*Bangkok Post* 1999a). Modest budgets tended to aim too broadly, benefits going to those who were not so poor as well as to the very poor. Administrative costs absorbed about half of all spending (World Bank 1996, 37-50). The political muscle of local notables exacerbated the tendency for programs to fail to reach target clients. The Ministry of Agriculture and the Cooperatives Department of Agricultural Extension generally did a poor job of providing extension services. Extension officers lacked knowledge, had little contact with farmers, and were unfamiliar with ongoing research (Garforth and Suthsupa 1996, 266-276).

To combat poverty, promote democracy at the local level, and strengthen their own support coalitions, politicians tried a new approach to local development, beginning in 1975. Bypassing the Interior Ministry, Parliament allocated funds to local councils for spending on public works and the development of infrastructure. These schemes nominally were designed to soak up labor, thereby discouraging off-season migration to Bangkok and other cities, foster self-government, and improve rural infrastructure. However, these measures generally failed to produce the intended results. The impact, instead, was to enrich local, politically connected construction firms and administrators. Locally elected individuals, acting as offi-cials of the interior ministry, typically controlled the local councils.

After the economic collapse of 1997, officials launched large but slow-disbursing, foreign-funded initiatives to expand social safety nets, including a Social Investment Plan and a Social Investment Fund (*Bangkok Post* 1999a). The Social Investment Fund involved community development grants awarded on the basis of proposals generated by village organizations such as cooperatives, schools, and temples. Most new spending was based on existing health, school lunch, and job creation schemes (Cook, Kabeer, and Suwannarat 2000). The large foreign role in financing and initiating these reforms was akin to that of outsiders pushing judicial reforms in Latin America, as discussed by Mahon in Chapter Nine.

MASTER PLANS

Thailand's most productive government between the early 1960s and the Chuan Leekpai government of 1997-2001 was the first Anand Panyarachun administration (1991-1992; 1992). The military-backed Anand government drew on a broad elite consensus on the need for a variety of policy changes to implement a series of reforms in taxation, trade liberalization, and environmental and financial regulation. This unusually active government, however, did not focus its attention on administrative reform. The measures it did introduce were consistent with the civil service model long dominant in Thailand. In 1992, the government enacted a Civil Servants Act that further reduced politicians' discretion in top-level civil service personnel matters. The civil service bill also established new salary scales.[5] A Ministerial, Bureau, and Departmental Improvement Act and a Public Administration Act restructured the bureaucracy (Bowornwathana 1994, 159).

Various governments in the 1990s pushed for administrative innovations, particularly Prime Minister Chuan's first government. Initiatives included an Administrative Procedures Bill, a Freedom of Information Bill, plans for an administrative court, and revisions in the Counter Corruption Commission. Ultimately, however, despite cabinet approval, these measures did not become law before the Chuan government's collapse in 1995.

Late in 1996, Prime Minister Chavalit Yongchaiyudh (1988-1991; 1996-1997) promised to increase civil service salaries. In May 1997, he unveiled a "master plan" that called for reducing the size of the civil service by one-third by 2001, while gradually raising salaries to levels competitive with the private sector (*Bangkok Post* 1996b; *The Nation* 1997). At that time, Thai politicians continued to discuss a freeze on growth in public sector jobs. One scheme of the master plan, never implemented, limited agencies to replacing only one-fifth the number of officials who retired (Bowornwathana 1998).

The first hint of more sweeping administrative changes in Thailand emerged with the unprecedented mobilization of civil society groups that ultimately resulted in a new Constitution. Earlier pushes for administrative reform typically had come at the behest of government officials and usually involved tussles between politicians and bureaucrats or members of both groups on opposing sides, seeking greater control over resources. The new charter, however, was created by groups outside established political institutions and the state apparatus. This time, it was a combination of academics, social critics, the press, and a variety of Bangkok-based groups who pressed for changes in the Constitution to stop the rampant corruption that continually resulted in military coups. The Banharn Silpa-Archa government (1995-1996), eager to deflect criticism of its corruption and to enhance its standing among Bangkok constituents, backed the Constitution Amendment Bill in May 1996, paving the way for a Constitution Drafting Assembly (CDA).

The agenda of aborted reforms of the 1990s became embedded in the new Constitution, approved in 1997. The political forces mobilized in support of the Constitution created for themselves institutions capable of reducing the roles of corruption in administration and politics. By January 1997, the CDA established four committees to guide the process. The committees gauged public opinion and held extensive public hearings. The process did not fall under the sway of officials or politicians. Only members of the opposition Democrat Party showed that they were following the process closely.

While the second Chavalit administration held power, the drafting assembly wrote the new charter, and the economy unraveled. Economic collapse ultimately eased adoption of the new Constitution. Politicians who otherwise might have offered more resistance feared spooking investors by provoking further political unrest. Further, the politicians' scramble to protect their own financial assets, pummeled by the crisis, may also have distracted their attention. Economic bad times helped to spur groups to mobilize in support of the Constitution (Klein 1998, 14). The politicians' limited opposition to the new charter may have resulted, in part, from a conviction that ultimately they would be able to evade the new charter's provisions. Certainly, many politicians have shown every intention of doing so. Overt organized opposition to the Constitution was confined largely to village headmen and Ministry of Interior officials concerned about how the charter would undermine their influence, especially at village ballot boxes. Some politicians also charged that the Constitution was antagonistic toward the monarchy, although the royal family all but endorsed it explicitly and the king played a central role in its adoption.

The new Constitution is quite elaborate, going to great lengths to protect against the abuse of power. Like the U.S. Constitution, the Thai Constitution seems designed more to guard against excessive power than to facilitate effective governance. The Constitution is path-breaking in its recognition of individual rights and requires that state agencies provide information, explanation, and rationales for policies affecting the environment, health, quality of life, and other material interests of citizens. The Constitution also gives Thais a right to 12 years of free education, and the disabled and poor receive elderly rights to state incomes. Its directive principles call for decentralization, participation, fair income distribution, and the promotion of cooperatives, among other goals. Moreover, it calls for administrative and political decentralization and obliges the state to prevent monopolies, pursue free trade, and reduce regulatory hindrances confronting business firms. Constituents also can demand the removal from office of local elected officials. The members of an elected Senate are barred from having links either to the bureaucracy or political parties, and they are forbidden from serving consecutive terms.

The 1997 Constitution reflects a pervasive distrust of politicians, reminiscent of the urban government institutions introduced in the United States in the early twentieth century by the Progressive Movement in efforts to tame corrupt city politics. To curb corruption, instead of aiming primarily at further administrative reforms of the civil service type, the charter strives to strengthen accountability mechanisms. Given widespread distrust of politicians, it is not surprising that these mechanisms focus on the creation of new institutions independent of the executive and legislative branches. Members of the CDA apparently were not very concerned about the degree to which their emphasis on accountability might undermine government efficiency.

The desire to protect the integrity of public institutions is evident in various constitutional provisions. The cumbersome processes for selecting members of the new independent watchdog agencies reflect this concern. The Constitution provides for an independent state entity to allocate radio, television, and telecommunications licenses. When the Senate, in 2001, created the new National Telecommunications Commission, an uproar ensued after press stories revealed that an aide to the Senate speaker had accepted bribes from some of the 14 nominees for the seven positions. The nominee selection process weeded out a widely respected economist, while choosing several prominent business figures, including some with bad debts (*Bangkok Post* 2001a).

The Constitution also created another independent group, drawn from NGOs and educational institutions, to pass judgment on the environmental impact of public projects. Still another independent group provides consumer representatives a voice in drafting consumer protection laws. As a result, local communities can participate in the management and use of natural resources, while individuals also have the right to participate in official discussions that may impinge on their rights as consumers. The Constitution's three most significant innovations lie in the creation of new, independent accountability institutions; provisions for administrative and political decentralization; and the new electoral system. The new charter created a Constitutional Court, an Electoral Commission of Thailand (ECT), a more powerful National Counter Corruption Commission (NCCC), an Administrative Court, and an Ombudsman. These entitities for the first time afforded an institutional base for advocates of a new, less clientelistic style of politics in Thailand.

For years in Thailand, academics and officials discussed setting up a French-style administrative court. A proposal during the first Chuan government was blocked in the cabinet by opposition from the Justice Ministry and court judges. The proposal for an Administrative Court also elicited considerable debate within the CDA. In the end, with backing from the Judicial Council and law professors, the Constitution provided for an Administrative Court, according to an adviser to Prime Minister Chuan Leekpai, interviewed in 1998. In 1999, the Senate rejected a list of candidates for the Administrative Court provided by the cabinet, and the issue went to the Constitutional Court. The administrative court began operating in 2001, hearing disputes among state agencies as well as grievances filed by citizens against the state. The Administrative Court is independent of the executive and legislative branches.

Other new institutions made their mark earlier. The ECT changed the way in which Thais conducted elections. In the 2000 Senate elections, repeated ECT findings that successful candidates violated election rules resulted in repeated rounds of polling before the Senate's 200 seats were filled. The process repeated itself in the lower House elections in January 2001. New violations among senators came to light in 2001, so that a new round of elections was necessary to replace one-third of the Senate that was disqualified due to election violations, false asset declarations, or other offenses. The NCCC, at least one of whose members was obliged to resign in the face of conflict of interest charges, was responsible for investigating politicians' asset declarations. In 2000, the NCCC judged the minister of Interior, a leader of the ruling coalition's dominant party, guilty of misconduct. He had to abandon his portfolio and party position. The NCCC also found that Thaksin Shinawatra had previously submitted a false declaration. With Thaksin heading his party in the elections early in 2001, the polls were held under a cloud of uncertainty, because the Constitutional Court had not yet ruled on his case. Nevertheless, Shinawatra's Palang-Darma Party won a resounding electoral victory, he became prime minister, and the court came under tremendous political pressure not to unseat him. Ultimately, in an 8 to 7 decision, the majority, citing two distinct and to some degree contradictory lines of reasoning, acquitted him. The voice of the electorate prevailed over the rule of law.

The Constitution created an elected Senate and changed the way Thais elect their representatives to the lower House. Under the new rules, 400 representatives are elected from single member districts and 100 from nationwide party lists. The 2001 election suggested that these changes, together with other regulatory adjustments leading to more effective poll monitoring, had a profound impact on Thai government. Candidates were far less successful in predicting election outcomes because their purchased votes were no longer reliable. The party-list elections (and Thaksin's influence) led to unprecedented discussion of policy issues. Probably for the first time, party stands on broad policy issues had a major impact on the election outcome.

The Constitution also mandated decentralization of administrative and political power to locally elected bodies. These processes are ongoing, and it is too early to be able to assess their impact. Since 1892, local governments had been under the firm control of the Ministry of Interior. Now, the National Decentralization Committee is responsible for monitoring the implementation of eight laws governing decentralization (Mahakanjana 2001).

It is difficult to predict the longer-term effects of the new Constitution. It will take time for Thai political actors to test the resiliency of the complex mechanisms of the new charter. It seems clear, however, that the constitutional framework with its extensive array of new institutions provides diverse means of blocking governance initiatives (see Kaufman's discussion of "veto gates" in Chapter Ten). Successful governance in this new context is likely to require robust political parties. The Constitution's electoral laws and the strengthening of election monitoring may indeed hasten the development in Thailand of political parties with stronger concerns for the tasks of governance through control over law making (rather than implementation).

The new Constitution's effectiveness depends heavily on its success in establishing an administration and politics of law. A wide gulf separates traditional Thai political attitudes and practices from those prescribed by the Constitution. The dimensions of this chasm suggest the need for a prolonged, sustained commitment to the charter's new institutions. The ECT's rejection of election outcomes, requiring successive election rounds to replace previously annulled results, already is wearying Thai voters and may be reducing turnouts. There is a strong possibility that reform in Thailand may enter its Thermidor[6] phase before the Constitution's new institutions are adequately established. Certainly this appears also to have happened in Italy when the "clean hands" (*mani pulite*) movement, launched in Naples in 1992 by Milanese magistrates to investigate political corruption, seemed to go on and on.

The revolutionary metaphor is apt in describing the changes that are being engendered in Thailand by institutions such as the ECT, NCCC, and the Constitutional Court. These bodies operate in a fashion reminiscent of Iran's Council of Guardians, a 12-member body with wide-ranging powers that include the ability to disqualify candidates for election who are deemed to fail to meet Islamic standards. While Thailand's new institutions certainly are more accountable than the Council of Guardians, they are similar in their efforts to compel a shrinking of the gap between normative injunctions and habitual practices. The ECT is a particularly vulnerable target. Members of the House and Senate whose electoral victories have been repeatedly disqualified by the ECT bear it particular animus. Evidence that a Thermidor might indeed undermine the new institutions came in 2001, when a House committee pondered creating a watchdog agency to police the new watchdogs.

The new Constitution also may diminish governments' capabilities. While such a development would curb rent-seeking and might suit the interests of some businesses and the middle class in Bangkok, it would make it more difficult to reduce poverty in Thailand or to meet the needs for infrastructure and other collective goods. The evidence to date, however, suggests that offsetting the impact of still more veto gates in Thailand is the influence of the new electoral laws. Thailand's new Prime Minister, Thaksin Shinawatra, a particularly skilled politician, was able to use the new electoral system to win very close to an outright majority in the 2001 election for his Thai Rak Thai Party. This was an unprecedented development in Thai politics, where weak parties and weak multiparty coalitions have been the rule. Stronger parties may yet make the new institutional landscape conducive to effective governance.

CONCLUSION

Administrative reform in Thailand was limited in scope between 1960 and 1997. Unlike, for example, in Argentina, Brazil, or Mexico, fiscal constraints in Thailand did not play a central role in driving the piecemeal reforms of this era or those introduced by the new Constitution. Foreign exchange concerns were more significant, however. Private firms facing competitive international markets were able to exert pronounced pressures for enhanced state service delivery.

Consistent with the expectations of Heredia and Schneider's hypotheses, Thailand's economic collapse of 1997 had the effect of boosting the influence of central government agencies, at least in the short-term. In particular, regulators increased their sway over legislators and their clients, pushing for the adoption of more transparent accounting procedures. The crisis also reinforced the structural power exercised by exporters and holders of liquid assets. With greater trade openness, exporting firms enjoyed enhanced influence.

Heredia and Schneider's hypotheses relating to regime type, party fragmentation, and coalitional bases are of limited utility in explaining outcomes in the Thai case. Given the very rudimentary degree to which policy processes outside the bureaucracy were formalized in Thailand, it is difficult to assess these hypotheses. Political parties were not vehicles to mobilize coalitions aimed at securing power in order to make lawsor influence formal regulation. Rather, parties provided access to the rents controlled by ministries. While Thailand has a parliamentary system,[7] the weakness of cabinet coalitions and political parties makes it hard to argue that the cabinet and Parliament were fusd. Did pronounced party fragmentation help explain low levels of administrative reform? Clearly, as noted above, the brief tenures of most governments impeded the implementation of administrative reforms. With coalitions' tenures hostage to half a dozen parties or a score of factions, the number of potential vetoes soared. For example, the Chart Pattana, as part of the the Chavalit government coalition, fended off critical financial sector reforms (MacIntyre 1999).

In Thailand, however, it is not clear that fewer effective parties would have produced significantly different outcomes. Kaufman sensibly notes that hypotheses roted in the assumption of competitive elections have no bearing in nondemocratic settings (Chapter Ten). While elections in Thailand are competitive, we need to pay careful attention to the nature of the political actors and the fruits for which they contend. Typically, we think of parties competing for control over the legislature's law-making powers. Even logrolling[8] requires a coalition that can gain control over the legislature. The logic of minimum winning coalitions applies to the numbers needed to establish a ruling coalition. In Thailand, of course, majority coalitions also are necessary. The goal, however, is not legislative control but access to portfolios. Control over the cabinet s the name of the game. Benefits, as a result, are relatively more divisible among coalition members, and the logic of minimum winning coalitions is associated as much with the far smaller numbers of members of Parliament necessary to hold portfolios as with those necessary to establish ruling coalitions. The result is that in many respects, including election finance, factions rather than parties are the key political actors in Thailand.

If the issue of party fragmentation was of limited importance in Thailand in the past, recent developments suggest this opinion may change. The frst parliamentary elections under the new electoral system in January 200 featured far more discussion of policy issues and produced a far less fragmented ruling coalition. The hypothesis that with a small number of parties having comparably large electoral bases it becomes easier to insulate the civil service may yet have significance for the Thai case. In fact, the formation of coalitions has more immediate importance in the case of Thailand's administrative reform process. Heredia and Schneider note the prominent role played by coalitional bases of support in other countries, for example, public unions in Argentina. These authors give less emphasis to the impact of the middle class in the reform process because, typically, most parties vie for the middle class vote. (Hence, the middle class is not a captive constituency.) They note, however, that northern Mexico's National Action Party (Partido Acción Nacional – PAN) is an exception to this generalization. In Thailand, the Democrat Party over the last decade also has been something of an exception, though it has not been a conspicuous champion of administrativereform.

While Thai governments have had neither strong rural or labor backing, business support was very important in the country's history. Under all regimes, business influence clearly played a major role in driving administrative reforms. Because the structural power of business was fairly constant across regime types, it is difficult to explain changing administrative reform outcomes in terms of an argument about business coalitions. There was some variation in institutional arrangements governing business access, however, ranging from more corporatist patterns in the early and mid-1980s to more pluralist and clientelist ones in the 1990s. We can understand business influence in terms of capitalists' structural power, where politicians and officials acting as "guardians" — as described in Plato's *Republic* — serve business interests in order to boost domestic investment and foreign exchange earnings. We can also view politicians as responsive to newly powerful business constituents. In either case, it is clear that Thai businesses involved in export and more complex services as well as manufacturing (as opposed to the also influential smugglers, operators of protection rackets, and those procuring various rents) expanded their policy influence through political parties and business associations and by means of unmediated access to officials.

The packaging of administrative reform initiatives in Thailand was less crucial than in other countries. A crucial unintended instance, however, was evident in the case of the Constitution, which, of necessity, encompassed a broad range of reforms that aimed, among other goals, to increase democratic accountability in Thai public administration. As a byproduct of concerns to enhance participation and to curb abuses of power, stronger accountability provisions may also enhance state service delivery. Another example of strategic packaging of reforms involved officials' use of two-level games — using IMF pressures in bargaining with domestic interests — in pushing administrative and regulatory reforms.

Serendipitous conjunctures associated with honeymoon periods were important to the process of administrative and regulatory reforms in Thailand in the 1990s. Under military rule, the Anand government used considerable public support, military backing, and momentary timidity on the part of poltical opponents to push through a large number of important reforms. The Chuan government used pressures from the IMF and the mood of crisis engendered by the economy's collapse in 1997 to implement key policy changes. The timing of the economic crisis was critical to the adoption of the new Constitution.

The impact of ideas was evident in the case of pressures for greater democracy and, in particular, stronger accountability. In the wake of the economic crisis, pressures for market transparency, internationally standardized accounting, and other forces increased sharply in Thailand. Perhaps more significant than the ideas themselves, however, was the ability to draw on concrete foreign models of institutional design in attempting to create political and administrative systems less pervaded by corruption and more accountable to civil society.

At this time, the world's most far-reaching set of reforms are found in Thailand's new Constitution, a product of radical departures from traditional political practices. The Constitution represents the aspirations and organzation of a small part of the Thai polity that previously lacked an effective political vehicle. Although the Democrat Party increasingly spoke for that constituency, it was not sufficiently powerful to dominate parties with bases among the far more numerous rural voters still enmeshed in money-based politics. The Democrat Party's future is uncertain, following its defeat in the 2001 elections, the unfamiliar terrain established by Thailand's new electoral system, and Prime Minister Thaksin's Thai Rak Thai's introduction of a new campaigning style (money used to buy votes indirectly, thrugh media saturation, as well as directly). The middle class, however, now has a relatively secure base in an entirely new set of watchdog institutions created by the new Constitution. The new Constitution created a plethora of new institutional actors that could impede governance and stymie efforts to enhance state capacities. Offsetting the effects of additional "veto gates," however, may be the impact of stronger accountability mechanisms, including political parties. By limiting bureaucrats' goal displacement and mobilizing larger numbers of Thais' political demands, stronger parties could enhance state capacities. As to what the outcome of all these forces will be in Thailand, the jury is still out.

NOTES

1. For more on Max Weber, see Chapter Two, note 2, this volume.

2. A Hong Kong-based consulting firm ranked Thailand Asia's fifth most corrupt country in 2001. Transparency International ranked Thailand sixtieth among the 90 countries it surveyed. See *Bangkok Post*,2001c, "We Pay the Price of Our Apathy," March 22.

3. For more on managerial reform, see Chapter One, this volume.

4. According to one source, there is, apparently, no Thai word for "accountability" (the English word dates from at least the sixteenth century), a concept that presupposes relations of equality rather than hierarchy (Christensen and Siamwalla 1993.) William J. Klausner notes the large number of neologisms, such as *thammarat* for good government, in modern Thai (Klausner 1998).

5. The Civil Servants Act of 1992 raised lower-level salaries without addressing the problem of low salaries among higher level officials. As a result, these officials continued to exit for the private sector. Starting annual civil service salaries in 1997, depending on the level of education of the individual, ranged from about US$2,400 to $5,000, against some $36,000 for members of Parliament (and a per capita income of about $3,000). In 1990, real salaries for top level officials were about one-seventh those available in 1909 (although this neither accounts for alternative income sources, such as seats on boards of state enterprises, nor does it include officials in agencies such as the Ministry of Finance or, in particular, the Bank of Thailand, where officials earn higher salaries). World Bank, 1997, *World Development Report, 1997*, (Washington, D.C.: The World Bank), 9, 215. These U.S. dollar figures are based on exchange rates before the July 1997 devaluation. See *The Nation*, June 22, 1997, B3; and Christensen and Siamwalla 1993, 17.

6. The "Thermidor phase" refers to the period during the French Revolution following the murder of Jacobin leader Maximilien Marie Isidore Robespierre (1758-1794) by reactionary opponents to the revolution. The reactionary movement took its name from the month of Thermidor on the revolution's new calendar.

7. The new Constitution introduced elements of division between executive and legislative powers. Under the new charter, ministers will resign their seats in Parliament.

8. The term "logrolling" refers to "the trading of votes by legislators to secure favorable action on projects of interest to each one." *Merriam-Webster's Collegiate Dictionary*, 1994, 10th ed. (Springfield, Mass.: Merriam-Webster, Incorporated), 686.

REFERENCES

Adviser to Prime Minister Chuan Leekpai. 1998. Interview by author.

Anderson, Benedict. 1978. "Studies of the Thai State." Paper presented at The State of Thai Studies Conference, Chicago, March 30.

Bangkok Post. 1996a. April 3.

Bangkok Post. 1996b. December 11.

Bangkok Post. 1999a. July 31.

Bangkok Post. 1999b. November 30.

Bangkok Post. 1999c. December 11

Bangkok Post. 1999d. December 20.

Bangkok Post. 1999e. "MP: Chatumongkol Shifting Focus from Krung Thai," November 28.

Bangkok Post. 1999f. "Chatumongkol Won't Quit – Tarrin," December 2.

Bangkok Post. 2000a. August 21.

Bangkok Post. 2000b. September 6.

Bangkok Post. 2001a. "Sweeping Review Ordered: Panel to Scrutinize Selection Process," March 2.

Bangkok Post. 2001b. "Thaksin Is Getting Down to Business," March 8.

Bangkok Post. 2001c. "We Pay the Price for Our Apathy," March 22.

Bowornwathana, Bidhya. 1994. "Administrative Reform and Regime Shifts : Reflections on the Thai Polity." *Asian Journal of Public Administration* 16 (2).

Bowornwathana, Bidhya. 1995. "Response of Public Administration System of Thailand to Global Challenges." In *Globalization and the ASEAN Public Sector*, eds. Sirjuddin H. Suller and Ledivina V. Carino. Kuala Lumpur: The Asian and Pacific Development Center.

Bowornwathana, Bidhya. 1996a. "Thailand: The Politics of Reform of the Secretariat of the Prime Minister." *Australian Journal of Public Administration* 55 (4).

Bowornwathana, Bidhya. 1996b. "Democratic Reform Visions and the Reinvention of Public Officials." *Asian Review of Public Administration* 8 (1).

Bowornwathana, Bidhya. 1996c. "Political Realities of Local Government Reform in Thailand." In *New Trend in Public Administration for the Asia-Pacific Region: Decentralization*, eds. Susumu Kurosawa, Toshihiro Fujiwara, and Mila A. Reforma. Tokyo: The Local Autonomy College, Ministry of Home Affairs.

Bowornwathana, Bidhya. 1998. Interview by author.

Bowornwathana, Bidhya. 2000. "Government Reform in Thailand: Questionable Assumptions, Uncertain Outcomes." *Governance: An International Journal of Policy and Administration* 13 (3).

Bresser-Pereira, Luiz Carlos. 1999. "Managerial Public Administration: Strategy and Structure for a New State." In *Reforming the State: Managerial Public Administration in Latin America*, eds. Luiz Carlos Bresser-Pereira and Peter Spink. Boulder, Colo.: Lynne Rienner Publishers.

Bresser-Pereira, Luiz Carlos, and Peter Spink, eds. 1999. *Reforming the State: Managerial Public Administration in Latin America*. Boulder, Colo.: Lynne Rienner Publishers.

Campos, Ed, and Sanjay Pradhan. 1996. *Budgetary Institutions and Expenditure Outcomes*. Policy Research Working Paper 1646 (September). Washington, D.C.: The World Bank, Policy Research Department.

Chetchotiros, Nattaya, and Ampa Santimetaneedol. 2001. "Thaksin Vows Progress in 7 Weeks." *Bangkok Post*, April 9.

Christensen, Scott, and Ammar Siamwalla. 1993. *Beyond Patronage: Tasks for the Thai State*. Bangkok: Thailand Development Research Institute.

Christensen, Scott, David Dollar, Ammar Siamwalla, and Pakorn Vichyanond. 1993. *The Lessons of East Asia: Thailand, the Institutional and Political Underpinnings of Growth*. Washington, D.C.: The World Bank.

Cook, Sara, Naila Kabeer, and Gary Suwannarat. 2000. "Social Safety Nets in Asia: Addressing Exclusion, Challenging Orthodoxy." Report prepared for the Ford Foundation.

Garforth, Chris, and Paliboon Suthsupa. 1996. "Who Benefits from Agricultural Extension? 'Training and Visit' and the Role of Rural People's Organisations in the Upper North of Thailand." In *Thailand's Uneven Development*, ed. J.G. Parnwell. Aldershot, UK: Avebury Press.

Haggard, Stephan, ed. 2000. *The Political Economy of the Asian Financial Crisis*. Washington, D.C.: Institute for International Economics.

Haggard, Stephan, and Andrew MacIntyre. 2000. "The Political Economy of the Asian Financial Crisis: Thailand and Korea Compared." In *Asian Economic Crisis*, eds. Greg Noble and John Ravenhill. Cambridge, UK: Cambridge University Press.

Ingrisawang, Cholada. 2000. "Soon Hua Seng Chief to Face Suit: Banks Want to Recoup About B150bn." *Bangkok Post*, August 21.

Intarakomalyasut, Nondhanada, and Woranuj Maneerungsee. 2000. "Trade Competition: Decisions on Broadcasting and Beer Fail to Silence Critics." *Bangkok Post*, September 6.

Klausner, William J. 1998. A Glass Half Full—A Glass Half Empty. In *Thai Culture in Transition: Collected Writings of William J. Klausner*. Bangkok: Siam Society.

Klein, James R. 1998. *The Constitution of the Kingdom of Thailand : A Blueprint for Participatory Democracy*. The Asia Foundation Working Paper Series No. 8 (March).

Krongkaew, Mehdi. 1997. *An Alternative Interpretation of Economic Policy Determination in Thailand: An Important Interplay of Bureaucracy, Political Power, and Private Business*. Occasional Paper No. 9 (December). Tokyo: International Development Research Institute.

Kurosawa, Susumu, Toshihiro Fujiwara, and Mila A. Reforma, eds. 1996. *New Trend in Public Administration for the Asia-Pacific Region: Decentralization*. Tokyo: The Local Autonomy College, Ministry of Home Affairs.

MacIntyre, Andrew. 1999. "Political Institutions and the Economic Crisis in Thailand and Indonesia." In *The Politics of the Asian Economic Crisis*, ed. T.J. Pempel. Ithaca, N.Y.: Cornell University Press.

MacIntyre, Andrew. 2001. "Institutions and Investors: The Politics of the Financial Crisis in Southeast Asia." *International Organization* 55 (1).

Mahakanjana, Chandra. 2001. "The Impact of Civic Community on Municipal Reform in Thailand." Ph.D. dissertation proposal. DeKalb, Ill.: Northern Illinois University, Department of Political Science.

Ministry of Industry official. 1997. Interview by author.

Mosel, James N. 1979. "The Essential Character of the Contemporary Bureaucracy." In *Modern Thai Politics*, ed. Clark D. Neher. Cambridge, Mass.: Schenkman Publishing Company.

Nation, The. 1997. June 22. Bangkok.

Nation, The. 1998a "Bureaucratic Reform: A Question of Political Will," May 2.

Nation, The. 1998b. "Int'l Advisers to BOT Rescue," May 4.

Nation, The. 1998. "Analysis and Evaluation of Facts Behind Thailand's Economic Crisis." *Nukul Commission Report*. Bangkok.

Neher, Clark D. ed. 1979. *Modern Thai Politics*. Cambridge, Mass.: Schenkman Publishing Company.

Noble, Greg, and John Ravenhill, eds. 2000. *Asian Economic Crisis*. Cambridge, UK: Cambridge University Press.

Parnwell, J.G., ed. 1996. *Thailand's Uneven Development*. Aldershot, UK: Avebury Press.

Pempel, T.J., ed. 1999. *The Politics of the Asian Economic Crisis*. Ithaca, N.Y.: Cornell University Press.

Prasith-Rathsint, Suchart, ed. 1990. *Thailand on the Move: Stumbling Blocks and Breakthroughs*. Bangkok: The Thai University Research Association and the Canadian International Development Agency (CIDA).

Riggs, Fred. 1966. *Thailand: The Modernization of a Bureaucratic Polity*. Honolulu: East-West Center Press.

Samudhavanija, Chai-Anan. 1986. "A Summary of the Final Report on Improvement of Government Practices in Public Facilitation." Submitted to the NESDB by the Public Affairs Institute (December). Bangkok: National Economic and Social Development Board.

Samudhavanija, Chai-Anan. 1990. "Administrative Reform." In *Thailand on the Move: Stumbling Blocks and Breakthroughs*, ed. Suchart Prasith-Rathsint. Bangkok: The Thai University Research Association and the Canadian International Development Agency (CIDA).

Siamwalla, Ammar. 1998. Interview by author. Bangkok: Thailand Development Research Institute.

Srisumpundh, Kasem. 1998. Interview by author.

Suller, Sirjuddin H., and Ledivina V. Carino, eds. 1995. *Globalization and the ASEAN Public Sector*. Kuala Lumpur: The Asian and Pacific Development Center.

Theparat, Chatrudee. 1998. "Evidence Found Against 40 Execs; Cases Involve Losses and Damages of B10m." *Bangkok Post*, May 30.

Unger, Danny. 1998. *Building Social Capital in Thailand: Fibers, Finance and Infrastructure*. New York: Cambridge University Press.

Wit, Daniel. 1961. *A Comparative Survey of Local Government and Administration*. Bangkok: National Institute of Development Administration.

World Bank. 1990. *Technology Strategy and Policy for Industrial Competitiveness: A Case Study in Thailand*. Industry and Energy Department Working Paper. Industry Series Paper No. 24 (April). Washington, D.C.

World Bank. 1995. *Infrastructure Development in East Asia and Pacific*. Washington, D.C.: The World Bank.

World Bank. 1996. *Thailand, Growth, Poverty and Income Distribution*. Report No. 15689-TH. December 13. Washington, D.C.: The World Bank.

World Bank. 1997. *World Development Report, 1997*. Washington, D.C.

Yuthamanop, Parista. 2000. "Former Central Bank Chiefs in New Probe: Junior Officials Have Been Cleared." *The Bangkok Post*, August 26.

COMPARISONS
AND CONCLUSIONS

Chapter Eight

WHEN INSTITUTIONS MATTER: A COMPARISON OF THE POLITICS OF ADMINISTRATIVE, SOCIAL SECURITY, AND TAX REFORMS IN BRAZIL

Marcus André Melo

INTRODUCTION[1]

This paper analyzes the politics of state reform in Brazil in the 1990s, with special attention to the role of institutional factors. Social security, tax, and administrative reforms during this period exhibited both particular patterns of strategic interaction among decision-making actors and unique coalitional dynamics.

By contrasting administrative reform with other issue areas, I highlight the distinctiveness of administrative policy reform. Also, by comparing issue areas rather than countries, I assess the explanatory power of the selected variables. Comparing sectors in a single country holds constant other potential explanatory factors. One of the central conclusions that emerges from the comparison of the three types of reform is that federalism affects key actors in each issue area in ways that are crucial determinants of their chances for success. This conclusion might not come through as strongly in single case analysis of administrative reform, so the value added of cross-sectoral analysis is to identify these pivotal actors. Although this chapter discusses the role of institutional factors in determining policy outcomes, it also draws attention to the role of other variables, in order to show the limitations of purely institutional analysis and the need for an integrated approach that also considers the variables that are issue specific.

The paper is organized in five sections. In the first section, I discuss how the analysis of the institutional constraints to policy reform can be combined with a consideration of the policy dynamics of each issue area. The second section of the paper focuses on the formation of the agenda of state reform in Brazil in the 1990s. The third section provides a summary of the evolution of reforms and of the legislative process in the Chamber of Deputies and the Senate in each area. In the fourth section, I discuss the explanatory power of the variables selected. The final section offers a preliminary conclusion on institutional explanations of state reform.

THE POLITICS OF REFORM AND
THE ROLE OF POLITICAL INSTITUTIONS

The reform of the state in Latin America has attracted a number of empirical and theoretical studies (Haggard 1995; Kaufman 1997). A small but growing number of studies have focused on the institutional determinants of policy reform (Haggard and McCubbins 2001). This new institutionalism literature has inspired my approach; however, I also consider various dimensions associated with what Heredia and Schneider call coalitional approaches. I, therefore, follow Stephan Haggard (1995), who emphasizes the centrality of politico-institutional factors in shaping state reform, but I argue that the issue-specific incentive structures underlying actors' strategic choices are crucial for an understanding of how institutions matter.

In Brazil, institutional issues have acquired centrality in the research agenda as a result of the recurrent episodes of constitutional choice that the citizens have been exposed to in the last decade. These include the writing of the new Constitution in 1988; the plebiscite on the system of government, the Revisionist Constituent Assembly (Assembléia Revisora); and the constitutional reform initiated by President Fernando Henrique Cardoso.[2]

The research agenda on institutional issues has been organized primarily around the effects of the system of government (presidentialism) and electoral rules (open-list proportional representation) on policy outcomes. More recently, the internal organization of Congress and the legislative process have attracted a number of studies (Limongi and Figueiredo 1995; Figueiredo and Limongi 1995; and Figueiredo and Limongi 1994). Studies of policy formation in Brazil have largely ignored congressional dynamics. They have focused on the patterns of interest intermediation among organized interests, the bureaucracy, and the political executive. Under military rule, this focus was justified because Congress played a marginal role in policy formation. In contrast, Congress played a key role in the process of state reform in the late 1980s and 1990s, not only because of democracy, but also because reforms have required changes in the Constitution. While the procedural obstacles for approving constitutional amendments are less stringent than in most existing poliarchies, they are far more severe than for passing ordinary legislation (Melo 1998).

In light of the literature on the institutional determinants of policy outcomes, the cross-sectoral comparison of a successful administrative reform in Brazil is analytically relevant for two reasons. First, it allows us to examine how governments can enact reforms in a political system depicted by the comparative literature as an extreme case of political fragmentation. And second, this method allows us to investigate when and how institutions matter.

The argument that stresses fragmentation in Brazil predicts reform deadlock (Ames 2001). It is based on the effects of the following traits of the Brazilian political system. Open-list proportional representation encourages individualistic behavior by politicians and thereby undermines party leaders' ability to advance national party lines. Furthermore, this type of representation undermines ideological and programmatic orientations on the part of legislators. Parties have become a collection of factions and cliques that lack even minimal coherence. In addition, some argue that proportional representation fosters multipartism and hinders the formation of stable coalitions. Presidentialism is also a contributing factor. Because presidents and legislators are elected separately, they respond to different constituencies. Differing goals and interests of those in the executive and the legislative branches can produce gridlock.

Fernando P. Limongi and Argelina Figueiredo (1994) challenged this consensus, arguing that parties exhibit surprisingly high levels of vote coherence and are distributed consistently along an ideological continuum. The "efficient secret" of Brazilian presidential multipartism lies in Congress's internal organization and in the ways parliamentary rights and power over setting agendas are organized. The latter are strongly structured along party lines and inherently biased for the executive. These factors account for strong predictability in Brazilian presidential-legislative relations. This assumption hypothesizes high levels of success in policy-reform initiatives.

In light of the argument that stresses fragmentation, the relative success of Brazil's administrative reform is all the more puzzling. To get reforms approved, a constitutional amendment must leap a number of procedural hurdles, including roll calls, a qualified majority of three-fifths of the members attending, and two rounds of voting in each chamber. In light of the argument predicting high levels of success, the extremely time-consuming, erratic, and conflictive pattern of negotiations that surrounds administrative reform presents a paradox. More important, the apparent defeats in tax and social security do not fit comfortably in a general analysis. The distinct patterns of policy outcomes in the various issue areas, therefore, merit explanation.

To preview one of the key conclusions of this paper, the executive changed its preferences in the case of tax reform (an issue area in which actors are extremely risk averse), as a result of unforeseen developments and changing political and financial circumstances. Rather than abandoning the reform, the executive allowed it to run its anticipated course of defeat. Setbacks in social security can be largely explained by the fact that the government became involved in the difficulties associated with the politics of loss imposition and blame avoidance.

The second reason the following analysis is analytically relevant is that it allows us to investigate when and how institutions matter. Referring to the new institutionalism literature, Stephen Haggard and Mathew McCubbins (2001) aptly argue that while these lines of research "powerfully demonstrate that institutions can matter, the issue of when such institutions matter and how they affect policy outcomes has received much less attention. Institutions surely do not matter at all times and in all situations." I argue that the following analysis shows how this institutional analysis can greatly benefit by considering the particular dynamics of each issue area.

POLITICS ENGENDERS POLICY? ISSUE AREAS AND INSTITUTIONS

A central assumption in this cross-sectoral approach is that each type of reform generates specific reactions from political actors, depending on the redistributive losses and gains generated by the institutions. In other words, sectors or issue areas do matter (Melo 2002). Theodore Lowi's (1964) insight that politics follows policy, and not the reverse, as common sense might suggest, was an important analytical tool for the study of public policymaking. The commonsense notion that interests — politics — shape and influence policy decisions frequently leads the observer not to pay attention to the process of interest formation itself. Actors' subjective evaluations of the costs and benefits of policy decisions bring about interests. Lowi (1964) went further, arguing that the nature of policy determines the pattern of interaction between actors in a decision-making arena. His typology of arenas is essentially static, allowing no account of the strategic interaction among actors, and also proved to be of little use in analyzing concrete situations. Nevertheless, his basic insight is illuminating and should be retained.

Kenneth Shepsle, one of the central figures in new institutionalism, argues that Lowi's approach "does not fit comfortably with recent neoinstitutionalist analyses in political science and economics" (1985, 231). In fact, Lowi considers the role of institutions in policy formation as *tabula rasa*. I believe, however, as George Tsebelis suggested (1995, 307), that institutional analysis can benefit from a consideration of the characteristics of each issue area. In his analysis of veto players, Tsebelis (1995) contends that the "very number of veto players varies according to [the] issue."

Interests come into being as a result of the distributional characteristics of sectoral decisional arenas, and institutions facilitate or impede collective choice. Institutions also represent the incentive structure to which actors respond strategically (Shepsle 1989). The distributional effects — or the subjective perception of these effects — are crucial for determining when and how institutions matter for policy outcomes. For these reasons, I hypothesize that some institutions are crucial for determining the success of reform in one sector or issue area but not in others. Losses and gains of policy decisions, particularly in highly complex matters, are not immediately perceived by the actors and the objects of an individual cost-benefit calculation. Actors behave on the basis of ex ante expectations and bounded rationality, and these expectations are socially constructed.[3] Policy advocates and shared beliefs about causal effects of policy decisions are important factors underlying the social construction of these losses. Policy advocates play a crucial role in influencing actors' beliefs regarding policy outcomes. Through policy advocacy, processes like policy bandwagoning, selective emulation, argumentation, and persuasion, not to mention ideology, play important roles in the social construction of losses and gains. Because political actors want to be associated with policies that work, they are interested not only in sponsoring particular projects but also in good policy (Arnold 1990). Expertise and ideas about causal relations are, therefore, important for them.

An important theoretical implication of the arguments outlined above is that modal types of reform or political conflict exist in each sector. In spite of the important differences between these areas, discussed later in the text, the three cases under scrutiny can be categorized, paraphrasing R. Kent Weaver and Bert Rockman (1993), as loss imposition reforms. Because the reforms imply concentrated costs to constituencies, reformers seek to avoid blame (Weaver 1998). This seems to be a characteristic of second wave administrative reforms, which impose concentrated costs to losers and do not create natural support coalitions (Heredia and Schneider, this volume), because they do not have clear winners.

I contend that by specifying the characteristics of issue areas, we gain an understanding of when and how institutions matter. In addition, we are in a better position to analyze the timing and, above all, the specific content of reforms — questions about which pure institutional analyses are generally silent.

In the case of state reforms, two structural features of the Brazilian political system have attracted recent scholarly attention: presidentialism and federalism. The impact of presidentialism refers to the difficulties political executives have had garnering legislators' support for their proposals. These difficulties arise from the fact that the president and Congress respond to distinct constituencies (Mainwaring and Shugart 1997; Stepan 1997). The impact of federalism refers to the ability of state governors to undermine nationally defined party lines (Abrucio 1998; Samuels 2000). I hypothesize that the impact of these institutions varies according to the sectors or issue areas.

THE FORMATION OF THE STATE REFORM AGENDA IN POST-1988 BRAZIL

The formation of the agenda for state reform represented, to a large extent, a reaction against the agenda that had prevailed during the working sessions of the Constituent Assembly from 1987 to 1988. This latter agenda was dominated by a number of important issues: 1) a consensus on the need to decentralize and restructure current intergovernmental relations, granting more fiscal autonomy and decisionmaking capacities to states and municipalities; 2) a widely held view that it was necessary to enhance social control and transparency of public policy through participatory institutional arrangements; and 3) a consensus that the social debt should be redeemed and social policy should be granted high priority in public expenditures. This agenda would be replaced by a new one centered on market reforms. Central to this new agenda was the notion of reducing the Custo Brasil (Brazil Cost) — an imperative for the country's competitive integration to world markets. Custo Brasil required revamping public administration and making institutional changes in the judicial system, labor legislation, and tax structure. A major short-term priority was ensuring macroeconomic stability, as opposed to the former strategy of promoting growth, even if growth produced distortions such as inflation.

The sequence of stabilization, economic reforms, and democratization in Brazil produced a complex situation. The agenda of the 1980s reflected the new social and political demands engendered by the process of democratization. The fact that democracy preceded efforts at stabilization of the economy had important consequences because it empowered actors who could offer resistance to reforms, and it created a political environment inimical to market reforms. Important actors during the transition, such as trade unions and former opposition politicians, were pressing primarily for social spending and pro-growth economic policies. In a similar vein, financial decentralization and devolution of powers to state and municipalities were implemented before stabilization undermined market reform efforts. Responding to social demands and to the expanding political market, mayors and governors embarked on a spending frenzy that ushered the states into heavy indebtedness.

The new agenda's organizing principle was that of a governability crisis, which was viewed as having several dimensions (Melo 1995). In the area of public administration, the extension of tenure to all state employees, formerly called Labor Legislation Code (Consolidação das Leis do Trabalho — CLT) workers, through the Unified Legal System (Regime Juridico Único – RJU), was viewed as having created a rigid system of personnel that exacerbated state inefficiency. The RJU prohibited different pay levels for distinct performance levels by state employees. It established the principle of isonomy of pay for categories of functions at the state, municipality, and federal government levels. It also granted tenure and secured a 100-percent (in several cases up to 130-percent) replacement rate for civil servant pensions. In the new agenda, the 1988 Constitution also created or strengthened bureaucratic and time-consuming mechanisms for competitive bidding and personnel recruitment, thereby creating an incentive structure that encouraged inefficiency.

In the area of fiscal and tax issues, the emphasis was on the perverse fiscal effects of decentralization and the need for convergence dictated by globalization. The fiscal autonomy of governors, along with control of state banks and their ability to undermine central bank regulations, were seen as major threats to stabilization (Sola 1995). The states' newly acquired rights to set different rates for the Consumption Tax (Imposto sobre Circulação de Mercadorias — ICMS), a tax on the consumption of goods and services that accounted for one-third of the country's tax revenues, caused a fiscal war among them. The states' fiscal war was seen as undermining national and regional industrial policy and depressing the country's tax revenues, thereby exacerbating fiscal problems.

In the area of intergovernmental relations, excessive decentralization was deemed to have disorganized sectoral public policies and caused more inefficiency. The creation of over 1,200 new municipalities after 1988 was regarded as the symbol of centrifugal forces that fragmented the institutional system and expanded patronage. More important, it was argued that the dramatic increase in the share of the budget absorbed by social security payments, debt service, and automatic transfers to subnational governments had reduced the degree of fiscal liberty, ushering the state into an unprecedented public finance crisis. In the area of social security, several constitutional innovations were seen as jeopardizing the country's financial equilibrium, including those that equalized values of rural and urban pensions, universalized access to health care, and increased entitlement conditions generously.

This is the backdrop against which the constitutional reforms were formulated in the 1990s. The state reform agenda of President Cardoso's administration contains important similarities with past reform efforts by the governments of Fernando Collor de Mello (1990-1992) and Itamar Franco (1993-1994), particularly with the failed comprehensive reform initiative by the latter. It could be argued that Collor de Mello's were more akin to first wave reforms and Cardoso's to second wave reforms. From a comparative perspective, a distinctive feature of Brazilian reforms is that the country can be seen as a reform laggard (Haggard and Kaufman 1992; Haggard and Kaufman 1995); therefore, various types of reforms are conflated in time.

SUMMARY OF THE EVOLUTION OF REFORMS

This section presents summaries of developments in the three reform areas. In Brazil, administrative reform was relatively successful in contrast with social security and tax reforms.

Administrative Reform

The Cardoso administration presented its proposal for administrative reform in October 1995. It took Congress 32 months to approve it in a slightly revised form. The government learned from the vicissitudes of the legislative process for social security and submitted its proposal after a protracted period of negotiations, led by the architect of the reform, Finance Minister Luiz Carlos Bresser-Pereira. Unlike the proposals for constitutional amendments (*projeto de emenda constitucional* — PECs) in tax and social security, the administrative reform (PEC 173) was packaged as an integral part of a comprehensive and ambitious master plan of 1995, the Plano Diretor da Reforma do Aparelho de Estado (Plan for the Reform of the State Apparatus), drafted by Minister Bresser-Pereira.[4] Bresser-Pereira's advocacy for the proposal has been widely recognized by legislators and the press. The Plano Diretor was strongly influenced by new public management (NPM) or managerial reform, and Bresser-Pereira's policy advocacy made him a key actor in the dissemination of NPM ideas. While essentially informed by NPM, the Plano Diretor also had strong Weberian components: it aimed at insulating key sectoral bureaucracies that the master plan considered strategic and that controlled typical state functions, such as central banking, planning, and budgeting. Aiming explicitly at enhancing state capacity, it is much in line with second wave reforms.

Bresser-Pereira's strategy for the approval of PEC 173, the administrative reform component of the Plano Diretor, was designed in light of the fate of the reforms in social security. According to his own testimony:

> We looked at the Constitution's chapter on public administration. And then we started deleting the articles. I reached the point when I told my advisers 'delete them all.' Then I figured that the proposal would be considered a blank check for the government and that it could never get approved. ... Rather than withdrawing provisions from the Constitution, I had to propose new things, positive things. That was the problem with social security [reform], you cannot just de-constitutionalize, you have to propose. That was the role of the Plano Diretor (Bresser-Pereira, interview, 1996; see also Bresser-Pereira's Chapter Four, this volume).

In fact, the substantive content of the articles to be deleted from the Constitution would have to be voted on subsequently in ordinary bills (leis ordinárias e complementares) whose legislative process is far less stringent than the one used for constitutional amendments. The opposition viewed deletion of the articles as a blank check, because it would be easy for the government to resort to its power over the agenda to approve subsequent bills on the subject (José Genoíno, interview).

At the beginning, PEC 173 encountered fierce resistance in the Chamber of Deputies. The rapporteur for the Subcommittee on Constitutional and Judicial Matters (Comissão de Constituição e Justiça — CCJ) was Deputy Prisco Viana, of the Party of the Brazilian Democratic Movement (Partido do Movimento Democrático Brasileiro — PMDB) of Bahia. He argued that there were five unconstitutional provisions in the proposed administrative reform, including one pertaining to the most important single issue of the proposal: the flexibility of job tenure. This triggered an open crisis and intense political opposition in the CCJ.[5] As rapporteur, Deputy Viana changed the content of PEC 173 by introducing various amendments. Arguing that the CCJ should restrict its job to judging the constitutionality of the proposal, the president of the House of Deputies decided that the ad hoc Special Commission on Administrative Reform should work from the government's original proposal rather than rapporteur's version. This decision was entirely unprecedented, but the president of the House held the upper hand in all procedural matters that were not spelled out in the book of rules. A pivotal move by the government was Bresser's mobilization of the 27 governors, who signed a motion indicating their support.[6] This mobilization and power over the agenda combined to ensure PEC 173's approval.

The PEC's rapporteur in the Chamber of Deputies' ad hoc Special Commission, Rio de Janeiro PMDB Congressman Moreira Franco, delayed his final report until the official deadline. Similarly, a key issue on the negotiating agenda before the PEC was formally submitted to Congress involved the question of the flexibility of job tenure. The new proposal made firing public employees easier, allowing dismissal on grounds of bad performance, whereas existing legislation made firing very difficult, permitting it only in very special cases, such as commission of crimes. According to Bresser-Pereira, "Party leaders from the government's support coalition insisted that without changes in it, it would not be approved" (Bresser-Pereira, interview, 1996).

The solution was found when the government accepted a proposal by party leaders that permitted firing tenured employees only in cases when personnel expenditures exceeded 60 percent of net revenues for the federal government, the municipalities, and the states. This ceiling was the final target stipulated by the Camata Law and was to be applied to states and municipalities beginning in January 1999. If a state did not meet the target, it would be subjected to a variety of sanctions including, inter alia, not being eligible for federal loans. While conceding to pressures from party leaders, by linking the flexibility of tenure to the Camata Law, the government was also able to curb important foci of opposition within the federal bureaucracy. Personnel expenditures had been declining at the federal level since the early 1990s and reached 43 percent of net revenues in 1997. In addition, during the negotiations in the first plenary vote in the Chamber, the government agreed to exclude employees in planning and budgeting, among others, from the new dismissal rules. Federal employees were secured job tenure at least in the near future.

Additional changes were introduced to curb the opposition of members of the government's coalition. These changes were crucial because they would protect against the political costs of highly unpopular measures. The president of the CCJ, a prominent politician in the Liberal Front Party (Partido da Frente Liberal — PFL) who was a candidate in the upcoming mayoral elections, was the pivotal actor in the negotiations that secured the approval. He, however, was protected from the government and given the go ahead in his decision to abstain from voting.

In the course of the discussion of the reform, two distinct periods can be identified. In the beginning, the proposal acquired little visibility on the agenda of constitutional reforms and little support from the president and the Planning and Finance ministries. As a result of Bresser-Pereira's relative political isolation — he was criticized publicly by both the Health minister and the president's right-hand man, the Minister of Government (Chefe da Casa Civil) — political actors saw administrative reform as an individual crusade. They considered it a program based on an intellectual fad that had little centrality in the political agenda, except for isolated measures that generated strong resistance, such as those involving job tenure. With the exception of the issue of personnel, political actors also perceived administrative reform as not having short-term fiscal impact.

Two factors led to a radical change in the way the reform was perceived and helped to usher it into a new phase (Bresser-Pereira, interview, 1996). The first was the ex post incorporation of new political actors who proved to be crucial for the subsequent fate of reforms, state governors. The governors became increasingly interested in the administrative reform for two reasons:[7] 1) Making tenure more flexible would be instrumental for patronage games at the state level, and 2) the constitutional amendment allowing the reelection of incumbent governors, mayors, and the president had been approved. With these incentives, the governors could extend the time horizons underlying their political calculus. With the possibility of an additional term of office, the governors started to assess future fiscal benefits that could accrue to the states as a result of the reform.[8] In fact, personnel expenses in many states had escalated to the point where they consumed all state revenues. It is significant that the watershed in the relationship between governors and the executive was during the deadlock in the CCJ.

The second factor leading to greater centrality of administrative reform in the agenda was the debt crisis affecting the states, which had reached a critical point by the end of 1995. The crisis produced a realignment of forces for the proposal within the political executive. For the finance and planning ministries, the reform was an important opportunity to reduce the states' debt (Bresser Pereira, interview, 1996). The government exchanged the refinancing of the states' debt for support of the reform ("Reforma administrativa: Governo endurece. Até a renegociação das dívidas dos estados entra na barganha," October 17, 1995).

The legislative process of reform was also characterized by bargains involving the rapporteur's opposition to issues such as tenure and ceilings for pay levels and particularly its applicability in the cases of accumulation of more than one job position or pension. The setting of value for the extra teto (the value exceeding the legal ceiling) concentrated a great deal of the negotiations.[9] This ceiling imposed concentrated losses for 141 legislators who frequently received generous public pensions in addition to their pay for the elected office. After agreeing to these concessions, the Brazilian Social Democratic Party (Partido da Social Democracia Brasileira — PSDB) and sectors of the PMDB transcribed a document denouncing the agreement as spurious. After protracted criticisms against the agreement, President Cardoso endorsed it and argued that in a democracy, one is not able to approve reforms in total ("Reforma administrativa: FHC aceita alterações," April 1997). The provision of the extra teto was deleted from the proposal and put up for a vote, but some general wording was maintained to create a deliberate loophole that would postpone the prohibition for a number of years. In fact, this solution minimized political costs for the president and for members of Congress: for the president, the costs of making immoral concessions to legislators, and for the legislators, the costs of serving explicitly their own material interests.

The conflicts over pay ceilings also involved the judicial and legislative branches as autonomous entities, because the setting by the executive of municipal and state pay ceilings (subteto) was regarded as violating the constitutional separation of powers. Regarding these two measures, "the government had to give away the rings so as not to lose the fingers" (Bresser-Pereira, interview, 1998). In the vote on the subteto, the government had 301 votes in favor (7 fewer than necessary), 142 against, and 11 abstentions.[10]

The administrative reform was approved in the first round of voting by 309 votes, just one vote more than the qualified three-fifths' majority required for constitutional amendments. (Congress has 508 members.) In the second round of voting, the amendment was approved by 351 votes in favor and 133 votes against. In a similar pattern as had been seen in the vote on the social security reform proposal, a strong vote fractionalization occurred within the PMDB and the Brazilian Progressive Party (Partido Progressista Brasileiro — PPB), and medium to high cohesion was seen for the PFL and the PSDB. The opposition's ability to change specific provisions of the bill was severely undermined following the drastic reduction in the number of provisions for separate votes (destaques para votação en separado — DVS) that legislators were allowed to present. Through the DVS, a specific item of the bill was put up for vote, forcing the government's coalition to amass the votes necessary to secure approval for every DVS presented by the opposition, as happened during the vote on the social security reform amendment.

Along with the extra teto and the subteto, the government experienced defeat of the amendment on temporary hiring of personnel. This prompted the government to issue a provisional measure (medida provisória) on related aspects that did not require changes in the Constitution. This proved to be a much contested interpretation that led to very intense reactions from the opposition, societal actors, and the judiciary. As a trade union confederation put it, "With the dictatorship of the medida provisória, President Cardoso is closing the Congress as far as the administrative reform is concerned."[11] Although less contested, the government also resorted to medida provisórias for setting up the social organizations and executive agencies.[12]

The main issues of the reform package were finally approved. These included revamping the Unified Legal System or RJU, setting up the legal foundations for social organizations and executive agencies, performance contracts within the public sector, and the flexible tenure system. The final element of the package was aimed at mid- to low-ranking state and municipal employees.

It should be noted that the government resorted to its procedural powers to pass the ordinary bills that would complement the constitutional reform without much trouble. On November 11, 1999, *O Globo* reported that the bill on hiring personnel under more flexible contracts (the so-called CLT rules) had passed:

> Although the issue had been included in the agenda, the party leaders did not come to the point of announcing the issue for vote in advance, as they usually do with important matters like this. A motion for the suspension of the discussion was approved, the vote proceeded, and in less than an hour the bill was approved. Little discussion and little mobilization led to a polarized result, with an impressive number of 'no' votes, but one that secured approval of a bill that required just a simple majority.

This suggests a pattern consistent with the idea of an executive that can overcome a fragmented legislature. Two years after the reform was approved, its implementation was still limited, with distinct impacts at different levels. At the federal level, only two institutions had become social organizations: the Sincroton Lab in Campinas and the Roquette Pinto Foundation. At the state level, however, many such organizations were created in various locations, including Tocantins, São Paulo, Bahia, Pernambuco, and Paraná. The same occurred with the executive agencies. Only one institution of this kind was created at the federal level — the Inmetro, the federal agency for industrial standards and norms.[13] Many of these initiatives were in fact closely associated with the Ministry for Administration and State Reform (Ministério da Administração e Reforma do Estado — MARE).[14] Cardoso's decision to close the ministry at the beginning of his second term of office was a severe blow to the reform effort at the federal level. Many states, however, have adopted the executive agencies' format.

At the state level, significant reductions in personnel did occur (Veja, May 2, 1997; Abrucio and Costa 1998), but because enabling legislation has not been enacted, they cannot be attributed directly to the reform. Much of it has to do with the use of the existing legislation, but the reform was instrumental in legitimizing these initiatives.

After Bresser-Pereira's departure from government, fiscal issues came to dominate the reform agenda. In July 1999, following the Real crisis, the government issued a provisional measure (MP 1917) aimed at reducing personnel expenses through voluntary retirement and reduced working hours. In addition, it prepared the Fiscal Responsibility Bill (Lei de Responsabilidade Fiscal — LRF), followed shortly thereafter by the Fiscal Responsibility Crimes Bill (Lei de Crimes de Responsabilidade Fiscal — LCRF). The latter was a separate extension of a section of the former, following a suggestion by Congress. Modeled after New Zealand's Fiscal Responsibility Act (1994), these bills contained provisions regulating public-sector debt and stipulating severe sanctions, including imprisonment for mayors and governors who authorized increases in personnel expenses in the last year of their administrations. In addition, the laws authorized mayors and governors to reduce the salaries of public employees or to do away with positions if personnel expenses exceeded 60 percent of net revenue. The bills also prohibited mayors and governors from the following: borrowing or using future revenues as collateral in their last year in government, starting public works projects that would not be completed during their term of office, and granting tax abatements without indication of new sources of revenue to compensate for the loss.

In the Chamber of Deputies, the Fiscal Responsibility Bill, or LRF Bill, was the object of heated legislative debates. The rapporteur rejected 100 amendments (93 of them in their entirety) and incorporated 23. After a protracted process, the final proposal had 77 articles — 33 fewer than the original bill. Of key importance to the approval of the bill were the more than 150 federal deputies who were mayoral candidates in the October 2000 election. It was in their best interests to oppose overspending in the municipalities, because those who were elected would have to suffer the political costs of austerity.[15] The bill prohibited expenses or pay raises to be effective from the moment the bill was approved (May 2000), thereby reducing the ability of incumbent mayors to use public funds for electoral purposes. During the final vote in the Chamber, the leaders of the parties of the government coalition managed to withdraw 129 proposals from members of these parties for separate voting on items (DVS). The withdrawn proposals included one supported by the Confederation of Brazilian Municipalities that would have created a transition period for the bill to come into force ("Lei de Responsabilidade Fiscal é Aprovada," 2000). This strategic withdrawal of proposals made the approval of an otherwise extremely cumbersome process possible. In the Senate, the rapporteur rejected all 13 proposals presented in the plenary, alleging that "the mayors' lobby is exceedingly strong; we'd better run [with the vote]" ("Lei de Responsabilidade Fiscal é aprovada, mas deputados aliviam penas," 2000).

Although the bill's provisions for personnel expenses were similar to those of the Camata Bill, the value-added of the bill for the government was that it stipulated severe sanctions, from imprisonment to prohibition from participation in elections.

Social Security Reform[16]

The constitutional amendment proposal for the Reform of Social Security (PEC 33) was presented to Congress in March 1995, shortly after President Cardoso's inauguration, and Congress was still considering it in the second half of 1998. The legislative process for PEC 133 exhibits an unusual path. It acquired high visibility because it was the only reform area in which the government was defeated in 11 separate rounds of voting. The proposal was voted on in two rounds in both the Chamber of Deputies and the Senate, and then following changes in the Senate, it returned to the Chamber. In fact, the Senate was able to reformulate the entire new version (*substitutivo*) approved by the Chamber and proceed with a new one prepared by a loyal senator.

The first defeat for the government was procedural rather than substantive. The rapporteur for the Subcommittee on Constitutional Matters suggested that the proposal be disaggregated into four pieces. A clause that granted the president exclusive rights in proposing legislation on social security was judged unconstitutional. The central issue of contention in the CCJ and subsequently throughout the legislative process primarily concerned the issue of future rights, that is, benefits that should accrue for current workers in the future. Resistance from legislators and organized interests, including pensioners' associations and trade unions, was greater than the government had anticipated.[17] As a result, the government decided to proceed cautiously and to make concessions. In the words of the government's chief political architect, "The commanding order is less speed and more discussion."[18]

Setting up the Special Commission on Social Security was strategically delayed for almost five months, and the negotiations became extremely politicized. Even though the commission's rapporteur and its president were members of the government's support coalition in Congress (from the PMDB and PFL, respectively), they were openly critical of the proposal. Their professional experience allowed them independence and political autonomy. The president of the Commission had been a minister for social security and had served as president of the National Institute for Social Security (Instituto Nacional de Seguridade Social — INSS). The rapporteur had been a federal deputy from the state of Amazônia, who had links with one of the most important interest groups in the arena of social security, the National Association of Social Security Tax Inspectors (Associação Nacional dos Fiscais da Previdência Social — ANFIP). The reform lacked a strong policy advocate, in part because Minister of Social Security Reinhold Stephanes, himself a beneficiary of early retirement, lacked the necessary legitimacy to persuade opponents of reform of the inequities of the system.

In line with the strategy adopted by government, the president invited trade unions to debate the reform. The two largest labor confederations, the progovernment Syndical Force (Força Sindical) and the more militant and leftist Unified Workers Union (Central Única dos Trabalhadores — CUT) participated in the debates. After demonstrations from the rank and file and accusations of treason, the unions withdrew from the roundtables. In fact, the government's strategy backfired because the very design of the proposal strengthened the public employees' coalition of sectoral interests and the much larger group of private sector employees. As most of the changes in social security were to affect public sector employees and only the abolition of retirement for time of service or early retirement affected private sector workers, the government expected to exchange support from the unions for concessions in its proposal for private sector workers. This de-linkage, however, was not viable because the PEC encompassed the proposed changes in private and public sector pensions, so both had to be voted on at the same time. As recognized by one of the chief presidential advisers, the proposal was somehow doomed by this mistake in reform packaging strategy: "To make changes in both pension systems through the same PEC helped the reform enemies from the public sector to manipulate the private sector workers and use them as shock troops against the reform."[19] Another key problem in the design of the proposal was that it deleted articles in the Constitution tout court, without introducing new proposals. As mentioned earlier, the central issue in de-constitutionalization was not simply the substance of reform but, more important, its procedural dimensions.

The rapporteur's substitutivo was submitted to the Special Commission with changes in the original proposal. Noting that the reform was becoming politically unfeasible, the government resorted to highly contested procedural mechanisms. When an open conflict broke out between the leader of the government coalition and the Commission's president, the president of the Chamber of Deputies said that the time limit of 40 sessions had been reached, dissolved the Special Commission, and sent the proposal to the floor of the House. The rapporteur's substitutivo, which incorporated many changes but retained the basic points of the reform, was defeated by 190 votes for the proposal, 294 against it, and 8 abstentions. Rather than following the Chamber's rules of procedure and voting on the government's original proposal, party leaders of the government coalition submitted a newly formulated proposal that was eventually approved.

The second round of voting centered on a reformulated proposal, called the *emenda superaglutinativa,* that merged the original proposal and amendments. During this phase, despite government efforts to amass the majority required for approval, the reformulated proposal was defeated eight times in a total of 33 voting rounds on specific items of the proposal[20] (Figueiredo and Limongi 1997). Two of the most important items were defeated, including one prohibiting early retirement and requiring an age limit for entitlement, and another imposing reductions of up to 30 percent in the replacement rate of pensions exceeding US$1,200, which was then at 100 percent of the value of past salaries.

The government was also defeated in its fourth attempt — the last one through Provisional Measure 1720 — to collect social security contributions from retired workers.[21] Shortly after this defeat, the government embarked on a new attempt to this end through an ordinary bill. The bill was finally approved in the Chamber of Deputies by 335 "yes" and 147 "no" votes. Two factors led to the approval of the bill. The government resorted to a procedural mechanism at its disposal, the urgency status rule (*regime de urgência*), which allows a regular bill (but not a constitutional amendment) to jump the line and be voted on immediately. The second factor was the national state of emergency, created by the financial crisis that led to the exchange rate crisis of February 1999, and the subsequent rescue package orchestrated by the International Monetary Fund (IMF). The press blamed the legislators, calling them traitors who were jeopardizing the macroeconomic situation. The social security deficit was mentioned in virtually all press coverage of the crisis.

The social security reform bill's approval proved to be short-lived because the judiciary became the veto point in the way of the reform. Following a wave of 1,050 collective and individual legal suits filed against the bill, along with 16 public civil actions (in a collective action mechanism created by the Constitution), the Supreme Court ruled the bill unconstitutional ("STF derruba contribuição de inativos," 1999). The litigation and Supreme Court ruling paralyzed the bill's implementation, causing a sharp drop in short-term expected revenues from R$267 million to R$5 million and produced an estimated total loss of R$7.6 billion in 1999 and 2000 ("Um exemplo discutível de Justiça," 1999; "Ações afetam 95% da arrecadação com servidores," 1999). The ensuing argument, which questioned the constitutionality of the bill, came from three separate suits filed by the Workers Party, the Bar Association, and the National Confederation of Public Servants ("STF decide se servidores inativos vão contribuir," 1999).

The Supreme Court's ruling took place when the newly elected governors faced very serious cash-flow problems due to a recent increase in personnel expenses, particularly in the case of retired employees. Most of the states had begun to tax retired employees following the approval of the bill in the Congress, 11 months prior to the Supreme Court ruling. This fait accompli reinforced the interest and motivation of the newly elected governors to find new sources of revenue in a post-election situation, when they could afford the political costs of imposing the tax on voters. In fact, the governors signed a petition for the taxation of retired personnel. The Forum of the State Government Secretaries for Administrative Affairs also circulated a motion supporting the tax.[22] Backed by the governors, the government attempted for the fifth time to tax retired public employees. This time, it proposed a constitutional amendment rather than an ordinary bill or provisional measure. The government sent the amendment to the Chamber of Deputies' Legal and Constitutional Affairs Committee, which approved it by 27 "yes" to 18 "no" votes. However, the proposal had not been voted on by the Congress. The new climate produced by the governors' mobilization contrasted sharply with the prevailing situation during the process of reform.

The government took a different path to circumvent the Chamber of Deputies' resistance to imposing a minimum age for retirement. The government tried to achieve its desired results by resorting to a scheme whereby the choices regarding retirement age would be limited. In line with reform efforts in other Organization for Economic Cooperation and Development (OECD) countries, such as Italy, France, and Sweden (Weaver 1998; Myles 1998, 243-244), the government proposed a factor (*fator previdenciário*), which would allow it to adjust the replacement rates of pensions, according to three variables: life expectancies of the pensioners' cohorts, average past earnings, and age. Under this scheme, early retirements would be penalized, and late retirements would be rewarded. The minimum age requirement would then be a matter of choice; however, the choice would be constrained.

This factor scheme was proposed through ordinary legislation, again under the urgency status procedure. The rapporteurs' report, prepared by Communist Party legislator Jandira Feghali, was defeated in the Chamber's Social Security Committee by 29 "no" and 12 "yes" votes, following the substitution of several members from the PMDB, who proved to be less than favorably disposed toward the proposal. In addition, the government published an official statement indicating the selection of a new rapporteur. Reacting against this interference with the committee's work, its president appointed yet another rapporteur. The new report, which introduced a transition phase of five years for the bill to be fully implemented, was approved by 305 "yes" to 157 "no" votes. According to the Ministry of Social Security, the ". . .government gave in to the extent that was possible; more would have been impossible" ("Fator previdenciário é aprovado," 1999). The judiciary, however, confirmed the constitutionality of Bill 9876 in a decision prompted by an action brought by the three parties (PCB, PSB, and PDT), which alleged that the bill reduced the real value of pensions and that because it had been modified by the Senate, it had to return to the Chamber of Deputies ("STF garante fator previdenciário," 2000). The fiscal implications of the introduction of the factor scheme were significant: the estimated social security deficit would be reduced by 2 percent of gross domestic product (GDP), from 5 percent to 3 percent.

Tax Reform [23]

The tax reform proposal of the Cardoso administration was submitted to Congress in August 1995 and was discontinued by the government, following a protracted process of resistance by various actors and inter-bureaucratic infighting. The developments were determined, to a large extent, by the role of governors in the process, but the intrinsic characteristics of tax as an issue area help explain it. In addition, this case study clearly shows the limits of purely institutional analysis: when they anticipate defeat, reformers may retreat and decide not to go ahead with their proposals. Alternatively, there could be an endogenous change of preference: changing circumstances may lead to the abandonment of the proposal. The analysis of approval rates of executives in the legislative arena cannot overlook this fact.

The Constitutional Amendment for Tax Reform (PEC 175) was presented shortly after the Social Security Proposal was put forward for discussion. Unlike social security and administrative reforms, the constitutional amendment took an exceptionally long time in Congress, and the rapporteur's amended PEC (*substitutivo*) was never formally presented by party leaders for vote in the ad hoc Special Commission; consequently, it never reached the floor.

The government abandoned the proposal as a result of three developments. First, the Finance Ministry, which had opposed the Planning Ministry's proposal from the outset, became the key actor in the reform agenda. The Finance Ministry was extremely risk aversive due to the country's serious financial instability and favored the status quo over risking moves toward an uncertain outcome. Second, the government managed to secure unprecedented levels of taxation through the Contribuição Provisoria sobre Movimentação Finaceira (provisional tax on banks' transactions). Third, the government managed to reform the corporate income tax to streamline tax collection for small businesses and to reduce the taxation of exports.

The amendment's rapporteur, a member of the PFL, was a former tax bureaucrat and state finance secretary for the northeastern states of Piaui and Ceara, and he enjoyed the support of key northeastern politicians.[24] The government's ability to negotiate with the rapporteur was undermined by infighting within the executive branch among pivotal actors, such as the Internal Revenue Service (Secretaria da Receita Federal — SRF), and the Planning, Finance, and Health Ministries.[25] Formulated by the Planning Ministry, the reform envisioned a transition stage for the new tax system to be fully implemented, whereas the Finance Ministry favored a more radical approach. In the version that was eventually presented, the Tax on Industrialized Products (Imposto sobre Produtos Industrializados — IPI) would be eliminated, and the federal government would be able to collect a tax similar to the Consumption Tax, called the ICMS. The Finance Ministry's proposal would abolish the ICMS and replace it with a newly created Value Added Tax (Imposto sobre Valor Adicionado — IVA). On several occasions, it became apparent that the government lacked a policy advocate.

A large number of legislative developments have to do with the aggregation problems associated with collective decisions in Brazilian federalism. The governors were the central players in these conflicts, which involved three issues of the reform agenda: 1) Taxes were eliminated on exports. 2) The governors proposed changes in location of ICMS collection from the state where a product is manufactured to the state where it is consumed. 3) They introduced a provision that set a national rate for ICMS. This provision effectively cancelled the effects of lower taxes set by state governments when they were struggling to attract investment during the so-called "fiscal wars."[26]

A stalemate resulted, prompting the government to design a new strategy to save at least parts of the reform. Recognizing that the elimination of export taxes did not require changes in the Constitution, the government submitted an ordinary bill with this purpose. With the government's backing, Deputy Planning Minister (and subsequently Planning Minister) Antonio Kandir proposed setting up an ad hoc Subcommission on Tax Reform to examine the various bills on the matter. The Subcommission, made up of legislators with interests in tax reform, many of whom were also economics professors, was a clear strategy to undo the deadlock. Kandir conducted a survey on its members' policy preferences, which returned important results. Ninety-three percent of those interviewed were against changes in the revenue sharing mechanism enshrined in the Constitution. Seventy-three percent favored a standard national rate for the value added tax, and 60 percent opposed changes in the place of taxation from place of production to place of consumption. Bearing in mind that these legislators were typically "preference outliers" or "high demanders" and that the high level of technicalities involved tend to produce consensus among specialists, the results indicated strong levels of opposition to the reform.

The government proceeded then with the bill on the elimination of the ICMS in exports and discontinued initiatives on other specific issues. However, by then, party leaders had at their disposal a variety of procedural mechanisms that guaranteed agenda power and "irreversibility" of policy decisions, as in the case of executive provisional measures, the *medidas provisórias*. The proposal was then approved, and the bill that came to be known as Lei Kandir (law 87/96) was finally enacted. After several failed attempts, the government's party leaders managed to vote it in, using the urgency status rule.[27] The most controversial aspects of this proposal were mechanisms that stipulated compensation for concentrated losses incurred by some states.

Three years after the proposal reached the House, the government made public its intention to proceed with the reform. The new proposal was formulated by the Finance Ministry, and it implied more radical changes in Consumption Tax than the proposal by the Planning Ministry. It called for the creation of a new Value Added Tax (IVA) to be collected by the federal government. This was regarded as an infringement of the states' constitutionally guaranteed prerogatives. The rapporteur insisted, "If there are no basic conditions that ensure that the state's revenue would not decline, I will not make concessions in my report."[28] In addition, he was against changing the privileged tax conditions of Manaus, a tax-free zone in the Amazon, and other regions. If the rapporteur did not incorporate the changes in his *substitutivo*, the government would have to submit a new PEC, which, in turn, would have to follow the legislative routine from the beginning, implying significant and unpredictable delays. More important, the government would have to bear the costs of defeating the *substitutivo*. As a legislator pointed out, "There emerged a confrontation climate, and the *substitutivo* will have to be defeated."[29] The other strategy the government adopted was the "no vote" strategy, which ushered in a deadlock situation. And then, the government postponed the reform until its next term of office.

In Cardoso's second term of office, the government presented a new tax reform proposal through the Ministry of Finance.[30] However, there has been little interest in submitting it for a vote, and the former president of the Banco Nacional de Desenvolvimento Econômico e Social (National Economic and Social Development Bank — BNDES) declared that the government was boycotting the proposal. Although leaders from the PFL announced that they would go ahead with legislative procedures, they have made no moves in that direction. The measure designed to combat the fiscal war was partially incorporated into the Bill for Fiscal Responsibility. It stipulated that tax abatements, that is, deductions, could not be granted by mayors and governors unless they stipulated a new source of revenue to compensate for losses in the subsequent two years. To a certain extent, despite having abandoned the tax reform, the government managed to secure approval of a number of specific measures through ordinary bills that required a simple majority vote. The government systematically instructed party leaders, although there were defections from the PMDB, not to participate in the workings of the Special Commission (Melo 2002, 94-97). The executive also managed to pass the Fiscal Stabilization Fund (Fundo Fiscal de Establzação), which imposed losses on municipalities and states and demonstrated the executive branch's power to enforce its agenda. A recent government move, aimed at overcoming the gridlock on tax reform, illustrates the constraints on reform in this area. Through federal Deputy Antônio Kandir, whose authorship of the reform is itself significant, the government submitted a constitutional amendment creating an ad hoc Mini-constituent Assembly. This assembly was empowered to make constitutional changes pertaining to a limited number of issues: division of powers among municipalities, states, and the federal government; taxation; judicial matters; and the electoral system.[31] According to this amendment, the assembly would gather for a period of six months and would be unicameral, thereby canceling the role of the Senate. It would adopt a simple majority rule rather than the three-fifths currently required.

EXPLAINING DIFFERENTIAL PATTERNS OF POLICY REFORMS

In this section, reforms are discussed from a comparative perspective. Tables 1 and 2 present a summary of key factors affecting reforms in the three issue areas and contain a summary of their important characteristics. The data help us to analyze the differing effects of institutions in each issue area.

Reforms in the three issue areas impose important concentrated losses for key constituencies. Paul D. Pierson and R. Kent Weaver (1993) aptly called the politics of these kinds of reforms the "politics of loss imposition" (see also Arnold 1998). Administrative reforms entail concentrated losses in the case of flexibility of job tenure, cuts in public sector salaries, and the introduction of new administrative procedures. The losses become significant in first wave reforms because of their emphases on downsizing. In second wave reforms, by contrast, the losses are less

Table 1.

Characteristics	Social Security	Administrative Reform	Tax Reform
Duration of legislative process	46 months	34 months	Abandoned by the government
Number of defeats in legislative process	12 (2 in Justice Committee; 2 in the Plenary of House; 8 in item vote, DVS); plus 1 in the Supreme Court	Two	Not voted
Legal statute	Constitutional amendment 20/98 (December)	Constitutional amendment 20/98 (June)	

pronounced but equally important. These reforms entail long-term realignments of institutions, incentives, and coalitions that affect power and privilege. Heredia and Schneider (Chapter One, this volume) argue that in the first type of reforms, the opposition is weakened because when key actors, such as public sector employees, lose their jobs, they also lose the capacity to resist. In the second type of reforms, actors retain the command of important organizational resources and are, therefore, in better condition to resist. These reforms are more likely to face problems in implementation than in policy formation.

In the Brazilian case, a crucial constituency was to be affected by one of the items of the reform package, when a group of 141 legislators accumulated pensions and pay for elective office in excess of the stipulated limit of R$12,000 (about US$10,000). In fact, this group was able to block a few sessions until this particular provision was eliminated. However, this was not a defeat for the executive because it was negotiated between the executive and its allies.

Administrative reform, however, produces benefits to important groups, including governors; core bureaucracies in planning, budgeting, and other areas; and public sector managers. This more mixed balance of losses and gains stemmed directly from the combination of managerial and Weberian dimensions of the Brazilian reform. Governors were crucial to success in administrative reform and defeat in tax policy. Their incentive structure changed when the possibility of reelection opened up in the second semester of 1996 and was finally promulgated in June 1997. In the case of administrative reform, this new condition turned them from potential losers to potential winners. Following the reversal of the Supreme Court decision, they became potential winners rather than indifferent actors.

The career civil servants in the federal police and the federal budgeting, planning, and finance sectors (*carreiras típicas*) would also potentially benefit from

Table 2. Issue Areas of the State Reform

Explanatory Variables	Social Security	Administrative Reform	Tax Reform	Enabling Conditions for Success
Coalitional characteristics and actors involved	Institutional and societal actors (bureaucrats, experts, public employees, trade unions)	Institutional (governors) and societal actors (bureaucrats, public employees, trade unions)	Predominantly institutional actors (governors, mayors, bureaucrats, experts). Business associations, trade unions (weak)	
Distribution of losses and gains	Concentrated in losers (existing pension funds, legislators, public sector employees) without clear winners	Concentrated in losers (public sector employees, legislators) with clear winners (governors, public managers)	Concentrated in losers (states); uncertainty about gains generates inherent status quo bias.	Diffuse losses and/ or clear winners
Compensation to losers	No	Yes, selectively	Not credible	Yes
Influence of federalism	Moderate (governors support it)	Strong (governors support it)	Strong (governors oppose it)	Strong (governors support it)
Policy advocate	Yes (weak)	Yes (very strong)	No (very weak)	Strong if ideas matter
Consensus within the executive	Medium	Medium to high (increasing during reform)	Low	High
Fiscal implications of reform in the short run	Very significant gains	Very significant gains	Very significant clear costs, high uncertainty possible gains	Very significant gains
Role of fiscal crisis	None in reform initiation, very important in reform acceleration	None in reform initiation, very important in reform acceleration	None in reform initiation, medium in reform acceleration	Important in initiation and acceleration
Policy bandwagoning and convergence	Medium	Yes (positive)	Medium	

the tax reform. The demands from this group were articulated by the Forum for Civil Service Careers (Fórum das Carreiras Típicas de Estado — FCTE). FCTE was set up at the beginning of Cardoso's term of office, in 1994, to press for the specific demands of career senior civil servants who worked in offices of the "core governmental functions." Good packaging helped the government attract support for the tax reform from this group, despite increasing conflict between the FCTE leadership and the government. The government's strong signaling of support for civil servants, as in pay raises and the opening of new posts to be occupied through competitive examinations, was instrumental in that respect. In the language of new economic institutionalism, this is not surprising because administrative reforms can be construed as attempts by the president and Congress to reduce agency losses between these actors as principals and public employees as agents.[32] The proposed flexibility of tenure, in fact, was aimed at lower rank career employees. As Ronald N. Johnson and Gary D. Libecab (1994, 8) argue regarding the United States, there are minimal gains from "shielding low-ranking public employees from political competition and manipulation, because they play a peripheral role in policy formation and execution." The rules that protect these individuals came about largely from federal unions in Brazil and, according to Johnson and Libecab, the United States. This is a direct consequence of the 1988 Constitution, which permitted unionization of public sector employees for the first time in Brazil's history.

Support from FCTE for the tax reform declined gradually for several reasons. First, FCTE faced an identity dilemma regarding its stance vis-à-vis the encompassing public employee unions. The government made it clear that the reform would entail losses for low-ranking public employees, while benefiting those in "core careers." The big unions would withdraw their support for FCTE if it endorsed measures that implied favored treatment of some careers in terms of pay raises and other benefits. In addition, as Zairo B. Cheibub (1999) argues, some careers faced collective action problems because the very selection of careers that would receive core career status was an open issue. The government was not prepared to define this issue in the Constitution, preferring to specify it in the enabling legislation,[33] effectively pitting some careers against others.

Second, FCTE's support for the reform declined because the unions were either controlled or greatly influenced by the Workers Party, which opposed Cardoso's reform agenda. This led to a gradual confrontation between FCTE and Bresser-Pereira. Third, Bresser's ability to negotiate with FCTE was undermined by the fact that the Casa Civil, the president's chief of staff, and/or the minister of Finance were allowed to decide upon some of the issues in this reform (Bresser, interview). Fourth, support from the core career civil servants was also affected by the fact that the social security reform imposed losses for public-sector employees. Cheibub (1999) argues that the social security issue gradually came to dominate the FCTE agenda because it was overwhelmingly made up of retired public employees. It should be noted that there is no collective bargaining in the public sector in Brazil, so the lack of any institutional arrangements in this area is the primary cause of the erratic path of negotiations between FCTE and the government.[34]

Public sector managers were to benefit from the reform because of the increased autonomy they would enjoy. Reformers from MARE did not anticipate this support. In fact, the large number of public organizations that consulted with MARE in order to adopt the "social organizations model" voluntarily surprised top officials in this ministry (interview with MARE's advisers). A survey of high-ranking bureaucrats shows strong support for the reform; 75 percent of Managerial and Advisory Positions (Direção e Assessoramento Superior — DAS) holders supported the reform. Fifty percent of respondents in a survey of elite groups and 66 percent of respondents in an Ibope poll supported the proposed flexibility of tenure.

Social security reforms of the 1980s and 1990s, because they have as leitmotif the fiscal problems caused by a combination of demographic and financial problems, caused current pensioners and workers, public sector employees, and other groups to sustain severe losses. In most industrial countries, these costs are distributed linearly, through changes in retirement age, social security rates, introduction of stricter eligibility conditions, or elimination of certain benefits. In Brazil, besides incurring these costs, many of the measures affect smaller groups of beneficiaries, as in special pensions for certain occupational groups, such as teachers and legislators. Not only were these groups affected by provisions prohibiting accumulation of pensions and pay for elective office, they were also able to form a loose coalition with private sector workers. In both social security and administrative reforms, many losses were perceived as social and individual rights rather than privileges. Even in the case of special privileges, it was widely held that future rights were constitutionally guaranteed.

The judiciary played an indirect role through articles and speeches by its members, signaling possible attempts at nullifying legislative decisions in the courts. Existing private pension funds were also important losers. The pension funds of public sector companies were under attack from the government, which was attempting to restrict companies' generous payments to the funds, but they could only offer diffuse resistance.[35]

For tax reform, losses were highly concentrated in the states. The gains were nonspecific, to be generated in the future from an increase in competitiveness of the country as a whole. A collective action problem comes to play here because these gains were actually public goods intended for the population as a whole. In the case of the elimination of the ICMS on exports, some states that were heavily dependent upon export revenues would incur potentially colossal losses. Total losses were estimated at between US$1.5 to 3 billion (Table 2). For the states of Pará and Amapá, these accounted for losses of 29 to 35 percent of their revenues from the ICMS. The proposed solution involved the creation of a compensation fund through an ordinary bill (Lei Kandir) and is surrounded by intense reactions from the governors as a result of the difficulties in measuring losses to be compensated in the future. Although "each governor examines the proposal with a calculator in his hands" (Industry Minister Francisco Dornelles, interview, 1996), there is an inter-temporal dimension involved. As noted by Governor Antonio Britto, "Nobody will agree to paying cash for the losses and to getting deferred credit for future compensations."[36]

Though the Lei Kandir created the compensation fund, the difficulties in implementing it suggest the issues involved. Protracted conflict over the compensation scheme led to changes in the mechanisms for compensation. The states were adamant in their opposition to the scheme and alleged that they incurred severe losses, so the government finally changed the scheme in 1999.

A stalemate resulted from the federal government's inability to commit to a credible compensation scheme for losses resulting from the change in the location of ICMS collection. The elimination of the ICMS on exports primarily affected small and predominantly backward states; consequently, the amount of compensation was relatively small. In this case, losses would be borne by the most industrialized states, in particular, São Paulo.

An important dimension of any successful tax reform is the multidimensionality of the reform package. No winning coalitions can be built, because actors who win in one dimension lose in the other. Also, multidimensionality exacerbates problems of preference cycles. A proposal that might defeat the government proposal could be rejected in favor of maintaining the status quo of doing nothing.[37]

Although the conflicts in the arena of tax reform were significant, they acquired little visibility because the actors were primarily institutional — governors, mayors, associations of state finance secretaries — and the issues highly technical. Although low visibility potentially facilitates consensus building, the fact that the losses were highly concentrated and had short-term effects seemed to have blocked the possibility of consensus for the tax reform.

The same pattern of resistance is found in the case of the losses resulting from the setting of similar rates for the ICMS and from replacing the ICMS with the IVA. Governors strongly resisted both changes because they faced what was essentially a prisoner's dilemma. The states would individually benefit from lower taxes through attracting investment, but they would lose collectively because the changes would weaken their position vis-à-vis firms. More important, the above changes would push down the national tax revenue. Even future gains for states are uncertain because they depend on jobs created and future revenues not yet determined or earned. Neither social security nor administrative reform offered the possibility of compensating the losers. The crucial difference between the two areas is that administrative reform did have some winners.

The evidence from Brazil's experience confirms Heredia and Schneider's argument (this volume) that fiscal crisis does not play a crucial role in the initiation of administrative reforms. However, fiscal crisis did play an important role in the timing and acceleration of reforms. As noted, the reform took a new direction when the finance ministers perceived that it would help in the negotiation of states' debts. The same holds true following the devaluation crisis regarding social security and tax reforms.

The reforms differ greatly in their short-term fiscal implications. The gains from second wave tax reforms are diffuse and deferred to the future. More important, uncertainty about the effects of changes in taxation upon revenues collected blurs the perception of gains. It also explains the widely shared belief among tax bureaucrats that "good taxes are old taxes." A bias in favor of the status quo, therefore, is inherent in tax politics. As the mentor of the tax reform proposal

Table 3. Concentrated Costs Associated with Tax Reform

State	Percent Losses*	State	Percent Losses*
Pará	34.84	Ceará	3.78
Amapá	28.46	Rondônia	3.30
Espírito Santo	22.01	Rio de Janeiro	3.09
Maranhão	15.12	São Paulo	2.73
Paraná	13.03	Pernambuco	1.87
Mato Grosso	10.19	Amazonas	1.55
Minas Gerais	10.14	Piauí	1.12
Alagoas	8.37	Acre	0.98
R.G. do Sul	7.50	Roraima	0.74
M.G. do Sul	6.14	Sergipe	0.72
Santa Catarina	5.32	Paraíba	0.52
R.G. do Norte	4.06	Tocantins	0.49
Goiás	4.03	D. Federal	0.08
Bahia	4.44		

Source: Subcomissão de Reforma Tributária do Congresso Nacional.

* Relative losses: ICMS tax on exports as percent of total ICMS. These are estimates of losses incurred by the states from the elimination of the tax on exports.

put it, "The reform is timid because we have to evaluate the impact of the introduction of the 'federal ICMS' on total revenue . . . and only then proceed to reduce the number of taxes collected" ("Porque a reforma tributária é tímida," 1995).

Gains from second wave reforms refer to increasing systemic efficiency and competitiveness, not tax increases. Tax reform implies short-term losses for the central government, as well, because of lost compensation. Only short-term benefits relate to improving the country's reputation in international markets and among multilateral institutions. In contrast, the reforms in the other issue areas generate short-term savings.[38] These savings acquired high visibility on the political agenda and were exploited recurrently by the actors involved with the Plano Real.

Fiscal gains from the social security and administrative reforms were a key issue in political discourse during the negotiations. A number of governmental and societal institutions, including business associations, presented estimates of savings resulting from various measures contained in the reform packages.[39] The vote on the taxation of retirement income was approved against the backdrop of the crisis of Plano Real and the politics of blame avoidance among the actors involved. At the same time, the press and the government pointed to those responsible for the imminent financial collapse of the country. The sudden support from the elected governors who faced significant losses from the prohibition of taxing retired public servants in the states was also crucial (Table 4).

**Table 4. State Governments' Losses Caused by Supreme Court Rulings
against Social Security Contributions from Retired Public Servants**

States	Contribution Rate*	Estimate of Losses
Acre	4.5	1.2
Amazonas	14.0	27.1
Amapá	8.0	0.2
Roraima	8.0	2.5
Tocantins	9.0	1.3
Bahia	5.0	30.4
Pernambuco	15.0	116.5
Sergipe	10.0	10.0
Mato Grosso do Sul	10.0	17.5
Espírito Santo	10.0	23.8
Minas Gerais	7.0	127.2
Rio de Janeiro	11.0	196.0
São Paulo	6.0	405.0
Paraná	12.0	138.0
Rio Grande do Sul	7.4	112.2
Santa Catarina	10.0	54.4
Total		1.264 billion

Source: Ministério da Previdência e Assistência Social. MPAS/DPS/DEDSP.
*Contribution rates charged to retired public servants by the states that had been set up prior to Supreme Court rulings against its legality.

As discussed earlier, the perception of losses has an important subjective dimension in so far as it is socially constructed.[40] Policy advocates and shared beliefs about causal effects of policy decisions are important factors underlying the social construction of these losses. Policy advocates play a crucial role in influencing actors' beliefs regarding policy outcomes. Several factors affect their ability to accomplish this, including policy bandwagoning, emulation of international success stories publicized by multilateral institutions (Melo and Costa 1995; Saint-Martin 1999; and Figueira and Martínez 1999), and policy legitimacy conferred by epistemic communities.[41] In these three arenas, the politics of ideas was quite pronounced. As suggested by B. Guy Peters (1991, 4), politics in the arena of tax policy may involve mustering experts as well as mustering interest groups (Beam et al. 1990).

The roles of international consultants [42] and multilateral institutions[43] were important in the administrative reform process, but they were incorporated ex post in the process and did not actively promote reform. As suggested by Denis Saint-Martin (1998), institutional variables can facilitate the degree of permeability by outside expertise. In the Brazilian case, MARE and the National School of Public Administration (Escola Nacional de Administração Pública — ENAP) served as important entry points for the incorporation of these actors within the executive, but this was limited due to the overwhelming concern with fiscal issues within the executive as a whole.

Policy advocacy proved to be an important factor differentiating the three cases. The evidence suggests a continuum from very strong in administrative reform, to very weak in tax reforms, with social security falling in the middle. The role of Minister Bresser-Pereira as a policy advocate is suggested by an editorial from the conservative *O Estado de São Paulo*: "The victory should be credited to the tenacity of Minister Bresser-Pereira . . . and his capacity for persuasion, which guaranteed almost total fidelity to the original proposal. . . . To the victor, Bresser, the spoils" (May 19, 1998).

Policy advocacy is made difficult when there is intense bureaucratic infighting and fragmentation of reform leadership within the executive. The case of administrative reform is particularly relevant here. At the beginning, the proposal enjoyed little support within the executive. The managerial aspects of the reforms — the setting up of semiautonomous bodies, social organizations, and executive agencies — were regarded as irrelevant by the other ministries. Paradoxically, this contributed to advance the reform because, despite lukewarm support, it was opposed by virtually nobody within the executive. A pro-reform coalition began to coalesce, however, when the governors, along with planning and finance ministries, were attracted by its potential fiscal benefits. The approval of the proposal for the reelection of governors and the timing of the roundtables on the refinancing of the states' debt were instrumental in providing a new incentive structure favorable to the reform. Bresser-Pereira proved to be very capable in exploiting this new incentive structure. The concern with the fiscal gains of the reform increasingly dominated interest in potential managerial and efficiency gains.[44]

An entirely different picture emerged in the case of tax reform. Tax reform was plagued with dissent among the various branches of the executive, including the Planning Ministry and its Institute for Applied Economic Research, the Finance Ministry, the Internal Revenue Service, and even the Health Ministry. This lack of sponsorship is consistent with the findings in the literature on tax policy. As Peters (1991, 4) put it, "A distinctive feature of tax policy is that politicians can rarely use this policy area for their advantage in electoral politics."[45]

However, there is strong evidence that the executive did not abandon the tax reform because it anticipated defeat. As noted, despite the difficulties in coming through with a consensus proposal, the chief reason for abandoning the reform was that the executive changed its preferences, as a result of changing reform circumstances.

The strategic choices of state reformers in shaping the political costs of different types of reforms is evident in Bresser-Pereira's decision not simply to delete articles in the Constitution ("de-constitutionalize"), but also to stress the innovative and positive points of his proposal. Conversely, the linkage between reforms in public and private sector pensions produced perverse effects, namely an alliance between the powerful private sector Confederation of Trade Unions (Centrais), representing Central Única dos Trabalhadores (CUT) and Força Sindical, and the much weaker public sector unions. As mentioned, the consequences of this linkage were not anticipated by reformers ex ante but by a top presidential adviser ex post.

Strategic packaging is perhaps the single most important variable in the politics of "loss imposition" and "blame avoidance." The solutions for the deadlock in the episodes of *extra teto* and of the minimum age of retirement through the factor scheme are emblematic of "reform by stealth" (Weaver 1998). Changes are approved that minimize the visibility of the losses to important constituencies (Weaver 1998).

There appears to be an inverse correlation between the role of leadership and advocacy and reform sustainability. Because sustainability has to do with the difficulties of implementing reform, if leadership disappears, reform sustainability is at a risk. Although it is too early to formulate conclusions in relation to the reforms, it could be argued that social security and administrative reform are polar opposites. Social security requires relatively little administrative capacity, and its implementation primarily entails changes in rules of entitlement. In contrast, administrative reform implies long-term realignments of institutional arrangements, organizational power bases, and resources. In addition, it exhibits a much higher technical complexity, requiring monitoring and compliance mechanisms. As suggested earlier, the implementation of administrative reform has been rather limited at the federal level but fairly significant at the state level.[46] President Cardoso's decision to close MARE at the beginning of his second term of office was a severe blow to the reform effort. Without its chief architect and its organizational basis, the administrative reform has lost much of its momentum.[47] Although less problematic than administrative reform, it could be argued, following Peters (1991, 4), "that a great deal of tax policy is made while it is implemented." Thus, administrative reform is likely to experience less severe but equally important implementation problems and permutations.

The fates of tax policy and social security reform can also be partially explained with reference to the role played by policy legacies in setting path dependency in policy developments (Pierson 1996). A comparison with the relatively smooth transition to the value-added tax (VAT) in Argentina is illustrative (Eaton 2002). The shift to VAT in Argentina was made possible by the fact that this shift would entail a substantial rise in revenue for the states. This was made possible because Argentina's tax system was relatively underdeveloped. The tax burden in Argentina before the introduction of VAT in the mid-1990s was 14 percent. In contrast, in Brazil the tax burden was twice as high. The more developed tax system of Brazil, which boasted the developing world's highest tax burden, precluded such a solution because the tax burden was unanimously seen as very high and had been locked into the alternatives to zero-sum-game solutions. Brazil, therefore, had to adopt a solution that would entail concentrated losses rather than gains for all of the states.

In the case of social security, one of the reasons for the government abandoning a radical move toward private pension funds was the system's maturity. The more mature a system, the higher the transition costs to the new system and the higher the political opposition to the change because of future pensioners' sense of entitlement to a given level of earned benefits.

Table 5. Rice Index* of Votes for Selected Constitutional Reforms

Parties	Issue Area				
	Admin- istrative Reform	Social Security	Legal Statute of National Enterprises	State Monopoly of Telecom- munications	State Monopoly of Oil Production
PDT	1.00	0.85	0.96	0.96	0.96
PFL	0.85	0.75	0.93	0.97	0.88
PMDB	0.58	0.16	0.60	0.46	0.57
PPB	0.71	0.31	0.92	0.84	0.81
PSB	1.00	0.92	0.62	0.92	0.77
PSDB	0.98	0.73	0.99	0.79	0.74
PT	1.00	0.96	1.00	1.00	0.94
PTB	0.98	0.34	0.79	0.86	0.79

Sources: Secretaria da Mesa da Câmara dos Deputados. Vote on the *substitutivo* in the Plenary of the House (first round).
*Rice index: Ri, x = percent of yes votes minus percent of no votes.

The most important evidence that issue areas matter is offered by an analysis of the voting pattern during the constitutional reform. Table 5 contains data on vote fractionalization in several areas of the reform, including other issue areas not considered in this paper, using the Rice Index (the absolute value of percentage of "no" votes minus the percentage of "yes" votes). The data suggest extremely differentiated fractionalization patterns across issue areas. Extremely high levels were found in the cases of social security and administrative reform, reaching the highest levels in the cases of the PMDB, PPB, and PTB. Even within the most loyal party, the PFL, fractionalization was high and reached 0.75.

Conclusions

This chapter analyzes the role of institutions in determining policy outcomes in Brazil in the 1990s. The current literature in this debate offers two polar types of explanations. Some argue that fragmentation and veto points in the political system (associated with the combination of multiparty presidentialism and open-list proportional representation, noncooperative federalism, and consocialist elements in the political system) block political and policy change. Other scholars are increasingly critical of this type of explanation and point instead to the internal organization of Congress as an integrative factor that enables the executive to pursue its agenda successfully in the Congress. This second body of literature has focused on aspects such as party discipline and cohesion, the ideological consistency of parties, and the executive's agenda powers.

These two patterns of explanation are not mutually exclusive in general terms. Although the second bloc of literature — the one that stresses the role of the internal organization of Congress — is essentially correct in criticizing the alleged effects of the open-list proportional representation and presidentialism on policymaking in Congress, the generalizations made in relation to the political system as a whole are unwarranted. Although my findings are consistent with the literature that stresses the preponderance of the executive, the executive's ability to impose its agenda is generally exaggerated. The most important flaw regarding the current debate is methodological. By limiting the analysis to voting patterns in Congress, it makes the substantive content of policy *tabula rasa* before the vote and during the formulation of policy. Furthermore, policymaking cannot be adequately studied with reference only to executive-legislative relations.

This chapter also tracks the vicissitudes of the constitutional amendment proposals in three issue areas, suggesting that many factors lead to fragmentation and consequently to gridlock, but others guarantee the prevalence of the executive agenda. The "fragmentation variables" have to do with federalism but also with issue-specific aspects and policy legacies of tax policy. These factors have great analytical power to explain the patterns of policy formation and implementation. The very fact that the policy outcomes are different in the various areas suggests that other factors beyond simple systemic traits, such as the electoral system, are shaping the policy process. There is strong evidence of concessions granted to gain support for reforms during policy formation and intense mobilization on the part of the executive to shepherd reforms through Congress. Policy proposals in Congress reflect bargains struck before voting and should not necessarily be viewed as revealing the policy preferences of the executive. The discussion presented here thus points to the limitations of pure institutional analysis for explaining policy outcomes. The fate of the tax reform is particularly emblematic of how case studies of reform in issue areas can illuminate the discussion. The government did not abandon the reform because it anticipated defeat but because it changed its preferences and could not reach consensus on the proposal within the executive.

Institutions matter as much as issue areas, but issue-specific incentive structures underlying strategic choices by the actors are crucial for an understanding of how institutions matter. These incentive structures are embedded in policy legacies and coalitional dynamics of a specific policy domain. The preceding analysis explored several important institutional features of the Brazilian political system — the role of governors and legislative and congressional dynamics, including the role of agenda and procedural powers in the legislature — in connection with the specific policy dynamics of each of the issue areas.

By focusing exclusively on political parties, existing political models of administrative reforms, such as Barbara Geddes' (1991; 1995), do not incorporate the important institutional variables of separation of powers, federalism, or the internal organization of Congress. I contend that these factors along with issue-specific mechanisms have strong explanatory power.

The relative success of the administrative reform, vis-à-vis the other reform initiatives discussed in this chapter, can be partially explained by the fact that governors became interested in the reforms as a result of the significant change in their incentive structure, caused by the approval of the constitutional amendment allowing their reelection. Once this provision was approved, they realized that the flexibility of tenure would be instrumental for patronage games at the state level in a new term of office. That unanticipated development significantly extended the time horizons underlying their political calculus. In the case of social security reforms, the crucial support of the elected governors for the taxation of retirement income produced a much more favorable environment for the approval of a very difficult proposal, which had been defeated four times before. This was not enough to secure the support of the judiciary, which ruled against the constitutionality of the bill, but it did guarantee success in the first hurdle of approval, the CCJ. As noted, agenda power, coalitional factors, packaging, and policy advocacy were all instrumental for the success of the administrative reform. The outcomes in the administrative and social security reforms underscore the roles of blame avoidance and politics by stealth: these strategies were chosen because of their potential to minimize the visibility of political costs to specific constituencies and, consequently, to survival-seeking legislators.

In sum, institutional analysis contributes significantly to our understanding of policy outcomes but has important limitations, as noted by Kaufman (Chapter Ten, this volume). The most important of these refers to making *tabula rasa* of policy content. General analysis is unable to determine whether a policy outcome, such as a deadlock or veto, has to do with the fact that it was too ambitious or too cautious. Therefore, policy outcomes can greatly benefit from issue area analysis. This expanded type of analysis helps to explain, as Heredia and Schneider maintain in the Introduction to this volume, not only whether a reform actually took place, but also why it happened when it did, what model it followed, how comprehensive it was in scope, and how it fared in the process of implementation.

NOTES

1. I would like to thank Ben Ross Schneider and Blanca Heredia for detailed critiques that greatly helped me to improve the chapter. I would also like to thank the participants in the preparatory meetings of the research project, especially Stephan Haggard, Bob Kaufman, Judith Tendler, and Susan Rose-Ackerman, and last but not least Professor Bresser-Pereira for helpful comments and suggestions. Needless to say, he is not responsible for my interpretation of his comments. I also thank my coauthors and partners in related projects, Pedro Barros e Silva and Sérgio de Azevedo for numerous discussions whose findings are somehow reflected in the paper. The usual disclaimer applies.

2. Institutional analysis acquires relevance and attracts continuing and systematic interest only in the context of democracy. Institutional volatility and the weakness of the electoral connection in authoritarian regimes reduces the explanatory power of institutions. However, their very volatility allows us to study institutions as endogenous and to explore key conceptual questions regarding institutional choice (Bates 1990, 47).

3. I am indebted to Robert Kaufman for comments on this point. See also Weir 1992.

4. For an analysis of the Plano Diretor as a rhetorical strategy, see Gaetani 1998.

5. The rapporteur's amendments were to be voted on separately by the plenary. See "Bresser Inicia Lobby contra parecer de Viana," 1995; "Bresser ameaça abandonar reforma e 'ir à praia,'" 1995; "Reforma começa já pem clima de guerra," 1995.

6. "Bresser inicia lobby contra parecer de Viana," 1995; "CUT diz que terceirização é um golpe no Congresso," 1997; "MP é solução para reformas," 1997.

7. See "FHC pede apoio de governadores," 1995; "Lula fica irritado com os governadores" 1995; "Planalto busca apoio de governadores," 1995.

8. For a similar conclusion regarding tax reform, see "Possibilidade de reeleição reduz resistência a projeto," 1998.

9. See "Parecer mantém a estabilidade do servidor," 1996; "Governo fará emenda contra a estabilidade," 1996; "Fim da estabilidade divide base governista," 1996; "FHC já admite acordo para estabilidade," 1996; "Acordo facilita dispensa do servidor," 1996; "Líderes governistas fecham propostas flexibilizando estabilidade do funcionário público," 1996; "Líderes recuam e mantêm estabilidade," 1996.

10. Despite losing the vote, the government approved in the same package tenure for 10,800 employees from the former federal territories (now states) that were recruited in patronage deals. This was part of the negotiations involving the support of the legislators from these states for the reform.

11. "CUT diz que terceirização é um golpe no Congresso," 1997; "MP é solução para reformas," 1997.

12. This led to a legal problem because the MPs would have to be voted on before PEC 173. If PEC 173 were approved first, the MPs would lose their effect. This was the case

because in 1995 Congress passed a constitutional amendment prohibiting the issuance of MPs on matters contained in constitutional amendments.

13. Although not legally an executive agency, Inmetro signed a performance contract in 1998 with the federal government and operates virtually as the one institution of that kind.

14. MARE used a World Bank loan to hire a consultancy firm to advise institutions in the transition to the social organizations format. In the case of the Roquette Pinto Foundation, it helped prepare the performance contract. An English consultant was also hired within the context of a technical assistance project to support the executive agency team. MARE set up an interministerial Reform Support Group to implement the executive agency project (Grupo de Apoio a Reforma). For case studies of the developments at Roquette Pinto and Inmetro, see Ventura, Igarasi, and Lima 1999; Melo and Marcelino 1999; and Lemos Filho, Russo, and Moreira 1999.

15. Franco, one of the architects of the Real Plan and former president of the Central Bank, put it aptly when he said, "If it were not for the 150 federal deputies who are candidates, the bill would not have passed that easily" ("A revolução fiscal apenas começou," 2000).

16. This section draws on Silva, Melo, and Matijascic 1998.

17. The reform was resisted by private pension funds that were also important losers. Attempts at setting a much lower ceiling for the value of public pensions (currently US$1,000) — thereby opening up a market for private pension funds — would affect the funds because their policies would cover the difference from an average of past salaries and this ceiling.

18. "Sarney aprova medida do governo de priorizar a votação na área econômica," 1995.

19. Eduardo Graeff, confidential memorandum to President Cardoso, 1995. He went on to advise "separating out the issues in order to divide the enemies."

20. In August 1998, three items (DVSs) were still up for vote.

21. This is a unique result because MPs are very rarely rejected by Congress ("Congresso derruba R$bilhões do Ajuste Fiscal," 1998).

22. For the Forum's petition, see "Secretários insistem em taxar inativos," 1999.

23. For a detailed analysis of tax reform, see Azevedo and Melo 1997. In the following section of this chapter, we discuss the reform of the taxation of consumption and not of personal income because it was not included in the constitutional reform package.

24. See "Estados perdem com a proposta," 1997; "Relator quer Mudar Emenda Tributária," 1995; "Para Relator, emenda do governo não passa," 1995.

25. The problems of health financing in Brazil acquired an unprecedented visibility and, following several scandals, became the central issue in the political agenda during 1995-1996. This issue of interdependence between health financing and tax reform overloaded the tax reform agenda. See "Proposta de Mudanças Tributárias ainda Divide Fazenda, Planejamento, e Receita," 1995; "Briga Entre PSDB e PFL Atrasa Reforma," 1995; "Reforma Tributária em Clima de Guerra," 1995; "Estados vão Definir a Reforma Tributária," 1995.

26. For a broader view of this, see "Estados Fazem Exigências para a Reforma," 1995; "Governadores cobram Detalhes do Projeto," 1995; "Fundo de Compensação poderá ter R$6

bi," 1995; "Governadores querem mudar Projeto. Perda dos Estados ainda Preocupa," 1995; "Governadores Querem Controlar o IVA," 1995.

27. The implementation of Lei Kandir has been extremely controversial and became political currency in important political negotiations in Congress in other issue areas. Cf. "FEF transforma-se em moeda de troca contra lei Kandir," 1997.

28. "Relator já admite assumir proposta de Parente," 1998. For the states' opposition, see "Estados resistem a aceitar propostas sobre tributos," 1998; "Mudança tributária gradual pode ser mais viável," 1998.

29. "Reforma Tributária: secretário executivo diz haver espaço para negociação," 1998. See also "Fazenda e Câmara mantêm divergências sobre o tema," 1998.

30. "Reforma Tributária. Nova reforma do Ministério da Fazenda, Minifaz," mimeo, January 12, 1998.

31. Cf. "Governo apoia a Mini-constituinte em 1999," 1998.

32. See Kiewiet and McCubbins 1989.

33. During the negotiations of Bill 248/98, the number of careers included in the "core" status changed significantly.

34. See Cheibub 1999.

35. Although the government did not propose to privatize the system, the funds were important veto players in this connection. Attempts at setting a much lower ceiling for the value of public pensions (currently US$1,000) — thereby opening up a market for private pension funds — would affect the funds because their policies would cover the difference from an average of past salaries and this ceiling.

36. It should be noted that the states faced a moral hazard problem because they would have an incentive to collect fewer taxes and a disincentive to increase tax collection ("Estados resistem a aceitar propostas sobre tributos," 1998).

37. This occurred in tax policy formation in the United States. Cf. Murray and Birnbaum 1988.

38. For assessment of the gains from administrative reform and costs of tax reforms from several relevant actors, see "Tática do Planalto será atrasar ajuste Tributário," 1996.

39. The National Industrial Confederation (CNI) estimated the gains as 1.5 percent of GDP (US$12 billion) and MARE's as 0.5 percent of GDP (Confederação Nacional da Indústria, 1997).

40. I am indebted to Bob Kaufman for insightful comments on this issue.

41. These factors have been stressed in the institutional sociology literature (Kaufman, this volume).

42. MARE hired Osborne and a number of British consultants, but not the big international consultant firms, as was the case in Argentina (Cf Rinne, this volume).

43. In the area of administrative reform, there was a division of labor between the Inter-American Development Bank and the World Bank, through which the IDB assisted the states in pursuing reform and the World Bank assisted the federal government (Interview with IDB Senior Representative, November 1997). In the area of income tax reform, Brazil's Income

Tax Secretary Everardo Maciel remarked, "Representatives from the IMF told me that we went further than it was advising governments to do" (Interview, April 23-24, 1996).

44. Rezende (1999) in a recent contribution comes to a similar conclusion, namely, that the concern with what he calls fiscal performance overshadowed the concern for institutional change. The former was associated with actors at the Finance and Planning departments, whereas the latter was associated with MARE. The administrative reform failed because the macro-environment was primarily dominated by the issue of fiscal stability.

45. For a new institutionalist analysis of tax policy, see Steinmo 1993; and Steinmo and Tolbert 1998.

46. The gains in terms of efficiency cannot be assessed yet. Existing evidence suggests cost reduction at Roquette Pinto after it became a social organization (Ventura, Igarassi, and Lima 1999; and Lemos Filho, Russo, and Moreira 1999). Although many of the institutions that were selected as candidates for executive agency status, such as IBAMA, CNPQ, Fiocruz, CAPES, and INS, have not changed their legal status, they are increasingly adopting managerialist styles.

47. The focus in this paper is on policymaking rather than on the implementation of reforms. Administrative reform capacity refers not only to policymaking, but also to implementation. While policymaking has to do primarily with the ability of the executive to impose an agenda on the legislature (depending on institutional veto points and so on), implementation has to do fundamentally with the degree of autonomy of the bureaucracy in a state (Knill 1999).

REFERENCES

Abrucio, Fernando Luis. 1998. *Os barões da federação, os governadores e a redemocratização brasileira*. São Paulo: Hucitec/USP.

Abrucio, Fernando, and Valeriano Costa. 1998. *Reforma do estado e o contexto federativo brasileiro*. São Paulo: Konrad Adenauer.

Ames, Barry. 2001. *The Deadlock of Democracy in Brazil*. Ann Arbor, Mich.: University of Michigan Press.

Arnold, Douglas. 1990. *The Logic of Congressional Action*. New Haven, Conn.: Yale University Press.

Arnold, R. Douglas. 1998. "The Political Feasibility of Social Security Reforms." In *Framing the Social Security Debate*, eds. R.D. Arnold et al. Washington, D.C.: The Brookings Institution.

Azevedo, Sergio, and Marcus Melo. 1997. "A política da reforma tributária: federalismo e mudança constitucional." *Revista brasileira de ciênciais sociais* 35: 75-100.

Bates, Robert. 1990. "Macropolitical Economy in the Field of Development." In *Perspectives on Positive Political Economy*, eds. James E. Alt and Kenneth A. Shepsle. Cambridge, UK: Cambridge University Press.

Beam, David R., Timothy J. Conlan, and Margaret T. Wrightson. 1990. "Solving the Riddle of Tax Reform: Party Competition and the Politics of Ideas." *Political Science Quarterly* 105: 2 (Winter): 193-217.

Bresser-Pereira, Luiz Carlos.1996, 1998. Brazil's Minister of State Reform and Administration interviewed by the author. Brasilia, March 26, 1996, and September 23, 1998.

Cheibub, Zairo B. 1999. "Reforma administrativa e relações trabalhistas no setor público: Dilemas e perspectivas." Escola Nacional de Administração Pública (ENAP). Mimeo.

Confederação Nacional da Indústria. 1997. "A reforma administrativa e a redução das despesas com o pessoal do setor público." Brasília. Mimeo.

Dornelles, Francisco. 1996. Interview by author. Brasilia, March 23.

Eaton, Kent. 2002. "Fiscal Policymaking in the Argentine Legislature." In *Legislative Politics in Latin America*, eds Scott Morgenstern and Benito Nacif. Cambridge, UK: Cambridge University Press.

Figueiredo, Argelina, and Fernando Limongi.1994. "O processo legislativo e a produção legal no congresso pós-constituinte." *Novos Estudos Cebrap* 38: 65-89.

Figueiredo, Argelina, and Fernando Limongi. 1995. "Mudança constitucional, desempenho do legislativo e consolidação institucional." *Revista Brasileira de Ciências Sociais* 29: 175-200.

Gaetani, Francisco. 1998. "The Reform of the Brazilian State Apparatus: An Ex-ante Analysis." London: London School of Economics and Political Science. Master's thesis.

Geddes, Barbara. 1991. "A Game Theoretic Model of Reform in Latin America." *American Political Science Review* 85 (June): 371-392.

Geddes, Barbara. 1995. *Politician's Dilemma: Building State Capacity in Latin America.* Berkeley, Calif.: University of California Press.

Haggard, Stephan, and Mathew D. McCubbins, eds. 2001. *Presidents, Parliaments, and Policy.* New York: Cambridge University Press.

Haggard, Stephan, and Robert Kaufman, eds. 1992. *The Politics of Economic Adjustment: International Constraints, Distributive Conflicts, and the State.* Princeton, N.J.: Princeton University Press.

Haggard, Stephan. 1995. "The Reform of the State in Latin America." Paper presented at the Annual Bank Conference on Development in Latin America and the Caribbean, Rio de Janeiro, June 12-13.

Haggard, Stephan, and Robert Kaufman. 1995. *The Political Economy of Democratic Transitions.* Princeton, N.J.: Princeton University Press.

Inter-American Development Bank Senior Representative. 1998. Interview with author. Washington, D.C., October 23.

Johnson, Ronald N., and Gary D. Libecap. 1994. *The Federal Civil Service and the Problem of Bureaucracy: The Economics and Politics of Institutional Change.* Chicago: University of Chicago Press.

Kaufman, Robert. 1997. "The Politics of State Reform: A Review of Theoretical Approaches." New Brunswick, N.J.: Rutgers University. Mimeo.

Kiewiet, Roderick D., and Mathew D. McCubbins. 1989. *The Logic of Delegation.* Ann Arbor, Mich.: University of Michigan Press (and in 1991, Chicago: University of Chicago Press).

Knill, Christoph. 1999. "Explaining Cross-National Variance in Administrative Reform: Autonomous versus Instrumental Bureaucracies." *Journal of Public Policy* 19 (2): 113-139.

Lemos Filho, Egas Murilo de Sousa, Fátima Ferreira Russo, and Normando dos Santos Moreira. 1999. "Modelo de administração pública gerencial para as agências executivas." Paper presented at the Meeting of the National Graduate Association for Reasearch in Administration, Foz de Igaçu, Brazil, September 19-23.

Limongi, Fernando P., and Argelina Figueiredo. 1995. "Partidos políticos na Câmara dos Deputados." *Dados* 38: 497-526.

Limongi, Fernando, and Argelina Figueiredo. 1997. "Processo decisório no congresso e comportamento parlamentar: Plano Collor e a reforma da previdência." Paper presented at the XVII National Meeting of National Graduate Association for Research in the Social Sciences, Caxambu, Brazil, October 20-23.

Lowi, Theodore. 1964. "American Business, Public Policy, Case-Studies, and Political Theory." *World Politics* 16 (July): 677-715.

Maciel, Everardo. 1996. Brazil's Income Tax Secretary interviewed by author. Brasilia, April 23-24.

Mainwaring, Scott. 1997. "Multipartism, Robust Federalism and Presidentialism in Brazil." In *Presidentialism and Democracy in Latin America*, eds. Scott Mainwaring and Matthew S. Shugart. Cambridge, UK: Cambridge University Press.

Mainwaring, Scott, and Matthew S. Shugart, eds. 1997. *Presidentialism and Democracy in Latin America.* Cambridge, UK: Cambridge University Press.

Melo, Julia S. de C., and Gileno F. Marcelino. 1999. "A experiência do contrato de gestão frente a cultura administrativa do estado brasileiro." Paper presented at the Meeting of the National Graduate Association for Reasearch in Administration, Foz de Igaçu, Brazil, September 19-23.

Melo, Marcus. 1995. "Ingovernablidade: Desagregando o argumento." In *Governabilidade e pobreza no brazil*, eds. Lícia Valladares and Magda Prates. Rio de Janeiro: Civilização Brasileira.

Melo, Marcus. 1997. "As reformas constitucionais e a previdência social, 1993-1996." In *Reforma do estado e democracia no brasil*, eds. Eli Diniz e Sérgio de Azevedo. Brasilia: Editora da UNB.

Melo, Marcus. 1997. "O jogo das regras: a política da reforma constitucional, 1993-1996." *Revista brasileira de ciências sociais* 33 (fevereiro): 63-87.

Melo, Marcus, and Nilson Costa. 1997. "A difusão das reformas neoliberais: Análise estratégica, atores e agendas internacionais." In *Pluralismo, espaço social, e pesquisa*, eds. Elisa Reis, Maria Hermínia T. de Almeida, and Peter Fry. São Paulo: Hucitec/Anpocs.

Melo, Marcus. 1998. "Constitucionalismo e escolha racional." *Lua Nova* 43: 55-79.

Melo, Marcus, and Sérgio de Azevedo. 1998. *A política da reforma constitucional: O processo decisório das reformas da seguridade social e da reforma tributária no brasil, 1990-1996*. Cadernos Para Discussão. Brasília: Escola Nacional de Administração Pública.

Melo, Marcus. 2002. *Reformas constitucionais no Brasil: Instituições políticas e processo decisório*. Rio de Janeiro: Editora REVAN.

Ministério da Fazenda. 1998. "Reforma tributária: Nova reforma do Ministério da Fazenda." Brasilia: Minifaz. Mimeo.

Murray, Alan, and J. Birnbaum. 1988. "Lawmakers, Lobbyists and the Unlikely Triumph of Tax Reform." *Congress and the Presidency* 15: 28-47.

Myles, John. 1998. "Comments to Weaver." In *Framing the Social Security Debate*, eds. R. Douglas Arnold, Michael J. Graetz, and Alicia Munnel. Washington, D.C.: The Brookings Institution.

North, Douglas. 1990. *Institutions, Institutional Change, and Economic Performance*. Cambridge, UK: Cambridge University Press.

Peters, B. Guy. 1991. *The Politics of Taxation: A Comparative Perspective*. Cambridge, UK: Blackwell.

Pierson, Paul D., and R. Kent Weaver. 1993. "Imposing Losses in Pension Policy." In *Do Institutions Matter? Government Capabilities in the US and Abroad*, eds. R. Kent Weaver and Bert Rockman. Washington, D.C.: The Brookings Institution.

Pierson, Paul. 1996. "Path Dependence and the Study of Politics." Paper presented at the American Political Science Association meeting, San Francisco.

Rezende, Flávio C. 1999. "Administrative Reform, Permanent Failure, and the Problem of External Support: MARE and the Reform of the State Apparatus in Brazil." Cornell University. Ph.D. dissertation.

Rinne, Jeffrey. 2002. "The Politics of Administrative Reform in Menem's Argentina: The Illusion of Isolation." Chapter Two, this volume.

Saint-Martin, Denis. 1998. "The New Managerialism and the Policy Influence of Consultants in Government: An Historical-Institutional Analysis of Britain, Canada and France." *Governance* 11: 37-61.

Samuels, David. 2000. "Concurrent Elections, Discordant Results: Presidentialism, Federalism, and Governance in Brazil." *Comparative Politics* (October): 1-20.

Santos, M.H. Ma. das Graças Rua Castro, and E.M. Machado. 1993. "Interesses sociais, poderes constituídos na política fiscal e tributária dos governos Collor e Itamar Franco." Brasilia: Brasilia National University. Mimeo.

Shepsle, Kenneth. 1985. "The State in Politics: The Relation between Policy and Administration." In *Regulatory Policy and the Social Sciences*, ed. Roger Noll. Berkeley,
Calif.: University of California Press.

Shepsle, Kenneth. 1989. "Studying Institutions: Some Lessons from the Rational Choice
Approach." *Journal of Theoretical Politics* 2: 131-147.

Silva, Pedro Luis Barros, Marcus Melo, and Milko Matijascic. 1998. "Reforma da seguridade
social no brasil." Research Report. Núcleo de Estudos de Políticas Públicas. NEPP/
University of Campinas (UNICAMP).

Sola, Lourdes. 1995. "Estado, regime, fiscal, e ordem monetária." *Revista brasileira de
ciências sociais* 27: 29-59.

Steinmo, Sven. 1993. *Taxation and Democracy: Swedish, British and American Approaches
to Financing the Modern State*. New Haven, Conn.: Yale University Press.

Steinmo, Sven, and Caroline Tolbert. 1998. "Do Institutions Really Matter? Taxation in
Industrialized Democracies." *Comparative Political Studies* (April):165-187.

Stepan, Alfred. 1997. "Toward a New Comparative Analysis of Democracy and Federalism." Paper presented at the Conference on Democracy and Federalism, Oxford
University, June.

Tsebelis, George. 1995. "Decision Making in Political Systems: Veto Players in
Presidentialism, Parliamentarism, Multicameralism, and Multipartism." *British
Journal of Political Science* (July): 289-326.

Ventura, Elvira C. F.; Lizarda Y. Igarasi, and Silvio A. Lima. 1999. "Organização social e
contrato de gestão no contexto da reforma do estado brasileiro." Paper presented at
the Meeting of the National Graduate Association for Reasearch in Administration,
Foz de Igaçu, Brazil, September 19-23.

Weaver, R. Kent, and Bert Rockman, eds. 1993. *Do Institutions Matter? Government
Capabilities in the US and Abroad*. Washington, D.C.: The Brookings Institution.

Weaver, R. Kent. 1998. "The Politics of Pensions: Lessons from Abroad." In *Framing the
Social Security Debate*, eds. R. Douglas Arnold, Michael J Graetz, and Alicia
Munnel. Washington, D.C.: The Brookings Institution.

Weir, Margaret. 1993. "Ideas and the Politics of Bounded Rationality." In *Structuring
Politics: Historical Institutionalism in Comparative Analysis*, eds. S. Steinmo, K.
Thelen, and F. Longstreth. Cambridge, UK: Cambridge University Press.

Newspaper Articles

Folha de São Paulo. 1995."Estados fazem exigências para a reforma." August 8.

Folha de São Paulo. 1995. "Governadores cobram detalhes do projeto." August 8.

Folha de São Paulo. 1995. "Fundo de compensação poderá ter RS6 bi." August 10.

Folha de São Paulo. 1998. "Governo apoia a mini-constituinte em 1999." September 19.

Folha de São Paulo. 1998."Reforma tributária: Secretário executivo diz haver espaço para
negociação." March 3.

Folha de São Paulo. 1998."Estados vão definir a reforma tributária."August 7.

Folha de São Paulo. 1999. "Para relator, estados perdem com a proposta." October 7.

Folha de São Paulo. 1999. "Para relator, emenda do governo não passa." November 8.

Gazeta Mercantil. 1995 . "Bresser inicia lobby contra parecer de viana." October 9.

Gazeta Mercantil. 1995. "Porque a reforma tributária é tímida." September 28.

Gazeta Mercantil. 1995. "Bresser ameaça abandonar reforma e 'ir à praia." August 27.

Gazeta Mercantil. 1995. "Relator quer mudar emenda tributária." October 10.

Gazeta Mercantil. 1995. "Sarney aprova medida do governo de priorizar a votação na área econômica." March 29.

Gazeta Mercantil. 1995. "Proposta de mudanças tributárias ainda divide fazenda, planejamento, e receita." March 8.

Gazeta Mercantil. 1995. "Lula fica irritado com os governadores." October 16.

Gazeta Mercantil. 1995. "Reforma administrativa: Governo endurece. Até a renegociação das dívidas dos estados entra na barganha." October 17.

Gazeta Mercantil. 1996. "Parecer mantém a estabilidade do servidor." July 10.

Gazeta Mercantil. 1996. "Governo fará emenda contra a estabilidade." July 11.

Gazeta Mercantil. 1996. "Fim da estabilidade divide base governista." July 12.

Gazeta Mercantil. 1996 "FHC já admite acordo para estabilidade." July 16.

Gazeta Mercantil. 1996. "Acordo facilita dispensa do servidor (Líderes governistas fecham propostas flexibilizando estabilidade do funcionário público)." July 18.

Gazeta Mercantil. 1996. "Líderes recuam e mantêm estabilidade." July 21.

Gazeta Mercantil. 1997. "Reforma administrativa: FHC aceita alterações." April.

Gazeta Mercantil. 1997. "FEF transforma-se em moeda de troca contra lei Kandir." September 3.

Gazeta Mercantil. 1998. "Congresso derruba R$ bilhões do ajuste fiscal." December 3.

Gazeta Mercantil. 1999."STF derruba contribuição de inativos." October 15.

*Gazeta Mercantil.*1999. "Um exemplo discutível de justiça." June 1.

Gazeta Mercantil. 1999. "Ações afetam 95% da arrecadação com servidores." November 7.

Gazeta Mercantil. 1999. "Secretários insistem em taxar inativos." October 11.

Gazeta Mercantil. 1999. "Fator previdenciário é aprovado." October 7.

Gazeta Mercantil. 2000. "Lei de responsabilidade fiscal é aprovada." May 26.

Gazeta Mercantil. 2000. "Lei de responsabilidade fiscal é aprovada, mas deputados aliviam penas."April 12.

O Globo. 1995. "FHC pede apoio de governadores." September 29.

O Globo. 1995. "Reforma tributária em clima de guerra" August 1.

O Globo. 1995. "Planalto busca apoio de governadores." August 24.

O Globo. 1995. "Briga entre PSDB e PFL atrasa reforma." August 3.

O Globo. 1999. "STF decide se servidores inativos vão contribuir." September 30.

O Globo. 1995. "Governadores querem mudar projeto." e "Perda dos estados ainda preocupa." August 23.

O Globo. "Governadores querem controlar o IVA." July 26.

O Estado de São Paulo. 1998. "Tática do planalto será atrasar ajuste tributário." February 8.

O Estado de São Paulo. 1998 . "Possibilidade de reeleição reduz resistência a projeto." May 19.

O Estado de São Paulo. 1998. "Relator já admite assumir proposta de parente." April 12.

O Estado de São Paulo. 1998. "Fazenda e câmara mantêm divergências sobre o tema." March 11.

O Estado de São Paulo. 1998. "Estados resistem a aceitar propostas sobre tributos." May 14.

O Estado de São Paulo. 1998."Mudança tributária gradual pode ser mais viável." April 14

O Estado de São Paulo. 1998. "Estados resistem a aceitar propostas sobre tributos." May 14

O Estado de São Paulo. 2000. "A revolução fiscal apenas começou." February 13.

Veja magazine, May 2, 1997.

Chapter Nine

REFORMS IN THE ADMINISTRATION OF JUSTICE IN LATIN AMERICA: OVERVIEW AND EMERGING TRENDS

James E. Mahon, Jr.[1]

In the 1990s, as part of a remarkable surge of legal and administrative renovation around the world, Latin America saw the acceleration and broadening of efforts to reform the justice sector. In Latin America, as elsewhere, institutional reforms have been linked to both the return, or, in some cases, the establishment of electoral democracy and the countries' status as emerging markets. To an unprecedented degree, international actors from advanced industrial countries have funded and advised these reforms. The primary funding sources have included lawyers and academics, in addition to government aid organizations, such as the United States Agency for International Development (USAID), international non-governmental organizations (INGOs), and intergovernmental organizations (IGOs) (Carothers 1996; Carothers 1998). Among the last, international financial institutions (IFIs), primarily the World Bank and the Inter-American Development Bank (IDB), have become increasingly prominent in supporting reforms of justice sector institutions in Latin America.

In recent years, important intellectual currents have recognized the significance of a well-functioning justice system as crucial to the consolidation of democracy and a market economy (for a good summary, see Rubio et al. 1994, Chapter One). The political left has revalued legal equality and administrative efficiency. Democratic reformers have bemoaned the fact that in the arenas where most people deal with power — in their daily contact with the police, bureaucracy, or courts — they often face officials who, if they are present at all, disdain, extort, or harm them without being held accountable (Castañeda 1996; Rosenberg 1994; O'Donnell 1995). Other scholars have emphasized the bad economic effects of complex and overabundant laws, unstable regulations, and arbitrary, grasping states (most famously, DeSoto 1987; North 1990). Drawing on the new institutional economics and the law and economics movements, proponents of this school of thought have argued that economic analysis of legal disputes can aid in arriving at efficient decisions and in writing "good" laws, that is, laws conducive to economic development. These same scholars assert that the goodness of a country's laws and institutions explain much of its economic performance and, thus, its level of development.[2] In the absence of adequate judicial institutions, a lack of trust stifles business initiatives and attenuates commercial networks.[3]

In regions with a civil law tradition, judges tend to act more like functionaries than they do in common-law jurisdictions. In the latter, we might expect many similarities between judicial reform and measures aimed at the executive branch, and, to a great extent, the expectation is borne out. Governments have pursued both executive and judicial administrative reforms widely and seriously in the region, especially since about 1990. Many reforms of the justice sector also fit usefully under the headings used in the opening chapter to describe those in the executive: civil-service, managerial, or democratizing reforms. In one important sense, from the standpoint of the international financial institutions supporting them, reforms of justice administration are also rightly called second-stage reforms, appropriate sequels to stabilization and structural adjustment. They could also be considered part of a second stage in the building of democracy, to be undertaken once the electoral process has become institutionalized.

Important differences, however, also exist. Reforms of the justice sector often express new ideas about justice itself: substantive changes to constitutions and codes, which go beyond questions of administration. With regard to timing, several major justice sector reforms in the region responded not to fiscal crises but to political ones, thereby preceding economic liberalization. Thus, to refer to these early initiatives as second-stage reforms would be somewhat misleading, if this is to imply a connection to structural adjustment. Still, as I will argue in the second half of this chapter, the label may become more accurate as time goes on if IFI sponsorship assumes a more central role and reforms with economic purposes take precedence over those aimed at consolidating democracy.

What conditions bring about reforms in the administration of justice? While this chapter, confined to Latin America, covers a broader range of cases, its conclusions support several hypotheses mentioned in the editors' introduction. The presence of a large middle class, especially one rooted more in the private sector than in state employment, seems to favor judicial reform. Partisan balance and coherent parties also appear to make reform more likely. Like reforms of the executive sector, justice-sector reforms rely on small, committed change teams. These teams may be located in the ministry of justice, economic ministries, or the highest court, but they invariably need presidential support to succeed. Hence, the programmatic commitments of these reformers and of the president clearly affect outcomes. Finally, this chapter supports the claim that in many Latin American countries international agencies have acted as much more than providers of best practice wisdom. They have often initiated the reform process where domestic initiative was lacking, and governments have frequently used an IFI imprimatur to reassure foreign investors of progress in establishing juridical security.

This chapter begins with a summary of the *status quo ante*, highlighting major problems with the justice sector in Latin America. The second section describes recent reforms. The third, drawing on rough comparative measures of the degree of successful implementation and the relative importance of domestic versus foreign initiative, suggests explanations for reform. The next section describes emerging patterns, suggesting that reforms aimed at institutionalizing market relations, especially those important to foreign investors, may become more important than those aimed directly at consolidating civil liberties and democracy. The final section considers some of the issues that arise when we try to describe and assess the international influence on reform.

PROBLEMS IN THE JUSTICE SECTOR IN LATIN AMERICA

The need for reform arises in large part because justice systems in Latin America have generally enjoyed very little public esteem. Surveys of popular attitudes in the early 1990s showed massive dissatisfaction, with the many respondents complaining that judicial processes are corrupt, open to party influence, formalistic, inaccessible, and slow.[4] Real problems, some of long-standing, lurk behind these complaints. With some exceptions, the following picture describes the principal problem areas (Hammergren 1998a, 16-21; Rico and Salas 1992, 6-8; Prillaman 2000; Rubio et al. 1994).

Corruption

The rich and the military historically have been able to manipulate or ignore the formal civilian justice system. Additionally, in this century, political parties have often further undermined the system's integrity by filling jobs in the justice sector on the basis of partisan patronage, likely deepening problems of corruption, which now range from tips for routine administrative tasks to the selling of judicial decisions. Partisan judges are also frequently accused of failing to provide equal justice to their political opponents.

Dependence and Formalism

At the national political level, the executive has dominated the judiciary since Independence in nearly every country of the region. This situation is only partly a consequence of the civil law system, which tends to restrict the spaces for adjudication by precedent and for judicial review (a defining aspect of the difference between civil and common law systems). Executive domination has manifested itself not only in externally instigated hirings and firings, but also in self-imposed restrictions on sectoral power aimed at preserving an independence confined to issues of no political significance. This lack of judicial independence has also been an important cause of excessive formalism, in which judges look for technicalities in order to avoid difficult or politically salient questions of jurisprudence.[5]

Failure to Serve the Majority

Apart from obviously corrupt monetary influences on the legal process and despite constitutions that enshrine equality before the law and legal aid, most justice systems in Latin America do not serve the poor majority. High fees and bribes, long delays, and, in the countryside, long distances reduce effective access to the justice system. In Venezuela, most estimates place 85 percent of the population outside the formal judicial system (Ungar 1996, 4n8). In Mexico, a similar figure has been calculated for the Federal District alone (Rubio et al. 1994, 132 n1, citing Valdés 1993). When the poor do have contact with the system, it is almost always as defendants. Here, they face a strong likelihood of a several-year prison term before trial. Judges across the region have tended to interpret preventive detention and bail statutes very strictly (Rico and Salas 1992, 30-31). As existing case backlogs ensure a long wait for trial, the majority of prisoners in Latin American jails have been accused but not convicted.

Congestion

The problem of rising court backlogs has become much more acute in the last 15 years, placing the quality of justice at stake. Prison congestion damages public respect for the system: "Justice delayed is justice denied" is becoming a common expression and a widely accepted norm. Of course, this affects not only criminal cases, but also civil and commercial ones. The delayed disposition of a commercial debtor-creditor case can ruin the creditor and often encourages various types of creative and unpleasant extralegal solutions. In the commercial sphere, some of the problems result from liberal economic reforms, which, by broadening the sphere of the market, increase the number of legal disputes (Dakolias 1999, 25).

To what extent can these four problems be ascribed to deficient administration? Certainly, in the justice sector, "pure" administration does not exist in any real form. Its goodness or badness is a result of priorities that are decided and acted upon politically. In a broader sense, however, all of the justice sector's problems might be considered administrative, as each is mirrored, in some form, in executive branches across the region.

Many connections between administration and performance are evident. Political appointees usually do not make the best or most efficient judges, their lack of independence notwithstanding. Low budgets and inefficiency mean less money for legal aid or additional courts, while corruption imposes additional costs not covered even when legal aid is available. As noted above, congestion affects the quality of judicial work. It may force judges, especially those in the upper levels of the system, to spend more time administering courts than deciding cases. In a context of an inherited emphasis on written procedures, judges have perversely responded to congestion by delegating effective control to nonprofessional staff, who compose the case summaries often tendentiously or ineffectively (Hammergren 1998a, 16).

JUSTICE SECTOR REFORMS AND THEIR CHARACTER SO FAR

Given this panorama, it is no surprise that reforms in the administration of justice resemble more general public administration reforms. They aim to promote both effectiveness and efficiency in judicial proceedings, with efficiency conceived not only in terms of the use of sector budget allocations, but also in terms of the costs users of the system incur. Table 1 presents the main reform efforts undertaken in 17 Latin American countries and the main institutional actors associated with them. The second column enumerates the most common reforms since 1982. Judicial councils, separating adjudicative and administrative functions, have been established or given new powers in the majority of countries. In most places, they nominally control not only day-to-day court administration, but also much of what

Table 1.
Major Justice-Sector Reforms in 17 Latin American Countries Since 1982

Country	Reforms-Years*	Main Types of Reform
Argentina	82 computerized case management, civil; 91 commercial (87) 92 criminal code oral procedure 94 constitutional amendments: presidential power 96 ADR	Substantive and Managerial
Bolivia	(91) task force on reform created 94 Ministry of Justice created 98 Judicial Council; (99) procedural code, criminal	Civil Service, Substantive, and Democratizing
Brazil	88 Constitution: judicial review, procedural reform; 95 small claims courts	Substantive, Democratizing (Civil Service)
Chile	(89) 92 computerized management (91-96) Judicial Council; judiciary school (98) 99-02, criminal code, procedural code; Public Ministry	Substantive, Managerial (Civil Service)
Colombia	80s ADR 91 Constitution: prosecutor, criminal code reform; Judicial Council reformed; reduction of civil delays	Substantive, Managerial, (Civil Service)
Costa Rica	89 Constitutional Court 94 judicial career strengthened 93-96 administrative reforms, Judicial Council	Managerial, Civil Service, Substantive (Democratizing)
Dom. Rep.	94 constitutional amendments: Judicial Council, judiciary school; 98 reform task force	Managerial, Democratizing
Ecuador	(92) constitutional reform: Judicial Council, increase in judiciary budget, training (95) ADR 98 Constitution: Judicial Council	Civil Service, Managerial, Democratizing

Notes: *Years (proposed) or enacted; reform types in parentheses denote significant reforms of those types before 1982; ADR = alternative dispute resolution.
Sources: USAID 1991-2000; NCSC 1996; WB 1994; IDB 1997, 1999; Dakolias 1999; Hammergren 1998; Arantes 1997; *FBIS*, 1982-99; LCHR/PROVEA1996; LCHR 2000a, 2000b; Dezelay and Garth 1999; Comisión Andina de Juristas 1999; interviews.

Table 1. —continued

Country	Reforms-Years*	Main Types of Reform
El Salvador	91 constitutional amendments: Judicial Council, judicial training 94-95 Supreme Court reform; family, juvenile codes reformed 98 criminal procedure code reform: accusatory	Substantive, Managerial, Democratizing
Guatemala	(92) 94 criminal procedure: oral, accusatory; public defender created 96 Reform Study Commission 98 (reversed 99) judicial career	Substantive, Managerial
Honduras	93 Public Ministry created 95 Inspector General's Office created (99) procedural code reform, criminal: oral	Substantive, Civil Service, Democratizing
Mexico	94 (Fed) Supreme Court reformed; judicial review broadened; Judicial Council	Substantive, Managerial, Civil Service
Panama	90 Judicial Council-like separation of admin. tasks 91 criminal procedure code; creation of public defender 93 judiciary school	Substantive, Democratizing, Managerial
Paraguay	(92 Constitution) 94 Judicial Council, administrative tasks separated; judicial career	Managerial, Substantive
Peru	(91) code of procedure, criminal: oral 93 Constitution: Judicial Council stronger, new civil procedure code 95-98 administration; loss of independence	Substantive, Civil Service 94- Managerial
Uruguay	89 procedural code, civil: oral 92 computerized case management	Substantive, Managerial (Civil Service), (Democratizing)
Venezuela	(90) administrative and code revisions 93 administration, judicial training 94 Justices of the Peace 96 criminal procedure code 97 Supreme Court reformed 98 ADR- arbitration	Managerial, Civil Service

Notes: *Years (proposed) or enacted; reform types in parentheses denote significant reforms of those types before 1982; ADR = alternative dispute resolution.

defines the judicial career — lower-level nominations, judicial discipline, and justice sector budgeting (Fierro and Zamudio 1996; Salas and Rico, n.d.). Code revisions have also been quite common. Most have begun with criminal procedures, and many of these have introduced oral arguments and some adversarial elements. Commercially oriented alternative dispute resolution mechanisms (ADRs), involving arbitration and mediation services associated with chambers of commerce, have been successfully promoted across the region. Many countries have undertaken computerization of court calendars and records as a part of programs aimed at advancing active case management, an area in which international agencies have developed a great deal of expertise.

With regard to administration, recent justice sector reforms can be usefully described under the three rubrics noted in the opening chapter: civil-service, democratizing, and managerial reforms. In the first class belong the region's oldest reform movements: efforts to establish a judicial career with appointments based on some objective criterion of merit, training programs for judges and support personnel, measures to place court administration in the hands of professionals other than judges, and judicial stability in office but with effective discipline against clearly defined malfeasance. Judicial councils have been prominent here. Such reforms should improve administrative efficiency and provide institutional insulation from political pressures coming from the legislature and, in particular, the executive branch (Wheeler 1979, 140).

The second group of reforms includes measures to broaden access to the justice system and make it more accountable to the majority of the population. These reforms include broader provision of free legal aid, easier avenues for obtaining injunctions or filing *amparo* claims (claims for judicial protection), the creation of local justices of the peace or other affordable alternative dispute resolution mechanisms, and the popular election of lower-level judges. The last type has included efforts to manage cases actively, outsourcing of some support activities, organizational changes that make it easier to measure judicial productivity, and the use of information technology. The main goal of most of these reforms has been to reverse the trend toward increased delays in case disposition.

This threefold typology, however, does not cover every reform of the justice sector. Many recent revisions of legal codes and Constitutions must be considered substantive, and not just administrative, changes. The most important of these involves reforming codes of procedure to allow oral trials, to permit judge interpellation of witnesses during testimony, and to give the system more of an adversarial character in other ways. The main intent has been to make court proceedings more public and transparent. In many countries, this reform began with criminal rather than civil courts, even though it was more complicated to reform criminal than civil procedure (Vargas in NCSC 1996, 55). Other examples of reform include the Bolivian initiative to eliminate debtors' prison and several countries' moves to prevent confessions obtained by torture.

While efforts to promote judicial independence might require civil-service type changes, independence is also a substantive concept. In general, as these examples suggest, substantive reforms reflect changes in prevailing ideas about the definition of justice. Though they may affect administration, as when moving to adversarial procedure implies an enhanced role for the Public Ministry, they are not primarily administrative reforms. (Reform types appear in the last column of Table 1.)

It is also no surprise that these goals may conflict with one another, as seen in the tradeoff between access (democratization) and speed (efficient management). Efforts to increase the former, by eliminating fees or by reforms that make *amparo* or *tutela* (judicial protection) suits easier, may dramatically increase congestion. Speed may also be at odds with transparency in some spheres, at least during the early stages of reform: the introduction of oral procedures in some Argentine federal criminal courts produced a backlog seven times higher than in unreformed courts (USAID 1994a, 5). Another area of potential conflict arises as democratization, in the form of elections for lower-level judges, violates the usual civil-service connotation of "merit" while opening the door to political interference (Wheeler 1979, 140-41). As managerial reformers have often pointed out, the traditional civil service structure may not yield the most efficient results; however, by the same token, some managerial reforms, such as judicial councils, may open up the judiciary to a new form of politicization through the control of judicial careers (Saez 1998, sec. VIII; Hammergren 1998a, 8-13, 271; for discussion, see Pásara 1996, 50-52). For these reasons, one observer has persuasively argued that reforms will not succeed unless they advance on several fronts simultaneously. Otherwise, "negative synergies" develop as, for example, a lack of independence compromises democratizing efforts or inefficiency leads democratizing reforms to have the opposite effect — a clogged, frustrating, and ultimately inaccessible system (Prillaman 2000).

A broader conflict inhabits most reform processes, as well. Judiciaries are supposed to be conservative; "their contribution to the maintenance of a legitimate order lies in their lesser vulnerability to short-term fluctuations in social preferences and the relative power of social groups" (Hammergren 1998b, 3). When reform originates from outside the judiciary, it may serve to weaken judicial independence, one of the very things reformers are seeking to promote (for discussion on Brazil, see Prillaman 2000). Ministerial reformers and their international allies may sustain, in form if not in content or intention, a powerful tradition of executive meddling that has weakened judiciaries. This reflects another important difference between justice sector reforms and those focused on the executive branch.

EXPLAINING THE DEGREE OF REFORM: DOMESTIC AND INTERNATIONAL INFLUENCES

Assessing the degree of recent reform requires skepticism about the degree of progress actually achieved in the welter of reform initiatives. Laws and institutions might express aspirations or the cynical manipulation of domestic and foreign opinion without regulating everyday practice (Karst and Rosenn 1975, 57-66).[6] As Hammergren (1998a) cautions, a lot of the new institutions have been merely cases of "repackaging," or they soon find themselves moribund. Some important aspects of implementation, such as the degree of judicial independence, are understandably hard to measure, though, and real changes take a long time to

Table 2. Major Donors, Extent of Reforms, and Prime Movers of Reform

Country	Major External Donors, Projects, and Amounts			Extent of Reform	Prime mover(s)
	USAID	World Bank	IDB/ MIF		
Argentina	90-94 procedural code, criminal: oral; administration, ADR	93 sector review, LTA 20 98 model courts, administration, training (00) strengthen Judicial Council	94 sector review 97 administrative reform pilot, 7 98 legal digest, crime-fighting, ADR, 10.5	Mod	Both
Bolivia	88-93 criminal code; public defender, Judicial Council, pretrial release, administration, ADR	92-94 LTA 93 prepare reforms 0.5 96 administration, civil ADR, constitutional reform, Ministry of Justice 11.5 (00) judicial school, access	95 administration, code form; labor law 10	Mod.	Int'l
Brazil	98 organized crime task force	none	none	Low	Dom
Chile	none	none	none	High	Dom
Colombia	88-92 Public Order Courts, access to justice ADR; 92 training, equipment 36	(00) civil procedure code, other law reform, training, ADR 10	95 Attorney General administration; reduce delays, 9.4 95 ADR commercial 98 criminal courts, 50	Mod	Both
Costa Rica	88-96 administration, training, computers, ADR	94 administration, criminal procedure and Supreme Court	95	High	Both
Dom. Rep.	97 administration, judicial independence, public defender; 98 pilot program	98 administration, access to justice 15	97 civil society support, property titles administration, 32	Low	Int'l
Ecuador	93- coordination of assistance, constituency building; 96- access to justice ADR	94 sector review 97 management, administration access to justice, ADR 11	96 ADR, 0.7 98 judicial training, code revision, prosecutor, 2.5	Low	Both

Notes: Donor programs by year approved or (year proposed to begin); amounts in $US millions; ADR = alternative dispute resolution; LTA = legal technical assistance. Extent of Reform: low/moderate/high. Prime movers: domestic, international, or both. MIF is the Multilateral Investment Fund of the Inter-American Development Bank. "None" = no substantial reform programs funded by these donors.

Table 2. —continued

El Salvador	84 criminal procedure code 85 administration, public defender, oral adversarial procedure, access to justice	(00) administration, access to justice 12	96 modernization, reduce juvenile delinquency, 22.2 96 ADR, 0.7	High	Int'l
Guatemala*	86-91 administration, access to justice 93-99 criminal procedure code, training of judges, prosecutors	(98) administration, access to justice, reduce corruption, ADR 33	97 access to justice, administration	Low	Int'l
Honduras	88-97 judicial independence, training, computers, public defender, prosecutor, access to justice, 7 97 code implementation	88 LTA mortgages, 25	96 code revision, administration, access to justice, 8.7 96 ADR, 0.5	Low	Both
Mexico	98 administration	95 LTA financial sector, 19	none	Low	Dom
Panama	90-97 administration, training, career, access to justice 10 99 complement IDB, 3	none	97 commercial ADR 98 administration, information, access to justice ADR	Mod	Both
Paraguay	90-95 administration, procedure (oral), judicial career, ADR	92 public enterprise reform	96 civil registry, 22 98 administration	Low	Int'l
Peru	90-92 human rights, judicial independence, procedural code, ADR	94 sector review 97 civil and commercial court administration; judicial independence, access, 23 (98: terminated)	96 commercial ADR, 1.5 97 access to justice, 20	Low	Int'l
Uruguay	87-91 procedural code: oral; administration	none	95 commercial ADR 97 crime prevention, 12	Mod	Dom
Venezuela	none	92 administration, training, 30; 98 Supreme Court, 5	98 criminal justice administration, prisons, 25	Mod	Both

*Reform aid coordinated by the United Nations.

Sources: USAID 1991-2000; NCSC 1996; WB 1994; IDB 1997, 1999; Dakolias 1999; Hammergren 1998; Arantes 1997; *FBIS*, 1982-99; LCHR/PROVEA1996; LCHR 2000a, 2000b; Dezelay and Garth 1999; Comisión Andina de Juristas 1999; interviews.

develop. Still, the benefits of a rough comparative judgment seem to outweigh the obvious risks.

The next-to-last column in Table 2 gives estimates in the form of a comparative index (low-moderate-high) of how far each country has come in the reform process since the mid-1980s. For example, if a government created a judicial council or appointed new judges but made few other changes in substance or administration, the country would show a "low" index. Dramatic changes in procedure, for example, creating a prosecutor's office, training judges, building new court facilities, and developing new rules for administration, would merit a "high" reform index. As this is a comparative index, high does not necessarily indicate that a justice system has been thoroughly remade. "Moderate" might also describe an ambitious reform agenda that has been seriously undermined by politicization and corruption (such as Argentina under President Carlos Menem) or a narrower one that has stalled (El Salvador). Table 2 shows a high reform index for Chile, thanks mainly to the sweeping criminal code reform in 1999-2000, and Costa Rica, followed by moderate reform achievement in Argentina, Bolivia, Colombia, and several other countries. These rough indices are based not only on the breadth and depth of ongoing initiatives, but also on local press reports and international agency documents describing progress in implementation.

What explains significant reform? Several authors have noted that a crisis seems to be an important cause. The important questions are crisis for whom, and what kind of crisis? In a sense, justice has always been in crisis for the poor. Moreover, fiscal crisis does not seem to be a proximate cause here, in contrast with first-stage reforms. Simply put, the predominant thrust of reform in the justice sector has entailed more government spending, not less, over the short and long terms. Justice sector reform, in contrast with other second-stage reforms of the executive, cannot promise eventual efficiencies in the use of public funds; measures of justice sector efficiency are likely to be confounded by gains or losses in its effectiveness in serving changing public purposes, which today include, among other things, the improvement of private sector efficiency.

What constitutes a crisis relevant to justice reform? Elites accustomed to manipulating or ignoring the system may consider that a crisis exists only when decay has reached the point of potential harm to them. This may come about as a result of strife that threatens to turn the system into an instrument of vengeance or because of a crime wave that the system cannot handle. In Costa Rica and Colombia, the initial concession of judicial autonomy followed civil wars; the 1991 reforms in Colombia, in fact, took place in a context of societal breakdown. In the limited sense just suggested, a sense of crisis may also come about simply as a result of a loss of elite control (Hammergren 1998a).[7] In addition, it may also reflect strong criticism, from inside and outside the institution, of the judiciary's role under dictatorship, as in Chile or Brazil.

Can similar considerations account for the institutionalization of reform over the longer term? In considering the reforms that advance judicial independence domestically, there is some confirmation for Negretto and Ungar's suggestion (1997), that two factors are necessary for judicial independence: first, enough partisan balance to make future benefits from patronage or politicization of the judiciary uncertain (cf. Geddes 1994) and second, effective societal defense of judicial independence, so that true judicial independence — rather than politicization by turns, as parties alternate in government — actually becomes the result.

What are the conditions for this defense? Hammergren's hypothesis (1998a, 264) that justice works better where middle classes are larger (for example, in Costa Rica, Chile, and Uruguay) may be part of the answer. A large middle class would constitute the bearers of the aforementioned sense of crisis in the judiciary. However, in Latin America, a close connection has existed historically between the rise of an urban middle class and the expansion of public employment. This kind of middle class may regard the state less as a rule-maker and more as a patron and thus be less critical of judicial failures. Hence, it may be more appropriate to compare countries in terms of the size of that portion of the middle stratum that is not economically dependent on the state in terms of employment. Such an independent group would be more likely to constitute the kind of critical public that Negretto and Ungar's (1997) analysis indicates is necessary. Here, for example, Colombia, with four major cities and a relatively low ratio of public spending to gross domestic product (GDP), appears to score higher than it would on a measure based simply on GDP per capita or urbanization. Chile, in turn, scores higher than Argentina.

In Costa Rica, the influence of these variables was indirect: they conditioned changes before 1982 that led to a degree of judicial autonomy, and, thus, because justice sector officials are crucial to following through on reform, these same changes enhanced the implementation of judicial autonomy after that date. According to Hammergren, the strong judiciary in the 1949 Constitution was the result of "an effort by each of the conflicting factions to keep it out of the hands of the other" (1998a, 222). This led to the early development of *de facto* judicial careers and, by 1957, an amendment stipulating that 6 percent of the national budget would go to the judicial sector. By the 1980s, as a consequence, the Costa Rican judiciary had the independence, professional identity, and resources to initiate reform itself (Wilson and Handberg 2000). The argument could also be extended to Uruguay in its democratic years.

In Colombia, a 1957 plebiscite ratified the National Front's agreement to grant independence to the Supreme Court and administrative courts, though it was tacitly understood that they would respect partisan balance. The judiciary, able to achieve significant budgetary autonomy only in 1989, was overwhelmed by the country's social and political crises. By then, judicial independence had served mainly to attenuate its response and to create a broad coalition against it. Still, this coalition included reforming lawyers and judges who, as members of the key drafting committee, managed to help preserve the sector's independence, even as it was reorganized under the Constitution of 1991 (Hammergren 1998a).

Some confirmation of the hypothesis can also be found in the 1994 judicial reforms in Mexico. Introduced immediately after Ernesto Zedillo assumed the presidency and passed soon thereafter, these included a federal judicial council with nomination and discipline powers, a re-composition of the Supreme Court, and new judicial review powers for the Court in some constitutional disputes and in *amparo* claims. Though the reforms did not advance judicial independence immediately — they involved sacking the entire Supreme Court — they did create a space for the

Court to overturn acts of Congress, upon a petition of one third of that body, and to overturn administrative law when a claim of unconstitutionality is upheld by eight of 11 justices (Finkel 1997, 5-8; Taylor 1997, 158-164). Finkel argues that political uncertainty among the Zedillo-led technocratic faction of the Institutional Revolutionary Party (Partido Revolucionario Institucional — PRI) and its allies in the National Action Party (Partido Acción Nacional — PAN) motivated the reform. The possibility that PRI would lose hegemony or that an alliance of PRI populists and elements of the Party of the Democratic Revolution (Partido de la Revolución Democrática — PRD) would re-establish it led Zedillo to craft a reform that would institutionalize his priorities. Significant here is not only the fact that the new Court proceeded to help the Zedillo faction and hurt its opponents politically, but also that the reform explicitly excluded the North American Free Trade Agreement (NAFTA) and electoral law, the key bases of economic and PRI continuity (1997, 22-24).

As with executive branch reforms, the programmatic commitments and strategic choices of presidents and change teams appear to matter very much. In Argentina, Menem's determination to politicize the courts ultimately negated much of the benefit of his administration's managerial and democratizing reforms. In Chile, the support of two presidents and the strategic decision to advance reforms on several fronts simultaneously led to a comparatively successful outcome (Prillaman 2000, 111-161).

How important have international agencies been? It is impossible to answer this question with precision. In the first place, measurements may not be reliable, as local government sources have reason to understate their accuracy or usefulness, while the international agencies, at least when justifying their expenditures, may have reason to overstate their importance. Second, international factors may operate obscurely across a wide range of cases, and they may be visibly decisive in none or only a few. If so, their influence might be underestimated.

Yet, many observers agree on the leading role of the international agencies. While the agencies officially describe themselves as supporting various government-proposed projects, to one reformer the agencies' presence "helps explain why, for the first time in Latin America, there exists such a coherent policy on judicial matters in the region, and why the strategies for changes are so strikingly similar among various countries" (Vargas in NCSC 1996, 57). Evidently, international agencies have served as more than just convenient repositories of best-practice institutional wisdom. Another observer has written, "In Latin America it is difficult to identify one government which demonstrated a major interest in reform predating a donor decision to sponsor one" (Hammergren 1998c, 2).[8]

In countries most dependent on foreign initiative, nobody pretends that reforms can become effective and lasting without domestic support and participation. Yet, even in these cases, international agencies also support and have helped to create local non-governmental organization (NGO) counterparts that advocate for reform and scrutinize its implementation. For example, USAID's program in Ecuador included support for the Latin American Development Corporation (Corporación Latinoamericana de la Desarrollo — CLD), the most important advocate of judicial reform. In the mid-1990s, the IDB and World Bank added "civil society" components to their state reform programs to encourage local interlocutors to help set reform goals and, many hope, become effective constituencies for the institutionalization and "ownership" of reforms in the future. Having identified weak societal support as a problem for judicial reform, international agencies have been engaged in remedying it, attempting to translate popular dissatisfaction into local organized advocacy.

The last column on Table 2 refers to "prime movers" in an index of the relative importance of international, as opposed to domestic, actors. It is based on the same sources as Table 1. On this measure, Brazil, Chile, Mexico, and Uruguay showed the greatest relative initiative of domestic actors. In some cases, local efforts were somewhat limited, but foreign-supported ones were even less extensive. Mexico before 2000 fits this description, and Peru has also undertaken several reforms in the last two decades, but foreign assistance was important mainly in the 1960s and has been again since 1994 (Hammergren 1998a, 23). Similarly, in many other countries — Bolivia, El Salvador, Guatemala, for example — very little judicial reform took place until USAID, the World Bank, the United Nations (UN), and/or the IDB became involved, starting in the late 1980s. (It should be noted that the UN's help was especially important in Guatemala.)

We can describe the reform process with reference to several key actors, beginning with the judicial institutions, the executive, and the international agencies. Reform stands the best chance when all three are on board, along with a fourth heretofore less prominent actor, civil society, which keeps the executive focused on the task (Hammergren 1998c). The executive can carry out reform, it seems, with little participation from judges or foreign agencies, as it did in Mexico in 1994-1995 (Garcia Ramírez 1999). However, such reform is both difficult and damaging to judicial independence. Reform can begin with a crusading minister of justice who gains some allies within the judiciary and draws on the support of international agencies, as happened in Bolivia, but it may falter when the crusader steps down. Isolated reformers in the judicial sector, in alliance with external donors, can, at the very least, initiate reforms, as in El Salvador in the 1990s or Venezuela during 1993-1994, but their implementation may later face political obstacles (Hammergren 1998a, 271; LCHR/ PROVEA 1996). A group of reforming judges, in alliance with civil society organizations and with a little foreign help, can also lead the process, as was done in Chile. Even in this relatively favorable case, though, reform has taken a long time.

EMERGING TRENDS IN JUSTICE REFORM

At the 1995 Montevideo conference on judicial reform, World Bank consultant Edgardo Buscaglia expressed his serious concern:

> We might imagine important improvements in the judicial services provided in commercial courts, used by firms linked to foreign investors. But if we do not come face to face with the lack of access to justice among the broad, marginalized sectors of society — where local vested interests and regional *caciquismo* [political bosses' domination] prevail — this will impede any further strengthening of liberal democracy in the region (IDB 1997, 34).[9]

Coming from Buscaglia, an expert on this topic and a fellow at the Hoover Institution, this warning deserves our attention.

Is this concern regarding the lack of broad access to justice justified? Several factors compel us to expect the future of judicial reform in Latin America to look different from the past, particularly from the period before 1992. First, a shift in international leadership in the support of these programs has taken place, with the IDB and the World Bank assuming the role of a weakened USAID. Second, governments, as part of an overall strategy to maintain growth and macroeconomic balance, have become acutely aware of the need to soothe investor fears about legal predictability and transparency. Additionally, in criminal law, the formerly dominant concern with human rights has been largely replaced by a fear of crime. Let us consider each in turn.

The Passing of External Leadership from USAID to the IDB and World Bank

USAID was the first important external funding source in the recent wave of judicial and legal reforms in Latin America.[10] Beginning in 1984, under the rubric of "administration of justice," the agency focused on the training of judicial personnel, revision of legal codes, efforts to improve court administration and data collection, assistance to police, and prison construction, as well as popular access to justice, including legal aid and the introduction of alternative dispute resolution (ADR) mechanisms (Table 1; Costello in NCSC 1995, 153; Vaky in IDB 1997, 435; Younger 1996, 3-4; and Ungar 1996, 7-10). These efforts expanded in the early 1990s, especially after 1992, as the Clinton administration broadened USAID's focus on access to justice. However, since the advent of a Republican majority in the U.S. Congress in 1995, USAID has undergone major cuts, just as the World Bank and IDB have been expanding their state reform activities (Table 2). By 1997, the IDB had surpassed the World Bank in lending for state reform programs throughout the hemisphere, and both banks' lending exceeded the amount granted by USAID (USAID 1997 CP; interviews, IDB).

For the multilateral banks, the current state reform movement is not only unusually ambitious, it also extends well beyond their traditional activities.[11] Beginning with a concern for governance, arising from experiences in Africa, the World Bank has taken on state modernization projects in Latin America, Eurasia, and Africa (World Bank 1995a; Frischtak 1994; and Rowat, Malik, and Dakolias 1995).[12] The Bank entered the game in earnest after a 1990 decision by its senior counsel that justified lending for institutional reform as integrally connected to the development mission of the Bank's charter (Shihata in Rowat, Malik, and Dakolias 1995, 219ff). The IDB, which has been less constrained by such considerations, began to emphasize this priority under the leadership of Enrique Iglesias in 1991. The proposition that "the renovation of the state cannot be achieved through isolated efforts of modernization that overlook important aspects of the government, the legislature, or the judiciary" (Tomassini 1994) has guided the IDB. Officials at the two banks have also said that state reform was next on their agenda simply because legal problems were now more visible and it was now feasible to attack them, as most governments had stabilized prices and reformed economic policies (interviews, July 1996).[13]

Official IFI documents, as might be expected, given their economic purposes, argue the justification for judicial reform most strongly in institutional-economic terms. One World Bank publication asserts, "The credible protection of property rights through a well functioning and transparent court system is a key element for encouraging investment and ensuring the sustainability of the new economic regime" (Burki and Edwards 1996, 13).[14] Similarly, in its governability program in Bolivia, the IDB sought to strengthen the juridical and institutional framework in order to encourage private investment, especially by making public policies more effective and legally bound, raising economic confidence, and, therefore, increasing the level of investment.[15] Unofficially, the picture is more complicated. IFI project staff sympathize with the human rights agenda. The banks also possess significant autonomy to promote changes in justice systems beyond the areas directly connected to trade and investment, based on expertise, funding, and a broad interpretation of their mandates. A great deal of overlap also exists between the USAID and IFI priorities regarding oral adversarial procedure, judicial councils, and computerization.[16]

Still, while the effect of the new IFI prominence is complicated and difficult to predict, it is likely to move the reform agenda toward economic areas. IFI charters can be reinterpreted only so far, and even in the best of cases, institutional reforms are slow to develop and hard to evaluate. If institutional reform programs show meager success, external criticism could push the banks to re-emphasize their traditional missions.

The Justice Sector and International Investors

For some governments, judicial reform is part of a deliberate strategy to soothe investors' anxieties about the legal environment. For example, according to the director of the office of Mexico's Supreme Court Chief Justice, the 1994 reforms were motivated by a desire to provide greater transparency to investors in the areas of trade law, taxes, and patents (Finkel 1997, 18). In 1991, Bolivian President Jaime Paz Zamora called for judicial reform "not just for ethical reasons," but also to attract investments requiring a "trustworthy system" (*FBIS Latin America*, May 29, 1991). More recently, Paraguay's interim President, Luis Gonzales Macchi, said he would give priority to judicial reform because "... this is the only road we can offer to foreign investors." He promised "a country of rules, a country of order" (*Journal of Commerce*, May 7, 1999). This reasoning, moreover, may respond more to foreign than domestic investors, in part because powerful locals have other mechanisms to achieve their goals. Buscaglia observes that while the international financial community is "ever more preoccupied with judicial reform" and has local allies, many locals still profit from a lack of the rule of law (1995, 33-34).[17] Luis Pásara echoes this sentiment, noting that international capital needs further transparency because it is "less skilled at moving in the corridors of local power" (1996, 158).[18]

In this context, governments may turn to IFIs not only for advice and support, but also in order to give their assurances of transparency the additional credibility that comes from tying them to IFI conditions. In the words of the *1997 Annual Report* of the International Monetary Fund (IMF):

It was clear, Directors agreed, . . . that external financing, both official and private, was tied closely to issues of governance. . . . [T]he Board also noted that country authorities were increasingly looking to the Fund for assistance to support their efforts to improve governance through strengthening both their institutional structures and their administrative procedures (1997, 41).

One can infer that at least some country authorities have come to the following conclusion: while it may be a good thing, in the eyes of the foreign investor, to improve country governance, it is even more attractive to investors for the IMF to supervise that improvement.

The most prominent example involves Argentina. In July 1997, the IMF and Argentina agreed to a loan conditioned on reforms of governance, including tax and judicial administration and budget transparency (*New York Times*, July 15, 1997). The Argentine government reportedly sought the agreement not because it needed or planned to use the money, but in order to make its commitments public and binding while tapping IMF expertise. As the *Times* reporter commented, "Presumably, [the 1997 loan agreement] would also attract more foreign investment since the changes sought by the IMF would provide more protection for business" (*New York Times*, July 15, 1997). The World Bank's subsequent project summary for Argentina's judicial reform pilot loan described its goals in similar terms: "These reforms are geared towards institution building required to reduce poverty, improve governance, and solidify credibility and access to international private capital markets."[19] Still, we should not overstate the power of such apparently self-imposed conditionality; by the end of the decade, the Argentine government had fulfilled few of its promises.

IFI involvement does not necessarily mean that governments are pursuing reform in order to spur foreign investment or that they are pursuing reform at all, but a lack of IFI involvement does not mean that they are ignoring investor concerns, either. Especially with regard to arrangements like Argentina's 1997 agreement with the Fund, for some governments, the domestic political costs will be greater and more certain than the economic benefits. What has changed since the 1980s is that governments now see judicial reform as a way to impress foreign investors, if not with immediate results, then at least with good intentions.

Changes in Priorities for Criminal Justice

As countries emerged from civil war (El Salvador, Guatemala, and Nicaragua) or dictatorship (Argentina, Brazil, Chile, Panama, Paraguay, Uruguay) over the course of the 1980s, a key concern in justice sector reforms was to protect human rights, especially civil liberties. In administrative terms, this meant establishing independent checks on presidential and military power, often including ombudsmen or special procurators. These changes generally had well-organized domestic and international backing, both from NGOs and from agencies such as USAID and the UN. Even though an effective crusade for justice reform can still bring political and human rights gains and NGOs are still strong, there have been important changes since the judicial reform movement began.[20]

Chiefly, the urban middle and upper classes now worry less about human rights and civil liberties and more about crime. In El Salvador, for example:

The new laws are described in the media as "made in Switzerland" and totally inappropriate for El Salvador's "tropical" social reality. They are said to tie the hands of the police by imposing too many due process guarantees. In a Gallup poll of 1,200 Salvadorans carried out between August and October of 1999, 7 out of 10 respondents said they believe the laws protect criminals more than victims (IDB, 1999, "Justice for Whom?" IDB web site).

El Salvador's situation is not unique. Vocal opposition to democratizing reforms of codes and administration exists in many other countries. As Hammergren puts it, "As the countries have moved out of an era of rampant and dramatic human rights abuses, the urgency that might have been felt by the ordinary public diminished, replaced by concerns with corruption, impunity of common criminals, or the apparent irrelevance of the ordinary legal processes" (1998a, 272). Additionally, in the poor neighborhoods affected most directly by crime, mafia-style dispute resolution and lynchings have dramatized the growing gulf between the urban masses and the formal justice system.

Some democratizing reforms may be particularly vulnerable. Despite the dissatisfaction registered in opinion polls, the public has rarely effectively demanded any kind of judicial reform in Latin America. Pásara describes the average citizen as "passive and disorganized" on the subject, someone who "finds himself at the mercy of the administration of justice without being able to modify the machinery" (IDB 1997, 169; see also Vargas in NCSC 1996, 68; William E. Davis, personal communication, May 1998).[21] Second, tradeoffs between the goals of increasing access and reducing backlogs are real, and some of these might become especially controversial during a crime wave. Given that judges already consider most indigent defendants dangerous enough to warrant setting unreachable bail, the provision of effective free legal counsel to such people would often be criticized as helping criminals clog the courts at public expense. These attitudes could derail any reforms of criminal justice that lack a clear link to crime fighting. They may encourage reformers to turn to pursuing measures closely linked with commerce and investment, or, indeed, to pursue crime reduction in the name of investor confidence.

In summary, three trends — the assumption of external leadership by the World Bank and IDB, the use of judicial reform to spur foreign investment, and a growing fear of crime — seem to presage a growing emphasis on reforms with a strong economic aspect, while not necessarily justifying pessimism about the rule of law in Latin America. The same reforms would also help consolidate both democracy and a market economy in a host of other important areas, including judicial honesty and knowledge, sectoral independence, legal transparency and certainty, and prudent speed in the disposition of cases. Corresponding reforms include the training and merit-based selection of judges, the prohibition of unilateral or *ex parte* communication (between judges and only one of the parties at trial), judicial councils, the expansion and computerization of law archives and official digests, computerized case management, ADRs, and oral and adversarial procedures.[22]

In addition, these trends may be compatible with a simultaneous "judicialization of politics," whereby political and societal actors discover the courts as a powerful resource or as a way to avoid dealing frontally with controversial issues (Smulovitz 1995; Faro de Castro 1997). Judicialization of many issues might well take place at the highest levels of the national or federal court system at the same time as reforms focused mainly on improving the efficiency of commercial dispute resolution.

More controversially and mainly for certain commercial cases, the new economic emphasis may lead to the fragmentation of court systems, resulting in speedier, more specialized, or more transparent adjudication. ADRs, for example, offer the reformer the prospect of quick results. In recent years, the most enthusiastic and effective practitioners of ADR have been business groups. The Bogotá Chamber of Commerce, which has the most active conciliation center in Colombia (Davis and Crohn in NCSC 1996, 78-81), is a good example.[23] The IDB's Multilateral Investment Fund (MIF) has set up similar projects in several other countries in the wake of the Bogotá program's success (see Table 2). In a similar spirit, the World Bank has sponsored the creation of separate debt recovery courts in Asia, designed to bypass the clogged regular courts. Regarding Latin America, a Bank official suggested in 1995 that with the delays in the rest of the system, it may be appropriate to establish separate courts to handle cases of antitrust under new competition policy statutes (Rowat in Faundez 1997, 122). Some fear that this would divert the political impetus for broad reform, leading to a two-tiered justice system (Cranston in Faundez 1997, 249). Taking a more optimistic approach, others might argue that reforms would spread as techniques diffused and the example of transparency caught on, even if the reforms were confined to commercial areas at first (William E. Davis, personal communication, May 1998).

A final point in favor of an optimistic position concerns the length of time it takes for justice sector reforms to become effective. After all, equality before the law took centuries to be relatively well established in Western Europe, and even today in the United States it is far from being realized in practice for all citizens. In Latin America, a region in which states have shrunk but social challenges have grown, the direction of reform today is unmistakably toward the delivery of more transparent, speedy, and equal justice. Such reforms begin by changing institutions, but they are neither effective nor durable if they do not change attitudes as well. Frustration at the slow pace of reform, felt by many in civil society and the justice sector itself, indicates that at least some minds have changed and that the ideals of reform are alive, and this may be the most hopeful sign of all.

POSTSCRIPT: THEORIZING INTERNATIONAL INFLUENCES

Insofar as justice sector reform is seen as the consequence of a growing nonstate middle class, partisan balance, and political crisis, it can be understood adequately through the existing literature on the reform of the state. However, I have suggested above that international agencies and investors have been important, too, and here the connection to prevailing ideas about the development of states seems less obvious. It is worth pausing, by way of a postscript, to elaborate on the role of international forces.

It is widely observed that the forces of globalization, especially rising global bond issuance and flows of direct investment, have created strong incentives for countries to conform to international standards in regulating trade, intellectual property, and investment. Whether they call it progress or a "race to the bottom," critics and advocates alike commonly connect policy and institutional reform to this international competition.[24] In fact, for some advocates, an effective tool of institutional reform is the pursuit of other reforms that raise a jurisdiction's exposure to market opinions.[25] Apart from direct IFI influence on the reform agenda, liberal economic reforms have raised governments' sensitivity to international investors, while contributing to the rising caseloads and, thus, the perception of a justice sector in crisis.

How do we understand this analytically? In the sense of international competition driving bureaucratic rationalization and the extension of the rule of law, it recalls Weber and the German school of historical sociology.[26] In another sense, we could understand it with reference to rational-choice models of institutional development in early modern Europe. Theory states that rulers who were fighting wars conceded rights, law, and parliaments to their subjects in exchange for taxes, especially as the subjects began to hold their taxable goods in more mobile forms (Tilly 1975; Levi 1988; Kiser and Hechter 1991; Bates and Lien 1985). The availability of external resources might, in some cases, undermine this bargain, however (Tilly 1985; Centeno 1997, 1569). In other cases, though, it might not do so. Drake (1989) relates the history of the Kemmerer missions in the 1920s, when Princeton economist Edwin Walter Kemmerer, together with friends on Wall Street and in the U.S. Treasury Department, established central banks and offices of the comptroller in several Andean countries. Through these actions, while simultaneously putting the countries back on the gold standard, the missions opened the way for new inflows of U.S. and other foreign capital. Instead of serving to discourage institutional development, the availability of foreign resources encouraged it, for the simple reason that the foreign investors were able to tie institutional change to the use of these resources under the direction of a respected North American expert. Foreign investors, not domestic investors, were the state's key counterparts in a resources-for-institutions bargain. Today, the IFIs try to play the same role Kemmerer did, mediating the exchange between investors and governments.[27]

A final way to understand the influence of globalization draws on the conclusions of the last section of this chapter. The most successful single kind of judicial reform in Latin America has probably been the adoption of alternative dispute-resolution, principally mediation, in commercial cases. Learning from the success of a program attached to the Bogotá Chamber, the IDB has replicated this model widely in the region. What accounts for its relative success? Looking at the experience with a similar reform in Argentina, Dezalay and Garth cite a knowledgeable local observer in concluding:

> . . . from the positions of businesses who through the opening to foreign investment have gained a strong position in Latin America, this move can satisfy the fact that 'they want guarantees' through legal institutions. A formalization of private dispute resolution can help provide such guarantees . . . around the public institutions of the state (1999, 95).

In an obvious sense, this brand of state reform resembles the privatization of economic assets, in that it hands over state functions to the private sector. In the Argentine case, these functions are handled by law firms with a cosmopolitan outlook and long experience as go-betweens for international capital (Dezalay and Garth 1999). Looking at this in historical perspective, we may think of it as reflecting the conditions for successful legal and institutional diffusion. That is, it may be true that in many areas of life, law, institutions, and informal practices reflect "the spirit of a people," but in others, agents are motivated to treat law pragmatically, as Alan Watson noted, making them open to foreign models.[28] In Latin America, it increasingly appears that the most compelling pragmatic motivations for judicial reform are coming from the international economy.

NOTES

1. Department of Political Science, Williams College, Williamstown, Massachusetts, 01267. The author would like to thank the editors as well as William E. Davis and Linn Hammergren for their comments on previous drafts.

2. The groups share common antecedents in Frank Knight, Ronald Coase, and Friedrich Hayek. It has been argued persuasively that, like the argument in comparative law, these "new" trends were also prefigured by (and through Hayek and Knight, were largely derived from) nineteenth-century German scholarship (Pearson 1997). On the question of deriving foundations for comparative law from economics, see Mattei 1997.

3. The literature on trust in the economy also goes back to German scholarship, such as Weber's "The Protestant Sects and the Spirit of Capitalism" (Weber 1946, 322ff). Recent works in the new institutionalist vein are Gambetta 1988 and, most famously, Fukuyama 1995. As an example cited by reformers, Shihata tells of a Venezuelan banker who spoke of having to restrict his commercial contacts to a narrow sphere because of his lack of confidence in the courts to enforce contracts he might make with strangers (421-422 in IDB 1997).

4. For Peru, common complaints included first, corruption and second, delays. Instituto de Apoyo 1993, cited by Eyzaguirre in IDB 1997. Other surveys cited in Rowat, Malik, and Dakolias 1995; Buscaglia 1995, 9; Pásara 1996; and Prillaman 2000.

5. For a discussion of independence, the civil law tradition, a judiciary under dictatorship, and the competing concepts of independence early in the Chilean reform process, see Vaughn 1993, 578-80, 599-601.

6. Many lawyers have opposed oral procedure in part because it requires them to appear in court themselves, whereas now they may send a subordinate to the court with written statements (Vargas in NCSC, 58). Regarding this last point, a Brazilian observer has described one function of a constitution to be, along with the regulator of government functions, "the master plan of an enterprise that ends when its goals are reached" (Borja 1993, 28).

7. Hammergren reports that "private economic actors and members of large law firms became interested in judicial reform when they began losing cases they had formerly won with a little political pressure or a bribe" (1998a, 295 n36).

8. When asked about the relative importance of domestic and international actors, a USAID official said that USAID and the banks did not have the active role, but rather that "ownership is local" (August 1996). A prominent consultant, who has worked under USAID and IDB contracts since the 1980s, flatly opposed this notion, saying that "nothing happens without AID," as money for reform is scarce and reformers are politically isolated in an environment in which "power elites" have vested interests (May 1998). As the discussion below shows, I am more inclined to agree with the latter, somewhat unexpected comment. On law reform and its implementation, see Thome 2000.

9. Patrick McAuslan echoes this concern. He sees the multilateral banks as being the most powerful forces for judicial reform at work right now and is dismayed by their emphasis on efficient markets, not [democratically] accountable governments (McAuslan in Faundez 1997, 27).

10. I skip over earlier periods. In the 1960s and in connection with the Alliance for Progress, USAID and the Ford Foundation funded U.S. legal specialists inspired by the "law and development" movement, seeking to revamp legal systems they considered antiquated. The reformers ended up frustrated not only by the obstacles to reform, but also by the uses to which their activist notion of law was put by authoritarian regimes (Gardner 1980). Other phases of USAID involvement are summarized in USAID 1994.

11. It should be noted that these have long concerned themselves with institutional design with regard to the more strictly economic institutions of the state. For example, the International Monetary Fund's Fiscal Affairs Department and a similar department in the World Bank, have for many years advised interested member governments on the design of their tax codes. The standard economic recipes for stabilization and adjustment have often included or implied institutional changes in economic ministries and central banks, and their scope increased as trade liberalization and privatization were added to the list in the 1980s.

12. For a particularly pointed statement, see Burki and Edwards 1996, for whom the "populist state" stands opposed to the solution of economic problems, including the effective delivery of public goods to the majority. Therefore, in their view, the populist state must be "dismantled."

13. It may also be speculated that the flood of private finance has left the banks needing new, complementary areas in which to lend in order to justify their level of funding.

14. The key document is Weder in Rowat, Malik, and Dakolias 1995, 21-26. For an earlier work in this vein, see Borner, Brunetti, and Weder 1993.

15. Project number BO-0112, IDB commitment US$10 million, March 10, 1995, section I.1.2.

16. USAID publications seem to be sensitive to this. "USAID works closely with these [multilateral development banks] and encourages them to expand lending in the social sectors, democracy and governance, and the environment" (USAID, 1999, Congressional Presentation, overview).

17. Among the local allies in Argentina, business organizations such as IDEA and FIEL were early leaders of a movement to make the legal environment more stable (Asselin in NCSC 1996, 96). It should be noted that, as in the case of democratizing reforms, the broader public has had little input. In the former, this was due to lack of organization, while in this area it is because the issues have little resonance for most people. Consequently, as in antitrust law and regulation, new policies have been introduced or significantly changed in many countries, with experts and external advisors "left free to draft legislation consistent with best practice" (Faundez 1997, 16).

18. Putting it more strongly, a World Bank researcher stated that international investor pressure, given voice perhaps through an ambassador, was necessary to overcome domestic vested interests (personal communication, May 1998). Another consultant, however, noted that while international investors might well persuade finance ministries, they would have more trouble with legislatures (personal communication, May 1998).

19. Project ID ARPE50713, October 10, 1997.

20. On popularity, see the profile of former Justice Minister of Bolivia René Blattmann (Rotella 1997).

21. Why the gap between citizen outrage and citizen action? Buscaglia ascribes it to the limited access to justice enjoyed by most of the population (IDB 1997, 44). Hausmann speculates that although there is no "natural" opposition to reform in the public at large ("everyone prefers better justice to worse justice"), the beneficiaries of reform are only occasional and not everyday users of the system (Hausmann in IDB 1997, 69-70).

22. See, in general, NCSC 1995 and IDB 1997, especially Buscaglia in IDB 1997, 38.

23. Enrique Iglesias, the president of the IDB, discusses ADR in connection with the IDB's mission in the economic realm, seeing ADR as a way that the private sector "lightens the duty of [formal] justice" (IDB 1997, 5).

24. To its boosters, the increasingly rapid international movement of capital disciplines governments by raising the costs of bad policies and the benefits of good ones — including institutional reforms such as increased central bank independence (Wriston, 1991; McKenzie and Lee 1991, 243ff; see also Morris 1987, 12; and Maxfield 1994, 9).

25. Burki and Edwards refer to the need for transparency and efficiency in subnational jurisdictions in the region (1996, 25, citing the model of "market-preserving federalism" in Weingast 1994). Many of the strongest proponents of reform apparently do not themselves believe in the power of persuasion unless it is supported by the structural constraints they seek to fortify. This poses a problem for those who ascribe the reform movement to ideology.

26. Weber saw international rivalry as the main spur to administrative rationalization, with the demands of modern capitalism also playing a role: "Military discipline gives birth to all discipline" (1968, 1155). Bureaucracy displaces patrimonialism and clientelism because it is technically superior, and states are more likely to adopt superior solutions when strategic threats prod them. In the modern period, "the bureaucratic tendency has been promoted by needs arising from the creation of standing armies determined by power politics and from the related development of public finances" (972). Although bureaucracy fits more readily in a milieu that rejects privilege, bureaucratization under threat need not entail a general societal shift toward equality before the law (1946, 231). On war, see also Dorn 1940 and Porter 1994.

27. Cf. Domingo 1994. I discuss these ideas at greater length in Mahon 2000.

28. Watson 1974, 1994. Watson saw such pragmatism in the widespread and rapid adoption of Roman civil law, especially as it affected the private law observed by merchants; see also Ewald 1995; and Faundez in Faundez, ed., 1997.

price-fixing by the leading steel company executive officers — good Republicans all — after President Kennedy castigated them for raising prices. Now he seized the chance to make big Republicans in the oil industry uncomfortable. The Justice Department started the antitrust suit against Richfield in October 1962, about seven months after W. Alton Jones was killed. Charles Jones, Richfield's chief executive, decided to fight, but by 1965 he faced a catch-22. Contesting the case to the end would run up tremendous legal fees that would weaken the company and surely imperil its ability to proceed in Prudhoe Bay. Yet the only way to buy out Cities Service and Sinclair would be to sell or merge, which meant he would lose his company.

Jones reluctantly agreed to hunt for a merger partner so he could buy out the two minority partners. "Then a funny thing happened," Jones later wrote in his autobiography. "One of our Washington lawyers wrote to tell me that a Mr. Cladouhos, an antitrust division lawyer assigned to the case, had suggested that Richfield settle the suit by merging with Atlantic Refining Co." Why, Jones wondered, was the Justice Department recommending merger, and why with Atlantic Refining? Jones never got his answer, but he was astute enough to sense that it would be prudent to follow the advice.

Atlantic Refining Company, then the nation's thirteenth-largest oil enterprise, was based in Philadelphia and had assets of $900 million. Its chairman, Robert O. Anderson, had been described in *Business Week* as a "loner with a Midas touch" who possessed "an incredible sense of timing." He also was America's largest individual landowner, controlling about 1.02 million acres of cattle ranges in New Mexico, Texas, and Colorado.

The merger between Atlantic Refining and Richfield Oil occurred on September 16, 1965, much to the distress of many proud Richfield employees. They felt they were on the verge of beating the industry to one of the world's great oil finds. Now, Atlantic Refining, which had been outsmarted at just about every stage of the race to the North Slope, stood to become a major beneficiary of Richfield's daring and talent.

On February 27, 1966, the new company, now known as Atlantic Richfield, drilled its first well at Prudhoe Bay. Dubbed "Susie," the site was in the foothills of the Brooks Range, well south of the arctic coast on the edge of the Sadlerochit formation. Despite all the high expectations, it turned out dry.

"It was a blow," Charles Selman, the seismic crew leader, recalls. It came on top of the experience of BP and Sinclair, which had drilled six wells—all dry—within the last eighteen months. The luster of the North Slope was now fading fast. Skeptics at Atlantic Richfield urged that no more money be spent on this remote region of Alaska, pointing out that all the other majors had given up. "After Susie failed, we were the only act in town," Harry Jamison concedes. "No one else was drilling."

But Jamison was unwavering in his belief. He put his career with the merged company on the line, insisting that they drill just one more hole. His confidence impressed Thornton F. Bradshaw, the Atlantic executive who had become president of the reorganized company. Bradshaw persuaded the board that one more well would not require a new infusion of capital. The company would have to pay for dismantling the equipment and flying it out to Fairbanks in any event. Why not drill a second well while it still had an assembled drilling rig sitting on the slope?

A mixed team of Richfield and Atlantic oil searchers met in Los Angeles to pick a drilling site. Jamison, Selman, district geologist Don Jessup, and district exploration manager John Sweet studied the strata on a map drawn by Rudy Berlin, a geophysicist, and reached a consensus. "After drilling Susie, we were sure that oil had migrated farther north," Jamison says. "We decided that it had left the marine soils of the cretaceous field in the south and was trapped in the Paleozoic, an older and different kind of rock formation that characterizes the north of Prudhoe Bay. That's where we pinned the new location."

Tennessee Miller's Cats moved the drilling rig 65 miles to the north, almost to the shore of the Arctic Ocean, and drilling on the new well began on April 22, 1967. Marvin Mangus, Atlantic's veteran slope geologist, and Gil Mull, Richfield's young geologist, were among those who took turns "sitting on the well," monitoring the samples of soil, rocks, and moisture as drilling progressed.

The first big break came on Mull's watch. "It was the day after Christmas, 1967," Mull says. "We opened a hole to let the fluid flow to the surface. Out came a tremendous burst of gas. It ignited at the end of a two-inch flow pipe and it blew a fifty-foot flare into the teeth of a thirty-mile-per-hour wind. A gas flow doesn't necessarily mean you have liquid, but that kind of pressure is characteristic of a major reservoir." Two months of drilling later, samples at 8,820 feet had all the signs of a major oil find. Harry Jamison, now bearing the title of Atlantic Richfield's general manager for Alaska, was confident enough to call in the press on February 16, 1968. "It looks extremely good," he said. "We have a major discovery."

Alaskan newspapers splashed the big oil strike in sixty-point headlines. The residents of Fairbanks—the closest city, 390 miles to the south—turned out to celebrate in the streets. Governor Walter J. Hickel, then serving his first term in the capital, hailed the "great news" and predicted big enterprises to come.

At first, Wall Street was reasonably calm. Stock analysts cautioned investors that the find might be a fluke. A confirmation well was drilled on a site 7 miles away on the Sag River, the area where young Richfield geologists Mull and Pessel first spotted oily sand. Mull was the "sitter" on this well, too, and once again spectacular things happened on his watch. "It shot out a full column of oil," Mull says. "This meant that the entire huge formation underneath had oil." Prudhoe Bay was no fluke.

No one shared in the joy of discovery more than British Petroleum. P. E. Kent, chief BP geologist, concedes that the company had been ready to cut its losses and leave Alaska. British Petroleum had finished dismantling its equipment and was seriously considering an offer from Atlantic Richfield to take over BP's Prudhoe acreage when news of the first discovery came in. Then, as Kent put it, "our technical assessment did not encourage easy capitulation to our main competitor."

By holding out a few months longer, BP saw the second Atlantic Richfield well come in, but it took a year more to realize the full magnitude of the decision. And the realization was a stunning one: When BP finally struck oil in March 1969, it found that its leases on the flanks of the Prudhoe Bay structure would contain the greater share of oil deposits in what became North America's largest oil field. Five smaller companies also discovered their first North Slope oil soon after. Mobil came in with a find that would enable it to become an 8.5 percent partner in building a pipeline system; Phillips and Union Oil each qualified for 3.25 percent, Amerada Hess for 3 percent, and

Home Oil of Canada for 2 percent. The combined companies estimated that this 350-square-mile field at Prudhoe contained about 22 billion barrels of original oil and 30 trillion cubic feet of natural gas in an overlying gas cap.

This time the news from Alaska created tremors on Wall Street. Disregarding all cautions from analysts, speculators rushed to buy stock in the discovery company. Atlantic Richfield stock shot from $90 a share to $162 during the five months from discovery to confirmation. Action became furious and rumors ran thick on Wall Street. *New York Times* writer Robert S. Wright tried to call for calm in his "Market Place" column on July 10, 1968: "Fantastic reserve figures [in the Alaska discovery] are making the rounds of Wall Street. The Umiat Chamber of Commerce, if there is one, could not be reached for comment ... but even if the North Slope discovery turned out to be a major source of oil, many problems and many years would be required to get the petroleum to market."

Wright was more than correct. The problems to come would be greater than anyone envisioned.

One obstacle that was already becoming apparent was the impact of oil development on Alaska's environment. Soon after the discovery at Prudhoe, in the name of helping to develop the state's new leading industry, Governor Hickel slashed a highway to the North Slope. The ill-planned road followed much of the route bulldozed by Boyd Brown and his Cat train. But Boyd and his crew at least had cut their road in winter conditions, so they had not damaged the permafrost. Nature would have healed the surface wounds in time. Hickel, however, tried to make the highway an all-season road by bulldozing into the permafrost. That made the damage permanent. The sun melted the surface in summer, turning the road into a canal, and without a bulldozer to buck the drifts, it remains impassable in winter. The road became derisively known as "Hickel Highway" and is seldom traveled today.

"We honestly believe Hickel built that road just so a contractor pal of his in Alaska could get his equipment up to the slope ahead of the others and get a jump on the business," says Celia Hunter, a pioneer conservationist who helped form the Alaska Conservation Society, the first statewide environmental watchdog group. "There were no permits taken out to build the road, no public hearings and no chance to be heard. Hickel just built it.

"So much environmental damage was done without public knowledge," she says bitterly. "We couldn't catch up to it until after the fact. Then all we could do was try to spread the word in our newsletter."

The problems would become even more complex. The threat to Alaska's wilderness was growing larger than arrogant governors and reckless Caterpillar skinners. The biggest names in the oil industry were readying to skim the riches of a land they didn't even own.

CHAPTER 5

The Settlement

ONE EARLY spring day in 1962, three Athabaskan Indian trappers set out from Tyonek, their remote, poor Native village on the west side of the Cook Inlet, to search for signs of lynx and fox in the thick forest that lines the rugged western shore. As they climbed a knoll of black spruce and birch about 6 miles from the village, they came upon a sight that stopped them in their tracks.

There, in the midst of a newly cleared plot of land on their ancestral hunting grounds, stood an oil drilling rig with several white people moving about it. "What the hell goes on?" Bill Standifer whispered to his companions, George and Alec Constantine. The three Natives dropped their traps and ran back to alert the village that white men were stealing their land.

Emil McCord, a muscular, bushy-haired officer of the Tyonek Village Council, quickly rounded up a band of villagers, vowing to drive the intruders off the reservation. They marched to the site and surrounded the rig. Emil climbed a ladder to confront the drilling crew. "What are you doing here? This is our land!"

"It's none of your fuckin' business," a driller shouted back. "Get off the equipment or we'll throw your ass off."

The Settlement

Emil's inclination was to storm the drillers and bash the one spewing obscenities. However, cooler heads calmed him down. "We decided to go back to the village and radio for Stanley," he says.

Stanley McCutcheon was a white Anchorage attorney with a social conscience, a liberal activist who understood service to country well before President John F. Kennedy's call made it politically fashionable. A bush pilot as well as a lawyer, McCutcheon would voluntarily fly a relief plane from Anchorage during the harsh winters. When word went out that the people of Tyonek were starving, Anchorage grocery stores would set aside barrels to help the Indians; people deposited canned goods and packages of food, which McCutcheon delivered.

Despite the repeated threat of starvation, the 260 villagers preferred poverty to giving up their traditional subsistence life-style. Their ancestors had hunted, trapped, and fished in the area for centuries, handing knowledge down to each generation about the patterns of the creatures that inhabited the forest and rivers and the ways to outwit them. In 1915, President Woodrow Wilson sealed their right to the land by signing an order setting aside 24,000 acres as the Moquawkie Reservation, one of the few ever created in Alaska.

The reservation had no roads or railroads leading to it. For years, the Tyoneks lived there in peaceful isolation, taking the moose, salmon, and other resources the land gave up and enduring the hardships when it did not yield enough. With more people exploiting the shrinking frontier, however, subsistence living became tougher over the years. Moose and furbearing animals grew scarcer, and in 1952 the government sharply cut back the season for commercial salmon fishing, the town's main source of cash. By the 1960s, Tyonek had turned into the Appalachia of Alaska.

Francis M. Stevens, a BIA child welfare specialist assigned to Tyonek in 1960, found the people living in hovels, sometimes as many as ten crammed into drafty, one-room tar-paper huts. The only water supply was a communal spring. They also had to carry out their body wastes, since the village's only flush toilet was in the school, a run-down building maintained and manned by the BIA. There was only one store in town, run by the BIA and stocked once a year by its supply boat, the *North Star*. Tyonek became a company town, and the company was the dreaded BIA, the subgovernment within the federal government that operated the welfare programs for Natives in Alaska.

Stevens was appalled by the federal bureau's insensitivity to the plight of the troubled Natives. It often removed children from their parents' custody without court process, usually on the mere word of a public health nurse or a BIA teacher. The children would be placed in group care facilities run by "Bible-thumping fanatics from out-side," as Stevens described them. They collected $250 a month per capita from the government for housing as many as forty children at a time. "These were pretty decent white people, but they all had some kind of hard religious bent. They came to Alaska to do good, but they did well," Stevens observed after seeing the government payments.

Stevens, who held a graduate degree in social work from the University of Minnesota, challenged the BIA's bureaucratic smugness. At one point, following a drunken bash in the village, Stevens was directed to tell the villagers they would get no more welfare until they stopped drinking. "I refused to do it," he said. "I was willing to go along and say, 'No more cash welfare,' but cutting off food and bringing starving families to their knees was not my way of dealing with the problem."

Now, the appearance of the mysterious oil rig on Tyonek land was about to force a showdown that would challenge the BIA's long hold on the reservation.

When Stanley McCutcheon heard about the rig, he saw an opportunity to help his friends obtain a measure of retribution. Ever since the first oil field had been discovered at Swanson River on the east side of the Cook Inlet in 1957, oil companies had pushed their explorations westward. Productive oil and gas wells were found in the inlet and new ones were discovered ever closer to the western shore, where the Tyoneks lived. The reservation was the next obvious step in exploration.

McCutcheon went to federal district court without even discussing a fee. He expected none, and, in fact, the village had only $14 in its treasury at the time, according to Emil McCord.

McCutcheon succeeded in exposing the BIA's extraordinary high-handedness and insensitivity. In 1962, without notifying the villagers, the BIA had leased a section of the Tyonek reservation to the Pan American Oil Company (since merged with Amoco). It placed the money in a government fund, also without telling the village. A swift court injunction stopped the drilling. Then McCutcheon sued the Department of the Interior, parent agency of the BIA, to prevent it from executing oil and gas leases on the Moquawkie Reservation without consent of the Tyonek Village Council.

The victory was stunning. The BIA was barred from making further deals without the village's permission, and it was forced to loosen its grip on any village money held in trust. Tyonek had finally regained a measure of control over its own future. With an embarrassed BIA doing the paperwork, the village proceeded to renegotiate all oil exploration leases on its reservation.

Because of Tyonek's proximity to the new oil finds in the Cook Inlet, major oil firms bid eagerly and heavily. The new leases generated about $12.5 million of the $14 million that would eventually swell the village treasury to undreamed-of wealth. This was the same land that the BIA had been willing to lease for $1 million.

The business acumen of the Tyonek Natives exposed the BIA's incompetence. Once the administrator of education, health care, and welfare for all Alaska Natives, the BIA had been reluctant to dismantle its bureaucratic empire, even though many of its services were to be transferred to Alaska under the provisions of statehood. The Tyonek incident provided new reason to hasten the transition. "All of us on the council went to Anchorage and rented rooms at an old hotel on Fourth Avenue," McCord recalls. "Then we all got drunk toasting our victory over the BIA — the Bastards Inflicted on Alaska."

The Tyoneks used their newly gained wealth to replace their hovels with modern houses, to erect a school as up-to-date as any in Alaska, and to ship tons of rice to poor villages in the north. Sadly, the boom was short-lived and ended as soon as the money ran out. Today Tyonek is struggling to keep its culture intact, but it takes great pride in its victory over the BIA and in its status as an exclusively Indian village.

Willie Hensley saw even greater rewards in the Tyonek victory. Here, he sensed, was a foot in the door to a further restoration of Native rights.

Up to now, the issue of Natives' rights to their land had been largely dismissed by most Alaskans as a local battle of vested interests: homesteaders and miners staking claims in the wilderness versus Natives claiming encroachment on their hunting grounds. Over the near-ly one hundred years that Alaska had been an American territory, much lip service and vague language had been given to the rights of aboriginals, but it was not until 1959 that Natives received the first tangible indication that they had a right to recover for the loss of prop-erty or rights in property.

That breakthrough occurred in the United States Court of Claims, which ruled in favor of the Tlingit and Haida Indian groups in Alas-ka's southeast. It awarded them $7.5 million for the 20 million acres that the government had appropriated to create the Tongass Nation-al Forest and Glacier Bay National Monument in the early 1900s. But the Tlingit-Haida claim had lingered in the courts for more than twen-ty years. The Tyonek victory had taken less than three years, and it had broken important new ground.

McCutcheon had won by demonstrating that the Interior Depart-ment's administrative policies were oppressive. He showed that the Tyonek Indians had been treated as second-class citizens when such treatment was being repudiated across the United States in the civil rights revolution. The case had brought national attention to Alaska Native rights. With the country's mood shifting to their side, Willie Hensley felt it was time for Natives to fight the white man with his own techniques.

Willie enrolled in graduate school at the University of Alaska Fair-banks in 1966. He spent much of the year researching a thesis he ti-tled "What Rights to Land Have the Alaska Natives?" The premise was that no treaty or act of Congress had ever extinguished Natives' title to their land. Yet Alaska had gone about selecting the 103 mil-lion acres granted under the Statehood Act of 1958 without consid-ering Native rights to those lands.

Unless help came soon, Willie feared, Native lands in Alaska would go the way of Indian lands in the lower forty-eight. It is a sordid fact of history that the government appropriated or sold more than 90 mil-lion acres of Indian property between 1887, when treaty-making stopped, and 1934, when the Roosevelt administration managed to halt further land grabs. "We felt that was our land and most Native people felt it was their land," Willie says. "But we had no idea of what transpired in the past … what legal, political activities had taken place. We didn't know anything about protecting our ownership."

The Settlement

In the spring of 1966, while baby-sitting for a friend from college, Willie saw a story in the *Fairbanks News-Miner* that inspired him to raise the issue publicly. Alaska's Senator Ernest Gruening, alarmed that some Natives were protesting state land selections around their villages, was quoted as saying the government probably ought to pay off Natives so the state could get on with its development. "Here, finally, was a U.S. senator agreeing that we deserved some compensation," Willie thought to himself. "So that means he must agree that we have some rights to the land. And if we have a right, then we have a right to say what kind of settlement we want."

The next day Willie sent a letter to Senator Gruening and mailed copies to all major Alaska newspapers. It read:

> Dear Senator Gruening,
>
> You cannot pin the responsibility for the present chaotic state of affairs of Alaskan lands on the Natives. There has been ample time since the Treaty of Cession in 1867 to interpret its provisions. Now that we are finally taking limited action on an issue which has been allowed to ride, I pray that the claims will be allowed to be heard and a just and equitable settlement be made in real property or in cash, depending on comprehensive hearings with full participation of Alaskan Natives.

The newspapers reprinted the letter and Senator Gruening promptly invited Willie in for a talk. Willie was scared, but he welcomed the chance to press his case upon one of the most prestigious and powerful figures in Alaska.

"We met at the Nordale Hotel, in the room where he lived, just the two of us," Willie says. "I told him of my research, that our title to the land had never been extinguished, either in the purchase treaty with Russia or in the statehood agreement. And therefore we had a right to say what kind of settlement we wanted. He was very nice about it. He said he was a friend of the Natives and reviewed his record as territorial governor in which he fought racism in Alaska and helped get rid of those signs in theaters and restaurants that had segregated Natives."

Willie said he didn't question Gruening's position on racism, but he felt a chill when he got to specifics on Native land claims. "I feared he wanted to do the traditional thing—go to the court of claims or the Indian Claims Commission, pay the Natives fifty cents an acre, and then move on. He had no feeling that we wanted to retain land." Gruening made no promises, except to say Natives deserved something. Willie left the meeting feeling that Alaska's more liberal senator was more a colonialist than a champion of Native rights.

Willie graduated with his master's that spring, with high praise for his thesis from one of the university's most respected teachers, Judge Jay Rabinowitz. Then he borrowed the money to return home to Kotzebue. There, still virtually penniless, he declared his candidacy for the Alaska legislature. At twenty-five, Willie had grown into distinguished adulthood. He was trim and neat, his manner both engaging and refined. And no one could speak more authoritatively—or persuasively—on the problems facing Alaskan Natives.

Borrowing $10 for paper and stamps, Willie wrote to all village leaders in the Kotzebue–Yukon Delta area, his legislative district, which has one of the greatest densities of Natives in Alaska. He invited them to a meeting, telling them that land their people had lived on for centuries might soon pass to state ownership and then be offered to public sale or lease.

"A lot of people didn't read too well," Willie says. "One guy from Noatak came seventy-five miles by boat to ask what the letter was all about." However, a strong local showing from Kotzebue enabled Willie to organize a Native group, which its members named the Northwest Alaska Native Association. Willie was chosen its first executive director. Now he had a forum and base. At the group's third meeting, Willie asked, "What should we do about our land?" "Claim it!" a chorus shouted.

Very little land in Alaska had actually been surveyed, despite the leasing frenzy. So Willie took a big, black pencil and drew lines on a map, circling what he felt was the drainage area of the Kotzebue region, and submitted the claim to the Bureau of Land Management and the Alaska land office.

There had been another Native land claim earlier that year, by the Arctic Slope Native Association. The group had been organized also on the spur of the moment by Charles Edwardsen, an unkempt, hard-drinking young Eskimo from Barrow. He claimed title to 96 million acres, which consisted of practically all of Alaska north of the Brooks

The Settlement

Range and covered all the potential oil fields the oil companies were exploring. A product of Mount Edgecumbe, the BIA high school in Sitka, Edwardsen had the smarts to go to college, but had dropped out. Copying the style of civil rights demonstrators of the era, he became an Eskimo radical, decrying "white trespassers" and suggesting that violent means might be necessary to save the land. Edwardsen wrote to Willie urging that the Kotzebue Natives team up with their fellow Inupiats in the north. But Willie was not ready to endorse Edwardsen's brand of activism. He felt he could win only if he played by white man's rules.

Willie made land claims his campaign issue in Kotzebue and then carried his crusade to Anchorage, hoping to find support for making it a statewide concern. There he met Emil Notti, one of the few other Natives in Alaska with a college education. Notti, short, dark-haired, and half Athabaskan, has scars from his left cheek to his neck, remnants of an attack by a dogsled team when he was growing up along the Yukon River in the interior town of Ruby. Four years in the Navy provided him with his escape into the outside world, and the GI Bill enabled him to earn an engineering degree from Northrop University in California. Notti had sensed social injustices to his people ever since a BIA school taught him how to read. "You would see pictures of famous people coming to Alaska, such as Roy Rogers, and they would have a picture taken with their trophy bear or moose," Notti says. "Inevitably, the Native person in the picture would be identified only as 'the Indian guide.' No name, even though he probably located the animal or even shot it for him. The Indians didn't have names, so you assumed they were not a person."

When he met Willie Hensley, Notti already was organizing a Native association in the Cook Inlet region, covering principally southwestern Alaska. Both men agreed that only a statewide organization of Natives could stop the seizure of their lands, but neither of their organizations had the staff or the money to assemble village leaders from across Alaska. Most Natives lived in villages with no access roads — although Alaska is more than twice the size of Texas it had only 6,500 miles of roadway — and to fly them in would cost too much money. Few villages could underwrite trips of such distances for their leaders.

However, both men had heard of the deeds of Tyonek. "Emil Notti and Willie Hensley came down and said they needed money," Emil McCord recalls. "They said Natives had to start doing things on their own or we were going to lose our land. We loaned them a hundred thousand dollars with a handshake." The Tyonek Village Council also agreed to pay the travel and room expenses for the delegates and arrange a meeting place in Anchorage as well. With a barrage of publicity and editorial support from Howard Rock, the revered editor of the *Tundra Times,* the weekly publication for Natives, the prospect of Alaska's first Native summit meeting became real.

However, the prospect of a consensus was something else. Alaska's Natives were isolated, splintered, and poorly educated. Because of the vastness of the state, communication among groups was possible only where borders touched. The profusion of languages and dialects alone threatened to doom any statewide conference to a cacophony of confusion. Nevertheless, on October 6, 1966, three hundred Native delegates from all parts of Alaska packed a deserted storeroom above Miller's Furs on Fourth Avenue in Anchorage, and the Alaska Federation of Natives (AFN) was born.

The anticipated chaos did not occur. The determination to save their lands overcame the groups' differences. The conference coalesced into a mission in which every Native group would have a role. Flore Lekanof, an Aleut from the Pribilofs, became permanent chairman. Roy Peratrovich, president of the Tlingit-Haidas in the southeast, headed the education committee. Richard Frank, leader of the Tanana Chiefs Conference from the Athabaskan interior, was named a director. Even the radical Charles Edwardsen made the team as chairman of Native employment.

The conference was held virtually on the eve of statewide elections, and political candidates swarmed among the delegates seeking votes. It was an eye-opener for many of the Natives, who were getting a speedy lesson in election clout. Alaska had fifty-five thousand Native votes to court.

Emil Notti, the first AFN president, quickly created a land claims committee and appointed Willie Hensley to head it. Then the committee drafted a position statement that was released to the press and sent to Alaska's congressional delegation. The statement contended that all Alaska Natives were being victimized and they wanted reparations.

The Settlement

Most whites in Alaska reacted indignantly to the news that Natives were claiming land title and money as compensation for acreage being selected by the state. Although the position paper stated that AFN only wanted input in the settlement, reports spread that Native leaders were demanding 60 million acres and a billion dollars. Governor Hickel added to the public furor, declaring in a statewide radio address, "Just because somebody's grandfather chased a moose across the land doesn't mean he owns it."

Months went by and still no member of the congressional delegation reacted to the AFN position paper. In April 1967, Notti sent telegrams to all three members of the Alaska congressional delegation. Senator E. L. Bartlett responded immediately. Senator Gruening responded two weeks later, and Representative Howard Pollock's response came shortly afterward. They agreed to place the Native claims issue before Congress in the form of Senate bill 2020. It was the first of eight bills that would be introduced before Congress finished its own soul-searching on the lands issue.

Meanwhile, Willie Hensley had been handily elected to the state legislature, defeating four strong candidates in the primary and a respected Republican in the fall election. He promptly used his new position to fight the state's arbitrary land selection. Stanley McCutcheon, his legal expenses paid by Tyonek, traveled to villages from Nome in the Arctic to Kodiak in the southwest to press the same cause, joined by his law partner, Cliff Groh, Sr. They helped Native organizations become legal entities so they could file land claims and block state selection of their regions.

By 1967, Native organizations had claimed more land than there was in the state of Alaska, completely stymieing the state's process. In response to this chaos, Secretary of Interior Stewart L. Udall declared a land freeze for all Alaska. He refused to accept further selections by the state until the Native claims issue was resolved.

The freeze halted all development. Cries of "greedy Natives" were interspersed with various stories of individual hardships caused by "federal tyranny." Many Alaskans still insisted that Natives had no right to compensation whatsoever. The powerful *Anchorage Times* editorialized that land and money demands being made by the Natives would cripple development for all Alaskans. The devastating economic effect of Udall's edict drove Governor Hickel, who was counting on land sales to balance his budget, to desperate moves. He tried to lift the freeze by suing Udall in federal district court. Then he attempted to get a quick fix in Congress. Nothing worked.

Udall's genuine sensitivity to Native claims and the national mood charged by the Johnson antipoverty pledges and the civil rights demonstrations of the 1960s were big pluses for the Native cause. But it is doubtful whether the Native land claims would have survived the hostility in the state during this era had they not coincided with the epochal discovery of oil at Prudhoe Bay in 1968.

Suddenly, the oil industry became an overpowering — if unlikely — booster of Native rights. Realizing it could not tap the massive oil field on the North Slope without a clear land title, the industry applied its considerable muscle to Congress. Newfound concern for Native rights in Alaska suddenly started emanating from Governor Hickel, from Congress, and, starting in 1969, from the inner sanctum of the Nixon administration. John Ehrlichman, who as a Nixon campaign strategist had discovered the advantages of helping the oil industry, was particularly emphatic. Congressional library shelves bulge with transcripts reflecting the millions of words that went into the deliberations on Alaska Native land claims bills, including a presidential commission field study, the testimony of scores of witnesses called before the Senate Committee on Interior and Insular Affairs, and letters and reports from interested parties ranging from environmentalists to sportsmen's councils. Even with the high-level response to the oil industry's urgent call, the Native land claims settlement was a tortuous process.

Walter Hickel developed a change of heart the hard way. As governor, he could afford to oppose the land freeze and vacillate on the land claims issue. However, when President Nixon nominated Hickel as his secretary of the interior after the 1968 election, Hickel needed Native support to counter the outrage among environmentalists who protested that his appointment would be like installing a fox to watch the henhouse.

Emil Notti, then president of the Alaska Federation of Natives, recalls being asked to visit Hickel's home late in December 1968. He was driven there by Cliff Groh, the AFN's attorney. They found a troubled Governor Hickel with Larry Fanning, editor of the *Anchorage Daily News*.. Fanning was holding an advance copy of a column

7 0

by Drew Pearson, Washington's leading muckraker and then the nation's most widely syndicated columnist. Pearson had written that Hickel did not deserve to be secretary of the interior because of his shameful treatment of Eskimos in Bethel, a western Alaska Native community on the Kuskokwim River. Clearly, Hickel needed to blunt the attack.

He asked Notti if he had contact with Indian groups. Notti replied that he had. "Do you think you could get an endorsement from them?" Hickel asked. Notti said he would like to be able to help, but he reminded Hickel of their running battle with him over the land freeze. What about an endorsement from the AFN? Hickel wanted to know. It would be the same with that group, Notti responded.

Notti says Hickel then promised to extend Udall's land freeze until Native claims were resolved. Notti wanted the promise in writing. Wasn't his word good enough? Hickel countered. Notti said that was not good enough, and left.

Groh was furious when they got to the car. "You called the governor a liar!" he exploded. Notti reminded Groh of Hickel's recent statement at a Seattle airport press conference: "What Udall could do with a stroke of a pen, I can undo with a stroke of a pen when I become secretary."

A few days after the meeting at Hickel's house, Notti called a special meeting of the AFN board to act on Hickel's plea for an endorsement. He recalls that a three-way phone call was set up with Hickel on one end, Cliff Groh on another, and a speakerphone in the board meeting room. The conversation ended without a commitment from the board. Apparently, Hickel thought the board had signed off, because suddenly the governor's angry voice came blaring over the speakerphone: "Cliff, you made a promise. When the hell are you going to deliver them?"

"That just jolted us," Notti says. "I had thought about going Outside for counsel earlier because of the way Congress jerked our local lawyers around. Hearing that exchange between our lawyer and Hickel convinced me we had to reach Outside."

Notti said the AFN sent him to the Hickel confirmation hearings before the Senate Committee on Interior and Insular Affairs with the authority to endorse, withhold endorsement, or oppose, depending on what Hickel said about maintaining the land freeze until Native claims were settled. Hickel dodged questions on the freeze for the first two days of the hearings. At the end of the second day, January 18, 1969, Senator Henry Jackson, chairman of the committee, put the question to Hickel directly:

> Governor, during yesterday morning's session, I asked you a number of questions concerning your intentions on dealing with the land freeze in the state of Alaska. Now as I understand your answers ... we had arrived at a clear understanding that no action would be taken by you as secretary of interior to lift the land freeze or otherwise change the status quo ... I have been informed that while I was out of the meeting yesterday you responded to the questions of Senator [George] McGovern and other senators on the same subject. The concern has been expressed that in your answers you may have modified somewhat the understanding which I thought we had attained. I would appreciate it if you would clarify this matter for me once again.

Hickel faced his worst moment in the hearings. As governor only a few months before, he had sued the Interior Department to lift the freeze. He had hoped to parry questions and leave himself an escape. Now he knew that his confirmation rode on how he satisfied Jackson. Yes, he said, Jackson's first understanding was correct and he would abide by it. That statement under oath was also enough to wrest the endorsement of the AFN.

Notti and Hensley estimate they and other Native leaders made about 120 trips to Washington to protect Native interests as the Alaska delegation negotiated and Congress debated land claims bills. More tiring than the traveling and negotiating, though, were the growing internal disagreements that threatened to shatter the fragile AFN. The disputes were fanned by a battery of lawyers who, sensing a gigantic legal payout, maneuvered to get a piece of the action. Notti says that at one point fourteen attorneys, each representing a separate region, were advising their clients what to demand to satisfy the needs of their regions in any land claims settlement act. Each attorney, of course, was expecting a slice of the settlement.

Many of the provincial demands were unreasonable, but pertinent issues also emerged. Emotional debates developed over protection of hunting and fishing rights, over how land shares would be apportioned, and over the diversion of funds from housing programs to pay for the mounting expenses of the claims fight. However, at the root of the friction was the struggle over which local attorneys got to represent the AFN in the congressional hearings. "These guys were working for ten percent of the land and the money in any settlement," Notti said. "They stood to make a lot of money."

Robert Goldberg, a young attorney who came to Alaska in 1967 and landed a job with an Anchorage law firm, told his father, former Supreme Court justice Arthur J. Goldberg, about the Native concerns and about the many attorneys trying to board the Native claims gravy train. He asked his father to help.

Goldberg had visited Alaska and had grown fond of the state. After confirming his son's reports, Goldberg offered to represent the Native claims without pay. Later he was joined by former attorney general Ramsey Clark, also working on a pro bono basis. Together they saved the AFN from possible disintegration and provided immense credibility for the Native case. "Up until then, we were a bunch of wild Natives trying to claim Alaska," Willie Hensley says. "Their defense of our cause made an impression on everyone—the Senate committee, the media, and the public. Keep in mind that just a short time ago, Ramsey Clark as attorney general was on the other side of the fence, fighting against Indian claims. His willingness to work for us made quite a statement."

On April 29, 1969, Goldberg made a masterful opening statement at the hearings of Senator Jackson's Senate Committee on Interior and Insular Affairs: "The Alaska Natives came to their nation—and it was their nation at the time—thousands of years ago. By sheer determination and ingenuity, they have endured, indeed they have conquered, an arctic semicontinent without the benefit of modern technology, without electricity or planes, or matches or modern heating equipment. They survived under conditions which might have destroyed any other group in the world."

Then Goldberg considered the plight of Alaska Natives in relation to the national War on Poverty, a comparison that struck a nerve in Congress: The average Alaska Native died at the age of 34.3 years, and thus had half the life expectancy of other Americans; death for Natives from influenza and pneumonia occurred at twenty times the rate for Alaskan whites; fifty-two out of every thousand Native

Alaskans died before reaching their first birthday, and the Native infant mortality rate was twelve times that of white Alaskans; more than half of the Native work force was jobless most of the year. And out of some seventy-five hundred residential dwellings in Native villages, seventy-one hundred needed replacement. Goldberg's powerful assessment of the Native land claims drew virtually no arguments. All that remained was the determination of the size of the settlement.

At the outset of the hearings early in 1968, the AFN had proposed that the aboriginal land claims be settled with 40 million acres and $500 million, an award that even its own supporters never thought they could get. On December 14, 1971, with the House voting 307–60 for a compromise package and the Senate whipping it through on a voice vote, Alaska Natives received 40 million acres of land and $962 million in cash. It was the largest land claim settlement in the history of the United States. (Subsequently, through a series of special-purpose amendments to include burial grounds and traditional sites, the total acreage grew to 44 million.)

Many whites in Alaska thought it was too much. Some Natives were displeased by the lack of specific commitments to the continuance of subsistence hunting and fishing rights. Charles Edwardsen's group, the Arctic Slope Native Association, felt it deserved mineral rights to Prudhoe Bay. But most observers agree that ten years earlier, before oil had been discovered, the Natives would have won nothing at all. Ten years later, they would not have received so much land, because the discovery of oil made it so valuable.

With a telephone call to the AFN meeting in Anchorage, President Nixon signed the bill into law on December 19, 1971. Twelve regional corporations within the state and one at-large corporation for nonresidents were designated to distribute the benefits. Anyone with one-fourth Native ancestry — just one Native grandparent — would receive shares, although nonresidents of the state would not be entitled to land. Alaska Natives had become Alaska capitalists.

CHAPTER 6

Birth of
the Pipeline

Even in June, snow still covers the gentle peaks of Sugarloaf Mountain across the inlet at Valdez. Tour boats leave rippling wakes as they head out of the harbor carrying the season's early visitors to see the Columbia Glacier and the marine life that abounds in Prince William Sound. In town, a pleasant man behind the counter at the Hook, Line and Sinker bait shop swaps stories with idling customers as he fills fishing-reel spools with new line for the imminent first run of pink salmon.

A deep-port town of about three thousand people, Valdez sits at the head of Prince William Sound, which lies at the top of the Gulf of Alaska and is one of the most magnificent ocean waterways in the world. Humpback and killer whales play in the waters. Halibut and lingcod thrive in its depths. A great variety of birds, from bald eagles to tufted puffins, live on the cliffs of the many islands. Bears and goats live on the mountains that rise as high as 13,000 feet from the edge of the sound. Blueberries, cow parsnips, and herbs, among other edible plants, carpet the forest floor and alpine tundra.

The Chugach Eskimos, descendants of the Aleuts, first populated shores of the sound. They pursued orca whales in the sea, trapped salmon at the mouth of the streams, and hunted otters and seals. Whites first set foot in Alaska in 1741, when Vitus Bering led a Russian expedition that came ashore at Cordova at the extreme southeastern end of the sound. Bering's ship ran aground on the return trip and he died of scurvy, but those who made it back to Russia told of the abundant sea otters, setting off a rush in the fur trade that led to the near decimation of the species.

In 1778, Captain James Cook sailed up the sound trying to discover a northwest passage. In his published journals, he named the sound for the prince who subsequently became King William IV of England. The Spanish explorer Salvador Fidalgo, who also was searching for a northwest passage, stopped at the head of the sound in 1790. He gave Valdez its name, but Alaskans never used the Spanish pronunciation. They refer to it as Val-*deez,* and anyone calling it Val-*dez* is quickly stamped a stranger.

Valdez gained its first real notoriety at the turn of the century. When news of a big gold strike set off a stampede to the Yukon in 1897, more than twenty thousand people jammed into the little frontier town, turning it into a tent city. Valdez was not the shortest route to the Yukon, and the stampeders had to traverse 20 tortuous miles over a glacier, but it spared them interrogation at the Canadian border. Thirty-two churches vied for attention with a like number of bordellos until gold ran out and so did most of the people.

By the Depression, the town's population had sunk to five hundred, where it remained. Then on March 27, 1964, the worst earthquake ever to hit North America occurred, with Valdez 20 miles from the epicenter. Houses cracked, foundations sank, and massive tsunamis sent waves 50 feet high thundering across the waterfront. Thirty-two people died, and many residents abandoned their homes, the ruins of which are still visible today.

John Kelsey, lean and ruddy at seventy, is a Valdez pioneer who well remembers those days. He sits behind his desk at the Valdez Dock Company with a lake trout mounted on the wall behind him and talks of a lifelong commitment to the hardscrabble life in Valdez. A genuine Alaska boomer, he went to college at Stanford, he says, because even in tough times Valdez believed in education for its young. It helped that his family could afford tuition during the Depression.

For more than a half century, the Kelseys operated the Valdez Dock

Company, one of the few profitable businesses in town. The giant sea waves that surged in after the earthquake demolished their docks, nearly swallowing John Kelsey with them. But the Kelseys stayed on and helped rebuild Valdez on a more solid site 4 miles away. By the time they put in their new dock, however, John and his brother, Bob, were $500,000 in debt.

When John heard of the gigantic oil discovery at Prudhoe Bay in 1968, the boomer spirit leapt within him. He knew the companies would have to ship the oil south out of some port in Alaska. Valdez, now reduced to a shabby trailer town with an unemployment rate of 40 percent, was in disarray, but it had a rare prize—the northernmost ice-free harbor in Alaska.

Prince William Sound is about the size of Chesapeake Bay. To reach the port of Valdez, ships must sail due north about 40 miles after coming into the sound from the Gulf of Alaska. The countless fjords and islands make it a breathtaking trip, and it has long been a popular route for cruise ships. But Kelsey knew that the location was more than pretty; it was strategic. Not only was Valdez closer to the oil fields than any other port in Alaska that stays ice-free during the winter, but a paved road, the Richardson Highway, connected it to Fairbanks, providing a direct overland link to Prudhoe Bay. Valdez had all the advantages in the contest for the commerce in the coming oil boom on the North Slope.

Yet far more influential people and interests had their own plans for shipping oil out of Prudhoe Bay. Secretary of the Interior Hickel wanted to extend the Alaska railroad from Fairbanks to Prudhoe and transport the oil in tank cars to Seward. Exxon, then Humble Oil, a major player in the planning, had early visions of using a northern water route. It spent $50 million to send a big ice-breaking tanker, the *Manhattan,* on a mission to determine whether escorted tankers could navigate to American markets through the often ice-clogged channels of the Arctic Ocean. After two bad trips, Humble gave up the idea.

Meanwhile, the Wilderness Society, Friends of the Earth, and other major environmental groups whose voices were rising in the nation opposed any shipping of oil by sea. They urged the government to force the oil companies to explore building a pipeline or a railroad across Canada to Chicago as a way of avoiding marine spills. But certain Native leaders opposed a pipeline. They feared the impact on caribou herds and fishing streams would doom their subsistence existence, and threatened to go to court to protect it.

In Kelsey's view, they were all off base. "Hickel's idea was a pie in the sky," Kelsey says. "All I could think of was a line of tank cars from Prudhoe Bay to Seward. The Canadian land route was bad because we wouldn't have had control of our own pipeline. And the Natives who were concerned about the caribou and fish were not aware that stiff environmental controls were certain to be imposed on the oil companies."

Kelsey wondered how a little dock owner from Valdez could get the ear of the oil companies. Then he remembered. When he had been mayor (Valdez has many ex-mayors, because the term is only one year), company officials nearly always came to the phone when told a mayor was calling. "So I got George Gilson, the mayor, and Bill Wyatt, who ran a motel, into my office and we made some calls," Kelsey says. "We tried to reach the Humble Oil president. We called Atlantic Richfield and British Petroleum. At first they wouldn't talk to us because they thought we were a couple of characters out of the night. We kept badgering and only asked that they listen to us. Finally, they gave in and told us about a study group working in Alaska." Kelsey tracked the study group to the Captain Cook Hotel in Anchorage. He called their suite and said the mayor of Valdez would like fifteen minutes of their time and was on his way.

The study team was just leaving the bar when the mayor and Kelsey arrived late in the afternoon. By coincidence, they stepped into the same elevator. "They looked at us with all the maps under our arms and said, 'You must be from Valdez,'" Kelsey says. "And they reminded us we had only fifteen minutes."

Inside the room, Kelsey spread the charts on the floor and traced a line from Prudhoe Bay to the nearest ice-free, deepwater port, which, of course, was Valdez. Then he pointed out the possible pipeline routes to Valdez that could maximize the use of federal land, enabling the companies to avoid costly land settlements. He started to get their attention. "The fifteen minutes dragged into three hours until someone on the team said, 'I'm hungry,'" Kelsey says. "They invited us out to dinner, and before the night was over I knew they were falling in love with our harbor."

In mid-February 1969, the three major Prudhoe companies — Atlantic Richfield, Humble Oil, and British Petroleum — announced without specifying a port that Prudhoe oil would be transported by pipeline and that the delivery system would be entirely in Alaska. Walter B. Parker, a member of the federal field committee comparing pipeline options, said the strong insistence upon West Coast delivery by Robert O. Anderson, the president of Atlantic Richfield, swung the decision. The field committee, appointed by President Lyndon Johnson, did not have veto power, but its chairman, Joseph Fitzgerald, had Johnson's ear and probably could have blocked the decision had the committee disagreed. Engineers were to determine the exact route and terminal, but the conduit was to be a 48-inch-diameter pipeline stretching for about 800 miles. Hydrostatic studies had determined that using a 48-inch-diameter pipeline would require the fewest pumping stations.

The first estimated cost of the pipeline was $900 million. *The New York Times* described it as "possibly the largest single private construction project and private capital investment in history."

Kelsey says he was informed six months in advance of the public announcement that the oil companies, now organized into a construction company called the Trans-Alaska Pipeline System (TAPS), had picked Valdez for the terminus. He was overjoyed. He saw the salvation of Valdez, as well as his own business. Then he showed his gratitude by giving the pipeline project one more big assist.

In 1968, the Internal Revenue Service had changed the tax laws to address the abuses of tax-exempt bonds. Some congressmen had been angered by the way southern states were floating these bonds to finance new factories that were luring textile firms from New England. Bond issues for docks and environmental safeguards such as those planned for the pipeline terminal would not be affected, however. The state of Alaska had the enabling legislation, and Governor William Egan agreed to float the bond issue until it was pointed out to him that with bonds issued by the state, the oil companies would save three or four points in interest — a gigantic break for a construction loan certain to exceed a billion dollars. The governor's advisers urged him to claim 50 percent of those savings for the state. The oil companies balked.

When Bill Arnold, a friend of Kelsey's and an attorney for the oil interests, told Kelsey of the impasse, Kelsey urged that they explore the possibility of using the city of Valdez to float the bonds. A few days later, Arnold returned and told Kelsey that Atlantic Richfield's Anderson was wary of turning to Valdez for help. He feared Governor Egan would retaliate by asking the legislature to raise taxes on oil. Acting on his own, Kelsey went to Juneau to visit Egan, a long-time friend and a fellow native of Valdez. When he left the governor's office, he had a handshake promise of no retaliation.

With the oil companies agreeing to guarantee the bonds, the little city of Valdez floated $1.5 billion of a $2 billion bond issue to build the pipeline—the largest tax-free industrial bond ever issued up to that time. The windfall for Valdez, which gets a 1 percent dividend each time the bond is refinanced, enabled the city to establish its own permanent fund for city improvements. Valdez became a boom city. Modern public buildings, including a community college campus and an attractive convention center, were built with oil revenues, transforming a faltering downtown into a bustling urban center. That attracted private investors to build first-class lodgings, restaurants, and boutiques.

The financing cleared the way for purchasing the 800 miles of 48-inch pipe that would provide the artery for the pumping system. Such a prospect should have brightened boardrooms across the American steel industry, but it didn't. No U.S. company had a plant to manufacture 48-inch pipe, and no American company could guarantee to build a special pipe mill in time to accommodate the crash schedule set by the oil firms. But the Japanese were ready to oblige. A $100 million order for the first shipment of pipe was placed with two Japanese mills, with delivery to start within five months.

This should have been a lesson for the American steel industry. But Peter DeMay, vice-president for project management on the pipeline, says that a few years later, when a need arose for fabricated steel chutes, no domestic steel companies bid on the order. The Japanese firms, aware that they had no competition, came in with overly high bids. DeMay got Edgar Speer, the chairman of U.S. Steel, on the phone. "Here I am trying to order some fabricated steel—and all it is is fabricated steel—and I can't get a bid out of you." A surprised Speer promised to have someone call. "Not good enough," DeMay said. "We don't have that time." DeMay said he sent his people down to the West Coast with drawings and U.S. Steel agreed to expedite the job. "The order was one hundred eighty million dollars, probably the biggest they ever had," DeMay said. "And it had to be forced upon them."

With Interior Secretary Hickel, the state's entire congressional delegation, and the governor of Alaska working hard to clear bureaucratic obstacles, the oil companies confidently started work on the pipeline early in 1970 without waiting for permits. TAPS bulldozed a haul road from above Fairbanks to Prudhoe, built an ice bridge across the Yukon, and began to move hundreds of men plus much equipment and material to construction camps along the route. But just as the oil companies were gearing up a construction spectacular to start oil flowing, other forces were organizing a spectacular attack to halt it.

Congress had passed the National Environmental Policy Act, the most sweeping of its kind ever, in 1969, almost coincidental with the decision to build a pipeline. Major environmental organizations, working in concert with the Center for Law and Social Policy in Washington, seized upon the act as an instrument to stop the oil companies from carving an 800-mile strip across Alaska's fast-disappearing wilderness. In this first major test of the newly formed Environmental Protection Agency (EPA), three lawsuits were filed in Washington's federal district court, starting on March 26, 1970. They were brought in the name of the Wilderness Society, the Friends of the Earth, and the Environmental Defense Fund.

The first suit charged that TAPS was asking excessive rights of way in violation of the Mineral Leasing Act of 1920 (which, while outdated, is still a handy weapon for all varieties of obstructionists). Next, the plaintiffs sought to join their suit with requests for an injunction filed by several Native villages that were refusing to let the pipeline go through their property. Then the plaintiffs filed an amended suit saying that the Department of the Interior had not complied with the impact statement required by the EPA.

This legal barrage produced court injunctions that stopped the project dead. For the next four years, loads of pipe and expensive machinery sat idle at Prudhoe, and many suppliers that had stocked materials there on speculation went broke. The battle raged in the courts, in Congress, in the media, in offices and bars. To many, the pipeline had become a national symbol of the destruction of the country's last bastions of wilderness.

In January 1971, an Interior Department staff report concluded that the pipeline would create unavoidable environmental damage but recommended that the line be built. Oil, it stated, was that crucial to the nation. With Native claims now settled, the oil companies thought the Interior Department's endorsement cleared the last big obstacle. But Hickel was no longer secretary of the interior. President Nixon had ousted him from office months before, after Hickel wrote him an impulsive letter complaining that the administration's Vietnam protest policy was polarizing American youth. Hickel's successor, Rogers C. B. Morton, promptly stated he was not bound by the finding of a report started under Hickel, and wanted to know more about the risk of piping hot oil across the permafrost. *The New York Times* applauded the position, proclaiming, "Hot oil is dangerous enough without hot haste."

In February, the Interior Department scheduled pipeline hearings, first in Washington and then in Anchorage. Alaskan leaders lined up a formidable array of engineers, government officials (including Hickel), and Native leaders to testify. But a few days before the hearings opened, a full-page ad appeared in *The New York Times* bearing the signature of David Brower, president of Friends of the Earth. It stated that two thousand oil spills had occurred in U.S. waters in 1966 alone, killing millions of birds. "If oil is pumped out of Prudhoe Bay and then shipped down the west coast," Brower warned, "we will eventually have an oil spill leading to the greatest kill of living things in history."

The Washington hearings became a showcase of unyielding positions. Pipeline advocates claimed Alaska oil was economically essential and the levels of damage and risk acceptable. Conservationists pointed to the industry's record of marine spills and predicted the destruction of Alaska's pristine wilderness if the interior were opened by pipeline construction. By the time the hearings moved to Anchorage, some interesting embellishments had been added to the debate. Arguing for the pipeline, Mayor Julian Rice of Fairbanks testified, "God placed these things beneath the surface for a purpose. For us to say that we shouldn't use them is to be anti-God." And Senator Ted Stevens of Alaska was said to have told the Cordova fishermen who make their living fishing Prince William Sound, "Wernher von Braun, you know, the spaceman, assured me that all of the technology of the space program will be put into the doggone tankers and there will not be one drop of oil in Prince William Sound."

The Anchorage Times did a competent job of reporting the thrust of the arguments from the three hundred witnesses who asked to be heard in Anchorage. However, it, too, had its lapses into oil boosterism. "The fears about damage from oil spills are like the fears of Henny Penny when she ran to tell the king that the sky was falling," read one editorial.

The battle might well be raging today but for a gasoline shortage that gripped the American public in 1973. The official explanation for the crisis was that the OPEC cartel had imposed an oil embargo on the United States in retaliation for aiding Israel. Not everyone bought that explanation for the long lines at the gas stations, however. "I felt it was a contrived oil shortage then and I still think so today," says David Brower. "It was contrived to get congressional support for the pipeline."

Nevertheless, the nation's dependence on oil suddenly obliterated its budding sensitivity to the environment. Moving oil from Prudhoe Bay became a patriotic mission, and Congress took the cue. In several swift steps, it removed the obstacles stalling the pipeline. When the courts found for the environmentalists in their suit charging that the oil companies violated the 50-foot right-of-way limit in the Mineral Leasing Act of 1920, Congress simply amended the act to allow the secretary of the interior to increase the right of way temporarily "when any specific project merited it." And when it still appeared that new legal challenges under the Environmental Policy Act could delay the pipeline indefinitely, Congress introduced an amendment to the pipeline bill insulating its permits for construction from any new legal challenges. In the eyes of many senators, that was cutting the heart out of the EPA, and the vote was hung up on a 49–49 tie. But Vice-President Spiro Agnew came to the rescue, making sure he was there on July 17, 1973, to break the impasse.

Before Congress ended its 1973 session, the House passed the pipeline bill 361–14 and the Senate passed it by a vote of 80–5. President Nixon signed it into law on November 16, and Interior Secretary Morton issued the long-awaited construction permit on January 23,

1974. Five years after it was conceived, work on the pipeline legally began. And the estimated cost had grown from more than $900 million to $6 billion.

CHAPTER 7

Pipe Dreams
and Schemes

IN FEBRUARY 1975, Susan Blomfield, young, pretty, and bored, was just out of high school with a career that was going nowhere. She was making $2.75 an hour in an Anchorage florist shop and her boss was on her case for taking too much time on floral bouquets. That's when she walked out and headed for the pipeline hiring hall in Fairbanks. "If I'm going to be hassled, at least I'll get a decent buck for it," she reasoned.

Susan had watched a steady stream of acquaintances head north to Fairbanks in pursuit of big dollars on the pipeline. Her brother, most of the Friday night gang at Chilkoot Charlie's, and even the cook at the Westmark Hotel lit out for the boom. The word was that they were hiring everybody in the rush to get oil flowing from Prudhoe Bay.

When she got to Fairbanks, Susan learned differently. "After signing up at every union labor hall and getting no response, I began to worry," she says. They were hiring all the craftspeople they could find, true. In fact, there were more crafts jobs than there were experienced craftspeople in all Alaska. But workers with no training went to the bottom of long waiting lists. With temperatures regularly dropping to thirty degrees below, Susan shivered with other unskilled workers every morning in lines that stretched three blocks from the hiring hall.

Susan became one more hapless figure in Fairbanks, an overrun city that appeared to be bent on reliving a notorious past. Founded in the gold rush at the turn of the century, Fairbanks started as a supply depot for the nearby mining camps. It soon became a center for gouging merchants, roving con men, and sleazy saloons offering whiskey and women, all of them intent on parting the miners from their money. When gold ran out in the early 1900s, Fairbanks turned respectable. A railroad linking it to Anchorage and the ice-free port of Seward made it a legitimate trade center for the vast interior region. The military built two major installations nearby, Fort Wainwright and Eielson Air Force Base, after World War II. And tourism flourished, complete with gold rush tours and steamboat rides on the Chena River.

The oil strike at Prudhoe Bay, 390 miles to the northwest, turned Fairbanks into an uncontrollable boomtown again. Located midway along the 800-mile pipeline corridor from Prudhoe to Valdez, Fairbanks was an ideal site for the warehouses and hiring halls. By 1975, its population had doubled in five years to twenty thousand as word spread that the oil companies were paying high wages to whoever was willing to work in cold Alaska.

By the time Susan arrived, the town was overflowing. The airport was strewn with the sleeping bodies of Outsiders who had risked their savings on a plane ticket north. One-room apartments, when they could be found, were renting at $600 a month. A hamburger that would have cost 75 cents in Tulsa cost $4 here. Residents talked derisively about the influx of Okies and Texans, but businesses happily took their money. Despite the high prices, shoppers backed up daily at grocery checkout counters, and the bars on Second Avenue (known as "Two Street" by the regulars) were awash with the laughter of pipeline workers in town for their week off. They bought drinks with $100 bills and casually polished the bar with the uncounted change as they regaled one another with their experiences on the job. Women nursing long, pink drinks sidled up to the spenders and joined in the hilarity.

Meanwhile, Susan continued to wait in line at the hiring hall, and her anxiety continued to grow. She noticed that people with pointed shoes and southern accents kept being hired ahead of her. She had heard there was a law requiring pipeline contractors to hire Alaska residents first, and she wondered what had become of it. But the men at the union hiring table only shrugged or gave her a sly wink when she asked.

The Trans-Alaska Pipeline Authorization Act passed by Congress in 1973 had indeed specified Alaska hiring preference, but it was regarded as a joke at the hiring halls. A racket in counterfeit Alaska residency cards blossomed right from the onset of pipeline construction, and the unions helped it grow. "You know the right bar or the right girl working the streets and you find out where you can get a counterfeit residency card," J. Randy Carr, a state labor department investigator, recalls. "Illegal cards were going for a hundred dollars a pop and no one in the system seemed to be concerned about it." Carr says he was in on a sting operation in which the state caught one seller with two hundred counterfeit cards in his possession. He was charged with "uttering a forged instrument," but the judge threw out the case. His reasoning? The defendant had represented the cards as forged, so he hadn't attempted to hoodwink anyone.

The unions' willingness to accept falsified residence cards was only one of the obstacles between Susan and a job. Another was her gender. The Trans-Alaska Pipeline Authorization Act also specified that the project conform to the government's affirmative action program, which banned discrimination by sex, yet Susan noticed that only men seemed to be getting jobs at the International Union of Operating Engineers table. When she complained, the man behind the table put it to her bluntly: "We have never hired women and don't expect to start doing so." The Operating Engineers were represented by Local 302, based in Seattle. "You can imagine how hard they enforced the Alaska hire statutes," Carr comments, "since nearly all their members came from Seattle."

Susan decided to hang in and fight. She got a job waiting tables at the Grubstake. There she met a cabdriver who told her to see Randy Parker, director of the Equal Employment Opportunity Center, and tell him about her experience with the Operating Engineers. Parker called the Operating Engineers and read them the equal employment opportunity provision in the pipeline act. The union decided that hiring Susan might be less troublesome than defending a discrimination suit. Besides, there were other ways to deal with the problem.

Susan was hired—to operate Cat dozer number 7, a job calculated to send her packing. Nervous and unsure whether she could handle the mammoth machine, she nevertheless entered the training program and kept at it after hours. To the surprise of everyone, including herself, she passed the test. She was ready to join the massive invasion of men and machines slicing an 800-mile corridor north to south across Alaska.

There was an urgency to work on the pipeline that was like the fervor of a military expedition. Crews landed by land, sea, and air all along the route. Then they raced to see who could move fastest. Nineteen camps, with random names like Happy Valley, Kennedy, and Sheep Creek, were built along the route. Each had a narrow, prefabricated dormitory, complete with dining hall, rec room, and first- aid station. Support planes, barges, and trucks brought in a steady stream of supplies, from the latest tools to thick sirloin steaks. Top-notch equipment and plentiful food came with the job.

A new construction consortium called Alyeska Pipeline Service Company had replaced the temporary TAPS operation. It formed a joint command for the eight oil companies that planned to ship oil from Prudhoe. The chief executive was Edward L. Patton, a Humble Oil refinery builder whose blunt, no-nonsense leadership style was as military as his name.

Design plans for the pipeline had been laid in Houston, where the best minds in arctic construction got together in command rooms at an office building once occupied by famed wildcatter Glenn McCarthy. Geotechnical engineers studied how to move hot oil across frozen ground. Seismologists worked with civil engineers to protect the pipeline from earthquake shocks. Naturalists mapped ways to accommodate the migration of caribou. Out of it evolved a pioneering design—a pipeline technology that even its critics agree exceeded all past technical horizons.

The project contractors were world famous. Bechtel Corporation, based in San Francisco, became the chief contractor for the main pipeline. Fluor Corporation of Los Angeles would build the twelve pump stations and the storage terminal on the bedrock across the inlet at Valdez. They, in turn, assigned construction work to more than a dozen subcontractors. Together, they unleashed an army of twenty-one thousand workers with orders to build the pipeline, pumping stations, and auxiliaries as fast as possible. Welding applicants got first consideration. It was estimated that seventy-one thousand welds would be required to string the pipeline from Prudhoe to Valdez. At least two thousand welders were hired, who in turn required two thousand helpers. About three thousand operators were needed to run the machines—fleets of trucks, bulldozers, and myriad pumps and generators. And that meant hiring thousands of additional helpers, because every machine operator had to have an oiler. Just about every conceivable craft—from carpenters to electricians to millwrights—was represented in the more than eighty job classifications on the project. The largest group were the support forces, ranging from laborers to bull cooks, who handled the jobs that machines could not or craftsmen would not. All were represented by seventeen separate unions, each with its own contract and jurisdiction.

Everything was geared for speed. Alyeska was prepared to accept higher construction costs any time the alternative meant delay. Each day lost meant the sacrifice of profits from 660,000 barrels of oil, the estimated daily flow at start-up. No one attempted to peg the precise figure; it was impressive enough to say that at $10 a barrel, oil companies would be giving up $6.6 million of income a day.

The consortium of oil companies wanted the pipeline completed in three years, and it paid heavily to ensure that goal. No contractor in the construction link had to worry about going belly-up. The contractors worked on a no-risk, cost-plus basis, which provided an incentive to meet the deadline without the concern of holding down charges. Well in advance of construction, Alyeska also got the seventeen international craft unions to sign agreements that no strikes, picketing, work stoppages, slowdowns, or other disruptive activity would be tolerated. In return, the unions won the most lavish worker wages in the United States.

The lowest paid were the laborers, many of them right out of high school, their $10.67 an hour nearly double the $5.80 standard wage for construction labor in 1974. And that was before overtime. The usual workweek at the outset was a "7-10"—seven days a week, ten hours a day—with every third week off. That grew to "7-12" as contractors pushed to meet deadlines. Because every hour after the first forty hours was at time and a half, with double time on Sundays and holidays, even the lowliest worker made better than $1,000 a week. The elite were the welders, or "pipeliners," most of them imported from Oklahoma and Texas, who averaged about $90,000 a year. The welders didn't have to meet the residency requirement because few Alaskans had the necessary skills. They did have to pass a stiff test before they were hired, and their welds on the job had to pass not only visual checks but X-rays as well.

In tales of goldbricking on the pipeline, welders emerged as the most imaginative. One worker claimed he saw a welder go a full week without making a weld. He pretended he was working but actually spent the time drawing maps with a torch on a piece of pipe, which he later sold as souvenirs for $500 apiece. Ducking work was easy, because without incentives to hold down costs, contractors often over-hired. Jan Hansen, who became the state's workers' compensation hearing officer, worked on the pipeline as a timekeeper at Galbraith Lake, about 150 miles above the Arctic Circle. She says the place was so overstaffed that it was common to see people reading or sleeping on the job. One transferee from Atigun Pass in the Brooks Range sat and did nothing for a full week until someone noticed she was there. "And of the thirty-five people in our place, I was the only one who was ever an Alaska resident," she recalls.

However, nowhere was waste and greed more evident than in the domain of Teamsters Local 959. Led by Jesse L. Carr (no relation to J. Randy Carr), a union boss in the classic tough-guy mold, the union amassed a fortune in dues during the construction of the pipeline. At the height of its membership in 1975, the Teamsters banked about $1 million a week in its pension trust accounts at the National Bank of Alaska, according to news reports that the union did not refute. While some of that money came from Teamsters working in other occupations, Carr knew how to apply muscle to pipeline contractors. He won hundreds of featherbedding jobs by coercing deadline-pressured contractors to place more than the normal crew of workers on jobs in the name of safety or labor peace.

When decisions happened to go against the Teamsters, Carr was a master at circumventing the no-strike clause. He once demanded that Teamster-driven pilot cars accompany all trucks and that two Teamsters sit in each base ambulance, twenty-four hours a day. When

Alyeska refused, he pulled all Teamsters off the job for emergency "safety" meetings, stopping work as effectively as any strike. The costly pampering of long-haul truckers became a pipeline joke. Their base pay was a comparatively modest $10.67 an hour, but Carr demanded and won a stipulation that they be paid for eighteen hours per day no matter how many hours they actually worked.

The Teamsters' attempts to claim control over anything on wheels got them into a running fight over job jurisdictions with the International Union of Operating Engineers, which also manned driving equipment. When a Teamster challenged, the Operating Engineer would walk off the job in protest, or vice versa. To keep the work going, Alyeska arbitrators would usually end up assigning both men to the job or simply rule for the Teamsters. The arbitrators reasoned that the Operating Engineers would be gone after the pipeline was built, but Alyeska would have to live with the Teamsters, who at that time controlled a third of the state's recruitable work force.

Carr's Teamsters Local 959 was an empire. Besides the pipeline workers, it was also the bargaining unit for the Anchorage Police Department, the Alaska Hospital and Medical Employees, the Alaska Roughnecks and Drillers, the Anchorage Independent Longshoremen, and Skagway Longshore Unit No. 1. "Teamsters Local 959 thinks it runs the state of Alaska … and that's about right," Alyeska chief Ed Patton said in a speech following a string of Teamster-inspired jurisdictional disputes in 1975. Peter DeMay recalls that Jesse Carr violated the terms of the no-strike clause and binding arbitration so often that Alyeska had to take him to court.

The *Los Angeles Times* and the *Anchorage Daily News* both assigned reporters to investigate stories that Carr provided Teamster jobs for hoodlums and ex-cons, particularly at the Fairbanks warehouse complex where police said a large percentage of the material and tools shipped for the pipeline project kept disappearing mysteriously. The *Daily News*'s series on the inner workings of Local 959, published in December 1975, won the fledgling paper a Pulitzer Prize. Rumors of Teamster ties to organized crime spread in the summer of 1976 when two Teamster shop stewards were abducted from the Fairbanks pipeline warehouse in mob style. Their bullet-riddled bodies were found weeks later, but police conducted only a cursory investigation. They were not about to get involved in the union's internal affairs.

Thievery, rape, and other violent crimes were rising steeply along the pipeline, and the state police often felt powerless to deal with them. (Gambling and prostitution, while rampant, were not considered major crimes.) A big part of the problem, the papers reported, was that pipeline authorities were late in passing on reports. "Alyeska is willing to accept a certain level of theft in order to buy labor peace," State Attorney General Avrum M. Gross was quoted as saying in a *Los Angeles Times* piece of November 18, 1975. "They'll do nothing to provoke the unions. They just want to finish that line. They've stayed about ten miles away from state law enforcement people."

The contractors took their cue from Alyeska, even condoning blatant cheating on state income taxes by an estimated one fifth of their employees. The young state had neither the manpower nor the methods to deal with tax chiselers, and contractors simply grinned when workers claimed as many as sixty deductions on their state W-4 forms.

The state's impotence in cracking down on crime on the pipeline became so apparent that a federal organized crime strike force from California moved in with the FBI to try to clean up. In 1976, after a two-year investigation, nine persons were indicted, including a former assistant U.S. attorney who earlier had been forced from office for mishandling an investigation of Jesse Carr. All nine either had their cases thrown out or were acquitted. Alaska's image as a haven for lawbreakers and crooks on the lam survived intact during the pipeline years. Carr's empire would fall apart later, but not because any arm of the law caught up with him.

There were more poignant social costs as well. Many of the thousands of workers who flocked to Alaska were grateful for the chance at boom wages. They came with the resolve to tough out the long workweeks and the interminable subzero winters to save money to buy houses or set up small businesses when they returned home. However, the absence was tough on families. No one kept count of the marriages broken up or the infidelities, but they were the talk of the pipeline camps. And as bloated as the salaries were, hordes left their jobs with no more money than when they started. Stories abounded of paychecks squandered on drinking, gambling, and trips to Hawaii or Las Vegas for a few days in the sun or at the casinos.

In Anchorage and Fairbanks bars, you could find drugs for sale out in the open. "People didn't do the stuff on the job or they would be fired," one pipeline worker says. "But on their week off, after working three weeks steady, they would come into town and just lose it." Valdez was the handiest recreation spot for pipeline families. "You would see children of pipeline workers buy their lunch with hundred-dollar bills," a community college president recalls. He says hustlers siphoned entire family budgets with trays of questionable gems, dubious art, and all kinds of gold items whose real value was difficult to appraise. Even after oil started flowing, some workers stayed on just trying to hold on to the carnival mood.

Job turnover was a nightmare for the bosses. More than fifty thousand people had to be hired to maintain the twenty-one-thousand-job level. Some quit as soon as they stepped out into the numbing winds at their first work site. Dropout by Natives was particularly high. A general statement promising minority hiring had been written into the pipeline bill. The hope was that pipeline income, combined with training in particular crafts, would equip Natives to participate in the general economy after the pipeline was finished. The Alyeska Pipeline Service Company worked out the specifics with the Alaska Federation of Natives and agreed on a goal of three thousand Native hires. That was exceeded by about twenty-one hundred before the pipeline was finished, but the good intentions were never realized.

More than half of all Natives hired worked for eight weeks or less. Most simply could not adapt to a white man's regimen of twelve-hour days and a camp life far removed from family. Many left their jobs to fish when the salmon ran and to hunt when the caribou migrated. An estimated 46 percent of the Natives who left were "involuntarily terminated." Some of these dismissals involved jobs that were eliminated, but most were dismissals for cause, most commonly for drunkenness, absence, or tardiness. "Time meant nothing to them," one supervisor complained. "They were used to subsistence life-styles and would not change their habits." Most of the Native workers who did stick it out came from the larger villages, such as Kotzebue, Nome, and Dillingham, observed Charles Elder, Jr., a former vice-president of Alyeska. "They hung in there because they were being converted to a cash economy," he says. "They discovered what money was and what you could do with it."

Unfortunately, success bred cultural problems for some of the Natives who did hang in. With earnings ranging from $1,000 to $1,500 a week—and often more—many earned in one month what their entire families in the village earned in one year. (The median income for Native families in the villages was only $5,200 a year even in the mid-1970s, when they were already receiving dividends from their Native corporations.) The brief encounter with pipeline wages often caused estrangements at home. Some refused to return to the villages when the project ended, undermining the long-standing cultural tradition that called for family members to share their income, food, and energy for the benefit of all. This essentially left the elderly—the poorest and the weakest—to keep together the values, customs, and organizational structures of the community.

A good number who did return tell how their pipeline incomes enabled them to buy trailer homes, snowmobiles, and other luxuries. But they also developed an appetite for the cash economy, and that made them more aggressive in seeking changes to the old ways. And with some of those who returned, drugs came to the villages for the first time.

While Natives had the hardest problems adjusting to jobs on the pipeline, the nineteen hundred women hired on the project probably faced the worst obstacles. They had to overcome hiring discrimination, sexual harassment, and macho resentment.

Susan Blomfield knew all about it. Her first assignment was to Five-Mile Camp on the Yukon River near the Arctic Circle. Six hundred men were in camp and only eight women, including two prostitutes, two labor union staff workers, and four secretaries. Hookers operated openly, at a rate of $300 a customer, and Susan says she saw one man turn over his entire paycheck.

"A woman intent on doing the work for which she was hired found it hard to gain respect," Susan says. "We faced a constant threat from men. I carried a big crescent wrench wherever I went. Everyone sat around and got drunk after work. Men would come to the dorm, scratching on the doors and making propositions." The environment made it unpleasant for her to even ride the bus to the job site. The buses were driven by male crews who plastered the ceilings and inside panels with pictures of naked women and carried on a crude banter meant to be overheard.

Because she refused to sleep with her boss, Susan says, she often got the worst assignments. One day, with the windchill factor at one hundred degrees below zero, she was told to go out and make sure the Rollagon hadn't quit running. Rollagons are huge vehicles with broad tires that travel well in snow and do a minimum of damage to spongy tundra. They had to be kept running all night because starting them cold was impossible in the arctic winter. Susan waded atop 10-foot drifts to get to the machine. When she climbed into the cab, a gale blew the door shut and it was an hour before the wind died down enough for her to escape. Only the heat from the running engine had kept her alive.

After that, Susan says, they decided she should not go alone. "So they would tie me and a lovesick guy named Gilbert on a rope which was tied to the building. We would grope our way through the snow and he kept trying to kiss me all the way. I felt sorry for him. The men kept telling him that I really cared about him and that I would give in if he tried to kiss me."

Susan regularly made at least $1,000 a week. During one rush period when 160 pieces of equipment were needed at once, she and another operating engineer made $2,500 apiece for the week by working seven straight eighteen-hour days changing oil. Susan increased her savings by buying and reselling condos for fast profits on the steaming Fairbanks real estate market. She had amassed $100,000 by the time her pipeline job ended and it was time to move back to reality.

While working as a grade checker, Susan had met a dozer operator she liked. They got married, a fairly frequent ending for pipeline romances. (One bride clambered on top of the pipeline in a long white gown to exchange vows with her groom.) Susan now lives with her husband, Mike, in Fairbanks. Both closely monitor news about the pipeline they helped build.

But happy accounts of those years always seem to be matched by dark ones. Lori Keim, a pert, auburn-haired newspaper copy editor in her mid-thirties, saw her boyfriend, a bright student with an academic scholarship to Texas A&M, pour his income into drugs. "He was a smart and nice kid who just wanted to go to college," Lori says. "But his dad talked him out of it, said he'd be crazy to pass up the chance to earn big bucks. He could always go to college, he told him. So the boy got one of the thirty-dollar-an-hour jobs — he was a foreman working twelve-hour days. Before long he was drinking heavily and then deep into cocaine.

"Years later, when his brain was fully fried, he got a gun, held his dad hostage, and accused him of putting him on the road to ruin," Lori says. "Then he shot his father dead, and then himself. It was such a waste. That crazy, manic time took a toll on the people who worked on the pipeline and earned those incredible salaries."

The pipeline was completed in 1977. It made the three-year deadline despite a scary delay in 1976, when a subcontractor was caught trying to rush the project along by falsifying X-rayed welding reports. He had certified some with minor deficiencies as acceptable and failed to X-ray several other welds at all. Besides precious time, it cost Alyeska $50 million to dig up, redo, and recertify the welds to the satisfaction of the U.S. Department of Transportation and critics in Congress.

The final cost of the pipeline was $8 billion, nearly nine times the initial estimate. Unanticipated leaps in costs, plus steadily rising tanker shipping charges during the double-digit inflation of the 1970s, would have made the project nearly worthless had not the Arab oil embargo sent oil prices spiraling during the 1973–74 OPEC rebellion. University of Alaska economists estimated that the cost of shipping oil from Prudhoe Bay was now up to $10 a barrel, which was greater than the 1972 market value of crude oil delivered to refineries in the lower forty-eight. In fact, it took a second Mideast crisis — the 1979 Iranian revolution, which tripled oil export prices — to make the Prudhoe Bay development truly profitable for the oil companies and the state of Alaska.

Nevertheless, the pipeline is viewed as a technological marvel and has become a worldwide tourist attraction. It starts at pump station No. 1 on the tundra on the edge of the Arctic Ocean at Prudhoe Bay. On its journey south, it traverses the mighty Brooks Range at Atigun Pass, crosses the mile-wide Yukon River, and winds through cuts in spruce forests and river valleys until it reaches the Keystone Canyon outside of Valdez. There, it leaves the bank of the Lowe River and rises like an encased stovepipe up the steep canyon cliffs on its way to the storage tanks at Valdez. Wherever the pipeline crosses rock it is buried in a trench, and it is elevated on stanchions over unstable permafrost that would melt if it made contact with the 140-degree oil flowing through the pipe. Slightly more than half of the pipeline is above ground. Helicopters and ground forces maintain round-the-clock security the length of the line.

On June 20, 1977, *The Anchorage Times* reported in a banner headline, "FIRST OIL FLOWS (After 8 Years, 4 Months, 10 Days)." The metered tap was opened, but a faulty valve caused an inferno four minutes after oil started to run. One man was killed and the line was shut for nine days. "Oil's There at Last," read the headline on July 29. The first load of oil had reached the terminal and was on its way. On August 1, the tanker *ARCO* sailed out of Valdez with the first shipment and headed for California. The twelve pump stations began sending about 1.2 million barrels of oil a day from Prudhoe to Valdez. Soon, the pipeline would provide about 25 percent of the nation's oil needs, and fund about 85 percent of the state's budget.

Alaska became wealthy overnight—in fact, wealthier than anyone imagined. When world oil prices tripled, revenues poured into the state treasury by the billions. Poor Alaska had finally struck it rich.

CHAPTER 8

Days of Milk
and Barley

It IS LATE SUMMER. I am in my third year in Alaska, and the state is changing fast. I am about 65 miles out of Anchorage on the other side of Cook Inlet, and I have just run out of tarmac road. A dusty sign on the gravel says "Point MacKenzie," and the dirt road heads directly into a heavy cottonwood, spruce, and birch forest. Sleeping Lady, the crowning contour of Mount Susitna, is on the horizon.

This looks like good moose and bear country. For miles there is no sign of life, yet the deeper I drive into the woods, the clearer it becomes that someone intended this road to leave a permanent mark upon the land. I see torn-up clearings with mounds of dirt and stumps on either side of the road, evidence that man has tried to rearrange nature. And here and there in the wilderness I make out deteriorating barns, rusting farm machinery, and thousands of acres of fallow fields that are being reclaimed by weeds and scrub.

Far down the rutted road, I find a survivor, a sixtyish man who peers at me from under the hood of an old truck that sits in a muddy barnyard. Ducks, geese, and sheep scatter as I approach.

"Can you talk while you're working?" I ask.

"That's okay, I can take a break," he says. He seems happy to have a visitor.

He introduces himself as Harvey Baskin. The desolation I saw along the way, he explains, is the remains of Alaska's attempt to set up a dairy business. He hears the state has poured at least $100 million into its grandiose agriculture project, of which dairy farming is the heart, but the only thing it accomplished was to protect the jobs of bureaucrats. Harvey says he is but one of two of the original dozen or so homestead farmers whose farms haven't been repossessed. He, too, is behind on his loan payments and he doesn't know how much longer he can hold on.

The story of how Alaska tried to develop a dairy industry in the subarctic frontier involves adventurous men and women like Harvey Baskin. Their saga belongs alongside that of the miners and trappers, breeds who pride themselves on endurance. But the story also involves foolish decisions at high levels that created a costly and environmentally destructive boondoggle.

The state did not know what to do with the gusher of money that poured in after oil began to flow from Prudhoe Bay in 1977. Alaskans had expected the royalties would ease the lean state budget and flesh out capital expenditure. But even the most optimistic projections did not foresee the world events that would send oil prices into orbit. By 1981, oil had reached a high of $34 a barrel, an increase of more than 1,000 percent in thirteen years. As owner of the Prudhoe Bay oil fields, the state collected about 12 percent in taxes and royalties from the sale of every barrel piped to Valdez. During the Iranian crisis alone, Alaska's revenues tripled to $4.5 billion.

A few years before, the annual state budget had amounted to only $368 million, supplemented heavily by the federal dole. In 1969, the sale of Prudhoe oil leases had generated a modest windfall of $900 million. But that was a onetime bonus, quickly gobbled up by the long-starved needs of schools, hospitals, social services, and transportation.

Dealing with a steady stream of wealth was a task for which Alaska was not prepared, and a free-for-all promptly developed among the governor, the house members, and the twenty senators. The legislature—an assortment of fishermen, miners, lumberjacks, lawyers, real estate agents, small businessmen, and sourdoughs—began to act like a frontier version of Tammany Hall. The legislative committee chairmen met in secret to divide the largess, circumventing the normal budget process. Indeed, the revenue system was so overloaded that no one really knew how much money was coming in or being spent. Administrators and lawmakers accused one another of doctoring figures to their own advantage. The press made much of the disparities, some as high as $100 million, between revenue reports put out by the Republican administration and those of the Democrat-controlled legislature.

The oil industry watched quietly from the sidelines. The battle nicely diverted attention from proposals to adjust depletion tax allowances in the state's favor. They had less chance of passing as long as the legislature was in disarray.

Into this chaos stepped Russell Meekins, Jr., a thirty-year-old Young Turk Democrat from Anchorage who was the son of an auto dealer. He wooed other disenchanted Democratic legislators who had been ignored in the pie-splitting and quietly forged deals with the Republican minority, who had been utterly excluded. By the middle of the 1981 legislative session, Meekins had secretly formed an insurgent coalition. Seizing a moment when the speaker's chair was temporarily unoccupied, Meekins moved in, called for a motion to remove the current speaker, and declared the motion passed before the old guard, meeting in caucus, knew what had happened. His band of insurgents responded on cue.

In the uproar that ensued, shouts of "kangaroo court" and "banana republicanism" echoed in the chambers. The deposed Democratic leaders were certain the courts would restore their control. But incredibly, the courts upheld the coup, ruling in effect that they wanted no part in participating in the internal organization of another branch of government.

Meekins then supported a deal that everyone could understand. One third of the surplus from the oil revenues would go to the governor, one third to the senate, and one third to the house. It was understood that the governor would not question how the legislature spent its allocation and the legislature would not question how the governor disposed of his—an open invitation to conflict-of-interest governance.

No one took advantage of the deal more audaciously than Republican governor Jay Hammond. Elected to a second term in 1978, Hammond had barely survived a bitter primary, which he won by ninety-eight votes. A former hunting and fishing guide, he had been hammered hard by his critics — his primary opponent, ex-governor Hickel, foremost among them — for being a "no-growth" environmentalist. Hammond needed to blunt the charges, and an idea came to him. Why not use oil revenues to create an agriculture industry in Alaska? That would put a stop to the harping for more development, and it would also bring into the state a clean, green industry, consistent with Hammond's environmental leanings.

The governor called in his top strategist, Bob Palmer, and told him to make it happen. Palmer turned to the University of Alaska at Fairbanks for help. In time, Palmer had what he wanted: an authoritative-sounding feasibility study backing Hammond's dream. The report found "a general consensus that production of feed grain (principally barley) for export and to supply in-state livestock enterprises would be a logical thrust for development." The professors predicted that agriculture could make Alaska a national breadbasket, like the Midwest. The administration predicted that the state would be self-sufficient in eggs and milk by 1990.

No one questioned whether the finding might be slightly self-serving. The proposed barley farms would be virtually in the university's backyard and held out the ongoing potential for lucrative, state-funded consulting contracts. Nor did anyone ask how remote and undeveloped Alaska could ever get a competitive edge in the international barley market, or if, in fact, such a market existed. Only state senator Victor Fischer, founder of Alaska's Institute of Social and Economic Research, a think tank, came close to challenging the governor's plans. Noting that the state was preparing to bankroll farmers with millions of dollars in credit, he calculated it would cost an estimated $10 in state dollars to produce every $1 worth of agricultural goods. He politely wondered whether this might not be too high a ratio of subsidy. The governor told Fischer not to worry. After all, hadn't university experts endorsed the plan?

Hammond's great leap forward into agriculture designated 84,000 acres in the Delta area, deep in the interior just southeast of Fairbanks, as Alaska's barley-producing capital. About 70,000 of those acres were still in spruce forest and had to be cleared, but the program was in high gear by 1982. Alaskans of all sorts entered the lottery for barley-farm land. Easy loan money from the state's

Agricultural Revolving Loan Fund put them in business, and promises of an elaborate transportation system to link them to world markets in Korea, Japan, and Asian markets beyond further buoyed their hopes.

The state proceeded confidently. It bought $940,000 worth of railroad grain cars to carry Delta barley to Seward, where the footings for an $8 million grain terminal were being erected in the harbor. Although Delta was 60 miles away from the nearest railroad track, it was simply understood that adequate linkage would be provided once barley fields started ripening. Meanwhile, barley fever had so seized the state that Valdez, closer to Delta and accessible by the Richardson Highway, built a rival grain terminal in its harbor. This one initially cost $15 million, financed by municipal bonds. Not a bushel of barley had been ordered by any international buyer up to this point, but the governor and his advisers were confident that a great new industry was on its way.

It had been intended from the outset that Alaskans themselves would be large consumers of Alaska barley—or, rather, their cows would be. A few small, family-owned dairy farms had existed for years in the Matanuska Valley outside of Anchorage, but this was not the market Hammond had in mind. He wanted large-scale dairy farms with hundreds of cows. Their needs would assure a steady in-state market for barley, and, in turn, a steady supply of milk—or so the state promised. True to its word, the administration set aside 33,000 heavily forested acres on Point MacKenzie, excellent moose and bear habitat, for dairy farming. It held a second lottery to give away about 14,000 acres to would-be dairy farmers, who would become eligible for a million-dollar line of credit from the state. No prior farming experience was necessary. The state would issue each winner a set of instructions on how to establish a dairy farm.

Harvey Baskin didn't win, but his wife and daughter hit it big and happily turned over their acreage to him with the understanding that they would not have to live on the farm. A retired chief master sergeant, Baskin had high hopes of carving out a second career in the wilderness. He dug into his savings to meet the 25 percent collateral that made him eligible for the million-dollar line of credit. "The state gave us an opportunity you couldn't get anywhere else in the world," he says. Further, he claims, he was assured that the state-financed

Matanuska Maid creamery would buy all his milk at good prices. A state-financed slaughterhouse, Mt. McKinley Meats, would buy calves and other expendable livestock for market. And good-quality grain was promised from the state-subsidized farms in Delta; he would buy it through the state-subsidized supply store in Palmer.

Baskin says his doubts about the state's competence to administer such an ambitious agricultural project started the day he saw his land at Point MacKenzie. "All there was was a gravel road, some stakes the state had driven in, and no state employee to show you anything," Baskin says. "The land was so wet you couldn't get a tractor on it. Maybe a hundred fifty of those five hundred acres were farmable. And I later found out we were one of the few farms that ever put up honest collateral for our loan. Hell, I learned some got their farms without putting up a penny. They listed nonexistent gravel pits as collateral. The state never checked."

Baskin reasoned that feeding an anticipated herd of one hundred cows by hand did not make sense, so he brought in a dairy expert to automate the process. "The state inspectors hopped on me for changing the design," Baskin recalls. "They said it was a violation of my loan agreement, and they threatened to cut off the money. It made no difference that I told them this was standard design in Minnesota. I had to redo the alley in front of the stalls to please the local bureaucrats. So I'm feeding the cows by wheelbarrow."

Baskin lived by himself in a small trailer on the edge of a forest for eighteen months while he cleared the usable land. Operating his own bulldozer, putting in fifteen-hour days, and grudgingly conforming to the state inspector's nit-picking rules, he met the state's thirty-six-month deadline and had his dairy farm operating by the fall of 1985. But Baskin's herd of 102 holsteins had barely gotten to know their stalls when the Matanuska Maid creamery, the farm's main source of income, filed for bankruptcy.

The state creamery had been paying Alaska farmers a generous $23 per hundred pounds of milk at the outset of the Point MacKenzie program. However, this price became highly uncompetitive in Alaska's new oil-based economy. Increased demands generated by a growing and increasingly affluent population made it more profitable to ship in large quantities of fresh goods in huge, refrigerated container ships with fast roll-on, roll-off service. Ironically, it was Sun

Oil, an eastern firm that was not among the Prudhoe developers, that exploited this lucrative market. Its new 790-foot container ship *The Great Land* started service to Alaska in 1976 to deliver supplies to the pipeline, but quickly switched to hauling food in by truck-trailer. Eliminating loading and unloading by crews of longshoremen not only made service cheaper but allowed a guarantee of two-and-a-half-day delivery for perishables. By the early 1980s, Alaskans could buy milk cheaper shipped in from Seattle, some 2,000 land miles away, than they could from the local Matanuska Maid creamery.

Unable to adjust to the realities, the creamery nevertheless tried to maintain its promised price to Alaska farmers by borrowing on its assets, which essentially were the state's pockets. When it could borrow no more, it collapsed—$3 million in debt. The whole Point MacKenzie dairy project was now in deep trouble. The price of milk at the creamery dropped to $20 per hundred pounds. Angry farmers filed lawsuits, claiming the state had concealed the creamery's precarious financial position and, in effect, had misrepresented the economic potential of dairy farming at Point MacKenzie. When William Sheffield, a Democrat, succeeded Hammond as governor in 1982, he froze all plans for further agricultural subsidies pending a complete review. That further distressed the farmers who had cleared the land and had already started milking cattle.

Sande Wright, a contractor who grew up on a Montana cattle ranch, was the first dairy homesteader to go under. In his late thirties, with a thick crop of curly reddish hair and the body of an athlete, Wright has an easy smile, but it develops a nervous twitch when he describes his dairy adventure in Alaska.

Wright said he invested $500,000 of his own money—"everything I ever made in life"—to acquire and clear 640 acres of Point MacKenzie land. With the help of a million dollars borrowed from the Agricultural Revolving Loan Fund, Wright had modern dairy barns on the site and started milking a herd in excess of one hundred cows by the fall of 1985. He also brought in a double-wide mobile home from Anchorage and erected a handsome knotty pine front, establishing the finest residence in Point MacKenzie. It was just down the road from the new elementary school, which was part of the state's grand plan to develop a booming agricultural community.

Wright's vision of a good life on the edge of the wilderness began to blur even before the creamery went under. He discovered that the dairy farming techniques he learned from his father did not work in Alaska. For one thing, he found he could not afford to raise his own calves. "Because of the feed expense, it was costing us twelve hundred dollars to raise a heifer from the time she was dropped," Wright says. "We could buy really top heifers out of Canada for a thousand dollars or under, so we quit raising calves. We sold some and gave others away. And I would say half of the bulls we ended up knocking on the head. There was no market for them. We told the dog mushers on Knik Road to come and get them."

Wright tried to keep his farm going by pumping in money he earned with his earth-moving equipment, mainly his five bulldozers. When the creamery failed and the price of milk dropped, losses mounted to $15,000 a month. He now had no chance of meeting the $12,000 monthly payments on his $1 million loan. Wright filed for bankruptcy to stay the repossession of his farm, but there was no escape. "They dragged me into court four times trying to get relief from the bankruptcy stays so they could repossess the cattle," he says. "On the last try, I handed them the keys. They ended up butchering all of the cattle … told the slaughterhouse to take them all."

In the end, Wright lost not only his farm but his contracting equipment. His struggle to meet his loan payments contributed to the breakup of his marriage. And he owes the Internal Revenue Service $100,000 in unpaid withholding and Social Security deductions for his farm help. He cannot even start anew as a contractor because no company will bond a person in such fiscal distress.

The entire Point MacKenzie dairy development was soon plunged into financial jeopardy. In all, the state loaned about $20 million to the farmers. Few made even a single payment before their farms were repossessed. Outside of Harvey Baskin, who looks to his lawsuit against the state for salvation, only one other homestead dairy farmer remained in business by the beginning of 1991. That farmer was an Anchorage physician who managed to ward off repossession mainly because the state wiped out a $1.4 million loan in order to keep some Alaska milk flowing into the struggling state creamery. Even this sweetheart deal collapsed by midsummer. With unforgiven loans totaling $2.4 million, the physician walked away from his debts and gave the farm back to the state, leaving Baskin the sole surviving dairy farmer by 1992.

While advertising that it sells Alaska milk, Matanuska Maid stays afloat by purchasing most of its milk from Washington State. "You'd have to put it under a microscope to find the Alaska milk," Baskin says of the current product. Meanwhile, a court order has put a freeze on all of the repossessed farms, and they are deteriorating rapidly on this once unspoiled land. Vandals have torn Wright's handsome house to pieces. Windows have been smashed, appliances mashed into rusting parts, and a fire believed started by squatters has burned a hole through the roof. A reporter who walked into the stables a year after Wright departed found piles of manure still covering the floor and the skeleton of a calf in a pen where it had died. The elementary school where twenty-nine children once studied had been torn down. All that is left is a macadam lot littered with debris, a rusting swing stand, and a seesaw.

It was inevitable that the failure of the dairy farms would hasten the demise of Alaska's barley program in Delta. However, the barley farmers were in trouble long before the creamery failure knocked the stanchions from under the milk farmers. The eighteen grain cars bought by the Alaska railroad to haul barley arrived in 1982. They were painted a royal blue and bore the legend "Alaska Agriculture Serving Alaska and the World." However, they never delivered a grain of barley to either Alaska or any other part of the world.

Not only did Alaska fail to find an international barley market, but its sparse and uneven crop could not compete with grain from the Midwest in the lower forty-eight. Governor Sheffield halted construction of the $8 million grain terminal at Seward in 1982 when it was half built. Seward sold some of the I beams and bin-loaders to a Fairbanks dog food manufacturer in 1989, but recovered only a fraction of the investment. The rival grain terminal at Valdez fared worse. It was completed, costing the city an estimated $30 million when interest costs were computed. Never having housed so much as a grain of barley, it still stands in the harbor.

Like the dairymen, the barley farmers never got their production up to the speed envisioned by the state. Bulldozers readily cleared the trees from the 70,000 acres of land designated for barley in Delta, but it was not so easy to cope with myriad other obstacles. Voracious grasshoppers, extended droughts, dropping prices, and even roving bison beset the barley farmers. The Alaska bison, the largest native land mammal in North America, is descended from buffaloes transplanted to Alaska from Wyoming in 1928 to add still more variety to big-game hunting in Alaska. However, roaming across fields in groups of fifty or more, the bison became major pests for the barley farmers. Rather than extend the shooting season or relocate the herds, the state seeded a 2,000-acre barley field across the highway especially for the bison. It took the ton-sized animals all of a month to trample their own barley to the ground and discover better pasture in the farmers' fields.

In 1984, the most active barley farming year, only 16,700 acres in the 84,000-acre Delta region project were harvested. The planting dropped steadily after that, sinking to fewer than 5,000 acres by 1988. Matanuska Maid Farm Supply, the biggest customer in the state, had to start importing barley from the lower forty-eight to support its modest market of horse ranches and family farms. Most barley farmers started to make money only after they stopped planting. They found they could let the fields lie fallow and collect $37 an acre from the U.S. Agricultural Stabilization and Conservation Service under a subsidy program created by Congress in 1985.

Of the more than $40 million Alaska loaned to farmers since Governor Hammond set out to develop an agriculture industry in Alaska, $30 million is still delinquent. Counting the money spent on grain terminals, slaughterhouses, the creamery, and railroad cars, the state's expenditures exceed $100 million. And Alaska is neither agriculturally self-sufficient nor close to it. The only beneficiaries are the well-paid workers in the state department of agriculture, a cadre of about forty executives and support staff—about the same number as when the farm program started—most of them housed in a handsome office building in Palmer. As a bitter Harvey Baskin puts it, "The administration didn't know a damn thing about dairy farming. The program was administered by salary people in career-type jobs. It didn't make a damn bit of difference whether they were overseeing one or fifty dairy farms. They got the same amount of pay."

"We were going to make Alaska an agricultural state," Jay Hammond reflected after leaving office. "Frankly, had we not had oil revenues of the magnitude at the time, it would have been a gamble I never would have considered."

CHAPTER 9

Season of Gold

For a short period in September, Alaskans enjoy a spectacular season before summer moves into winter. The changing colors of the birch and aspen trees turn mountain foothills into unending vistas of gold. For a moment, Alaskans bask in the glory and try to ignore the shortening days and the snow that dusts the tops of the mountain ranges. These are precious days, and Alaskans make the most of them while they last.

A similar euphoria overcame the governor and legislature of the state of Alaska in 1982. Oil revenues were flowing in so copiously that the state found itself with $4.5 billion in the till, of which it needed only $1 billion to balance the budget. During the debate over the pipeline, some Alaskans had wondered about the downside of oil discovery. How much progress was good for the state? Would rapid development ruin the pristine land? Would the influx of Outsiders change the unique character of Alaska? But with oil revenues flowing in, the downside was forgotten. Instead, there was much talk of Alaska's becoming a "superstate." It now had the means to create an environment that would attract industry, bring lasting employment, and end the instability of a boom-or-bust economy.

Capital gap. That, nearly everyone agreed, had been the biggest obstacle holding back Alaska. "There is no capital for borrowing in Alaska" is the refrain Robert E. LeResche, a Dartmouth-educated cabinet member in several state administrations, recalls from the late 1970s and early 1980s. " 'Don't underestimate the strength of Alaska entrepreneurs,' people were saying. 'Just give them a chance and they will prove that Alaska is ripe for business that will create jobs that will last long after oil is gone.' "

Having rolled the dice on Alaskan agriculture, Governor Hammond wagered a substantial bankroll of oil money on Alaskan capitalism. "The best way to keep the wealth in Alaska is to sponsor research to develop technology and innovation to advance renewable resources," reads a press release issued from the governor's office on December 15, 1978. It announced that Alaska was henceforth placing 5 percent of its oil wealth in a fund that would sponsor research to "identify new products, markets, and technologies for renewable resource industries." On this high promise was born the Alaska Renewable Resources Corporation (ARRC). It was to become a deep well for venture capital, funding projects that normal financing institutions would not handle.

The state gave the new agency an infusion of more than $40 million, including $15 million earmarked for commercial fish processing assistance. The governor appointed three board members, at cabinet-level salaries of $75,000 each, and sent them forth to ensure the future viability of Alaska. They were led by William Spear, a lawyer turned lapel-pin designer, described by some as a dreamer. Spear and his colleagues had great visions of Alaska's future, but, as audits would show, a decided blindness to established procedures for investment activity.

One of the board's first acts was to bring in a Boston consultant, at a $38,000 fee, to set up skills tests to help screen the qualifications of loan applicants. He devised a three-stage aptitude test. Would-be venture capitalists were judged on how well they tossed rings onto a pegboard on the floor, how precisely they stacked building blocks (some of which had rounded edges), and how wisely they selected equipment to ensure survival in the wilderness.

Word of the tests created an uproar in the legislature. State senators castigated ARRC for playing "kiddie games" while ignoring important qualities such as work experience and credit ratings. The tests were soon abandoned, but controversy over how ARRC doled out the state's substantial lending resources continued to simmer.

Doubts about the agency's credibility grew with its first major loan, a $330,000 grant to a freshly organized venture company whose principals included three people who had recently been members of Governor Hammond's administrative staff. Known as Tepa, their company proposed to build a plant to develop a chemical method for turning fish scraps into commercial protein.

With an announcement heralding the project as possibly having global impact, ARRC did considerably more than a traditional lender would to help the company succeed. It provided a two-year moratorium on loan repayments and required no interest payments until the third year. While the much-publicized purpose of ARRC was to create jobs and products in Alaska, Tepa decided to build its plant in the friendlier climate of Coos Bay, Oregon. The company told ARRC that the out-of-state site was necessary because no year-round supply of fish wastes was available in Alaska. It was hard to see how this was going to help Alaska employment or why the ARRC people bought the sales talk, but no one pressed the issue.

After several infusions of state money, it soon became plain that the venture needed far more than a steady supply of fish waste. The plant never overcame cost overruns and start-up problems. It went bankrupt without ever producing a product or making a payment. Auditors listed the state's loss at $410,581. "There were a lot of politically influenced interventions in which we were told to disregard the parameters," Wayne Littleton, ARRC's first executive director, concedes.

ARRC's investment judgment hit bottom in the case of the Salamatof Seafoods, a fish processing plant in Kenai, which sits on a point midway up Cook Inlet. The agency poured $4,961,000 into the plant but could not save it from bankruptcy. After the business lost $2 million during the 1980 fishing season, ARRC moved in to salvage what it could of its investment. It ended up buying out the owner, Tom Waterer, whom Littleton describes as "quite a charmer." Waterer happily accepted a $700,000 loan forgiveness in exchange for 50 percent of his shares and left the state to put the company into bankruptcy and deal with dozens of angry, unpaid fishermen.

A state audit in 1981 found that with the exception of one plant, all of ARRC's numerous investments in seafood facilities had failed or were on the edge. The agency's loan losses exceeded $15 million. Poor management, inferior salmon runs, Japanese competition, and a botulism scare were among its more credible excuses for the dismal record. In one case, however, a sizable investment loss was blamed on the stubborn religious beliefs of a fishing fleet operator who refused to work on Saturdays.

ARRC also invested heavily in nonmarine ventures, but they fared no better. The agency sank $200,000 into a mushroom farm that grew excellent mushrooms but failed to turn a profit because the farmer insisted on delivering the orders himself, socializing excessively at cafés along the route. It put $150,000 into a fox farm at North Pole, southeast of Fairbanks, but disease killed the entire breeding stock of two hundred foxes and, with them, any likelihood of a return on the investment. It lost about $3 million in a politically mandated loan to a sawmill operator who was going to build wood-fired powerhouses in Haines. The struggling little town hadn't developed much of an economy beyond the tourism it drew as gateway to the historic Chilkoot Pass of gold rush fame. News of the state's investment raised high hopes for a year-round industry, but the sawmill went bankrupt before it could complete even one powerhouse.

Agency directors had a hard-luck story for nearly every failure, but state auditors found a pattern to the series of loan defaults: the agency dispersed money blithely (one man got a grant for a proposed dog-powered washing machine), and often without even checking previous business failures or demanding specific project plans.

When he succeeded Jay Hammond as governor in 1982, William Sheffield summoned Robert E. LeResche and put him on the ARRC board with instructions to "straighten out the terrible mess." LeResche and two other new board members phased out the agency. The state replaced it with the Alaska Resources Corporation (ARC), which tried to operate with more specific criteria and accountability for venture capital investments until it, too, was phased out by Sheffield. "The ARRC experience proved it was impossible for a public official to run a legitimate banking operation," LeResche says. "If you try to apply sound lending practices, people say to you, 'Come on, it's not your money. It's the state's. I want my share.'"

The experience also left LeResche unimpressed with the Alaska entrepreneur of the eighties. "These people learned how to squeeze the state tit—all in the name of free enterprise."

If the venture capitalism undertaking proved disillusioning, however, the hope of investing in self-sufficiency for Alaska lived on, fueled by desire on the part of the governor and legislative leaders to leave their mark on history. While ARRC and the Agricultural Revolving Loan Fund were lending millions to sea and land projects, timber cutters and commercial fishermen pressured the congress for their own funding agency. And so the Commercial Fishing and Agriculture Bank (CFAB) was formed as a kind of adjunct to the Farm Credit Administration, a federal loan agency that was broadened to include fisheries in the 1970s.

CFAB was to serve as a cooperative bank for Alaska residents, although what constituted residency was never defined. It would operate much like an independent bank, with professional standards, except that it needed $32 million from the state to get started. This would be deposited with the Farm Credit Administration via the Spokane (Washington) Bank for Cooperatives, thereby qualifying CFAB to acquire more lending funds from the federal system. Those who feared this might prove yet another way to siphon off money from the oil-rich state treasury were assured that the state was totally protected. Alaska would receive class C stock for its $32 million start-up investment with a guarantee that the state could cash in the stock for full reimbursement in the year 2000.

The cooperative bank was launched with "exuberant myopia," in the words of one director. To establish its credibility as a professional lending institution, the management team decided it had to exude professionalism. It spent $246,835 furnishing its Anchorage office. The motif was teak—teak executive desks, teak coffee tables, teak bookcases, and a teak cabinet with a refrigerator and a stock of liquor for the president's office. Commissioned paintings decorated the staff offices, and a large soapstone carving of a land otter with a crab sat atop a rosewood conference table that itself cost $16,220.

The fishermen, processors, and lone potato farmer who made up the board were financial amateurs. To broaden the agency's vision, they decided to take their spouses on an expense-paid fisheries tour of Denmark, England, Rome, and Paris. Next came an agricultural tour through Scandinavia and an administrative trip to London. Other trips were scheduled for Japan, Munich, and Hong Kong.

Lawmakers demanded an audit before CFAB had been in business even a year. The auditors found thousands of additional dollars spent on a private apartment maintained in Juneau, lavish dinners in Anchorage's best restaurants, and bonuses for staff and directors. "A significant number of the expenditures may be inappropriate for an entity subsidized by public funds," the audit noted. CFAB responded that it was a private business operating under standards of private business.

That was too much for state senator Arliss Sturgulewski of Anchorage, a down-to-earth woman not given to outrage. Expressing strong concern over "questionable management expenses," she asked CFAB how it intended to approach repayment of the state's investment. The response of CFAB's lusty chairwoman, Roseleen "Snooks" Moore, who regularly fished her own boat in dangerous False Pass in the Aleutians, was uncharacteristically subdued. Repayment, she wrote, is "a multi-faceted problem that must be approached carefully."

It turned out that CFAB was in financial trouble almost as soon as it started. It was no more judicious in its lending procedures than it was in its administrative expenditures. It had virtually shoveled out $100 million in loans by 1984, and 35 percent of those were "non-performing."

The cooperative lost millions financing crab boats at a time when Alaska crabs were disappearing from overfishing. "People were standing in line borrowing money for crab boats," Forest J. Paulson, then CFAB's chief executive, recalls. "There was about an eight-month lead time for boats to be built. We couldn't foresee that the crabs would vanish before the boats were built." Alaska commercial fishermen chronically complain that most of the profits from fishing go to the processors. So CFAB financed a fish processing consortium started by fishermen. But two thirds of the fishermen who were members of the limited partnership refused to sell to their own firm as originally intended. They wouldn't accept credit and sold their salmon for cash to a competing processor instead. That put their company under, taking down the state's $3 million investment with it.

Other large ill-fated loans were made to timber companies, including the Haida Native corporation. Neither the lender nor the borrower read the fading timber market correctly, and the Haida

1 1 3

corporation was thrust into bankruptcy, owing CFAB millions.

Naive judgments were probably even more costly than market factors. For example, agency officers concede they were "needlessly taken" for huge sums by an outfit known as the Owens Drilling Company, run by a Kentucky horse farm owner named Tom Owens.

Owens impressed CFAB officers with his plan to build roads and bridges for loggers eager to cut the prime timber in southeast Alaska. The vision of a year-round industry with stable jobs was so compelling that they continued to loan him money without taking even basic safeguards to protect the loans. "Owens would get a contract for, say, eight hundred thousand dollars to do roadwork for a logging company and we would give him the money on the spot," Ed Crane, the current CFAB chief executive, recalls. "Normally, you would give him a small sum up front and then pay the rest in stages as he completes the work. But he would get it all, buy some equipment, and go to a bank and get another loan on the equipment he bought with our money." CFAB was left holding the bag for millions in unpaid loans when Owens filed for bankruptcy. The cooperative investigated whether some of the Alaska money might have been misapplied to his horse farm. But it found he had insulated his Kentucky property as well as many of his other assets.

By the end of 1984, CFAB was tottering on the verge of bankruptcy. The Spokane bank sent up Crane, then a West Coast bank consultant, to investigate. He stayed on as the new president with orders to cut everything he could to save the agency. While Crane restored a sense of stability, he could not allay Senator Sturgulewski's worst fears. CFAB announced in 1985 that even with severe retrenchment it saw no way it could live up to its agreement to repay the $32 million in interest-free seed money advanced by the state of Alaska.

Part of the prevailing wisdom was that if Alaska was to become self-sufficient, it must look to the future. Consultants, engineers, and contractors converged on the state upon hearing of Alaska's spending spree. They convinced powerful legislators that the future demanded the creation of an alternative supply of energy to feed the state's coming industrial engines when oil ran out and the cost of other traditional fuels became prohibitive.

Such was the public explanation for the plan to build a hydroelectric project at Tyee Lake, in the sparsely populated alpine area near the head of the Bradfield Canal southeast of Wrangell. This was to be the state's entry into developing water power, a model for others in this land of abundant lakes and rivers. The first beneficiaries would be the small fishing and lumbering towns on the thin panhandle of southeastern Alaska that buffers Canada from the Pacific.

In 1979, the newly constituted Alaska Power Authority submitted a license application for the project to the federal Energy Regulatory Commission, estimating a cost of $39.6 million. Consultants recommended design changes the next year, raising the price tag to $51 million. The following year the first bids came in 90 percent higher than expected, inflating estimates to $96.7 million. Governor Hammond asked no questions about the alarming cost escalation. Having accepted his share of the oil windfall to spend as his administration pleased, he had abdicated control of the rest of the budget.

The legislature was silent for a different reason. Its leaders had made a deal to fund Tyee Lake in exchange for the southeast legislative delegation's support of a much more massive hydroelectric project in the works for Susitna, north of Anchorage. Ed Dankworth, a powerful senate leader from Anchorage, had even imperiously authored what legislators referred to as the "Susitna blackmail clause." It made appropriations for a four-dam pool in the southeast, of which Tyee Lake was the centerpiece, contingent on support for Susitna.

Only Ron Lehr, a banker and a new member of the power authority, spoke up: Had Tyee Lake ever been subjected to the Division of Budget Management review requirements? It hadn't. Had the state explored the cost of alternative power sources in view of the rising estimates of Tyee Lake? It hadn't. Had the state negotiated agreements to sell Tyee Lake power to even one utility beforehand? It hadn't. "I saw it didn't make sense to build it, but I wasn't able to stop it," Lehr says. "There were trade-offs in all these things."

The final cost of the southeast four-dam project was $450 million. But the local utilities had use for only 30 percent of the dam's overbuilt generating capacity. As the only customers, they had the state power authority over a barrel. They were able to negotiate subsidized rates so low that the state had no hope of ever recovering its investment equity. Fortunately, the massive Susitna dam, the cost of which had been projected at $15 billion, was never built. As oil prices started dropping, so did enthusiasm for the plan. But the decision cost the state $350 million in consulting fees and engineering studies.

The Alaskan public as well as its politicians deserves blame for the political exploitation and abject waste of those billions of dollars of Alaska's oil wealth. Had it been tax dollars that were squandered, the public outcry would have been deafening. But why fret over abuse of Big Oil's bankroll? Furthermore, people were too occupied with getting their own share of those dollars to complain.

State representative Ramona Barnes, a savvy, chain-smoking, sometimes raucous blonde, recalls the swell of voices across the state demanding that the oil windfall benefit all Alaskans, not just the special interests. Memories were still fresh of the $900 million jackpot from the Prudhoe Bay oil leases in 1969. Although the money did finance many worthy projects, the public perception was that it had been squandered. And people were aware that there was no master plan in place to deal with the new bonuses to the state when Prudhoe began to produce.

Barnes says she was among the legislators who demanded an end to the state income tax. But Governor Hammond, his expensive agricultural program just starting, wanted to keep the income tax and instead invest some of the oil money in a permanent fund that would pay future dividends to Alaskans. The money-flush legislature accommodated both. It repealed the income tax in 1981 and created a permanent fund in 1982. A voter referendum in 1976 had overwhelmingly amended the constitution to create a savings entity. Now the legislature gave it form by assigning 25 percent of the revenues from the mineral leases and oil royalties to a gigantic public trust. Further, it specifically protected the principal from future administrations or legislatures that might be inclined to raid it.

In 1982, the state sent a $1,000 check to every man, woman, and child deemed a citizen of Alaska—the first distribution of Alaska's Permanent Fund. (Among the recipients were untold numbers of Outsiders who had established mailing addresses in the state at the first whiff of the dividend program.) Since that year, Alaska has taken in no taxes from individuals. It has no income tax, no sales tax, and no wage tax. (Some Alaskan cities, however, have enacted their own sales taxes.) Instead, the state distributes a yearly Permanent Fund payment to all who have lived there for at least the previous two years. Though some public officials have tried to circumvent its sanctity over the years, the fund remains untouchable and its assets grow steadily each year. The dividends, which amounted to $952.63 a person in 1990, are something of a mandated relief program for rich and poor alike, unparalleled in the world. The state has also added an unprecedented $250-a-month bonus program for every citizen sixty-five years of age or over.

The state's population increased rapidly as people got news of its good fortune and generosity, from 414,000 people when oil started flowing in 1979 to 542,000 by 1986. In Anchorage, which grew more than 40 percent in that time, housing prices soared and living space became so scarce that even shacks and lean-tos became rentable property. The clamor for state-funded housing assistance became loud in the land.

William Parker, a self-described "early hippie" who served as a legislator in the early eighties, recalls the lament that young couples could not afford to live in Alaska. How could they be expected to stay and build the new state if they couldn't buy a house? "It was true," Parker says. "The smallest houses were going for a hundred thousand dollars in Anchorage and double-digit interest rates were driving mortgages out of sight. The banks wouldn't lend unless you came in with a good credit record and a big down payment, which most people here didn't have."

Alaska's legislature sympathized. For starters, it voted a $560 million appropriation in 1980 to subsidize mortgage interest rates, reduce down payments, and extend the time to pay. Fueled with the state's oil money, the Alaska Housing Finance Corporation (AHFC) moved in where no private lending institution would tread. Banks and the other traditional mortgage lenders in the early eighties were asking 15 percent interest, 20 percent down, twenty years to pay. The amenable AHFC enabled Alaskans to buy a house with a 10 percent mortgage, 5 percent down, and twenty-five years to pay.

Realtors, builders, and financial institutions made fortunes in the real estate boom that followed. The state's fifteen banks did particularly well. They received the applications, processed the loans, and sent them to the AHFC for virtually automatic approval. In return they received a generous 1 percent service fee and none of the risk—

the state guaranteed the mortgages. The AHFC bought almost all the new mortgages written in the state during the first half of the 1980s, underwriting more than $1.3 billion in housing loans in 1984 alone.

Jack Linton, an early-vintage Alaskan with a long career in banking, was one of the first executive directors of the agency. He remembers the political meddling that accompanied the free flow of state money into the housing market. "Since the state legislature was providing the funding, or the backup loans, the politicians wanted a finger in the pot," Linton says. "You would get a call from a senator who was complaining that his brother-in-law was turned down for a loan. I was supposed to look into it and make sure he got it." When he balked, Linton says, life soon became intolerable.

The breaking point came when politicians tried to force the agency to bend its liberal lending policies to take care of housing for one more segment of the population, those with the lowest incomes. Many of them were decent people struggling to get a start in life, but others were financial deadbeats and recent arrivals with credit records so vague they couldn't qualify for a car loan. But they were helping build the new state, too, the argument went. Didn't they also deserve to own homes?

The mobile-home dealers, a powerful special-interest group in Alaska, thought so. They pressed a plan upon their friendly legislators: Finance mobile homes with the same generous terms as real estate. Never mind that banks treat mobile homes as personal property with a far shorter life than real estate. Or that they demand far stiffer terms—25 percent down and seven years to pay. The enabling legislation gave the AHFC the flexibility to set its own financing rules, and the politicians knew it.

Linton says that the cochairman of the house finance committee, Russell Meekins, Jr., called him to Juneau and told him that if the AHFC was interested in its appropriation, it had better accept the proposed terms for mobile homes. He was also approached by the lieutenant governor, Terry Miller, and John Sackett, the chairman of finance in the senate, with the same request, he adds.

Linton says he told them he wouldn't do it because it violated all prudent lending practices. "Next, the chairman of the AHFC board calls. 'We have to do it,' he insists. 'If we want our appropriation, we have to do it.' They did it. Whereupon I resigned."

Season of Gold

The surge in mobile-home buying in Alaska created a fortune for dealers, benefiting among others the family of Russell Meekins, Jr. Meekins's father ran a mobile-home business in Anchorage.

Meekins, who abruptly quit Alaska politics after his term expired, now lives in Wellesley, Massachusetts, where he is a prominent civic leader. He defends his support of mobile-home financing and denies that he ever threatened to hold up AHFC appropriations or that his father's business affairs had any influence on his legislative decisions: "My actions were philosophically consistent with my record to help the little guy whenever I could."

All in all, Alaska financed a total of $6.1 billion in housing loans before the boom ran out of steam.

In 1986, world oil prices plunged from about $27 a barrel to less than $10. With the collapse came a deluge of loan defaults and bank failures. Only six of Alaska's fifteen banks survived. The boom parasites loaded up their pickup trucks and headed down the Alaska Highway to the lower forty-eight, leaving their houses with clothes in the closets, food in the refrigerators, and, often, pets in the backyards.

The state lost $1.128 billion in mortgage foreclosures by the end of the 1980s. Not surprisingly, the highest rate of defaults occurred among mobile-home owners. The financial damage to the state was relatively small in the context of the total losses that it had to absorb, but the battle that Linton had lost cost the state dearly in another way. Randy Boyd, who handled hundreds of trailer foreclosures for Alaska State Bank, remembers, "They would sell the washer-dryer, the kitchen chairs and table—all of which came with original purchase. That was their money out of town. Then some flooded the place before they left, smashed holes through the flimsy walls, or just trashed everything." A blight of deteriorating, abandoned trailers still mars the Alaska landscape, a jolt to visitors who come expecting pristine wilderness. It is a form of oil spill, state induced, a reminder of a foolhardy era.

The shining survivor is the Alaska Permanent Fund. It has assets of nearly $13 billion today and has grown each year, largely because it places its money in safe securities outside the state. It is prohibited by law from investing more than a quarter of its assets in Alaskan industries. Spared the obligation of helping Alaskan enterprises, the fund has built an impressive portfolio of bonds, government securities, and blue-chip stocks. Much of the credit for the shrewd stewardship of Alaska's nestegg belongs to two men: Banker Elmer E. Rasmuson, the first chairman of the fund's Board of Trustees, did extensive research at his own expense and persuaded the state to inflation-proof the fund. David Rose, the first executive director, then set high standards overseeing the investments until he left his position in the spring of 1992 to start his own financial consulting firm.

CHAPTER 10

Corruption, Alaska Size

A BRIGHT GLOW from the Prudhoe Bay oil pumping stations light up much of Alaska's North Slope during the winter darkness, but it runs out well before you get to Barrow. That's when ice fog generally takes over, as it does on this day late in November 1990, while our MarkAir pilot hunts for the Barrow airport. We land through the gloom just after noontime, and it is no lighter on the ground. I can see only a blur of a town. Its buildings are dim outlines in clouds of swirling snow and frozen steam from the exhaust of trucks and cars that are kept running even when people stop for lunch, for fear it will be impossible to restart them.

It is cold in Barrow in November. The temperature is twenty-nine below with a windchill factor of sixty below. As the northernmost city in Alaska, Barrow sits on the edge of the Arctic Ocean, hemmed in by ice much of the year. The sun disappears in mid-November and doesn't appear again until mid-January. Polar bears sometimes come into town across the packed ice floes in search of defenseless dogs tied in their pens.

It costs $915 round-trip to fly to Anchorage from here, bootleggers charge $50 for a fifth of whiskey, and gasoline is $2.80 a gallon. You

can't drive to Barrow. And nobody drives very far around Barrow—
the longest road goes only 12 miles. "Why would anyone want to live
here?" I wonder. Yet thirty-three hundred people do.

"It's peaceful here," replies Marie Adams, an amiable, college-ed-
ucated Inupiat whose father was a reindeer herder. One of twelve children, Marie got through Evangel College in Missouri with financial
help from the Assembly of God church, but she chose to return to her
subsistence family in Barrow instead of staying with a good job in
the lower forty-eight. She is a dedicated whale researcher and recently opened Barrow's first public information agency, which publishes a newsletter on community activities.

Marie is proud that her people have survived for thousands of years
in what some say is the world's most hostile inhabited environment.
Each generation handed down the skills to capture migrating caribou, net returning salmon, and identify edible plants on the tundra,
among other necessities for survival. The pride of the Inupiat to this
day is the harpooning of the giant bowhead whale. In 1977, the International Whaling Commission tried to put a moratorium on the
taking of bowhead whales, but so intense was the Eskimo protest that
U.S. authorities helped the North Slope borough obtain special quotas for subsistence harvest. Each catch of these monsters (they weigh
as much as fifty tons) is shared among the villagers and is an occasion for festivals and prayers.

The Eskimos in Barrow escaped contact with the Russian trappers
who came in the eighteenth century. Other Alaska Natives were not
so lucky. The invaders decimated the sea otter population and often
enslaved the aboriginals who lived in the Aleutians. But the Inupiats
had to overcome the hardships inflicted on their food chain by flotillas of American whaling ships that all but eliminated the whales that
migrate in the Arctic. Yet they continue to hang on to their harsh
world, to the perplexity of anthropologists and historians.

A visitor to Barrow quickly senses that Marie and much of the Native community are fighting harder than ever to save their culture.
Over the past fifteen years, the threat to their traditional way of life
has been greater than any they endured through centuries of famine,
disease, and natural disaster. The discovery of oil on the North Slope
has transformed these once primitive people into privileged people.
Their land has created billions of dollars of wealth, and they have

had serious problems dealing with it.

As the seat of the North Slope borough, which taxes all of the Prudhoe Bay oil fields, Barrow is the richest city, per capita, in the United States, and possibly in the world. In recent years it has also probably attracted the greatest number of unscrupulous people, per capita. That they have managed to extort many millions of dollars of Eskimo wealth is a scandal little known beyond Alaska.

Oil companies did their utmost to prevent the incorporation of the North Slope borough. Early in the 1970s, they sought injunctions in court, arguing that it did not make sense to create a municipality of 56.6 million acres (about the size of the state of Minnesota) just so a small band of once nomadic people could tax the Prudhoe Bay complex, plus every future oil well, the pipeline, and service centers across the entire top of Alaska. "Who Will Control the Dazzling North Slope Wealth?" one Anchorage newspaper headlined the battle.

With the several thousand oil company workers who had recently arrived in Alaska barred from voting, an essentially Eskimo electorate voted 402–27 in June 1972 to create the North Slope borough. Citing the terms of the state constitution, the Alaska courts validated the election, thereby certifying the largest local government in the world. The borough starts where Alaska meets the Chukchi Sea on the west and encompasses the entire oil-rich tundra north of the Brooks Range to the Canadian border on the east.

The fifty-seven hundred predominantly Inupiat Eskimos who occupied the eight isolated villages in this desolate land probably had no idea of the wealth that would be theirs. Newspapers estimated that the oil company facilities at Prudhoe Bay alone would swell the assessed value of taxable property to $10 billion. It reached $13.6 billion by 1987. Meanwhile, Outsiders scrambled even before the vote was in to advise the Eskimos on how such a solid tax base could be used to create instant millions for themselves, and, of course, their advisers. Investment houses were begging to sell municipal bonds backed with such guarantees of oil revenues.

The borough elected Eben Hopson, an Inupiat whaling captain and respected patriarch, as its first mayor. He had a clear vision on how to apply the money. "The caribou and the whale have formed the base of our existence, but cash has become a way of life," he stated. "We have been introduced to dwellings heated by oil, with running water and even indoor toilets." He pledged that the people of the North Slope henceforth would have all the amenities of Anchorage or Fairbanks. No longer would they have to carry their wastes to village tank trucks or hunt for blocks of blue ice to melt for drinking water. And never again would they have to worry about the caribou not returning or the salmon disappearing. There would be well-paying cash jobs for everyone.

As the center of his improvement program, Hopson authorized the Barrow Utilidor, an extraordinary sewer and water system that would be installed in heated tunnels burrowed beneath the permafrost. He promised to connect it to every home in the city. To give his people the finest education, Hopson started building the largest and most up-to-date high school in Alaska. It would occupy 119,532 square feet, and include an Olympic-size swimming pool, a college-size basket-ball auditorium, plus separate rooms for wrestling, gymnastics, and karate—an impressive facility for a district that averages about 250 high school students.

Hopson died in 1980. He did not live long enough to see either project completed. Nor did he live to learn of the massive corruption his well-intentioned building program would spawn. That sad distinction belongs to the administration of Mayor Eugene Brower, a boyish Inupiat who took office in 1981 at the age of thirty-three. Brower, also a whaling captain, had been the public works director, but had grown impatient with the slow pace of the capital improvements started by Hopson and the interim mayor, Jake Adams, another whaling captain. (Barrow has 144 whaling captains.) When the baton passed to Brower, he set out to take Barrow from the Stone Age to the space age as fast as he could get vessels and planes to ship the lumber and hardware from Seattle.

Coached by outsiders, Brower borrowed hundreds of millions of dollars—the debt swelled from $453 million to $1.2 billion during the three years he served—by floating bonds backed by the borough's oil property-tax base. This was quite a spectacular feat for a municipality of fewer than six thousand people. Moody's Investors Service rated the bond issues A or better. Wall Street bond brokers and their Alaskan agents feasted.

As the debt began to approach that of Philadelphia and other large cities, several alarmed lawmakers started to call for legislation to put a cap on Barrow's runaway borrowing. They feared the state could be left paying off the debt in the long term when oil revenues started declining and Barrow could no longer meet its payments. In response to these threats from Juneau, Brower signed multimillion-dollar construction contracts the way some mayors sign proclamations. And with about the same amount of scrutiny.

Brower, whose education was limited to BIA schools, could not have masterminded so massive a capital program by himself. Experts of all stripes from the Outside streamed in to help, and Natives often stopped to admire their shiny Lear Jets and Cessnas parked at the airport. But there were two figures who emerged from the shadows of Alaska's political life to grab the inside track from the day that Brower took office.

Lew Dischner, then sixty-five, was a portly, glad-handing political veteran who had been part of the power structure in Juneau for as long as Alaska had been a state. He had been appointed the state's first commissioner of labor in 1959 by Governor William Egan, a Democrat. Dischner left the post after a year and resurfaced in Juneau as a lobbyist for several large clients, including the Teamsters, the most powerful labor group in the state. Along the way, Dischner demonstrated an adeptness at getting government loans and state contracts to build a private business empire. He developed a waterfront mall in Juneau, won the contract to operate a laundromat in a state-owned residential high rise, and acquired a hotel that leased rooms to the state.

Dischner also built a network of influence. With the help of the Teamsters, he became a leading fund-raiser for the Democratic party and certain helpful Republican candidates. His ability to deliver hefty campaign contributions earned him a reservoir of return favors at all levels of local and state government, to be tapped when needed.

With the birth of the North Slope borough in 1972, Dischner headed north to the future. He arrived bearing a campaign chest for Eben Hopson, who rewarded Dischner by hiring him as a borough lobbyist. When Hopson died, borough assembly president Adams served out his term and was expected to win the next election, in October 1981. But Dischner decided the next mayor should be Brower, the young Eskimo rising in the public works department.

Dischner masterminded Brower's campaign, raising $100,000 to fund it. Much of the money was laundered, given in the names of a variety of people but actually coming from Dischner and an assortment of slope contractors who expected to be rewarded once their man was safely in office.

It was a daring gamble. Brower won by only twenty-four votes, but he lost no time in rewarding Dischner. He made the lobbyist consultant to the mayor on capital improvement projects, a lucrative combination that would set Dischner up to make $250,000 a year for lobbying services alone, two and a half times Brower's own salary.

The mayor's other confidant was Carl Mathisen, then forty-nine, a small-time political wheeler-dealer who dripped gold. As glum as Dischner was cheerful, Mathisen made his statement with what must have been a record-size wristwatch studded with gold nuggets, featuring two twenty-karat bears growling at each other across the timepiece. Mathisen had worked in the 1970s for the borough's bond counsel, Bob Dupre of Juneau. While helping Dupre reap a bounty of commissions by floating the $1.2 billion in bond issues, Mathisen had been laying the foundation of his own future. Though short on formal education, Mathisen had enough contracting experience in Anchorage to understand the ways of government and bureaucrats. He convinced Mayor Hopson to hire him as borough training program coordinator. That was how he got to know Brower in the public works department.

Mathisen became Brower's mentor, teaching the young Inupiat ways of government not found in textbooks. Mathisen also ingratiated himself with the Brower family, showering them with gifts and even became godfather to a Brower son. Brower reciprocated by persuading his father, yet another whaling captain, to appoint Mathisen a member of his renowned crew. The only white man ever to be so honored, Mathisen bowed out after he had a terrifying nightmare about a polar bear in camp on his first outing and injured his leg on the second.

But when Brower ran for mayor in 1981, Mathisen and his wife were in the forefront of his supporters, with a $5,000 check. One of Brower's first acts in office was to install Mathisen as a consultant to the mayor and to the public works director handling capital projects, a post that would pay him an average of $300,000 a year. His initial consulting contract paid him $156,500.

The two consultants were well paired. Dischner was skilled in siphoning money and Mathisen had the nuts-and-bolts savvy to provide respectable projects. Together they recruited a compatible cast of engineers, architects, technicians, and construction and service companies to do their business. Many were struggling specialty firms and some did not exist until the borough started letting contracts. But all were expected to abide by the house rules, which required them to systematically kick back 10 percent of every borough contract to Dischner and Mathisen.

Awed by the way his two advisers got things moving, Brower didn't question them when they picked a Seattle firm, the H.W. Blackstock Company, to purchase all materials, all shipping, and anything else that had to do with servicing the borough's capital construction projects. As an influence peddler, Dischner had had a long relationship with Blackstock. He took good care of his client.

Dischner engineered a contract that permitted Blackstock to tack 30 percent on top of the cost of anything it provided, an arrangement unheard of in municipal government or private industry. The president of the lucky company was Kenneth Rogstad, the former Republican chairman of King County, which includes Seattle. Dischner knew that Rogstad could be counted on to contribute to campaigns of well-positioned Democrats in Alaska as well.

"The consultants became the government," Chris Mello, then contract reviewer for the borough, says. A California native, barely thirty years old and fresh out of California Western School of Law in San Diego, Mello was working at his first real job. He admits he was puzzled by what he saw at first, and then was simply dismayed. "In my first meeting with Lew Dischner, he told me he was a blood brother to the mayor, and what he said went," Mello says. "Suddenly the borough was starting hundreds of projects and running them was wrested away from the borough employees and turned over to the consultants. We were reduced to clerks."

Brower signed contracts for more schools, firehouses, health clinics, roads, worker camps, incinerators, engineering studies, and architectural renderings, plus expensive change orders for the Utilidor and other projects in progress. At one point, the sparsely populated borough's capital budget soared to $300 million a year, which rivaled what the city of Chicago then spent for the capital needs of its millions of residents. "Consultants identified the projects," Mello says. "We were spending as much as a million a day. Projects were coming so fast that those that should have been bid were not bid. I was supposed to review the contracts before they went to the mayor. But sometimes those documents would arrive in the legal department already signed by the mayor. What was the point of reviewing them then?

"We hear rumors of kickbacks. Then we find out later that Lew and Carl formed their own companies to work on projects. The next thing you know they are negotiating contracts on behalf of the borough with their own companies, and the costs of the projects go way out of line."

Harold Curran, another young law-school graduate, was also among those who felt uneasy. He had come to Alaska as a VISTA volunteer and followed his girlfriend, an environmental planner with the Trustees for Alaska, a nonprofit public interest law firm specializing in Alaska environmental issues, to a project in Barrow. Hopson welcomed the talent and hired him as borough attorney. "When I found out that a sole-source contract was awarded for six health clinics, I advised Brower that it should have been a bid contract," Curran says. "At one point I wrote him a memo noting that some of the contracts that had not been bid seemed to be in the high dollars. Soon after, I got a letter from Brower's litigation counsel telling me that the price of a contract was not a legal issue."

Frustrated, Curran tried to interest John Larson, news director for Channel 2 in Anchorage, Alaska's largest television station, in looking at the way the borough handed out contracts. Larson said the station didn't have the staff to investigate a situation so far away. But the Eskimos in Barrow did not need media exposure to see that things were getting out of hand at borough hall, or that Outsiders were helping themselves to millions of dollars of their money.

The Utilidor was initially estimated to cost $80 million, but Brower's change orders helped send the total up to $250 million by 1984, when only 10 percent of the buildings were hooked up. (The cost had reached $330 million by 1991, when still only slightly more than half of the homes were being serviced. It is by far the most expensive public works project ever attempted in Alaska.) The bill for the high school, initially projected at $25 million, soared to $80 million, which amounts to $320,000 per student. In his book *Alaska*, James Michener gives the impression that it is an ugly building. To me, the appearance did not register as forcefully as did the distortion of educational priorities. An expensive, life-size bronze statue of Hopson greets a visitor at the entrance, and a $75,000 mural decorates an inside wall. Yet the library is no larger than the gym's smallest exercise room, its book supply is glaringly meager, and its current periodical shelf does not contain any out-of-state newspapers or even one from the state capital.

What attracted even more public attention than the skyrocketing cost of these projects, however, was the change in the mayor's lifestyle. Brower now traveled by private jet to Anchorage, Seattle, Palm Springs, and, it was rumored, the casinos in Las Vegas. After one trip, he returned sporting a huge diamond ring and expensive new suits. The mayor's new boat, worth at least $35,000 according to local mariners, was the envy of all who boated upriver to the caribou grounds. Brower also started showing off a new Browning semiautomatic shotgun.

The prevailing wisdom is that an incumbent mayor who provides full employment and more than the usual amenities for his constituents is bound to be reelected. Brower did all that and had a reelection war chest of $250,000 to boot, raised with Dischner's expertise. But the people of the North Slope could feel their fortune being drained by Outsiders, and quiet resentment was mounting. In the fall of 1984, they voted Brower out of office. The victory of George Ahmaogak, a borough worker who is only part Inupiat (but a whaling captain, of course), was the political shocker of the year.

During Brower's last five days in office, his administration pushed through more than $15 million in checks and signed $7.6 million in contracts. The frenzy was described in a story filed from Barrow by Bill White, business editor of the *Anchorage Daily News:* " 'There are planes leaving in a half-hour. Get the checks out,' outgoing mayor Brower barked at an accounting officer. While the planes waited, the men they had brought hovered over the mayor and the accounting clerks. They wanted checks for millions of dollars and they wanted them cashed before Brower left office." Among the principal beneficiaries were Dischner, Mathisen, and Kenneth Rogstad, the head of the H. W. Blackstock Company.

Incoming mayor George Ahmaogak immediately noticed that many borough files were missing. He assumed they were shredded, whereupon he went to the assembly and asked for an audit of borough finances. The audit, performed by the Fairbanks accounting firm of Main Hurdman, surprised even those who had expected the worst. Besides finding many contracts that had not been legally bid, the report showed that millions of dollars had been spent on services for which no invoices existed. It also identified an array of contracts with "an improper scope and fee relationship," meaning that the amount paid appeared to be too excessive for the service. The auditors particularly questioned the propriety of nearly $20 million of expenditures to H. W. Blackstock. Not only were many of the payments in cash, contrary to purchasing procedures, but sometimes goods were never delivered. Among the many discrepancies cited was a $365,134 payment for borough housing development furniture. Neither invoice nor furniture appeared to have been received.

The most eye-opening finding was that Dischner and Mathisen, while on the borough payroll as consultants, had set up firms of their own to get borough business. The largest, North Slope Constructors, had been favored with many millions of dollars in contracts. It was incorporated, with Dischner, Mathisen, and Rogstad as equal owners, one year after Brower took office. North Slope Constructors was able to shut out other firms by bidding low and then negotiating change orders. "That substantially increased the size of the contract without substantially increasing work to be done," the auditors reported.

The whiff of wholesale fraud inspired newspapers in Fairbanks and Anchorage to dig deeper. They soon exposed layers of lesser players — lawyers, architects, engineers, consultants, public-works employees, and even a state senator — who had benefited from the questionable payments, kickbacks, and tainted gifts that flowed like water in the Barrow building boom. Public attention inevitably shifted to Governor William Sheffield. What was he going to do about the North Slope corruption?

The governor's first response was that he was not aware that any state money had been involved. The *Anchorage Daily News* quickly challenged him, showing that more than $4 million of state money had been budgeted for a half-dozen projects questioned in the audit.

Then Anchorage representative Fritz Pettyjohn charged that state attorney general Norman Gorsuch was dragging his feet in investigating the matter because several of those who landed lucrative contracts in Barrow were heavy political contributors to Sheffield's campaign. Dischner himself was one of Sheffield's largest contributors. A secretary in the governor's office says Dischner walked into the office one day and tried to drop off a $60,000 check for the governor's campaign committee. The secretary, recognizing the illegality of the gift, refused to accept it. But the surprise was that Rogstad, a Republican power in the Seattle area, figured so prominently in raising money for Sheffield, a Democrat. According to newspaper reports, which were not denied, employees of Blackstock sent $7,000 in checks to Sheffield and the company helped organize a fund-raiser in Seattle to reduce the sizable campaign debt Sheffield carried into office.

Suddenly, the question of whether Sheffield would act became academic. By the spring of 1985, the governor himself was in deep trouble. Someone had tipped off the *Fairbanks News-Miner* that there was something shady about a ten-year, $9.1 million lease the state had signed for office space in a Fairbanks building. The specifications had been written so narrowly that only the one building had qualified.

Stan Jones, a reporter on the *News-Miner*, dropped the Barrow story and plunged into a round-the-clock investigation of the Fairbanks lease. He reported that a labor leader named Lennie Arsenault, who had helped raise $92,000 for Sheffield's campaign, had a financial interest in the favored building. Further, he found that Arsenault had had discussions with the governor regarding the lease and that employees within the state leasing office had protested the circumvention of leasing procedures.

The stories troubled state prosecutor Dan Hickey, a Georgetown Law School graduate who, like Curran and Mello in Barrow, was among the young lawyers who had answered ads for jobs in the emerging state of Alaska. He became chief prosecutor in 1975. In spite of Sheffield's public declarations of propriety, Hickey quietly started to investigate the Barrow mess without the governor's knowledge. But other disturbing events soon demanded his full attention. Two employees from the administration's procurement office visited Hick-

ey and bared their concerns about the Fairbanks lease. They also told
him Stan Jones had filed a request under Alaska's Freedom of Information Act to see the file, which, they said, was damaging to the governor.

Crusades against corruption in government have a poor record in
Alaska. In fact, the system seemed to find ways to abort aggressive
law enforcement, a fact no one knew better than Hickey. In 1982, he
had led a grand jury investigation into the dealings of state senator
Ed Dankworth, former head of the Alaska state troopers. While
cochairman of the senate finance committee, Dankworth and a business partner had bought the former Isabel Pass pipeline camp for $1
million and tried to sell it to the state for use as a correctional facility—at an asking price of $3 million. The grand jury indicted
Dankworth for conflict of interest, but the courts gutted the case, ruling that the senator was protected by legislative immunity. None of
his conversations or actions to persuade the legislators to appropriate money for the camp purchase could be used against him; they
were considered part of the legislative process. Hickey had no choice
but to dismiss the case.

Hickey was also well aware of what happened to another whistle-
blower, Representative Russ Meekins, Jr., the upstart who had captured the speaker's chair in the famed 1981 legislative coup. In the
spending frenzy of 1982, Meekins publicly accused state senator
George Hohman (D-Bethel) of trying to bribe him with promises of
a bag of money in exchange for support of a water-throwing plane.
Hohman was convicted and expelled from the senate. However, ten
years later he still had not paid his $10,000 fine and was gainfully
employed as acting city manager of Bethel. Meanwhile, Meekins's
brilliant political career suddenly came to a screeching halt. He did
not run for reelection and left the state.

These were parables Hickey could not ignore as he began to probe
the affairs of the highest officer in the government of Alaska. Nevertheless, he impounded all the leasing records in the procurement
office and launched a grand-jury investigation.

Governor Sheffield made two appearances before the grand jury.
Soon after the first, Hickey went to his boss, Attorney General Gorsuch, with an unappealing prognosis. The ramifications of the case
required outside expertise. A pained Gorsuch agreed. They looked to

Washington, D.C., and brought in George Frampton, who had worked as a special prosecutor with the Watergate grand jury that led to the downfall of President Nixon in 1974. Tensions in the state escalated as politicians and the public soon suspected that the inquiry into Sheffield's administration involved more than the lease of a building. The grand jury worked for ten weeks, calling in more than forty-four witnesses and preparing 161 exhibits as it built a case against Sheffield.

Meanwhile, two key state housing administrators died under circumstances many continue to find troubling. In February 1985, Bruce Moore, a department of administration services employee who complained superiors were pressuring him to process the Fairbanks building contract, was found dead on a sidewalk beneath the balcony of his condominium in Hawaii. He was an apparent suicide, though he left no note and friends noticed no indication of depression or ill health. Three months later, Lisa Rudd, a Sheffield cabinet officer who also had expressed skepticism at the building contract, died within hours of contracting a virulent bacterial infection. Investigations did ensue, but no evidence of foul play was found in either of the deaths.

On July 2, 1985, the grand jury returned a devastating report. It charged "a serious abuse of office" by Governor Sheffield and his chief of staff, John Shively, in their alleged intervention into the lease process and in their attempt to frustrate official investigations into the matter. Inspired, according to some, by the climate of the Watergate hearings, the jurors called Sheffield unfit to hold office and recommended the senate be called into special session to consider impeaching the governor.

Shaken by the finding, Sheffield stuck by his testimony that he did not remember meeting with Arsenault and that consolidating state offices in the Fairbanks building would have saved the state money. Nevertheless, about six hours after the grand-jury report, Gorsuch issued a legal opinion stating that the administration should cancel the lease because it was tainted by favoritism.

The attorney general, who had already said he wanted to resign, left office the next week. Sheffield quickly appointed Hal Brown, a lawyer from Ketchikan, to succeed him. One of Brown's first acts was to call in State Prosecutor Hickey. "I was told to get out quietly," Hickey says. He left, but not quietly. He issued a blistering parting message citing the work to be done, including the state's responsibility to investigate the situation at Barrow.

The senate impeachment debate took on even more strongly aspects of Watergate. The Republicans, who had 11–9 control of the Senate, hired former Watergate committee counsel Sam Dash to oversee the proceedings. Meanwhile, Sheffield also reached down to Washington for another Watergate pro, Philip Lacovara, counsel to Watergate prosecutor Leon Jaworski, to defend him.

Dash advised the senate that Sheffield's tampering with state leasing procedures might not amount to an impeachable offense, but perjury would. (The broad pattern of lying to cover up the crime rather than actual complicity in the Watergate break-in was the biggest factor in Nixon's ouster from the presidency.) Dash pointed out that Sheffield had testified four times that he could not recall ever meeting with Arsenault, while not only Arsenault but John Shively, the governor's own chief of staff, told the grand jury in detail about a meeting in which the governor and Arsenault discussed lease specifications.

Many thought Dash had made a case for impeachment, but at the moment of truth, the majority crumpled. Observers speculated that some didn't understand what was wrong with helping a campaign contributor, and others were bound to the unwritten political code that you don't stone anyone in your own circle today lest you be stoned tomorrow. Still others clearly saw official misconduct but simply did not have the courage to make a stand.

In the end, the senators not only rejected Dash's recommendation, but gutted a subsequent rules committee resolution denouncing Sheffield for questionable veracity and "significant irregularities." Instead, they called for a study into state procurement procedures and then added a rebuke to the investigators in the form of a resolution asking that the Alaska Judicial Council "study the use of the power of the grand jury to investigate and make recommendations ... to prevent abuse and assure basic fairness." Five years later, as memories faded, the legislature even reimbursed the governor for his legal expenses. A catchall bill, ostensibly passed to fund the state's longevity bonuses and legal expenses to recover disputed royalty payments from oil companies, included a payment of $302,653 for Sheffield. And when the Democrats regained the U.S. presidency in 1992, Sheffield emerged as President Bill Clinton's dispenser of patronage in Alaska.

The trauma of the Sheffield controversy plus the departure of Hickey doomed any state action against government corruption in Barrow. The new state attorney general had no appetite for searching out corruption in Bush villages, much less for the turmoil of another grand-jury investigation. By now just about every element in the protection system was prepared to do nothing about Barrow. The reason seemed clear to Roger McAniff, a University of Alaska engineering professor who, as a business consultant, had analyzed the inflated contracts let during the Brower years: "Alaska simply had no experience in dealing with white-collar crime."

But while the desire for money induces corruption, it can also counter it. The millions lost to favored contractors on the North Slope had infuriated many contractors who sought and were denied the chance to compete. Several refused to accept the affront without a fight. Reports of kickbacks for contracts and of the millions Eugene Brower had dished out during his final days in office came to the attention of the FBI. The bureau dispatched agent G. Bruce Talbert to Barrow to investigate. He came back with a harrowing story. The payouts appeared to be the desperate final stages of a sophisticated system in which a tight circle of white manipulators had been making personal fortunes by milking the newly rich Eskimo municipality. Only someone knowing how to match political greed with free-enterprise chicanery could have masterminded such a scheme, Talbert reported, and Brower's consultants, Lew Dischner and Carl Mathisen, had just those skills.

Meanwhile, North Slope's escalating bond indebtedness was receiving attention around the state. Representative Fritz Pettyjohn of Anchorage had been urging fellow legislators in Juneau to support a bill to cap the borough's extraordinary borrowing spree, lest the state eventually get stuck with the debt. Some Natives assailed Pettyjohn as a racist for denying Eskimos the right to use their own money to upgrade their living conditions, but their complaint was unlikely to pacify an uneasy legislature for long.

By the spring of 1985, the FBI, now joined by Internal Revenue Service investigators, was able to piece together a picture of the dimension of corruption. The bureau handed the Justice Department a bribery, extortion, and fraud case the likes of which the nation had rarely seen before.

Alaska's U.S. attorney was a tall, trim, low-key lawyer in his late thirties named Mike Spaan. His training was solid—Boalt Hall law school at the University of California Berkeley, two years as a legal assistant for Alaska's senior U.S. senator, Republican Ted Stevens, and six years with a private law firm. But he also was very conscious of whose turf he was treading on. While many of his peers would have jumped at the chance to establish a political reputation as a foe of crime and corruption, Spaan was reluctant to preempt the state. Further, he felt state laws could be applied more directly and effectively than the Racketeer Influenced and Corrupt Organizations (RICO) Act, the federal antiracketeering law that covers local corruption.

But the FBI gave Spaan little choice. It was possible, the bureau reported, that Alaska was sitting on the biggest bribery, extortion, and tax evasion case in municipal history. The FBI identified more than a dozen people—public officials, contractors, engineers, architects, and assorted lesser players—as members of Barrow's inner circle who had enjoyed grossly inflated contracts in return for which they'd kicked back a steady stream of millions to the masterminds in the mayor's office. The bureau wanted the authority to start subpoenaing records.

Whatever the difficulties of using federal law to crack a state corruption case, Spaan was persuaded. Appalled at the amounts of money and instances of public betrayal, he was further dismayed to find he did not have the staff to move against everyone at once. He could prosecute only in stages and hope that he could finish the job before the five-year statutes of limitations ran out. While much of the state's attention was still occupied by the Sheffield impeachment battle, Spaan moved quietly to start a federal grand-jury investigation into the North Slope mess.

Early in 1985, Spaan and Talbert began mapping out the first full-scale white-collar corruption case ever prosecuted by the U.S. attorney's office in Alaska. Spaan decided to move first against the lesser figures, hoping he could get them to plea-bargain for lighter sentences in exchange for a promise to testify for the government in the bigger cases.

Corruption, Alaska Size

On May 30, 1986, the federal grand jury finally handed down its first indictment. After more than a year of news reports of intense witness traffic in the federal building, it was an anticlimax. A lone Inupiat named Irving Igtanloc, Brower's public works director, was indicted on six counts of extortion, wire fraud, and income tax evasion. Nor was the substance of the charges particularly earthshaking. Igtanloc was accused of extorting gifts from a Washington State firm doing business with the borough, to wit: a remodeling job on his home, a .44-caliber revolver, and the mounting of an 18-inch lake trout his wife had caught while they were guests of the contractor at a fishing lodge.

Quite incidentally, Spaan announced, the man charged with providing the gifts to Igtanloc had been indicted for bribery but had pleaded guilty to a reduced charge in exchange for an agreement to cooperate with investigators. The lesser charge—illegal shipment of gifts of liquor—was laughable, especially in Alaska, but Spaan felt he had at least made a crack in the inner circle.

The name of the plea bargainer was Joseph P. Brock, and he had been a $250,000-a-year executive for a consulting group called MMCW. Based in Anchorage, the firm was a partnership of McCool McDonald Architects of Seattle and Anchorage and the Bellevue, Washington, engineering firm of Coffman and White. Dubbed "the engineers" in the FBI investigation, MMCW was a major player in the borough's capital improvement program. It had been handed an annual $7.8 million, no-bid contract to administer the technical side of the project development. MMCW determined the scope of the work and the estimated cost, then placed the contracts. Many of the contracts, the FBI found, were steered to architects and engineers within the MMCW family, at suspiciously lucrative terms. Brock was an important point man for the MMCW operation. But his feeble penalty—two years' probation and a $4,000 fine—made some wonder whether the state was in for another round of typical Alaska white-collar justice.

By the end of 1986, the indictments had picked up speed, and a picture of looting in the North Slope had finally begun to emerge. Martin Farrell, Brower's top lawyer, was charged with fraud for getting Brower to sign a $720,000 contract, with a $150,000 nonrefundable advance, two days before leaving office in 1984. Thomas Gittins, a contractor, was charged with kicking back 10 percent on all borough contracts to consultant Lew Dischner and with doing a $600,000 home remodeling job—at Dischner's expense—on the home of Myron Igtanloc, Irving's brother. Myron maintained an 8,500-square-foot Anchorage residence with gold-plated plumbing fixtures while serving as the North Slope's capital improvement projects coordinator. Myron Igtanloc himself was charged with three felony counts of tax evasion for failing to report $600,000 in income over a three-year period.

It was also disclosed at this point that Gittins claimed he had been paying an additional 3 percent on all contracts to a North Slope Native legislator, Al Adams, who soon after had been elected to the state senate. He at first insisted he had received "a little more than his legislative pay"—$45,000—for helping Gittins get contracts, most of which were funded by public money. Subsequent testimony would charge that Adams received at least $700,000 for services described as "public relations, ensuring compliance with local hire, and such other duties as Gittins might assign him." Those allegations did not figure into the indictment, nor did the Alaska state legislature find any breach of ethics after it made a cursory investigation.

The North Slope grand-jury investigation went on for two years before it touched principal figures. On February 2, 1987, ex-mayor Eugene Brower was indicted on fourteen counts of receiving bribes, gifts, and loans from contractors and lobbyists in return for preferential treatment. Several big names—Dischner, Mathisen, and Rogstad among them—were identified as having provided the favors, but they were not indicted, to the consternation of the public and the press. Spaan dodged the questions. As it turned out, he was buying time to negotiate with Brower in the hope that the ex-mayor would agree to reduced charges in exchange for testifying against those who extracted the heavy money.

For several months the ex-mayor held out, vowing to prove his innocence in court. Finally FBI agent Brent Rasmussen, who had worked with Talbert on the investigation, set up a meeting with Brower and showed him the government's evidence of the "10 percent clause," the secret deal Dischner and Mathisen had with the engineers, architects, and contractors under which the latter kicked back

10 percent of their payments from the borough. "I don't know if words can describe it," Rasmussen said. "Brower went into a state of shock. He broke down entirely, he was sobbing, and the interview had to stop. He was unable to continue."

Soon after, Brower pleaded guilty to a single charge of tax evasion and agreed to help the government. This time there was not only the uneasy feeling that a truly major player in the corruption case was getting off with a sweetheart deal, but a lingering question in the public's mind whether Brower might have feigned his remorse.

Nevertheless, Spaan was convinced he now had what the case needed—an Eskimo leader to testify against the white exploiters. On November 10, 1987, Dischner and Mathisen were indicted. The government alleged that their illegal take from the borough amounted to $21 million. Each was charged with thirty-six racketeering counts of fraud, bribery, kickbacks, and extortion in the North Slope borough.

The slope inquiry had so drained the short-staffed U.S. attorney's office that the state attorney general agreed to lend Spaan two lawyers from his staff to help out. An attorney named Peter Gamache had been assigned there earlier and now a second was urgently needed.

Karen Loeffler got the call. A petite, dark-haired, cheerful young woman only four years out of Harvard Law School, she had come to Alaska when she became bored with her job at a private law firm in Minneapolis. She landed a job with the oil and gas section of the state attorney general's office in 1985, when the gubernatorial impeachment controversy dominated the news. She had heard only a little about the North Slope, and since the state had at that point decided not to pursue the case, she had never dreamed she would become part of it.

As soon as she reported for duty, Spaan handed her a pile of grand-jury transcripts, exhibits, and financial records with instructions to read them thoroughly. The tone in his voice said, "From now on, Karen, the North Slope corruption case is your life."

Loeffler had limited experience as a prosecutor and very little exposure to criminal law. But she did not have to read very deeply into the North Slope file to discover she had been handed an incredible mission. For the next year, she devoted long days, nights, and weekends trying to put together blocks of the evidence in a way a jury of ordinary citizens could understand. She evaluated the grand-jury testimony of hundreds of witnesses. She pored over reports of FBI agents, often meeting with them and Peter Gamache to analyze prospective witnesses. She buried herself in a small mountain of documents to unravel the workings of complicated interlocking corporations.

On October 14, 1988, the racketeering trial of Lewis Dischner and Carl Mathisen finally began. In a crowded courtroom on the second floor of the federal building in Anchorage, U.S. attorney Mike Spaan stationed his erect six-foot-four-inch frame before the jury. "This is a case about fraud, bribery, kickbacks, extortion, and corruption," he said. "The sticky fingers of Dischner and Mathisen managed to grab twenty-one million dollars in public funds from the borough in just three years. We are going to prove that twenty-one million dollars dollar by dollar."

Mathisen smiled weakly. Dischner leaned over to confer with his attorney, Douglas Pope, giving the impression he was puzzled by what Spaan was saying.

"This entire case," Pope countered, "is here because the prosecution misunderstands the situation on the North Slope." The government was confused about the law, he said, and about the duties of Lew Dischner, "a man with a strong sense of values being unfairly prosecuted for his strong commitment to the people of the North Slope borough." Taking his turn, Laurence Finegold, Mathisen's attorney, declared, "This isn't a case about money. It is far more complex than the government wishes to have you believe ... It was not illegal payments that created expensive projects, but the [arctic] conditions ... In less than fifteen months Mathisen helped bring dramatic, if expensive, changes to the North Slope." The lawyers took about four hours to outline their cases, and then the court recessed for the weekend.

Brower was the government's first witness. In a hesitant, almost sheepish manner, Brower testified that while in office he had been showered with gifts by Dischner, Mathisen, and their contractor friends. Dischner provided him with the use of a home in a fashionable section of Anchorage. Brower also admitted to accepting a $45,000 diamond ring from him. Mathisen had paid for a customized 27-foot dory valued at $35,000. Brower's benefactors flew him to Las Vegas several times and on two occasions handed him $1,000 in gambling money. Contractors flew him to Palm Springs, where he was provided the use of a Cadillac, and he never asked who paid his hotel bills and airfare to Hawaii.

Brower admitted that many of the borough contracts he had approved were issued to companies totally or partly owned by Dischner and Mathisen. He conceded that he had pretended not to know of their involvement when he testified before the grand jury and had lied under oath to protect them. Yes, he said, he had known about Mathisen's ownership of Alaska Management Services, about Dischner's part ownership of North Coast Mechanical, and about both defendants' ownership shares in Igloo Leasing and North Slope Constructors, all big beneficiaries of Brower's public-works spending. Under questioning by Spaan, Brower even said he was aware that Dischner and Mathisen had started a jet service, called Tri-Leasing, with Dana Pruhs, a lobbyist for the nationally known Enserch contracting firm, which was based in Texas but also had sizable operations in Alaska. He conceded he had heard that North Slope contractors had to use the service or lose future contracts. (According to the indictment, Tri-Leasing extorted $570,979 from borough contractors in 1984.)

In cross-examination, however, the defense attorneys went to work. Incredibly, they got Brower not only to deny that the gifts were bribes or were used to gain his approval of contracts but to agree that the borough had benefited from them. By providing Brower with a house in Anchorage, where he had the free use of a telephone and a Cadillac, hadn't the defendants saved the borough money when the mayor was away on business? "Yes," Brower answered.

Lawyer Douglas Pope even sought to portray the gifts as part of an Eskimo *pamaq*, a Native gift-giving ritual that signifies a partner for life, with no expectation of something in return. Longtime Alaskans in the courtroom had to suppress chuckles. They knew that *pamaq* is based on helping those in need when food runs out or when disability restricts subsistence activity. A $45,000 diamond ring, a $35,000 dory, and $1,000 handouts to gamble in Las Vegas hardly sounded like aid to a Native in distress.

In short order, the defense attorneys reduced Brower to total confusion. Suddenly, what had seemed an open-and-shut case of bribery had been recast as big government coming down on well-meaning people who had tried to befriend the Eskimos on the North Slope.

The case became a trial of legal finesse. Spaan concentrated on building a paper trail showing calculated bribery. He placed in evidence an array of official records, painstakingly assembled by Karen Loeffler and IRS agent Ronald G. Chan, to show how money flowed to the borough, then to the contractors, and then in 10 percent increments to the bank account Dischner shared with Mathisen.

Spaan got some unexpected help from witnesses who suddenly began talking to save their own skins. Charles Hinson, a construction project engineer with Coffman and White of Seattle, which was part of MMCW, reluctantly testified that the engineering firm paid Dischner $1.3 million between 1981 and 1984—an amount equal to 10 percent of its engineering fees to the borough. Geoffrey Fowler, another member of the inner circle of consulting engineers, gave an even more vivid account of what it was like to do business on the North Slope. Testifying with immunity after having pleaded guilty the year before to a single charge of bribery, Fowler said his original firm, Frank Moolin and Associates, was down to a single employee in 1980 when he got a call from his brother to come to the North Slope borough, which was having design troubles with the underground Utilidor. It turned out to be a timely call. Fowler's struggling firm eventually redesigned the entire $330 million project and emerged as a flourishing business, but he had to play by the rules. Fowler testified that besides paying bribes to Dischner, he bought guns, portable dishwashers, and tape players for borough officials, raised campaign funds, and laundered campaign money at Dischner's behest, fully aware he was breaking laws.

Thomas Gittins, a self-made contractor who started as a janitor, already had his own indictment for bribery to worry about, but he testified without immunity to assist the government. He said he met Dischner and Mathisen in Palm Springs and asked them about lining up work in the North Slope. During the discussion, he said, Dischner agreed to represent him—for 10 percent. Gittins already was allegedly paying legislator Al Adams 3 percent on all contracts, but, according to Spaan, he needed Dischner for additional protection. Gittins was rewarded with a $6,155,000 service-area project that included building a well-appointed barracks for oil field workers. It didn't matter that oil companies already maintained their own living quarters—public money to build was there. (In a 1991 visit, I found the building vacant and apparently never used.)

But while the paper trail and witnesses had clearly established a

10 percent kickback pattern, for conviction under RICO the government had to prove that the municipality had been harmed. Spaan took no chances with the jury. He had hired Roger McAniff, an associate professor of engineering at the University of Alaska Anchorage, to do a project cost summary of contracts awarded to the inner circle principals on the North Slope. Working from a large chart that Spaan posted in front of the jury, McAniff analyzed twenty-three contracts involving nine projects, testifying that each was grossly overpriced. Blackstock had been paid $8,785,000 for its services in building health clinics, when a more realistic cost would have been $3,523,000. MMCW had been paid $24,435,000 for consulting, when McAniff's analysis showed that it had done about $13,200,000 worth of work. A firm named Olympic faithfully kicked back 10 percent of the $25,639,000 it was paid to build fire stations that could have been built for less than half that amount.

The defense attorneys pounced on McAniff. They grilled him for two months, attempting to show that he had greatly underestimated the cost of building on arctic permafrost. They cited the extraordinary costs of the high school and Utilidor, which had been started by Brower's predecessor. But while the defense attorneys parried with the witness, jurors were studying the project cost summary chart in front of them. Several could be observed doing their own math.

Finally, the government opened the subject of the defendants' personal wealth. Now jurors saw figures they didn't need a math course to understand. FBI agent Talbert, an accountant by training, calculated Dischner's net worth at $150,000 at the start of 1981. By 1984, he said, Dischner's net worth rose to between $11 million and $12 million and included properties in Anchorage and Palm Springs. The government introduced Dischner's income tax records, over strong objections by the defense attorneys. The returns showed that Dischner had listed the numerous companies associated with the North Slope constructions as "clients." The largest was H.W. Blackstock. In one year alone, Blackstock paid $1.6 million in fees to Trust Consultants, a business solely owned by Dischner. The government maintained that Dischner had not only failed to pay proper income taxes in 1981 and 1982, but had filed no tax returns at all in 1983 and 1984; his estimated income for those two years was $19 million.

In May 1989, eight months after it started, the longest and most expensive criminal trial in Alaska's history came to an end. More than one hundred witnesses, including nearly everyone who had any connection with the government in Barrow, had been called by the prosecutors. Thousands of documents and other items introduced as evidence filled the courtroom. Neither Dischner nor Mathisen took the stand, and the court had seemed relieved when Mathisen's defense attorney called only one witness. By the end, the attorneys, the jurors, and even the judge appeared on the edge of nervous exhaustion.

The jury deliberated for sixteen days. On May 23, it found Dischner, now seventy-three, and Mathisen, fifty-seven, guilty of more than twenty counts each of racketeering, fraud, bribery, and accepting kickbacks from contractors. U.S. district judge James M. Fitzgerald sentenced each man to seven years in federal prison and ordered them to forfeit more than $5 million in property.

But the euphoria in the U.S. attorney's office was short-lived. Exhausted, Spaan resigned, saying he needed a year off to refresh body and spirit with a trip around the world. An assistant, Mark Davis, was named acting U.S. attorney. It was up to him to direct the prosecution of the two major bribery cases that remained—against the MMCW engineers and the Seattle businessmen who ran the H. W. Blackstock Company, who together had profited more than anyone from the North Slope contracts.

The MMCW gang, architect Allen McDonald and engineers Peter White and David Coffman, had been indicted on thirty-nine counts of racketeering, bribery, and tax fraud. If convicted, they faced more than twenty years in prison. Their trial was initially scheduled for Fairbanks, but no judge was available because federal courts were too busy and recent retirements had drained the judicial ranks. The search for a federal judge elsewhere took on comic proportions.

First, the trial was moved to Los Angeles. The prosecutors in Alaska protested. Then it was moved back to Fairbanks, but the Los Angeles judge, a onetime amateur ski champion, balked because, among other reasons, he considered the skiing inferior in Alaska. The case was finally assigned to federal court in Portland, Oregon, where it simply evaporated in March 1990. Despite protests from his young assistant, Neil Evans, assistant U.S. attorney Stephen Cooper from the Fairbanks office negotiated and signed an appalling plea bargain.

Cooper agreed to reduce the thirty-nine-count indictment against the MMCW defendants to a single felony with no jail time, no fine, no community service, and, worst of all, no commitment to testify in the Rogstad corruption trial yet to come. In comparison, back in 1987, Geoffrey Fowler, a fourth member of the MMCW group who had agreed to testify for the government, was sentenced to six months in prison, a $10,000 fine, and one thousand hours of community service.

Acting U.S. attorney Davis claimed he had no idea such a plea bargain was being signed and said it was done without his approval. He sped to Portland in an attempt to get the presiding judge, James Burns, to rescind it. Judge Burns was incensed. He castigated Davis for "this thoroughly unedifying display" and threatened to reconsider the constitutionality of all the charges. The plea bargain stood, and a chastened Davis returned to Anchorage. Mike Spaan, back from his vacation and now in private practice, called the whole matter "unconscionable." Neil Evans, the assistant, resigned in protest. Cooper did not respond to media queries.

The third and last of the three major racketeering cases was placed in the hands of Peter Gamache, who was on loan from the state attorney general's office. In February 1990, Gamache had successfully indicted the two Seattle men who ran the H. W. Blackstock Company. Kenneth Rogstad, the president, and Wayne Larkin, the director of administration, were charged with paying more than $2.5 million in bribes and kickbacks to obtain $140 million worth of slope business during the Brower administration. If convicted, each faced twenty years in prison and the forfeiture of millions of dollars.

The case had more than usual media interest because Rogstad was a politically prominent former chairman of the Republican party in King County, which encompasses Seattle. Newspapers reported that he had connections to the White House through a Blackstock director, Seattle lawyer James Munn, who had run Ronald Reagan's 1980 presidential campaign in Washington State.

The case began to unravel before it began. Right off, the Seattle pair succeeded in moving the trial to federal court in Tacoma, Washington, roughly 3,000 miles from Barrow. Next, Peter Gamache unexpectedly resigned to take a state job in Kodiak. His departure further crippled the U.S. attorney's office. Almost by default, the case fell into the lap of Karen Loeffler. With barely a month to prepare, she would have to take on two nationally prominent defense lawyers—

noted San Francisco attorney Marc Topel, representing Rogstad, and Chicago attorney Thomas Decker, retained by Larkin. Both had had plenty of time to do their homework.

In September 1990, Karen Loeffler packed up three thousand pounds of documents and headed for the U.S. district court in Tacoma. A senior judge, Jack Tanner, had been assigned to the case. Karen soon discovered that Tanner, a retired jurist, was also an impatient judge. "The government's case depended upon building a forest of evidence as it did in the Dischner and Mathisen cases," remarked Hal Spencer, the Associated Press court reporter who covered the trial. "But every time Karen tried to produce a tree, the judge or the defense knocked it down."

Meanwhile, the government's Eskimo witnesses, Brower and Irving Igtanloc, were torn apart by the defense. Yes, they had received items of value ranging from $37,000 boats to groceries and free housing from Blackstock. No, they conceded, these were not bribes, only gifts. Yes, they had been billed for these items by Blackstock—after the government started its investigation in 1984. No, they had never paid. Several of the more experienced witnesses who might have helped, such as borough lawyer Chris Mello or Roger McAniff, were never called to the stand at all.

"There is no question that the mayor and the public works commissioner were bribed," Judge Burns commented after the prosecution rested its case. But, he said, whether Rogstad and Larkin had been involved remained at issue. Topel and Decker quickly built a wall of doubt for the jury. First, they argued that Blackstock had been paying fees to Dischner for years in return for consulting services. What Dischner did with the fees was of no concern to them. As for the items the company had given to Mayor Brower, those were not favors, they stressed, but items he was expected to pay for. It happened that Brower was something of a deadbeat, Topel declared, but Blackstock, however belatedly, had billed him for the boats and housing.

The trial of Dischner and Mathisen, which involved similar allegations, had lasted eight months. This one lasted two weeks. The jury acquitted both defendants. Afterward, a juror remarked, "We felt something was fishy, but the government never proved it."

It was a sad ending to a long and courageous investigation. FBI agent Bruce Talbert had devoted six years of intense work to the case and paid for it with a broken marriage. Karen Loeffler is now saddled with responding to eternal appeals as Dischner and Mathisen, among others, fight going to jail. She still manages to be cheerful, although she feels she was betrayed by a lower forty-eight jury with an ingrained perception that such doings were just normal for Alaska.

More than a dozen North Slope officials, contractors, and consultants were convicted. The Eskimo community still hopes to recover some of the splurged funds through a maze of civil suits that were still slowly moving through the Anchorage courts in 1992. But the only sure winners will be the lawyers.

Aside from Rogstad and Larkin, only one other defendant, Brower's lawyer, Marty Farrell, was acquitted. Dischner and Mathisen were ordered to begin serving their jail terms on March 2, 1993. Until then, the only ones to serve time were three Eskimos. Ex-mayor Brower, sobbing before the court, was sentenced to thirty days and three years' probation for tax evasion. Irving Igtanloc did six months in a halfway house for bribery. His brother, Myron, spent six months in a minimum-security prison in Washington State for tax evasion.

At best it was a cloudy victory that left Alaskans wondering why neither the U.S. Justice Department nor the state congressional delegation had helped arm the U.S. attorney's office to see the battle through.

CHAPTER 11

Anchorage
Meets Dallas

LIFE TURNED SOUR in 1982 for Rick Chiappone, a hustling, thirty-three-year-old paperhanger who had been doing well covering the walls of glitzy Las Vegas hotels and casinos. His marriage had broken up, he was under court order to pay off all of the leftover house bills, and his girlfriend was egging him on to make a clean break from Vegas.

So Rick packed up his tools, married his girlfriend, and headed for Alaska to start a new life. He had read that Anchorage was one of the ten fastest-growing American cities, and it lived up to its billing. "There were cranes and skeletons of high rises on the horizon, a bulldozer on every corner, and pickup trucks with Idaho, California, and Washington license plates at the construction sites," Rick says. "The roads were jammed with drivers who seemed impatient to get to where they were going."

Rick spent $1,500 that he'd salvaged from the bill collectors on a Chevy pickup. He painted a sign on the side that read, "Paper Hanging." Then he put down his last dollar to install a telephone in a tiny one-room apartment he felt lucky to rent at $450 a month.

"I just walked into places and started bidding, and the phone started ringing as soon as people heard there was another paperhanger in town," Rick says. "I stepped into a pot of gold. Public buildings and private houses were going up everywhere and anyone with any skill in construction could get a job. Up here people were geared to hanging paper only in bathrooms and kitchens. No one was geared to do the fast-paced wall installations I did in Las Vegas. Soon, my wife and I had all the business we could handle. She has a master's degree in anthropology and eight years' experience as a social worker, but she worked with me, covering walls. Our gross receipts hit two hundred twenty-five thousand dollars in two years, and I even got in some fishing."

Rick's success story was not unusual in Anchorage in the early 1980s. Unlike Barrow, which boomed from property taxes on oil facilities at Prudhoe, or Valdez, which prospered from the big pipeline payrolls and terminal revenues, Anchorage thrived on a later wave of prosperity that oil discovery brought to Alaska.

Through the hard campaigning of city fathers, with *Anchorage Times* publisher Bob Atwood leading the way, the oil companies were persuaded to locate their Alaska headquarters in Anchorage. Fairbanks, which was much closer to the Prudhoe oil fields, was the logical site, but, as Atwood says, "we were much more inviting." Anchorage civic leaders promised greater cultural opportunities and made much of facilities at the city's all-weather international airport. (The frequency and severity of Fairbanks's winter ice fogs were well known.) Meanwhile, Atwood says, Fairbanks business leaders were raising rents and otherwise preparing "to screw the oil companies."

The oil companies helped create the first cosmopolitan city in Alaska. In 1983, Atlantic Richfield (ARCO) finished a twenty-one-story office tower of glass and steel in downtown Anchorage at a cost of $65 million. Sohio, BP's domestic subsidiary, matched that with a handsomely landscaped fifteen-story midtown edifice costing $75 million. Nelson Bunker Hunt invested $45 million of Texas money in a twenty-story high rise within easy walking distance of ARCO. Lesser high rises sprouted all over the city. Acres of tiny cottages were bulldozed to make way for a forest of gleaming office buildings.

A few spirited citizens tried to persuade the city administration to consider saving a block of the older homes out of respect for heritage. A public hearing was set, but it became academic when one developer learned of it and moved in at dawn to bulldoze three historic homes in the block. ARCO did spare two frontier-era homes on its site and moved them at its expense to the city dump until Historic Anchorage Inc., a civic group formed to preserve the frontier legacy, could decide what to do with them. But the preservation movement lost steam when the city decided that private funds would have to take it from there.

By 1982, oil royalties and commissions from Prudhoe Bay pushed state revenues to $4.5 billion a year. The state spread the money around lavishly—not only for its own projects, but also as direct cash payments to municipalities. The distributions were based on a formula of $1,000 per resident, to be used any way the towns saw fit.

With about half the state's nearly five hundred thousand people, Anchorage found itself awash in money. True to its promise to the oil companies, it earmarked more than $250 million for the cultural amenities that would make it a world-class city—theaters, concert halls, libraries, and museums. The centerpiece of the undertaking, called "Project 80s," was the $75 million Alaska Center for the Performing Arts, which houses three state-of-the-art theaters. Critics of its design—of which there still are many—say the building resembles a "gigantic squatting toad." Nevertheless, star performers, from Jay Leno to the San Francisco Opera, regularly grace its stages, often with praise for the facility.

The George M. Sullivan Sports Arena ($34.5 million) seats eight thousand and can accommodate events from ice hockey tournaments to rock concerts. The majestic Loussac Library building ($41.6 million) is a versatile edifice, though some contend that more should have been spent on books and less on its elaborate Roman design and fountains. The Museum of History and Art ($25.5 million) became an important anchor on the edge of the refurbished downtown and a major visitor attraction. The Egan Civic and Convention Center ($26.8 million), across the street from the performing arts center, offers a convenient location that draws conferences.

The arts, which had always been lively in Alaska if largely homespun, became adventurous, polished, and exceptionally well heeled. Christine D'Arcy, who heads the Alaska State Council on the Arts, an allocating agency, says, "The biggest legacy of the oil money was the development of cultural facilities throughout the state. But what also happened was that the arts organizations were able to undertake sustained creative development and hire staffs to promote funding. As a result, today we have a twenty-three-million-dollar arts industry that provides income to four thousand people throughout the state."

In 1967, the newly created arts council's budget was $54,778; fifteen years later, oil revenues shot that up to $6.2 million, the highest per capita subsidy in the nation. Arts activities bloomed throughout the state, attracting artists from throughout the country. Anchorage, in particular, astonished visitors with its resident opera, symphony, and concert associations and especially its excellent repertory theater.

The cultural vigor of Anchorage undoubtedly made the harsh climate of Alaska more inviting to oil executives and other employees offered transfers from Texas and other southern states. ARCO and BP, the major Prudhoe partners, added substantial inducements of their own. ARCO, for example, gave bonuses of 45 percent on the first $24,000 of base salary and 25 percent on the remainder. Each adult received $1,300 toward air travel, and each child $1,000.

The influx of so many families from sophisticated Dallas and other oil-rich cities further rearranged the demographics of Alaska. Soon, blocks of elegant homes and condos appeared, some alongside the not-so-elegant jerry-built apartment houses, tar-paper shacks, and trailer courts that housed an earlier generation of Alaskans. Nordstrom, the Seattle-based chain of tony specialty shops, renovated the store it had bought in 1975 in anticipation of the affluent customers oil would provide. Boutiques, interior decorating shops, and trendy restaurants mushroomed where scrubby brush had stood. Workers who headed downtown over gravel in the morning were startled to find themselves driving home over freshly paved roads at night. The city's pace was frantic.

In 1983 alone, permits were issued for a billion dollars' worth of construction, exceeding the combined building permits issued that same year in the also-thriving cities of Seattle, Portland, and Honolulu. Bankers, from inside the state and out, stormed into the city as willing lenders, taking full advantage of state programs that guaranteed loans. Easy borrowing further fueled the boom.

Given such volatility, the area was rife with opportunities for immense private profiteering. It was inevitable that the action would attract the likes of Peter Zamarello, an Alaskan entrepreneur without parallel, who in a few brief years would rise from rags to become the richest man in Alaska.

Zamarello was born in 1927 to poor Italian parents on the Greek island of Cephalonia. His formal education ended in elementary school. He says he bribed a bureaucrat to get him a high school diploma so he could join the merchant marine. When his Greek freighter reached Albany, New York, in 1953, Zamarello jumped ship, headed for New York City, and within forty-two days married a Polish girl who had American citizenship. (When asked how a poor boy fleeing immigration authorities could sweep an American citizen off her feet in such a short time, Zamarello replied, "Don't you know the smartest people in the world come from Cephalonia? That's spelled C-e-p-h-a-l-o-n-i-a.")

His timely match kept the immigration authorities off his back long enough for him to work his way across the country as a carpenter until he reached his goal — Alaska. Zamarello's father was one of the immigrants who'd come to the tent city of Anchorage in 1915 to build the Alaska railroad, and he'd constantly talked of the wonders and potential of the land after his return home in 1924.

Anchorage in the 1960s was teeming with hustlers like Zamarello, many of them busy combing the oil scouting tip sheets for where the big plungers were leasing land. While the oil game tempted him, Zamarello soon saw a better way to make his fortune in Alaska. He wielded his hammer only as long as it took him to save enough money for a down payment on a loan to buy a parcel of land. He quickly discovered the weak underbelly of the banking bureaucracy. Credit checks in Alaska were so loose that when the money from one bank loan ran out, he found he could go to another bank and get another loan.

Zamarello's first construction loan — $150,000 in 1969 — enabled him to build a shopping center in Muldoon, a shabby but strategically located neighborhood near the gates of the huge Elmendorf Air Force Base. Pizza parlors, convenience stores, and other businesses were quick to rent when they noticed the steady traffic. Next, Zamarello bought a 568-unit trailer park. Convinced that imminent oil discovery would make the city boom, he used his new flow of revenue to buy cheap land around Anchorage. When pipeline construction started in the 1970s, he opened an office in Beirut, Lebanon, where he extolled the potential of Alaska to oil-rich Arabs, and, he says, successfully sold Alaska land to wealthy sheiks. (His landlord in Lebanon, he claims, was Jaber al-Ahmed al-Sabah, who became the Kuwait emir deposed by the Iraqis in 1990. In an interview at his Anchorage office in February 1991, Zamarello fumed over U.S. involvement in the Gulf War. "That Jaber Whatever-the-Hell-the-Rest-of-His-Name-Is had fifty concubines and two wives. Still, he was always trying to screw my secretary. And now we have the whole American army over there trying to save a guy like that.")

When the oil companies opted to build their Alaska headquarters in Anchorage, land values took off like a missile. Zamarello was perfectly positioned. His real estate leverage propelled him out front in the frenzy of development that transformed Anchorage and much of its environs. He borrowed, built, and borrowed some more—at least a billion dollars, by his own estimates—to create an empire of dozens of shopping centers, malls, office plazas, condos, and trailer parks. Banks in Alaska and Washington State courted him, rarely questioning his single-page, unaudited statement of financial worth. By 1985, Zamarello had become the largest and richest developer in the state. Known as "king of the strip malls," he employed a thousand workers. He could even boast that he owned city hall; he'd bought the building Anchorage leased for its principal municipal offices with an $8 million loan in 1984.

His personal fortune grew to a reported $292 million. He freely accepted the title of wealthiest man in Alaska—and did his best to live up to it. He lived in a $1.2 million mansion in Anchorage, bought condos for himself and his wife in Tacoma, and owned an $850,000 retreat in Honolulu. He invested millions in four financial institutions, acquired $1.4 million in Krugerrands, and collected a trove of art, expensive furniture, and jewelry valued at $11 million. His favorite bauble was an $80,000 gold-and-diamond watch. The only other one like it was said to belong to King Fahd of Saudi Arabia. Although a self-described atheist, he paid a large share of the bill for a $3 million cathedral that became the headquarters of the Orthodox diocese of Alaska. ("I did it to honor my parents.") A grade-school dropout, he pledged 40 acres of lakefront property and cash valued at $480,000 to Alaska Pacific University. ("I want others to have what I missed.")

He made a major contribution to build a mobile dental clinic for children in Greece. (The Greek government awarded him its medal of honor.)

Anchorage has paid dearly for Zamarello's rise to riches. The stamp of banality he put on the city has persisted. His dozens of strip malls and commercial centers, some with hazardous traffic entrances and many in incompatible neighborhoods, stand as testaments to the zoning and planning standards that were ignored while Anchorage boomed. Most of his malls and plazas are undistinguished rows of humdrum storefronts, strung together under elongated blue roofs. He threw them up wherever he chose, even in a suburb 40 miles from Anchorage, and because the city did not check the crazy-quilt pattern of its commercial development until it was too late, it is fated to live with them.

Zamarello refers to "the pygmy minds of people who run government" and boasts he paid thousands to insulate himself from "stupid" public officials who were in a position to challenge him. One day, he regaled the students in a University of Alaska Anchorage economics class with stories of his bribes and laundered campaign contributions to governors, mayors, and other public officials. In 1977, during the administration of Anchorage mayor George Sullivan, Zamarello says he even bribed two greedy building department employees by check. "I complained to the Anchorage assembly. They investigated. The ethics chairman said the inspectors used poor judgment. The two guys get fifteen-day suspensions—with pay," Zamarello says, with a contemptuous laugh.

In 1982, Tony Knowles, a youthful, Yale-educated native of Oklahoma, took over the mayor's office after a hard-fought victory, defeating a prodevelopment legislative leader backed by aggressive real estate interests. A biker, cross-country skier, and lover of Alaska's open spaces, Knowles campaigned on a promise to bring Anchorage's runaway building under control. The new mayor promptly cleaned out the zoning and planning boards, which had long been dominated by real estate people. Then he put across twenty-one revisions to the planning code, ranging from a policy to protect and, when possible, acquire wetlands to regional controls on strip zoning.

It was only a matter of time before Zamarello and Knowles collided. No sooner had the new mayor put his development restrictions in place than Zamarello announced that he intended to build a thousand-room hotel at the intersection of Minnesota Drive and Raspberry Road, which is a gateway to the international airport and on an easy access route to downtown. But the site was smack in the administration's newly designated wetlands area, and the city refused to give Zamarello a permit. The standoff intensified when a city employee inspecting the site found a duck nesting on a batch of eggs.

Zamarello responded in his usual flamboyant style. He rented a room in the name of "A. Duck" at the Captain Cook, the city's five-star hotel. Then he sent a copy of the reservation to city hall with an offer to house the "fuckin' duck" in the hotel room at his own expense until the eggs hatched. The Knowles administration would not be moved. Stunned by the rebuff, Zamarello vowed he would get even with the bird lover in city hall. (He waited until 1990, when Knowles ran for governor, to exact his revenge. As the campaign heated up, ethics became a pressing issue, whereupon Zamarello surfaced in the media, claiming that he had illegally laundered $27,000 in contributions to Knowles's 1984 campaign with the mayor's full knowledge. Knowles admitted receiving consecutively numbered cashier's checks in the names of Zamarello and his various employees but said he was unaware the contributions were illegal. He concedes that the allegations hurt him in the race, which he lost.)

By late 1985, university economists were warning that Anchorage was heading for a building glut. Some developers pulled back, but Zamarello declined to slow down. Inevitably, laws of economics kicked in and Zamarello's empire collapsed almost as spectacularly as it began. "The Anchorage area simply became overbuilt, and bankers permitted the overbuilding because they misread the nature of the boom," Arnold Espe, a surviving banker, recalls. "Too many buildings, too many barbers, too many everything. The boom never developed the underpinnings of permanent private employment. Population grew as long as government kept throwing massive amounts of money at virtually everything. When people saw that government no longer had the money to throw, they left the state almost as fast as they came in."

The steep dive in the price of oil early in 1986 hastened the exodus. Alaska crude fell from $27 a barrel to less than $10, which translated into a loss of more than $1 billion in already budgeted revenues in the space of six months. Governor Sheffield declared a fiscal emergency. He cut nine thousand jobs from the state payroll. "It was as though you lived in Detroit and Detroit closed its automobile plants," recalls Scott Hawkins, who runs the city's economic development corporation. "The immediate impact was less cash on the street, fewer people buying goods, and stores and businesses suddenly struggling to stay alive."

Yet even as other businesses started retrenching, Zamarello disclosed plans for an eighteen-story Anchorage bank building. He was particularly pleased by the location, he said, because his penthouse would blot out the view of the Chugach Mountains for the National Bank of Alaska across the street, the only bank in town that refused to lend him money.

But by 1986, Zamarello's store vacancy rates had increased drastically and his newest malls had no takers. Newspapers later reported that Zamarello's lease income dropped from about $13.2 million to $7.2 million in that one year. The banks that had lent Zamarello money on the basis of that one-page unaudited statement now began to look deeper. They soon found his business was in distress and worsening by the day as Alaska real estate began a free-fall. When a contractor sued to collect payment due and won a $4.3 million judgment against Zamarello, his empire was pushed over the edge. In August 1986, he filed for protection under Chapter 11 of the bankruptcy laws. The depositions revealed that Zamarello was swamped by debts estimated at about $150 million and pursued by about 250 angry creditors.

Before going broke, Zamarallo built 4 million square feet of retail space, which amounts to more than half of the retail footage in the state. Now he handed the state one more legacy—the most complicated bankruptcy case Alaska had ever encountered. Court-appointed examiners tried to untangle his seven interlocking companies and attempted to question Zamarello on the whereabouts of his fortune. It was tantamount to trying to revive memory in a man with a serious case of amnesia. He turned the bankruptcy proceedings into a comic skit so intriguing that even *The Wall Street Journal* devoted a front-page story to it.

Questioned about a rumor that his estranged (but still friendly) Polish wife, Patricia Zamarello, carried a suitcase containing $20 million out of the country and deposited the money in a Swiss bank, Zamarello laughed. "It's hard to get even one million dollars in a suitcase—I know, I tried it," he said. "If she could carry twenty million dollars, I'd put her in the weight-lifting Olympics." Had he transferred any possessions to his wife? Yes, Zamarello said, he did give a portion of his assets to his wife in exchange for other property in Beirut. "Don't go look for it," he told the examiners. "It's not there anymore. They blew it up." He claimed he had no job, no income, and no cash except the $8 or $10 on his person. Turning to the lawyer who was taking his deposition, he asked, "You want it?" At another point, he said he'd "rather be a pimp with a purple hat and a feather" than be associated with banking. After the bankruptcy was over, he added, he would apologize—to the pimps.

Zamarello's crash was one of the first in the severe recession that gripped Alaska in 1986, and the hardest. The tremors of his collapse were felt by banks, suppliers, and the entire real estate industry. The fifteen-year mortgages with variable interest rates many of the banks had stipulated became too stringent as the economy began to soften. Landlords unable to fill their units simply declared bankruptcy and left lending agencies to deal with the problem. Nine of Alaska's fifteen banks went broke or were forced into mergers soon after, most of them overleveraged in real estate and many of them carrying uncollectible loans made to Zamarello.

John Shively, who became chief executive of United Bancorporation, Alaska, Inc., after leaving Governor Sheffield's administrative staff, was among those who had the unpleasant task of informing stockholders their bank was going out of business. "We lost $83.7 million in the first six months of this year," Shively wrote in 1987. "That is a pittance compared to the billions of dollars the big boys are losing .... The majority of the people felt the real estate development boom would last forever ... but Alaska banks were financing the building of condos, houses, and shopping centers for the people who were building condos, houses, and shopping centers. When the building stopped and other sectors of the economy began to disintegrate, people working in the construction industry and other ailing businesses began to leave and now we don't need all those condos, houses, and shopping centers."

The Federal Deposit Insurance Corporation (FDIC) took over $1.5 billion in bad loans and defaulted property from the failed Alaska banks and thrifts. On a per capita basis, the government bailout rivals the national savings and loan scandal that would follow. In an attempt to recoup losses, the FDIC sued thirty-three former bank officers and directors in 1991 for $55 million. Charged with gross mismanagement, breach of duty, and reckless real estate lending, most of the defendants are pillars of the Alaska establishment. Among them were three top officials of Governor Hickel's administration, including his commissioner of revenue; former and current legislators; Native corporation leaders; and even the assistant publisher of *The Anchorage Times*.

While banks were the most spectacular failures, hundreds of other trades, professions, and individuals also flooded the bankruptcy courts. Employees were left stranded as businesses closed their doors. The carpetbaggers who survived were those who had other resources to fall back on. Among them was Rick Chiappone, the hustling paperhanger. His well-educated wife managed to get a job teaching school and her income paid the bills while they rode out the recession. The stable incomes of oil industry executives and office staffers kept Anchorage from flat-out collapse; the monetary excesses of those who had come just to cash in were already gone.

After three years in bankruptcy, Zamarello was back on the scene in 1989. His complex reorganization left him with only a fraction of his holdings. Most of his malls were becoming eyesores, with flaking paint and neglected landscaping. Unfortunately, the pattern he had set had inspired other developers to produce many more miles of urban blight. Zamarello, meanwhile, rejoined the business world, swearing that he would never build anything in Alaska again, "not even my tomb." Some contend that he must nevertheless be considered one of the lucky ones. While he lost an empire, what did he really lose? As one bitter banker observed, "Pete could have fared a lot worse. He could have lost his own money."

CHAPTER 12

The Iron Fist Of Jesse Carr

Ron Windeler, a thin, wispy-bearded son of a homesteading family, used to hear stories of ruthless characters in Alaska while growing up on the remote, moose-trampled acres of the Kenai Peninsula. But he never really knew the meaning of ruthless until he left the failing farm and met Jesse L. Carr, the boss of the International Brotherhood of Teamsters union in Alaska.

In 1972, Windeler, then twenty-three, got a job as a technician on the White Alice, an RCA/Alascom project that installed communications systems for radar stations on the mountaintops along the Bering Sea in Alaska. He had heard of Carr, the state's fastest-rising labor leader, and even benefited from his clout during his first year on the job. The aggressive Teamsters had just ousted the sleepy International Brotherhood of Electrical Workers (IBEW), and Carr promptly got the technicians a 41 percent raise—from $4.36 an hour to $6.16. And that was the year President Nixon had slapped a 5½ percent wage freeze on the nation.

Windeler was impressed, but he did not see the man in action until 1977, when he attended a Teamsters union meeting in Fairbanks at which Carr was presiding. He watched in awe as the burly, flushed man, alternating between bombastic invective and studied silence, kept a roomful of normally rowdy Teamsters in docile decorum as he discussed mounting an assault on Alaska's antiunion bastions.

The principal piece of business that required membership action was ratification of the new agreement with Alascom, the statewide phone company. The pact covered Windeler and the other technicians working on White Alice and Carr said he had pounded out a good contract. Windeler had a question, so he did what he thought any concerned union member would do—he raised his hand. Carr ignored him and went on. "We'll ratify by a voice vote," he announced.

Windeler rose to his feet. "I move we vote by secret ballot," he said. Carr scowled, slammed his gavel, and angrily ruled Windeler out of order. The members gave Carr the chorus of *ayes* he was waiting for. After the meeting, Carr approached Windeler. "How's it going, son?" he asked. Then he poked a finger in Windeler's belly and walked off.

When Windeler reached home that night, he noticed his car had a flat tire. The next morning he saw that a screw had been driven into the sidewall. The tire had held air while the car was parked, but the friction opened a leak as soon as the car began moving. "Someone skilled in inflicting damage did it," Windeler says. "You can fix a puncture in the tread of a radial tire, but when the side is pierced, the tire becomes unpatchable."

Windeler became all the more determined to make his presence felt at union meetings. He studied the bylaws and Robert's Rules of Order. He talked to members about defending their rights. He challenged procedural points from the floor. And over the next six months he had thirteen more flat tires, all the result of screws or nails driven into the sidewalls.

Windeler asked Fairbanks police for help. The police took notes, but nothing happened. Then he talked to reporters at the local daily, the *Fairbanks News-Miner*, and the paper obtained a tape recording of a night of Carr's dictatorial rantings, printing several of the more colorful quotes. At the next meeting, Windeler encountered two thugs in a hallway. One grabbed him from behind and crushed him in a bear hug while the other snatched his briefcase, scattering the contents on the floor. He had no tape recorder, but they sent him sprawling across the hall anyway. By now Windeler had learned a basic lesson: Jesse Carr ran a rigid union.

A high school dropout and ex-Marine, Carr learned the ropes under Southern California Teamster boss Dave Beck, who became president of the international Teamsters and eventually landed in jail. Carr came to Alaska in 1951 and drove a gravel truck for two years. In 1953, at age twenty-seven, he became business agent for the infant Local 959, which had about five hundred members and was several hundred dollars in debt. Seven years later, Carr persuaded the international union to merge all four Teamster locals in Alaska and put him in charge.

Oil explorations at Swanson River and the Cook Inlet had brought in new business and therefore new opportunities for organized labor in south-central Alaska. Carr did whatever he thought was necessary for his union's share. By the early 1970s, he had been hit with six felony arrests, on charges ranging from extortion to embezzlement. He beat every one. He was acquitted on four of the counts and the other two were dropped when, according to court records, "the principal witness had to undergo extensive medical treatment and was in no physical condition to testify at the trial." No explanation of what caused the disability was given to the media.

The aura of invulnerability added to Carr's growing prestige inside and outside the union. He became known as a master of intimidation. By the mid-1970s, the Teamsters in Alaska held an estimated five hundred contracts, many of them wrenched from management by their leader. Few companies dared to say anything publicly about Carr's tactics, but privately, they reported, he became a beast in contract showdowns. William Heintz, a Teamster, says Carr once drop-kicked a rubbish barrel through a window during negotiations with the trucking company Sea-Land Service.

Besides organizing the traditional truck drivers and haulers, the Teamsters became the bargaining unit for such unlikely groups as butchers, bakers, bank clerks, high school principals, and even the Anchorage police department. Every new member swelled the union treasury, and, Carr, as secretary-treasurer, controlled the purse strings.

By the time pipeline construction peaked in the middle 1970s, Jesse Carr had already become one of the most feared men in Alaska. Teamster membership in the state soared to twenty-three thousand, making the union the largest and most influential special-interest body in

Alaska. Carr cowed not only employers but important public officials as well. Former Alaska commissioner of labor Lew Dischner lobbied the legislature on behalf of the union and dispensed favors to the right people. Teamster money was distributed generously at election time, and candidates from both political parties vied for Teamster endorsements. Newspapers began to refer to Jesse Carr as "the most powerful man in Alaska ... his word [is] capable of shutting down the state."

Rumors about Teamster ties to organized crime surfaced during the building of the pipeline in 1976 after two of Carr's people working at the main warehouse in Fairbanks were abducted and murdered, but no one ever investigated. "One of my biggest regrets is having been too green to do what needed to be done in unraveling the double homicide associated with the Teamsters union and the warehouse terminal in Fairbanks," Dan Hickey, then state prosecutor, says. "Around this time, a union steward talked the parole board into freeing a man who was serving time for a botched paid hit. He is paroled and two people at the terminal disappear."

An FBI strike force from California conducted the only grandjury investigation into pipeline racketeering, but it concentrated on prostitution in Valdez rather than violence in the Teamsters union. Six Alaskans were indicted in 1976, but the closest the FBI came to Carr was arresting his former lawyer. He was subsequently acquitted, as were all five other defendants.

During pipeline construction, about $1 million a week flowed into Local 959's trust accounts, nearly all of which Carr dominated as an overpowering trustee. The largest of those entities was the pension fund, which collected $220 million in mandatory employer contributions by the time the pipeline was finished. It was evident that many workers paying into the pension fund were Teamsters only for the duration of the pipeline project. They were unlikely to stay in Alaska for the ten years stipulated for vesting. Jesse Carr saw the opportunities in those excess millions. He set out to literally build an empire.

In 1974, Congress had passed the Employee Retirement Income Security Act (ERISA), a long-sought curb on the extravagance of union leaders. It was designed specifically to protect the nation's twenty-three million private, nongovernmental workers from having their pension funds squandered on dubious real estate deals, speculative stocks, or questionable loans. ERISA forbids trustees to invest pension funds to benefit parties of interest, or to make imprudent or self-serving investments, or to surpass specified limits of investments in any one geographical area.

Carr trampled every key provision of ERISA in putting together his Teamster colossus. He organized a nonprofit subsidiary called the Teamsters Local 959 Building Corporation and went on a construction spree. He got Teamsters to buy building bonds at $50 apiece, and banks courted the business. Even the conservative National Bank of Alaska readily provided construction mortgages, comfortably aware that the union was backed by an overflowing pension fund.

At a cost of $32 million, the Teamsters erected the two-hundred-bed Alaska Hospital along the south bank of Merrill Field, one of the first sights visitors see driving into Anchorage from the east. Union members would receive free care here, from womb to tomb, and Local 959 would control the hospital. It would hire administrators who would hire doctors willing to negotiate fair fees. For $8 million more, a 4,000-square-foot professional building was built to house a medical center. It was connected to the hospital by a $6.5 million mall especially for Teamsters, complete with pharmacy, shops, restaurants, bank branches, and a fountain. Ribbon-cutters called it "a monument to the growing strength of the Teamsters union."

The most modern recreation center Alaska had ever seen went up next, alongside the new seven-story office complex that would be named the Jesse L. Carr Building and house the relocated Teamsters headquarters. Union members had the use of an Olympic-size indoor pool, tennis courts, an indoor running track, and, most important, a well-equipped bodybuilding room—Carr and his chief lieutenants believed in lifting weights to maintain the Teamster image. A similarly well-equipped recreation center was built for members in Fairbanks.

Despite rebels like Ron Windeler, who was usually ruled out of order, Carr raised union dues from 40 cents a compensable hour to 50 cents so the union could expand its air fleet from two planes to four. It was true that Teamster business agents had more territory to cover. But it wasn't strictly business that accounted for Jesse Carr's frequent out-of-state trips these days.

Tapping the pension fund, he built a $120 million country club–condominium development in Indian Wells, California, 10 miles from Palm Springs, where the nation's wealthiest go to enjoy the prime desert climate. Named the Desert Horizons Country Club, the 275-acre complex sported a championship golf course, a lavishly equipped clubhouse, tennis courts, and swimming pools. The condos started at $300,000, in 1970s money.

Unfortunately, Carr pointed out, Alaska Teamsters, including himself, could not expect to receive special privileges or a price break at the resort because this would violate the ERISA regulations. He asked members to view the country club as a shrewd investment that would return great financial rewards to the union. Of course, he would need a Lear Jet for regular trips to oversee this money-maker.

Few Teamsters were fooled. Carr and his wife, Helen, a champion amateur women's golfer, were starting to lead a double life. While they lived modestly in Anchorage, they bought a well-appointed (and heavily guarded) condominium in an exclusive section of Indian Wells about a block away from Desert Horizons and within walking distance of the starting tee at the golf course. And while Carr drove a beat-up Monte Carlo sedan in Alaska, he tooled around California in a gold Lincoln Continental.

Carr's new upscale existence was not altogether inspired by a need for respite from Alaska's harsh weather. It was part of his grand empire-building strategy. Because of his excellent performance in Alaska, he had won a director's seat on the western conference of the international Teamsters, and he had visions of going higher.

The struggle for leadership of the international Teamsters union traditionally had been a tug-of-war between the eastern and central conferences, which had the largest memberships. But pension-fund scandals, Mafia dealings, and bribery convictions toppled one international union president after another. Dave Beck went to jail. Jimmy Hoffa served time and his mob-style disappearance afterward further stained the Teamster image. Roy Williams was president in the early 1980s, but even he was fighting accusations of mishandling pension funds and arranging kickbacks for Mafia figures. (He, too, would later go to jail.)

By Teamster standards, Carr was squeaky clean. The international chose its presidents at that time by vote of the conference delegates rather than of the members, and Carr cultivated a wide circle of contacts. His aspirations growing, he hosted Teamster power brokers at Desert Horizons and at his Indian Wells home. His guests led him to believe his performance and his jail-free record made him a strong compromise candidate for the highest union office. That expectation was reinforced by news reports that the U.S. Justice Department was becoming impatient with the succession of tainted presidents of the international and was even considering action under the racketeering laws.

But Carr's streak of luck started to change in the early 1980s. With the pipeline built, Teamsters began leaving Alaska in droves, drastically reducing union revenues. And with so much heavily mortgaged real estate, Carr's empire began to show cracks. An auditor's report filed with the U.S. Department of Labor showed that at the end of 1979 the Teamster building corporation had a deficit of $6.8 million and had lost more than $5 million in the past five years alone. Its biggest property, the Alaska Hospital, drained money at an alarming pace. Bankruptcy was inevitable if the pattern continued.

The burden of bailing out Carr's building program was falling on the Teamsters who chose to stay in Alaska, and many started to resent it. Ron Windeler was starting to have more comrades in opposition. In 1979, with barely enough supporters to fill a phone booth, Windeler had organized an opposition group called ROOR, which stood for Ruled Out of Order. The ROOR opposition slates never won a single union office, but they did drum hard on the theme that Carr was building a personal empire while denying democratic rights to the rank and file. The grievance was considerably strengthened by the tough and persistent reporting of the *Anchorage Daily News*. Then the city's struggling second paper, it had managed to keep a running account of Carr's excesses. A series on the Teamsters during the pipeline days won the paper and its courageous publisher, Kay Fanning, a well-deserved Pulitzer Prize for public service in 1976. (So feared was Carr in that era that no critical Teamster or employer allowed his name to be used for publication in that series.)

The growing dissatisfaction within the rank and file finally surfaced in 1981, when Carr attempted to bulldoze through one more contract at Anchorage Cold Storage, the state's largest wholesale distributor of meats, beverages, and grocery products. The firm's fiercely independent owner, Milt Odom, had battle scars from previous confrontations with Carr, and he decided that he wasn't going to take any more from the Teamster boss. He offered a take-it-or-leave-it deal. The Teamsters, at Carr's urging, turned it down and struck the company.

While Cold Storage workers picketed the plant, Carr called on other Teamsters to join in boycotting major grocery stores that sold Cold Storage products. Odom didn't flinch. The voluntary effort failed to produce the numbers Carr had expected, and it fizzled. Furious, Carr tried to up the ante. At a packed union meeting in Anchorage, he called for thousands of Teamsters from other crafts to join the biggest picket line Alaska had ever seen. He proposed that every Teamster picket four hours a week or pay a $100 fine.

Murmurs of dissent filled the hall. Ron Windeler, now working with Alascom in Anchorage, was among those who tried to find a floor microphone that night. "The place was so packed that some people had to sit in an overflow room, and they were unhappy about voting on something they couldn't hear, much less understand. None of us from the other crafts ever knew the terms in that contract the Cold Storage members turned down. And Jesse sandbagged the mikes so we couldn't ask. Only his people could speak. It was as though someone had written a white paper and assigned one paragraph to each staged speaker.

"When Bill Heintz, one of our Alascom techs, did manage to grab a mike and try to speak against it, he was ruled out of order and physically dragged out of the room. 'That guy [Heintz] is a little teched in the head,' a shop steward shouted. I finally got a chance to say it was wrong to force people on the picket line. Some others who got through offered an amendment to reduce the picketing requirement. It all added up to total confusion."

On the verge of losing control, Carr invoked his infallible parliamentary maneuver. "We will now put the proposal and amendment to a voice vote," he announced.

Windeler leapt to his feet and shouted that the mandatory picketing and the $100 fine were two different issues and each required a vote by secret ballot. But Carr was ready for him. He turned to a person beside him whom he described as a "parliamentary expert." The "expert" ruled that a voice vote was proper as Carr proposed. "A chorus of ayes was followed by an equal volume of nays," Windeler says. "I thought it was a dead heat, but Jesse hops up and says, 'The ayes have it.' And then he gives us a benediction and tells us to report to the picket line." Windeler, who had picketed voluntarily before the mandatory assessment, decided he would continue to picket. But he refused to sign the roster sheets that would legitimize the outcome of the meeting.

On December 22, 1981, ten Teamsters, with Windeler's name at the top of the list, filed a class action suit against Jesse Carr and Local 959 "to enforce their procedural rights." Each had contributed $50 to a kitty to start the fight. Carr was not worried. He was used to court battles, and he was confident that the deep pockets of the union would wear down the little band of dissidents until they ran out of money. But he could not so easily shrug off a different court problem that surfaced about the same time. For years, the U.S. Labor Department had been quietly investigating reports of Carr's manipulation of Teamster pension funds. Now a Department of Labor task force led by John A. LeMay, the Seattle-based administrator for labor management, had provided sufficient basis for the government to start a civil suit against Carr, the other Alaska Teamster pension trustees, and certain alleged illegal beneficiaries, one of which was Desert Horizons, Inc.

The Labor Department charged violations of ERISA in just about every major investment of Teamster pension funds in Alaska. The trustees had allegedly breached their fiduciary trust by financing the Alaska Hospital complex and by permitting about $18 million in unsecured loans to the hospital's related welfare plan, in violation of ERISA regulations that require money to be invested with some expectation of profit. In developing Desert Horizons, they allegedly violated the government regulations in three major ways: by using pension trust funds to acquire the property, by becoming directors of the country club and causing it to be built, and by causing the pension plan to bear the total risk for the project. The trustees further were alleged to have breached their trust by making "party in interest" loans totaling in excess of $8 million to companies regarded as friends of the Teamsters union. These were firms that granted lucrative contracts in exchange for substantial loans from the Teamsters pension fund.

The court did not address the issue of whether Carr and the other trustees would have to pay back millions of dollars in lost pension fund investments, and the full details of its decision were sealed in a consent order that was not released until many years later, so only the union's inner circle had any idea of the magnitude of Carr's trouble. But the union was ordered to begin disposing of the prohibited investments immediately. "For Sale" signs went up on the Alaska Hospital property, the adjacent medical center, and the mall. The union managed to sell the hospital within the year to the Humana Hospital chain for $60 million, thereby showing that it was abiding by the consent order in good faith.

But in the same year, Carr was hit with a devastating setback to his ego and, potentially, to the union's pocketbook. On December 2, 1982, Windeler's group won a clear first-round victory in federal court. U.S. district judge James von der Heydt ruled that Carr's picketing assessment in the Cold Storage strike had been passed illegally. He issued a temporary restraining order barring the union from levying assessments in the Cold Storage strike and certified the legitimacy of the class action suit, clearing the way for it to continue on the issue of damages. The injunction pulled a good number of Teamsters off the picket line. More crucially, it deflated the aura of Teamster infallibility. Angered by the illegitimacy of Carr's actions, Cold Storage workers voted several months later to decertify the union, thereby ending the Teamsters' jurisdiction and effectively breaking the strike. The ouster of the Teamsters at Cold Storage sent a signal to many other companies: You could stand up to Jesse Carr.

By 1983, the Teamsters local was still $4.2 million in debt, and membership had slipped to 12,000. But if the empire of the most powerful man in Alaska was crumbling, you wouldn't know it from Carr. "This local's never been in trouble. We've got lots of assets," he told *The Anchorage Times*. His drive for power in the international union continued. In 1984, he was elected head of the 450,000-member Western Conference of Teamsters. Now he was potentially in line to succeed Teamster president Jackie Presser, who had been in trouble over his association with organized-crime figures from the day he assumed office. Alaska Teamsters say Carr's trips to California became more frequent and longer, leaving his confused lieutenants back home to wonder why the union empire kept losing money.

On January 5, 1985, Jesse Carr, age fifty-nine, was found dead on the living room floor of his Indian Wells home. His wife, Helen, found his body at 7:00 A.M. She said he had awakened at 3:00 A.M. complaining of pain, and told her he would take medicine and watch TV for a while. A coroner's inquiry attributed his death to heart failure.

The job of dismantling Carr's empire fell to Robert J. Sinnett and Jack Slama, two loyal business agents of Carr's. "That same January that Jesse died, Bobby and I sat down and started looking at our situation," Jack Slama says. "We saw we were losing an average of three hundred thousand dollars a month. The last bit of cash coming in was the five million dollars we received for the sale of the office building [to Humana Hospital]. That was eaten up so fast that on one occasion we were unable to meet the payroll."

They got more bad news from the courts. In the spring of 1986, a federal judge determined the union was liable for damages in the Windeler group's class action suit. The implication was tremendous. If every member forced to picket was to be compensated under the judge's formula, the Teamsters would have to pay out more than $10 million. In addition, an Alaska court ordered the local to pay five hundred thousand dollars more to a Fairbanks Teamster named Arlo Wells, who had filed his own suit over union threats when he refused to picket in the Cold Storage strike.

Having made the point that members suffered because of the lack of democratic process, Windeler says his group attempted to soften the financial blow to the troubled union. He said they offered to accept only a nominal settlement and to extend payments over six years. The final entry into the court record shows a judgment against the union of $4,898,000, plus $56,892 in costs and attorney fees.

It was the collapse of the real estate market in 1986 that proved the union's final undoing. The Teamsters Local 959 Building Corporation, the real estate subsidiary, had incurred heavy losses since its inception. It could find no buyers for even its most desirable remaining properties, notably the heavily mortgaged health clubs in Anchorage and Fairbanks. The union had no choice but to file for Chapter 11 bankruptcy reorganization before the year was out. "We came close to filing Chapter 7 [total dissolution], but we had too much pride to do it," Slama says.

The Alaska Teamsters emerged from bankruptcy court three years later with a plan that would allow the union to pay off about $9 million in debt over the next fifteen years. It did not need court prodding to liquidate the Desert Horizons condominiums and country club. "The country club investment and many of the other debts were a mystery to members," Jack Slama, who is currently secretary-treasurer of the union, says today. "But I firmly believe that Carr intended to pay off everyone. He was banking on becoming president of the international. It is not unusual for the international union to help out locals in financial trouble." Slama, who is as low-key as Carr was high-powered, has managed to reverse the financial losses by slimming staff, eliminating fringes such as the air fleet, and renegotiating the consent order with the Labor Department. ("Most of the charges were put on hold," he says.) But the Alaska union is a shadow of its former self. Its 1991 membership was estimated at seven thousand, a drop of 70 percent in fifteen years.

Many members left the state when construction stalled in the real estate bust. But just as damaging was the deflated image of the almighty Teamsters after Carr's setbacks in court and the Cold Storage showdown. The major oil companies opted out of contracts and continue to shun the Teamsters. Even traditional constituents such as truckers and warehouse workers are among those who have decertified the union. The decline of the Alaska Teamsters paralleled the decline of the union in the rest of the country; Carr's hunger for power and his rash, unrestrained expansionism are the corollary to the union's flagrant corruption and strong ties to organized crime on the national level.

The exodus of the Teamsters has delighted even some who never had a connection with the union, notably a dump-picker by the name of Emerson White. He can be seen on most winter weekends ice fishing on Finger Lake outside Wasilla. He wears $150 bunny boots, classic thermal coveralls, and expensive sealskin mittens — all retrieved at the Wasilla dump. "When those union guys headed for Texas or Oklahoma, I had it made," White says. "They didn't take back anything warm. They just drove up to the dump and threw stuff in by the carload. I guess it gets too warm down there to wear this stuff. Or maybe they just didn't want any reminders of Alaska."

CHAPTER 13

Eskimo
Capitalists

Natives of Alaska have had to adapt in many ways over the centuries to survive the harsh extremes of the Great Land. For at least ten thousand years, Eskimos in the north hunted and fished the gale-whipped Arctic coast. Athabaskan tribes roamed the forested interior and the southeast, following caribou and salmon migrations. And the Aleuts on the bleak Aleutian Peninsula subsisted for centuries in underground shelters, and endured slaughter and enslavement by the Russians. But nothing changed Natives' lives as swiftly or traumatically as the arrival of the oil age in Alaska.

Almost overnight, the Alaska Native Claims Settlement Act of 1971 transformed Natives into capitalists. In exchange for surrendering their claims to ancestral lands, the settlement gave the state's estimated seventy-five thousand Eskimos, Indians, and Aleuts $962 million in cash and 44 million acres, about four times what all the dispossessed Indian tribes in the lower forty-eight ever won from the Indian Claims Commission.

Recognizing its past mistake in having herded Native Americans onto reservations, Congress instead devised a unique social experiment. Alaska was divided into thirteen regions, including one designated as "at large" for those Natives who weren't affiliated with a village. Each region was empowered to establish a corporation to manage its new wealth and develop its land. Anyone with at least a quarter Alaska Native blood—a minimum of one Native grandparent—became a stockholder and received one hundred shares in the regional corporation. Forty-five percent of the claims money was assigned to the villages in each region. The villages would also be permitted to organize into corporations, though their plans for the claim money and land selections would be subject to approval by their regional corporation. In short, Alaska Natives would be allowed to control their own destinies, but within a legal structure devised by white men.

Eskimos and Indians, who before statehood had been barred from many saloons and forced to sit in separate sections in some theaters, suddenly became Alaska's most sought-after citizens. As hundreds of millions in reparation dollars started flowing into corporate treasuries, Natives were pursued by hordes of developers, land speculators and securities salesmen offering investment schemes, and a mob of consultants, bankers, and lawyers offering advice—for a retainer—on how to guard against those who would fleece them. "I can recall stock salesmen inviting Native leaders to lunch, plying them with booze, and making glowing promises of high return on investments, which, of course, carried high commissions," Ralph Papetti, a veteran stockbroker in Anchorage, says. "The Natives were also besieged by people selling them trucks and small airplanes. Transportation was very important in the bush. After years of using dogsleds, powered vehicles had great status."

Many Alaskans, resentful of the hefty settlement for a frontier they believed whites had largely tamed, predicted the Natives would be parted from their money and land in a matter of years. But few would foresee the social impact of their being catapulted into the twentieth century. Anthropologists call the transition "rapid acculturation." Since the early part of the century, hellfire-preaching missionaries, BIA school disciplinarians, and patronizing social agencies had steadily imposed alien values on Natives and stripped them of much of their heritage. The money generated by oil heaped on new ideas and expectations. Natives eagerly bought television sets and satellite dishes with their first land claims dividends, seeing on their screens a good life that failed to materialize.

Eskimo Capitalists

Men who had once provided for their families from what nature offered were now expected to look for cash jobs to pay for modern needs and conveniences. But except for the few village corporations that found oil on their property or could tax oil-producing facilities, the new order did not provide jobs for the masses. Many Native men moved into the cities to look for work, but few succeeded in getting into the mainstream. The sidewalks along Fourth Avenue in downtown Anchorage and the little park outside the old city hall are lined with disheveled men looking for a handout or sleeping off a drunk.

Back in the villages, women and their children can get along on welfare. The elderly collect Social Security. The modern market economy and government paternalism have robbed males of their self-esteem. They no longer are critical to family survival. For solace, and perhaps retribution, many men (and many women, too) have turned to comforts some of them learned working the pipeline. Alcoholism and drug addiction have given rise to hundreds of shelters, detox facilities, and abstinence programs. Troubled village leaders have made use of Local Option No. 4, which allows communities to drastically restrict or outright ban the use or importation of alcohol. The result has been significant population shifts, especially an influx of determined Native drinkers to the cities, as police and community service patrol squads can testify.

Particularly tragic is the record rate of suicide among young Native males who succumb to despair and the disorientation of drunkenness. Sporadic epidemics of suicide among teenagers are common in the villages. According to the most recent figures available, Native males between the ages of eighteen and twenty-four are killing themselves off at ten to fifteen times the rate of their peers in the lower forty-eight. Accidental death, in which alcohol is often a factor, occurs at five times the national rate. The suicide rate of young Native women is about five times the national average. But their dependence on alcohol raises other specters. Rates of both fetal alcohol syndrome and sudden infant death are more than twice as high as they are for the rest of the nation, and the consequences are costing the state millions.

Ann Walker, executive director of the Alaska Native Health Board, attributes much of the Natives' substance abuse to their sense of impotence in their changed roles. Uneasiness about their ability to succeed in the white man's world was, in fact, evident among Native

173

leaders from the outset of their venture into capitalism. "We lived for centuries on the land and on what the land could provide, and all of a sudden we are businessmen," Nelson N. Angapak, the son of an Eskimo reindeer herder and a director of Calista Native Corporation, recalls. "Now the Natives are supposed to leave the subsistence life and compete with Wall Street."

Compounding Natives' problems, exploitation of their newly rich corporations became a world sport. Angapak's Calista represents 13,308 shareholders in the second most populous region after the one represented by Sealaska. Its largely Yupik Eskimo population inhabits the soggy, almost treeless coastal and delta plains where the Yukon and Kuskokwim rivers flow into the Bering Sea in southwestern Alaska, embracing a territory the size of Michigan. The region, home of the Yukon Delta Wildlife Refuge about 500 miles west of Anchorage, is widely known for its large seabird rookeries and varieties of migrating waterfowl. (It is the home and nesting area for all of the Cackling Canada and Pacific white-fronted geese in the world.) Less known is that it is also the home of the most economically and socially distressed people in Alaska, and possibly in the U.S.A.

Forty-eight year-round villages, most of them clumps of crudely boarded tar-paper shacks, are scattered throughout the region. They are widely separated, with no roads connecting them to one another, much less to the sparse road system of the state of Alaska. The people live on fish and waterfowl and whatever land mammals venture close to the Bering Sea. Little village stores sell nonperishable items to supplement subsistence harvests, at prices about 50 percent higher than in Anchorage. Except in Bethel, the Kuskokwim delta city where forty-six hundred people live, there are no hospitals or libraries in the region. In short, the region looks much as it did in precorporation days.

When news spread that Calista would receive $80 million in cash and 6.5 million acres of surface land, there was rejoicing. Unemployment in most villages exceeded 60 percent. No one could accurately estimate per capita income, but it was fair to say that most Natives in the Calista region earned less than $2,000 a year. The region's health problems were the worst in the state, with regular outbreaks of hepatitis, meningitis, and tuberculosis. The Kuskokwim area also had the state's highest levels of violent crime, suicide, and accidental death. Finally, it seemed, money was in sight to address these problems.

In fact, a lot of money did come into the corporation. But most of it went out just as quickly, without touching the lives of Alaska's neediest citizens in any meaningful way.

Calista's first problem was one common to all the Native corporations. Having won the passage of the Native claims act, Native political leaders naturally took control of the newly formed corporations. But they were not businessmen, nor did they possess the skills or experience to select trustworthy, capable professional advisers. Their real expertise was in tribal politics, so it is hardly surprising that many of their business decisions were political decisions. The old traditional ways did not foster prudent financial practices, and they resulted in liberal amounts of patronage but few profits.

"We will pursue every available employment for shareholders," Calista stated in its 1974 report. But when it tried to form a construction company that would provide jobs for its people in the Anchorage building boom, all it got was a painful lesson and a lot of red ink. "We bought a lot of equipment and incurred a lot of debt service," explains Mike Niemeyer, who is part Yupik and a vice-president of the corporation. "Later, we found it would have been more efficient to lease equipment. We also hired a large permanent staff when we actually needed only a small core of permanent people. The costs started to pull us under." The company never returned a profit and was losing about $4 million a year when it went under in Alaska's real estate bust of the late 1980s.

Calista also ventured into the fish processing business. Many of its shareholders fish the king and chum salmon that migrate up the Kuskokwim and Yukon rivers. "We bought a couple of collector boats and raised the price [at which we] bought from our fishermen and sold to the Japanese," Terrence Reimer, chief operating officer of Calista, says. "We tried to create a better economy to help support the subsistence life-style. But the price of salmon dropped everywhere and we no longer could afford to sell salmon at huge losses to benefit only a segment of our shareholders."

Calista directors thought it would be a fine idea to train their people in hotel management, since tourism was certain to become a growing industry in Alaska. So they set out to build a palatial hotel that would be not only a training base but a symbol of Calista's economic presence in Alaska. The sixteen-story hotel was to be the centerpiece of an office-retail complex to be called Calista Square on the eastern edge of downtown Anchorage. The wife of an early Calista president was chosen to be one of the interior designers. While other prestige hotels in Anchorage highlight their lobbies with a trophy-size stuffed grizzly or polar bear, she ordered a $700,000 solid jade staircase. It turned out to be too slippery to walk on, however, so it had to be covered with carpeting.

Cost overruns put the hotel in deep financial trouble before it was half finished and brought construction to a standstill. The Native leaders went to Washington for help. They returned with a promise that the BIA would provide a 90 percent guarantee on a $34 million loan — said to be the largest in BIA history — on the condition that Calista sign up a major chain to operate the finished hotel.

After many inquiries, Sheraton emerged as the most likely partner. A committee went to Boston to iron out the contract. They were wined and dined, in the words of one Calista insider, and came back with a deal he describes as "no-win for Calista and no-lose for Sheraton." Sheraton agreed to operate the hotel and train twelve Eskimos in hotel management. However, it insisted on a management fee based on a percentage of the gross revenue, assuring it a comfortable return whether or not the hotel was profitable. Further, the Natives were required to buy many of the basics from Sheraton, including towels, sheets, and napkins bearing the Sheraton logo.

A handsome hotel was erected, but the arrangement made it impossible to return a profit. After five years, Calista could no longer afford to underwrite the losses. It sold the hotel in 1988 to a Korean syndicate at a total loss of $40 million, and with little to show in the way of training for its people. "It was not as successful as I had hoped," concedes Martin B. Moore of Emmonak, one of the Eskimo directors who negotiated the deal in Boston. "Yupiks did not like the confinement of the hotel business. Some couldn't pass the test. Others couldn't stand the life-style. It is in the Native people's blood to return home when the weather is good. We want to go back where the air is free and the country is wide open."

As settlement payments continued to pour in, Calista tried new ventures but could not shake its management problems. It lost more than $6 million on an ill-fated surimi analog (artificial crabmeat) processing plant that it built in Olympia, Washington, with a Korean firm as a minor partner. Mismanaged construction resulted in a ruinous overhead. Oscar Mayer acquired the plant at a bargain and runs it successfully today.

Spurred by speculation that the state expected to build a bridge across the Cook Inlet connecting Anchorage to the undeveloped Knik Arm, Calista began developing a six-thousand-homesite complex called Settlers Bay on a scenic knoll near where the bridge would lead. The bridge was never built and only a few homes were sold. When it could no longer cope with the financial drain, Calista unloaded Settlers Bay at a $12 million loss.

Calista lost an estimated $39,009,000 during the three-year period ending December 31, 1988. An audit of the corporation's fiscal status that year contained an ominous warning: "The factors . . . indicate that the Company may be unable to finance its operations or meet its obligations as they become due and, therefore, be unable to continue in existence." While responsibility for the bad investment decisions must rest with the Native board of directors, it usually dutifully followed the recommendations of its white advisers. (The board was so inexperienced that it got rid of one chief executive, who had performed so badly that he placed the very corporation in jeopardy, by leading him out of his office and changing the locks on all the doors. The board's lawyer later told him he was fired.)

If poor business practices and naive leadership dashed the expectations of Calista, other Native corporations encountered more sinister perils. Bering Straits Native Corporation encompasses the Bering seacoast and Norton Sound settlements north of the Calista region. While its winters are more severe and its sixteen villages are similarly isolated, Bering Straits is relatively better off than its neighbor down the coast, with far fewer people — only sixty-nine hundred stockholders. Many of them find jobs in its largest settlement, Nome, of gold rush fame. The city's thirty-five hundred residents today have a bustling community of government employment and service industries.

George Bell, a Nome Inupiat Eskimo, was an incorporator of Bering Straits and a loan officer of the only bank in town, the Alaska Miners and Merchants. He was chosen to accept the first disbursement under the claims settlement act, which he promptly deposited in his own bank. Alaska Miners and Merchants had just been bought by Alaska National Bank of the North, whose president was Frank Murkowski, later to become a U.S. senator. The Bank of the North elevated Bell to director of its department of Native affairs, in anticipation of the steady flow of claims payments from the government. Bell offered himself as financial adviser to his colleagues on the Bering Straits board, a position that enabled him to direct the millions in settlement money into the bank's coffers.

With $70 million assigned over the next decade, the Bering Straits Native Corporation's account became the bank's largest. However, as the money started to come in, Bering Straits neglected to turn any of it over to the villages, as mandated by the settlement act. Instead, it commingled all the funds and went on a spending orgy, making a series of investments through the Bank of the North. The bank, as a trustee, might have been expected to advise Bering Straits' directors whenever it had adverse information concerning a potential investment. But as a loan officer would later testify, the bank felt no such obligation. The list of unwise investments rapidly grew, and included a now defunct concrete conduit manufacturing company called Life Systems, which was having trouble meeting its payments to the bank even as it was unloaded onto the Native corporation.

Bering Straits lost $1.7 million on Life Systems, but that was minor compared to its other ill-fated ventures. Many more millions went down the drain when the corporation bought a construction company and its aging equipment from a white owner. The Natives hired a Panamanian to run it. He was instrumental in landing the company a big Seward dock project, but it underbid the job by an astounding $26 million, which it then had to pay to the bonding company. In an effort to cash in on the pipeline building boom in the mid-1970s, the Native corporation bought a tire-recapping company and started building a hotel in Fairbanks. Tire customers vanished with the completion of the pipeline, and the heavy debt incurred by the doomed construction company crippled the corporation's finances so badly that it never had the money to finish the hotel.

Newspaper accounts of depositions filed in a later court case indicate that during Murkowski's tenure the Bank of the North earned more than $1 million in fees and interest on loans to Bering Straits.

The corporation was a banker's ideal client. As the parent company, it had guaranteed all the debts made by its subsidiary companies. The bank reimbursed itself for the bad loans by simply dipping into the stream of settlement money.

By the early 1980s, the Bering Straits Native Corporation was battling to stave off bankruptcy. It might have wallowed quietly in its misfortune had not the people of Sitnasuak, the Nome village corporation, decided to make an issue of the bank's role in the rapid depletion of the regional corporation's bank account. In 1976, and again in 1977, Richard Atuk, Sitnasuak's general manager, had written requesting a status report on an estimated $2 million due the village. Each time the bank stonewalled. In October 1980, the village sued the Alaska National Bank of the North in superior court, charging that the bank, as a trustee of Alaska Native fund monies, had helped Bering Straits "to systematically dispose of the village funds for the benefit of everyone but the villages." Under a promise that it would repay the money due Sitnasuak, the Bering Straits Native Corporation escaped becoming a defendant, and, in fact, joined the village in suing the bank until it ran out of money a year later.

The village continued to press the suit for five years before it came to trial in 1987. Both sides brought in high-powered lawyers — Charles Cole, today Alaska's attorney general, represented the bank, and R. Collin Middleton, an experienced trial lawyer from New England, pleaded for Sitnasuak. The village won a devastating victory. "The defendant Alaska National Bank of the North as trustee breached the obligations imposed by the trust causing the loss to the beneficiary, Sitnasuak," Judge Mark C. Rowland ruled. He ordered the Bank of the North to pay the village, which had a population of twenty-six hundred at the time, $14 million in damages. The bank went into receivership soon after, and the responsibility for paying off the court award fell upon the FDIC — a shifting of the burden onto the public that has become all too familiar.

Frank Murkowski, by now securely seated in the Senate, never personally appeared as a witness in the case. Middleton was obliged to go to Washington, D.C., and seek a dispensation from the Senate to depose him. The thrust of the senator's deposition was that he had been aware that Bering Straits was spending and encumbering far more funds than it had. He remembered that he'd once even called a meeting to discuss it.

Bering Straits Native Corporation filed for the protection of Chapter 11 bankruptcy in 1986. A number of other Native corporations, notably Calista, were also teetering on the brink of bankruptcy. Concerns rose that Alaskan Natives would, indeed, be parted from their money, and eventually their land.

Out of those fears emerged one of the most unusual special-interest tax giveaways in U.S. history. The right to sell net operating losses (NOLs) for cash to any profitable U.S. companies desiring to lower their tax bills had been the law briefly for all U.S. corporations in the early 1980s. But the practice created such a tax loophole that Congress made it illegal in 1984. Lobbied by the distressed Native corporations, Alaska's senior U.S. senator, Republican Ted Stevens, managed to persuade his colleagues in Congress to pass a special tax law in 1986 that reopened the privilege only for Alaska Native corporations.

The tax break saved several of the Native corporations from extinction. Bering Straits sold more than $250 million of hard cash losses, including one $55 million sale to Del Webb Corporation, which had been rolling in profits from building Sun City in Arizona as well as Nevada gambling casinos. Those sales returned about $80 million in cash, giving Bering Straits the resources to pull out of Chapter 11 and even to settle its debt with Sitnasuak. Calista Native Corporation's heavy losses from the ill-fated Sheraton Hotel and Settlers Bay real estate ventures enabled it to sell $70 million in hard cash losses, for a return of about $33 million in cash to its depleted treasury.

This was the way the tax break was supposed to work. However, lawyers for other Native corporations decided to get creative. They persuaded Native directors that NOLs did not necessarily have to be in hard cash but could also be land devalued when oil or gas exploration proved unproductive. They contended that the falling prices of timber and oil made the land less valuable than at the time of conveyance by Congress, constituting a loss accrued to the corporations.

The Cook Inlet Region Inc. (CIRI), by far the most profitable and one of the best-managed of the thirteen Native corporations, promptly multiplied its wealth by testing the limits of the tax loophole. The corporation reaped $102 million from losses created from devalued oil and gas reserves, almost as much as its poor cousins, Bering Straits and Calista, collected on their total hard cash losses.

CIRI, the Native corporation serving the Anchorage region, had much experience in getting the most out of Uncle Sam. Its original share of the claims settlement was a modest $78 million in cash and 2.3 million acres of land. It selected promising oil and gas properties in the Cook Inlet area but soon ran out of available land. It could pick up only about half of its allotment because much of the land around Anchorage was already in private hands or claimed by state and federal agencies. In exchange for the unavailable acreage, CIRI persuaded Congress in 1981 to give it $200 million worth of credits to bid at auctions of surplus federal property. Newspapers tracking its progress estimate that by 1991 CIRI built up a billion-dollar real estate empire that included more than thirty former federal properties, ranging from beachfront acreage in Miami Beach and Potomac River frontage in Alexandria, Virginia, to extensive holdings in Hawaii and California. CIRI also took advantage of tax breaks offered to broadcasting interests that sell their businesses to minorities. It now owns major interests in television stations in New Haven, Connecticut, and Nashville, Tennessee, as well as radio stations in Boston, Washington, D.C., Chicago, Seattle, and three other metropolitan areas.

CIRI's president is Roy M. Hundorf, born of a Yupik mother and a German father. Dressed in a well-tailored gray business suit, he parks his slender six-foot frame behind a large desk on the executive floor of CIRI's gleaming Anchorage high rise, which is tastefully decorated with Native art and artifacts. Occasionally glancing out the window at the Cook Inlet, he sums up the corporation's formula: "Our policy is to run a successful business operation," he says. "To the extent that we can, we hire shareholders, but we don't overburden ourselves. If we fail in business we are worthless."

CIRI earned $237,953,000 through 1988, compared to the combined $16,506,000 earned by the twelve other regional corporations since Native claims settlement payouts started twenty years ago. CIRI was luckier than the others in that it was the only one to find substantial amounts of gas and oil on its property. It had the further advantage of the $200 million in federal surplus credits, which it invested wisely. And CIRI comprises only seven villages, which made it easier to get a consensus on its policy to seek good investments first and jobs second. No one doubts that CIRI is going to survive.

The Kotzebue region's NANA Regional Corporation, headed by Willie Hensley, is also posting an impressive record. Hensley, a tireless Native activist still, stressed creating jobs and preserving culture from the time the corporation was formed. He won wide acclaim for developing the Red Dog zinc mine, which employs three hundred of his region's people.

But economists who have analyzed the twenty-year record of Native capitalism find that the majority of the regional corporations are in real trouble. Besides bad investments, much of their money has been dissipated on legal fees, often incurred by fighting one another. Endless lawsuits over sharing of revenues derived from the sale of natural resources, over grievances filed by dissident stockholders, and over challenges to subsistence rights have enriched Alaska's lawyers. One corporation officer estimates that lawyers have skimmed off at least $100 million in fees from the original $962 million claims settlement.

The special privilege of selling NOLs for cash may have stemmed the demise of some of the corporations, but it can be blamed for accelerating the self-liquidation of others. And it is the root cause of an environmental massacre that is ruining much of scenic Alaska today. In pursuit of revenues from NOLs, many Native corporations denuded Alaska forests and sold the timber — principally to the Japanese — at bargain-basement prices so that they could profit by selling the red ink from their huge losses. Environmentalists have long focused public attention on hefty U.S. subsidies that benefited two big pulp mills logging in the Tongass National Forest, ignoring this furious devastation of much of Alaska's original-growth rain forest, even as they wage hard-sell fund-raising campaigns to save the rain forests in South America, Africa, Malaysia, and Indonesia.

A visitor flying over Prince William Sound sees thousands of acres of clear-cut patches where ancient hemlock and Sitka spruce once created a wilderness home for deer, bear, river otter, and nesting marbled murrelets. Farther south, in Yakutat, fishermen pass miles and miles of devastated rain forest on their way to the Situk River, famed for its run of steelhead trout. This stately forest, which contains three-hundred-year-old Sitka spruce, was leased for logging by the local Tatitlek village corporation. It was supposed to be a sustained cut of twenty years with about 10 million board feet to be harvested a year, but crews wielding 36-inch Stihl chain saws have taken down as much as 60 million board feet a year since cutting started seven years ago. Today there is little left to cut. "Every agreement that the timber industry ever made with the community has been broken," says Larry Powell, the mayor of Yakutat. "Stream protection. Annual allowable harvest. Size of clear cut. Providing a sawmill to employ twenty to thirty people." (A sawmill was built during the first year but its roof caved in under heavy snow the first winter and not a single board was cut. Instead, the logs go directly to Japan, Korea, or Taiwan.)

The greatest desecration, however, occurs in the vast Tongass National Forest in southeast Alaska, the embattled 16.9-million-acre preserve of moss-draped trees, mountains, glaciers, salmon streams, marshy estuaries, and habitats for grizzly and black bears, Sitka deer, and bald eagles. Loggers from the two beleaguered Outsider-owned pulp mills in the area, whose practices and subsidies have been reined in by wilderness legislation enacted late in 1990, are pleased to steer visitors to Native corporation clear cuts in the Tongass that go right down to pristine salmon streams—a practice for which the pulp companies would have been quickly hauled into court.

One of the boldest Native corporations cutting in the Tongass is Shee Atika, headquartered in Sitka. On the verge of bankruptcy only a few years ago, it has been hurriedly marketing its 23,000 acres of prime timber on Admiralty Island, one of the unprotected wilderness areas. In trying to regain its fiscal health, Shee Atika pushed the 1986 tax loophole to the breaking point: first, tax breaks for hard cash losses, next for devalued land, then for timber loss sales, and finally for the $10 million sale in 1981 of timber appraised at $175 million to a new business named Atikon Forest Products—which is 49 percent owned by Shee Atika. After an adjustment for some harvested timber, Shee Atika claimed a $152 million loss, which it sold to Quaker Oats Company for $57 million. Meanwhile, Atikon—and by extension Shee Atika—stood to profit from processing the undervalued timber.

The IRS audited Shee Atika's loss claim and hit it with a $60 million bill for back taxes in 1991. If upheld on appeal, it could drive the Native corporation into bankruptcy. Some regard it as the government's opening salvo in an effort to recover some of the hundreds of millions of dollars in tax write-offs obtained through questionable tax manipulating by Alaska Native corporations.

Congress did finally close the NOL loophole completely in 1988. But the damage it caused is far from ended. Having given their shareholders a taste of hefty dividends, the directors of the Native corporations, who depend upon shareholder votes to stay in office, are under pressure to maintain them. The only way to do so is to keep cutting until the forests are gone, which some Native leaders concede will happen soon.

In 1990, the incorporated Tlingit village of Klukwan, which once advertised tax losses for sale in *The Wall Street Journal*, declared a dividend of $36,000 for each of its 253 shareholders. The windfall came from clear-cutting majestic, old-growth Sitka spruce on Long Island in the Tongass National Forest, which it obtained after it ran out of land to select in the Haines area, where the village is located. "The island has some of the finest timber in the world, and we knew we were going to become timber barons," Irene Rowan, chairman of Klukwan at the time, says. "The Forest Service approved it. There were no environmentalists around. So the state signed it off to us in 1977. Now we are being pressured for easements, the environmentalists are on us, and the government is coming back at us through the Internal Revenue Service."

"Don't you worry about the destruction to the environment?" she was asked.

"Let me explain from an Indian standpoint," Mrs. Rowan replies. "Our land was taken away from us when they declared Tongass a national wilderness. We spent half of our lives trying to get the land back. Now we are spending the rest of our lives trying to hang on to it." Pressed on the subject of exploitation of tax loopholes by Native corporations, she adds, "Wouldn't you try to make as much money as you can now? Our people feel that it is only a matter of time before they again are going to take the land away from us."

Once the Native corporations run out of timber to cut, some of them will also run out of cash. What happens then? Amendments to the claims act protect the land from liquidation sales. But such protections have never been put to a legal test. With two of the largest timber-cutting Native corporations already in bankruptcy protection, the right to collect debts by attaching Native land looms as the next big battleground in Alaska. In 1993, restrictions against selling stock in the corporations are due to end. This will certainly invite another threat to Native ownership—hostile takeover attempts, which until now have been barred.

The Native Claims Settlement Act was supposed to provide security for present and future generations of Alaska's Natives. Corporations were expected to earn profits, create jobs, improve living conditions, and protect subsistence resources. Instead, half of them enter their third decade uncertain of their future. Bering Straits and Chugach struggle to recover from Chapter 11 bankruptcy. Four others—the Aleut, Calista, Bristol Bay, and Koniag corporations—are skeleton operations, scarred by business setbacks and now simply trying to stay afloat. The other six, led by the remarkable CIRI, have established solid fiscal foundations, but they also will face harder times as natural resources give out and the pressure to maintain shareholder dividends remains high. (The thirteenth corporation owns no land, and its assets have been distributed.) The NOL loophole provided an infusion of $445 million on top of the $962 million appropriated by Congress. Now, Alaska's Natives have no further payments and no further federal tax breaks to bail them out. Meanwhile, the state refuses constant offers from cash-drained Native corporations to sell back scenic holdings.

As Natives ponder their predicament, the chain saws keep tearing down Alaska's vanishing rain forests. Much of the irreplaceable beauty of this Great Land leaves on barges piled with 40-foot logs, heading west across the Pacific.

CHAPTER 14

Here Is Free

W HEN SUMMER COMES to Alaska, with it come great numbers of salmon on their journey from the Pacific Ocean into freshwater streams and lakes where they spawn and die. The migrating salmon sustain the river ecosystems, perpetuating a chain of life in which Dolly Varden trout wait in the eddies to devour salmon eggs, grizzly bears prowl the banks to feast on the weakening fish, and ravens swoop down to scavenge the carcasses.

This strange rite of passage has gone on for more centuries than anyone knows. The other animals who depend on it divide the spoils, whether the year is abundant or lean. Only humans battle with increasing intensity over who gets what share of the harvest. Alaska licenses about thirty-three thousand commercial fishing boats and bestows on about thirteen thousand of them the ultimate privilege — a limited-entry fishing permit. In 1990, this exclusive group alone hauled in 690 million pounds of the five species of salmon from Alaska's designated waters on designated fishing days.

That is the legal harvest. However, huge ocean trawlers from the West Coast and the Pacific Rim, many with vacuum-cleaning efficiency, intercept untold millions of pounds of salmon illegally. They respect neither designated fishing areas nor other restrictions designed to protect the species. The trawlers deliberately poach the young fish in outer waters before they head for their spawning grounds in Alaska. International law forbids this, but the demands of the marketplace and the difficulties of policing the open seas make risk-taking profitable.

There are also Alaskan Natives who assert their subsistence rights and claim immunity from the white man's fishing laws. They net more than one million salmon a year, which are supposed to be dried and stored to feed their families. But many Native fishermen do not resist the temptation to turn salmon into cash when willing buyers appear. In a rare crackdown, L. George Schenk, a Bellingham, Washington, fish supplier, was arrested in the summer of 1992 for buying 53,000 pounds of king salmon from Natives who sold their subsistence fish. He was fined $50,000, sentenced to six months in jail, and his fishing boats were confiscated.

The discovery of oil in Alaska has put still more pressure on Alaska's salmon stocks. The oil firms brought in waves of affluent, recreation-minded employees. And the boom generated gigantic state revenues that made still more citizens affluent and recreation minded. This expanded Alaska population, which also includes a steady and sizable flow of military personnel, accounts for most of the 350,500 sport fishing licenses that Alaska now sells each year. These rod-and-reel fishermen demand a crack at the salmon, too, and their numbers give them political clout. They've shown their determination to reduce the lopsided harvests of commercial and subsistence netters by fighting in the courts, in the legislature, and sometimes on the banks of the salmon rivers.

In the fall, about 835,000 caribou, comprising twenty-five distinct herds, leave their summer feeding grounds in Alaska's lower half and head for their winter retreats around the state. This annual migration also has been occurring since before recorded time. It, too, has been a support system for animals and man, particularly for Natives who live off the land. Though involving fewer people, equally bitter vocal and legal battles now split Alaska not only over who gets to shoot caribou but also over who gets the permits to develop near caribou habitats. The state's constitution guarantees that the fish and animal populations are common property resources and therefore belong to all. But each year more parties lay claim to them while more people engage in shrinking the environment that supports them. It's a dilemma with a long and intractable history.

During the first half of the century, the territory sold out to the cannery interests, which nearly decimated the salmon by intercepting them with huge, deadly efficient traps stretched across the mouths of rivers. Most Alaskans cheered when fish traps were banned by the first act of the first state legislature in 1959. However, curbs on the canneries brought on a flood of independent fishermen. They saturated bays with gill nets and blockaded the migration routes near the shorelines with setnets—all legal equipment, but with the same devastating effect as fish traps when used in such profusion. By the mid-1970s, overfishing caused salmon stocks to crash again. From 1970 to 1975, the catch of Alaska salmon fell from seventy million to twenty million—and the number of licenses continues to grow.

State senator Clem Tillion, a strapping, bushy-haired salt who fishes off Halibut Cove, the picturesque harbor across from Homer in Kachemak Bay, was among the first to sound a public alarm. In the early 1970s, he saw that salmon stocks were approaching record lows in the once rich fisheries of Cook Inlet and Bristol Bay, while the number of fishing boats kept multiplying. He started a campaign to persuade Alaska that for its own economic protection, it must preserve its salmon runs by establishing a permit system limiting the number of boats and setnets eligible to harvest the fish commercially. Immediately, an uproar was heard around the state. "Up to then, fishermen had been setting their own rules, and many refused to accept any interference," Tillion says. "Kodiak in particular balked at any kind of regulation. They would sing the cowboy song 'Don't Fence Me In,' and tell everyone not to let that happen to Alaska." Tillion's telephone rang constantly, sometimes with threats to his life. His children were harassed in school and someone managed to slash a niece's tires.

Tillion won. In 1972, voters approved an amendment to the state constitution rescinding a common resource section that barred the state from restricting the numbers of fishing boats. Then, in 1973, the legislature passed Tillion's bill. Henceforth, Alaska would regulate the number of commercial fishing boats, establish zones they could fish in, and set the dates and hours when fishing would be permitted.

The prevailing understanding was that any Alaskan who had fished commercially earlier was assured of a permit, and the influx of boats from Seattle and elsewhere would be curbed.

A logical method of issuing the permits might have been to award them on open bidding or at least to charge a fee based on an estimated commercial return. But that would have practically shut out Alaska's Natives. With the nation's conscience still tender over its treatment of dispossessed Native peoples, the state rashly decided to give away the fishing rights free of charge. A commission determined eligibility by using a point system, with priority given to those who had fished in areas where there was no alternative employment. This tilted the advantage to the Natives. Points were also given to those who had fished for the greatest number of years and to those who had fished the most in recent years. By the time this giant giveaway ran its course, the state had handed out thirteen thousand limited-entry permits, the exclusive license to fish commercially. The majority went to gill-netters, who drift their nets into schools of salmon on designated days. About two thousand permits went to setnetters, who trap salmon by stretching gill nets from shore and anchoring them at a specified distance from the beach. Purse seiners, who use two boats in tandem to encircle schools of fish, won about the same number of permits as the setnetters, and about eight hundred permits went to power trollers, who fish designated waters in vessels with baited fishing poles extended from their sides.

But the legislature, under pressure from the fishing lobby, placed no restrictions on resale of the permits and attached no provisions for returning permits to the state when the owner died or quit fishing. Not surprisingly, many rushed to cash in what they had received for nothing. Licenses were traded on the open market, creating a lively exchange that continues today. Purchasers currently bid as much as $300,000 for gill net permits and $15,000 for setnet licenses. Their collective value is estimated today at $1.2 billion, according to a recent survey by the House Research Agency of the Alaska legislature.

The attempt to help Natives fishing in areas of no alternate employment did not work as intended. "Some Natives never understood the limited-entry process and sold their permits for little or nothing," Tillion says. "They now work on a fishing boat, and the permit is probably owned by some doctor in Anchorage." He could add Seattle businessmen, North Slope oil workers, and university professors to the list of those who have acquired permits from their original owners. Those with means are today the principal holders of the right to catch and sell Alaska's precious seafood without returning any substantial royalty to the state.

While the number of commercial salmon permits remains constant, the competition to harvest other fish has not abated. Permits to catch other species are open to anyone, and in 1991 there were about twenty thousand applicants to harvest halibut, crab, pollock, and even sea cucumber. The permit renewal fees for Alaska fishing boats range from $50 to $750 a year, depending on the species and the area. Fishermen and processors in Alaska waters are supposed to pay a nominal tax on their catch, estimated at $1.7 billion a year, but cheating is rampant, the Internal Revenue Service says. The House Research Agency estimated that fishing-related industries paid $46.6 million in taxes and license fees in 1989, while Alaska spent more than $60 million on programs to help them. And that net loss does not include the environmental damage caused by fuel spills, discarded trash, or the torn netting that floats out to sea and smothers thousands of fur seals each year, as the National Marine Fisheries Service reports.

"We didn't adequately tax the fishing resource because in the glory of oil we gave up all tax revenues from other sources," Tillion admits today. "Yes, it's a robbery." And he feels that nothing much will change as long as the state has oil revenues to take care of 85 percent of its budget.

The sellout of Alaska's prized resources doesn't stop there. The state's generosity, coupled with widespread lack of respect for the environment, is causing big trouble on shore, where greedy real estate speculators, unethical fishing guides, and lawless bank fishermen also exploit Alaska's natural treasures. Collectively, they are trashing the waters and shores of North America's most famed salmon stream, the Kenai River in south-central Alaska.

The Kenai's glacier-fed, turquoise waters are renowned for record-size king salmon (the world record, a ninety-seven-pound, four-ounce chinook, is mounted on the wall of a Soldotna auto dealer's showroom). The river also has a generous run of the two other most widely sought species, the sockeye and silver salmon, as well as trophy rainbow trout. As the state's single largest recreational resource, the easily accessible Kenai draws fishermen from the world over. Its headwater is the breathtakingly beautiful Kenai Lake, which carries the runoff of the snow-topped Chugach Mountains, about 90 miles south of Anchorage. The river rushes for 50 miles through the aspen, birch, and hemlock forests of the Kenai Peninsula until it empties into the Cook Inlet. Its deep pools, swirling eddies, and white-water rapids are a fisherman's dream and an artist's delight.

The peninsula itself is the original land of the Kenaitze Indians and is rich with Alaskan lore and history. The harbor town of Kenai, where Russia and the United States once maintained military forts, has had mining and fishing booms, but by 1950 its population was down to 321 people. Most of the white residents were homesteaders, many of them beneficiaries of the Veterans Homestead Act, which was passed after World War II. They cleared the required 20 acres, staked a claim to an allowable 140 acres more, and lived in chosen isolation. The surviving Kenaitze, having been exploited by the Russian fur traders and largely disdained by their new American neighbors, also preferred to keep their distance. Few, if any, pinned down ownership of their land as homesteaders. It was not the way of their culture, and in any case it would not have occurred to them that lands they had lived on for centuries were not their own.

When the Richfield wildcatters struck Alaska's first commercially productive oil well at the Swanson River on the northwest edge of the peninsula in 1957, this peaceful land was suddenly overrun. The population shot up by 2,500 percent over the next thirty years. An invasion of noisy, hard-drinking boomers, gamblers, and other oil camp followers not only ended the solitude of the Kenai but also trampled whatever remained of the ancient Kenaitze culture. Loretta Breeden, a homesteader now in her sixties, had been a reporter for the *Cheechako News,* a Kenai weekly born in the boom. She recalls a night on the police beat: "There was a shooting, three knifings, and someone blew up a building where they were having labor trouble. And police were asked to look for a gal who took off with several thousand dollars after selling tickets at the local saloons for an evening with herself."

Kenai became the first oil capital of Alaska. Camps and trailer campgrounds cropped up overnight on the banks of the Kenai River. No one raised questions about sewage disposal, bank erosion, or wetlands protection. And that was just the beginning. A dirt road connecting the peninsula to the state road system had been opened in the early 1950s to help the homesteaders. The discovery of oil made it urgent that the state pave it all the way to Anchorage. That was a signal for real estate entrepreneurs to go into action.

The banks of the Kenai were targeted by hard-sell developers, who tempted struggling homesteaders with money they couldn't refuse. Most of the lots were at least a half acre, but many were cut into parcels barely big enough to accommodate a cabin, much less a cesspool or a septic tank. If a lot didn't have a view of the river, the owner would often cut down the trees on the banks to make one. Those who didn't have direct access to the river sometimes found a way to manufacture it. Campgrounds carved boat slips into the banks and rented them for the summer. And in a coup that would make any Florida developer envious, the Kenai Keys, a 120-lot riverside development with locked gates, actually got permission from the U.S. Army Corps of Engineers to gouge out three canals totaling more than a mile in length, creating scores of additional river-access lots that sell today for $40,000–$50,000 apiece.

Having a place on the Kenai became a sign of status in Anchorage, and with weekend cabins came weekend crowds. Most were content to fish, but some hauled down powerful jet boats. Soon, small flotillas roared up and down the world's most famous salmon river, leaving 8-foot-high rooster tails in their wake and pounding waves over the fragile banks. Swamped fishermen, canoeists, and homeowners watching their river frontage wash away eventually besieged the state to halt the abuse. The property owners claimed high-speed wakes eroded the banks so badly their cabins were in danger of falling into the river. A few did suggest that the siltation caused by erosion was smothering salmon spawning beds, but those concerns made little impact because everyone was still catching plenty of salmon.

Neil Johannsen, an environmentally sensitive California transplant, has been director of Alaska's state park system since 1983. His 3.2-million-acre domain is the largest in America—about one third of all the state parkland in the nation. Yet he found that by 1985 the state had lost control of all but 15 percent of the Kenai riverfront. Homesteading and land selection by Native corporations had transferred an estimated 66 percent of it to private hands, and the remaining shreds were owned by either local municipalities or the federal parks system.

Nevertheless, Johannsen drew up a bill and with the help of sports fishermen lobbied the legislature to create a special management area under which a joint board representing the state and the municipality of Kenai would govern the river. If government could no longer get control of the Kenai's troubled banks, at least now it could lay down rules for use of the water that runs through them. The board's most effective action so far has been to place a maximum thirty-five-horsepower limit on the size of outboard engines. But the measure is not enough to stop the deterioration of Alaska's famed salmon river.

No one feels the inadequacy more than Dan France, sixty-five, a longtime game warden who lives in a small house on a remote bluff where he can see miles of the Kenai. A short, round, energetic man with a full head of crew-cut gray hair, France remembers hiking with his schoolteacher wife, Mary, 3½ miles across a tangle of half-burned, fallen hemlocks to stake a homestead claim on this spot thirty years ago. Instead of a road, they built an airstrip, and commuted to their jobs by Super Cub until they could retire to the tranquillity of the river. They had expected some problems with bears, but soon learned that bears will stay away as long as you don't leave around food or anything plastic they can chew. Pine grosbeaks peck at the sunflower seeds in the feeders outside the window, and juncos and crossbills flit about the ground, eating the spill. An unsightly pile of lumber near the feeder is a hiding place for ground squirrels. France sits at his picture window for hours at a time, training powerful binoculars on the river. Watching the Kenai flow has not turned out to be the pleasure he expected. "We sit here watching the death of the river," France says, and Mary nods in agreement.

France dedicated twenty-five years to trying to save the river. Appointed a game warden by President Harry Truman, France had been assigned to Idaho and came to Alaska in 1954 as federal game warden for the territory. When the state troopers created a fish and wildlife protection unit, France donned their uniform and made the river his principal beat. His years of patrolling the banks left him with only contempt for the way Alaskans treat the Kenai. When the salmon start running, poachers go into action. They cover the mouth of a tributary with a seine at night, then send someone upstream to pour chemicals—usually Clorox—into the water. The salmon, which are highly sensitive to changes in the purity of water, try to escape downstream, where they are trapped in the nets.

France arrested hundreds of poachers each year. "Do you think it did any good?" he asks. "Let me tell you what I see out of this window." The problem starts with licensed fishing guides, he explains. About four hundred powerboat and drift guides offer services along the river when the salmon start running. They promise big fish and lots of them, and for a while the promise was easy to keep. "Many of them come up the river to fish right below me," France says. "I see the boat catch its limit of kings. They rush down the river, drop off their fish, and come back with the same people for another load. How long do you think this can go on before the fish give out?"

The drop-off boats, some of them run by guiding services, are also culprits. "These boats pull up to the banks near a likely salmon hole," France continues. "First the adults unload the beer and the soda, then the kids and the dog get out. More boats pull up. The same thing. The banks are pounded down by hundreds before the day is over. Banks crumble into the water. The bushes become a toilet. How much people-pressure like that can the river stand?"

Yet this destruction is mild compared to what occurs on the banks accessible from the highway. The confluence of the Kenai and the Russian River upstream of the Sterling Highway, about 90 miles south of Anchorage, attracts hordes of fishermen who stand elbow to elbow thrashing the waters. The mob scene is aptly known as "combat fishing." Signs say "Fly Fishing Only" and the law is that anglers can keep only those fish hooked in the mouth. Not only is the return rule widely ignored, but when night falls, whole families armed with lethal three-pronged grappling hooks snag salmon by the dozens.

Visitors from out of state—as well as many from Europe and Asia—come to the Kenai to fish for salmon on the cheap. They jam the adjacent $6-a-night state campgrounds, fill freezers with fish, and send loads of salmon back home. They boast that what they'll get for those fish from friends and relatives will pay for the trip. I asked one German why he didn't go to Norway to fish for salmon, since it was much closer. "Too expensive," he replied. "Everything there is private. Here is public. Here is free."

By the end of the salmon season, the banks of the Kenai resemble a battlefield, strewn with coils of monofilament line, fish lure wrappers, and discarded lunch bags and beverage cans. Paths through the bushes are filled with toilet paper and human waste. The streamside vegetation has been trampled and thousands of boots have left their scars on the banks. The damage caused by wading fishermen and churning motorboats particularly concerns Johannsen. "Out-migrations of smolt [juvenile salmon] occurs along the edges of the river," he says. "When banks crumble, siltation covers the gravel and robs the young fish of shade protection. And silt can smother any eggs that are hatching."

In the summer of 1990, Alaskans began to understand that the Kenai was suffering badly from the pressure. The return of king salmon, the largest and most prized species, dropped so severely that the state declared a catch-and-release-only moratorium — over loud protests from guides who make $600 to $1,000 daily in the king fishing season. The next summer, the number of kings had declined even more, by 35 percent compared with the poor season the year before. The state declared an emergency and again ordered fishing by catch and release only. Johannsen tried to cut the number of licensed guides to 250, but was overruled by the attorney general on procedural grounds.

Tim Hiner, a former Michigan guide who has worked the Kenai for the past fourteen years, concedes the river is in trouble. "As Kenai's population grew, more people fished it, and the Kenai's reputation for holding the world's largest salmon spread," he says. "Chances of catching a fish over fifty pounds are better here than anywhere in the world." Much of the blame rests with the greed of developers, he says. "The six miles below the Soldotna bridge [the stretch where salmon first enter the river] is virtually a slum. Trailers are parked up and down the banks. Rocks are rolled in where natural barriers are worn down. The aesthetics of this part of the river is terrible. There is no consideration for nature. People come up here and say, 'I never thought it would be like this in Alaska.'"

Hiner has strongly complained to the Kenai Special Management Board about the proliferation of guides as well. While state records show it issued only 280 permits for powerboat and drift boat guides in 1990, the scene on the Kenai at the peak of the salmon season makes a mockery of the figure. Boats are so thick from Soldotna on down a person could practically walk the 6 miles to the inlet by stepping from boat to boat. Hundreds of these vessels are owned by moonlighting guides who are content to take the small risk of arrest for the chance to make a fast $1,000 over a weekend. It is common knowledge that most of the time state police assign only one safety officer to patrol the entire river. "Let's face it. What river in North America has or needs more than 100 power boat guides?" Hiner wrote to the management board. A few days after he sent the letter, Hiner noticed a new neighbor, a guide who had just moved up from New Mexico. He hung out his shingle the same day.

"Overfishing has decimated the great king salmon runs in the Kenai but don't lay all the blame on guides," Hiner says. "There are also too many setnetters in the inlet and too many salmon are killed in deep-sea nets." He says he is seeing more kings arrive with scars from intensified netting. He posts pictures on his bulletin board showing salmon with noses bloody and twisted and tails split apart, signs they escaped the commercial netters.

Captain Phil Gilson, the chief fish and wildlife enforcement officer for the state troopers, readily concedes that the Kenai is underpatrolled, but feels the department must concentrate on catching the biggest offenders. "Is the state served best by having a man on the banks catching a couple dozen illegal snaggers, or by chasing commercial fishermen in closed waters where they might be taking three thousand salmon illegally?" he asks.

A fisherman himself, Gilson glumly notes that not only kings but even the silver salmon are not returning to the river in accustomed numbers. He blames the increasing perils that the fish confront as they try to reach their traditional spawning grounds up the Kenai. Young salmon start their journey to the sea after a year in fresh water. They depend upon shady, steeply banked corridors to help hide them from their natural predators, including Dolly Varden trout and mergansers and other seabirds. As the banks are worn down by people, their protective cover diminishes.

Things are no better once the survivors reach the ocean. "The usual stay at sea, which is four years, lately has been fraught with new danger," Gilson explains. "Japanese, Korean, and Taiwanese high-seas net drifters are fishing closer to Alaska. They let out miles of monofilament net forty to sixty feet deep. Supposedly they are fishing for squid. In truth, they catch anything that swims, including many salmon." Alaskan newspapers regularly report that American pollock fishermen, who operate on the high seas with giant sock trollers, are also becoming a high-seas menace as the market for bottomfish grows. Many king salmon, a protected fish, are jammed into the nets by the fast-moving boats, and only those caught at the very end survive. Since it is illegal to keep them, pollock boats dumped sixty thousand dead kings overboard in 1990, Gilson said, citing National Marine Fisheries Service figures.

Once the salmon make the turn into the Cook Inlet, they have to escape the licensed gill-netters. Hundreds of boats, each permitted to launch 900 feet of net, jockey for position as airplane spotters steer fishermen to the schools. Competing fishing crews have been known to level guns at one another.

Next, there are the setnet fishermen. Gilson says he doesn't think there is a vacant spot on the beach the entire 40 miles of the inlet during open season.

As the fish enter the mouth of the Kenai, the sports fishermen finally get a crack at them. The guides, who have made a science of salmon fishing, know how fast the fish travel, when the fish rest, and when they move. They can follow the schools all the way up to the confluence of the Kenai and the Russian River, where they stop—out of concern for their customers' safety amid the barrage of barbed, flying steel from shore.

"We will have to limit the number of users," Gilson says. "Catch and release is a possible remedy. Using only artificial bait could cut down the catch. I think we are seeing that the kings can no longer take the pressure." But Dan France is more pessimistic. "Forget the kings; they're gone," he says bluntly. "Concentrate on saving what's left of the river."

The intensity of the conflict over fishing is matched by the struggle over hunting that continues to polarize the state. The public perception was that under the Native Claims Settlement Act of 1971, Eskimos, Indians, and Aleuts relinquished claims to their ancestral lands in exchange for 44 million acres of land and $962 million. But most Natives never dreamed this would affect their right to hunt, fish, and gather plants in traditional style. Meanwhile, environmentalists didn't foresee the destruction of natural beauty that would occur when Natives started cutting old-growth forests and otherwise transforming their resources into income-producing assets.

In an attempt to appease both groups, Congress in 1980 passed the Alaska National Interest Lands Conservation Act (ANILCA), which set aside 104 million acres as national parkland and wildlife refuges. Hunting is generally restricted in such areas, but the federal law also mandated that Alaska allow subsistence hunting by rural residents and fishing preference for those residents on all federal lands. The act effectively wiped out millions of acres of prime hunting territory for all but subsistence hunters. Tensions mounted further when some Native corporations closed their land to hunting except by their own people. Other Native groups charged hunters a fee to cross their lands, and at least one village now posts a specific kill fee for non-Native hunters: $3,000 per bear, $2,000 for moose, and $1,000 for caribou.

Alaska hunting guides, who virtually guarantee a trophy with any $10,000 wilderness hunting trip, might have been expected to protest. But the fraternity knew when it was well off. In 1974, the state had established exclusive guiding areas, which it gave away free to favored guides in exchange for a pledge to protect the stock of big game on their domain. A politically appointed guide board handed out exclusive areas to about two hundred guides of their choice, causing scores of others who were shut out to complain that criteria were based more on political connections than outdoorsmanship. Further, the state passed a law making it a felony to guide without a license. (Illegally practicing law or medicine is only a misdemeanor in Alaska.) With airplanes helping them spot bear, moose, caribou, and wolves, guides with exclusive territories could gross up to $500,000 a year. Craig Medred, outdoor editor of the *Anchorage Daily News,* reported in an excellent series on guiding that it was not unusual for guides to make a further killing by transferring their areas to others for prices as high as $250,000, even though the state still owned the land.

The injustice of the system angered Ken Owsichek, a native of Kenosha, Wisconsin. Concluding he could not guide in Alaska on his talents alone, he sued the state, charging that it had conspired to create a hunting guide monopoly. Meanwhile, a hunter and angler named Sam McDowell stepped forth to challenge the law giving rural residents priority in hunting and fishing privileges. A Missouri farm boy who came to Alaska in 1948 with $6 in his pocket, McDowell lined up a Native and an urban resident as coplaintiffs and went to court. Hunters and fishermen, many seething at the privileges granted Natives, helped McDowell raise more than $200,000 to fight the case to the state's highest court.

In 1989, the Alaska Supreme Court found the state guide law unconstitutional, ruling that it restricted opportunities to kill wildlife in the state. The next year, the same court ruled that the state subsistence law was unconstitutional as well, in that it illegally discriminated against city residents, notwithstanding the federal government's guarantee of subsistence rights for rural residents on its lands. Three years later, Alaska officials are still dancing around the tender question of Native rights. To resolve the issue would require either amending the state constitution to comply with the intent of the federal ANILCA act or suing the federal government on the remote chance that the federal subsistence privilege might be ruled unconstitutional.

Two consecutive state legislatures, in 1990 and 1991, could not muster the political courage to address the subsistence dilemma. When a third legislature tried to duck the issue in 1992, Governor Hickel convened a special session and ordered the legislators not to adjourn until they passed a solution. He had to post state police at the Juneau Airport to stop legislators from sneaking out. But even that drastic measure failed. The legislators passed a meaningless bill that attempted to define a subsistence user but fell far short of addressing the Native rights issue.

The chaos has thrown all hunting laws and some fishing regulations into disarray. Tensions between Natives and urban sportsmen are boiling at the highest level since the debates over the Native claims settlements in the early 1970s. Subsistence hunters who used to get first crack at the Nelchina caribou herd have been made to wait until the season opens for everyone. Three Natives in the village of Togiak were arrested for forcing white fishermen at gunpoint to leave a remote river. Newspapers regularly report on defiant Native hunters who kill migratory birds and caribou in their traditional way, regardless of season or quotas. The village of Akiak even officially decided to conduct its traditional caribou hunt in the summer of 1991, when villagers knew it would be illegal. Meanwhile, the insensitive

Alaska Board of Game created a national storm in 1992 when it advocated reducing the Fairbanks area wolf population by authorizing a hunt from helicopters.

The polarization is enough to make Kreg Thometz, twenty-seven, an assistant hunting guide with Alaska Trophy Safaris for seven years, rethink his career. He fears that the controversy and the competition is putting big-game hunting in jeopardy. "Many guides are turning to fishing," he says. "I think I may too."

He promises to stay clear of the Kenai River.

Index

283

Index

Index

285

photo © Sam Kimura

John Strohmeyer earned national acclaim as an investigative reporter for the Providence, Rhode Island, Journal-Bulletin, and won a Nieman Fellowship and a year's study at Harvard along the way. Strohmeyer won the Pulitzer Prize for editorial writing while at the Bethlehem, Pensylvannia, Globe Times where he was editor for 28 years.

Strohmeyer is also the author of *Crisis in Bethlehem* which explores the rise and fall of the steel industry. He has written for Harper's, the Los Angeles Times, USA Today and numerous other national publications.

An Alaskan since 1987 when he came to the University of Alaska Anchorage as Atwood Professor of Journalism, Strohmeyer is presently writer-in-residence at the university. He has traveled (and fished) in all parts of this magnificient state and lives in Anchorage with his wife, writer Nancy. They have three grown children.